MUSICAL AUTHORSHIP FROM SCHÜTZ TO BACH

What did the term 'author' denote for Lutheran musicians in the generations between Heinrich Schütz and Johann Sebastian Bach? As part of the Musical Performance and Reception series, this book examines attitudes to authorship as revealed in the production, performance and reception of music in seventeenth-century German lands. Analysing a wide array of archival, musical, philosophical and theological texts, this study illuminates notions of creativity in the period and the ways in which individuality was projected and detected in printed and manuscript music. Its investigation of musical ownership and regulation shows how composers appealed to princely authority to protect their publications, and how town councils sought to control the compositional efforts of their church musicians. Interpreting authorship as a dialogue between authority and individuality, this book uses an interdisciplinary approach to explore changing attitudes to the self in the era between Schütz and Bach.

STEPHEN ROSE is Professor of Music at Royal Holloway, University of London. He is the author of *The Musician in Literature in the Age of Bach* (Cambridge, 2011) and editor of *Leipzig Church Music from the Sherard Collection* (2014). He is co-editor of the journal *Early Music* and active as a harpsichordist and organist.

MUSICAL PERFORMANCE AND RECEPTION

General editors
JOHN BUTT AND LAURENCE DREYFUS

This series continues the aim of Cambridge Musical Texts and Monographs to publish books centred on the history of musical instruments and the history of performance, but broadens the focus to include musical reception in relation to performance and as a reflection of period expectations and practices.

Published titles

Playing with History: The Historical Approach to Musical Performance
JOHN BUTT

Palestrina and the German Romantic Imagination: Interpreting Historicism in Nineteenth-Century Music
JAMES GARRATT

Eight Centuries of Troubadours and Trouvères: The Changing Identity of Medieval Music
JOHN HAINES

The Keyboard in Baroque Europe
CHRISTOPHER HOGWOOD (ED.)

The Modern Invention of Medieval Music: Scholarship, Ideology, Performance
DANIEL LEECH-WILKINSON

Performing Brahms: Early Evidence of Performance Style
MICHAEL MUSGRAVE AND BERNARD SHERMAN (EDS.)

Stradivari
STEWART POLLENS

Beethoven the Pianist
TILMAN SKOWRONECK

The French Organ in the Reign of Louis XIV
DAVID PONSFORD

Bach's Feet: The Organ Pedals in European Culture
DAVID YEARSLEY

Histories of Heinrich Schütz
BETTINA VARWIG

Engaging Bach: The Keyboard Legacy from Marpurg to Mendelssohn
MATTHEW DIRST

The Musical Work of Nadia Boulanger: Performing Past and Future between the Wars
JEANICE BROOKS

The Guitar in Tudor England: A Social and Musical History
CHRISTOPHER PAGE

The Guitar in Stuart England: A Social and Musical History
CHRISTOPHER PAGE

Musical Authorship from Schütz to Bach
STEPHEN ROSE

MUSICAL AUTHORSHIP FROM SCHÜTZ TO BACH

STEPHEN ROSE
Royal Holloway, University of London

CAMBRIDGE
UNIVERSITY PRESS

University Printing House, Cambridge CB2 8BS, United Kingdom

One Liberty Plaza, 20th Floor, New York, NY 10006, USA

477 Williamstown Road, Port Melbourne, VIC 3207, Australia

314-321, 3rd Floor, Plot 3, Splendor Forum, Jasola District Centre, New Delhi - 110025, India

79 Anson Road, #06-04/06, Singapore 079906

Cambridge University Press is part of the University of Cambridge.

It furthers the University's mission by disseminating knowledge in the pursuit of education, learning and research at the highest international levels of excellence.

www.cambridge.org
Information on this title: www.cambridge.org/9781108421072
DOI: 10.1017/9781108363280

© Stephen Rose 2019

This publication is in copyright. Subject to statutory exception and to the provisions of relevant collective licensing agreements, no reproduction of any part may take place without the written permission of Cambridge University Press.

First published 2019

A catalogue record for this publication is available from the British Library

Library of Congress Cataloging in Publication data
Names: Rose, Stephen, 1975- author.
Title: Musical authorship from Schütz to Bach / Stephen Rose.
Description: Cambridge, United Kingdom ; New York, NY : Cambridge University Press, 2019. | Series: Musical performance and reception
Identifiers: LCCN 2018054842 | ISBN 9781108421072 (hardback) | ISBN 9781108431286 (pbk.)
Subjects: LCSH: Composition (Music)–History–17th century. | Composition (Music)–History–18th century. | Authorship.
Classification: LCC ML430 .R67 2019 | DDC 781.30943/09032–dc23
LC record available at https://lccn.loc.gov/2018054842

ISBN 978-1-108-42107-2 Hardback
ISBN 978-1-108-43128-6 Paperback

Cambridge University Press has no responsibility for the persistence or accuracy of URLs for external or third-party internet websites referred to in this publication, and does not guarantee that any content on such websites is, or will remain, accurate or appropriate.

For Lucy, Imogen and Oliver

Contents

List of Figures	*page* viii
List of Music Examples	x
Acknowledgements	xii
Author's Note	xiv
List of Abbreviations	xv
Introduction	1
1 God, Talent, Craft: Concepts of Musical Creativity	16
2 Between *Imitatio* and Plagiarism	48
3 Signs of Individuality	81
4 Rites of Musical Ownership	116
5 The Regulation of Novelty	158
6 Authorship and Performance	187
Conclusion	213
Bibliography	216
Index	237

vii

Figures

I.1 Heinrich Schütz, *Erster Theil kleiner geistlichen Concerten* (Leipzig, 1636), Primus partbook, title page with composer's annotations. Wolfenbüttel, Herzog August Bibliothek, 13.1 Musica 2° (1) *page* 2

I.2 Output of printed music from German-speaking lands by decade, 1550–1699, using data from RISM A/I and B/I 8

1.1 Spiridion (Johann Nenning), *Nova instructio pro pulsandis organis*, vol. 1 (Bamberg, 1670), p. 3. Brussels, Bibliothèque royale de Belgique, Fétis 2.940 C (RP). Copyright Bibliothèque royale de Belgique 39

3.1 Johann Hermann Schein, *Opella nova Ander Theil* (Leipzig, 1626), Tenore partbook, title page. Munich, Bayerische Staatsbibliothek, 4 Mus.pr. 2696, urn:nbn:de:bvb:12-bsb00091037–6 90

3.2 Johann Adam Reincken, *Hortus musicus* (Hamburg, *c.*1688), title page. Staatsbibliothek zu Berlin, Preußischer Kulturbesitz, Mus.ant.pract. R283, http://resolver.staats bibliothek-berlin.de/SBB0001CB5A00000000 92

3.3 Watermark in Heinrich Schütz, *Symphoniarum sacrarum secunda pars* (Dresden, 1647), Prima Vox, leaf after p. 62. British Library, F.21. By permission of the British Library Board 94

3.4 Heinrich Schütz, *Königs und Propheten Davids Hundert und Neunzehender Psalm* [*Der Schwanengesang*] (Dresden, 1671). Sächsische Landesbibliothek – Staats- und Universitätsbibliothek Dresden, Digitale Sammlungen, Mus. 1479-E-504, p. 37 98

3.5 Johann Jacob Froberger, *manu propria scripsi* sign. Vienna, Österreichische Nationalbibliothek, Mus. Hs. 18706, fol. 12r 99

List of Figures

3.6 Michael Praetorius, portrait in prefatory insertion
bound with *Musae Sioniae* (Regensburg / Wolfenbüttel,
1605–10). Wolfenbüttel, Herzog August Bibliothek,
2.5 Musica (1), fol. 1v   103

3.7 Johann Kuhnau, *Neue Clavier Ubung* (Leipzig, 1689),
title page. Leipzig, Bach-Archiv, Rara II, 727-D.
Heritage Image Partnership Ltd / Alamy Stock Photo   105

3.8 Johann Hermann Schein, *Venus Kräntzlein* (Wittenberg,
1609), portrait in Tenor partbook, sig.):(3v. Wolfenbüttel,
Herzog August Bibliothek, 46.3 Musica   106

4.1 Fair copy of Saxon printing privilege issued to Johann
Hermann Schein, 17 November 1628. Leipzig,
Stadtgeschichtliches Museum, A/4298/2009.
By permission   132

4.2 Engraved title page of Heinrich Albert, *Achter Theil
der Arien* (Königsberg, 1650). British Library, G.61.
By permission of the British Library Board   147

4.3 Johann Caspar Kerll, *Modulatio organica* (Munich, 1686),
start of thematic catalogue. Munich, Bayerische
Staatsbibliothek, 4 Mus.pr. 37847, urn:nbn:de:bvb:12-
bsb00090323–9   156

Music Examples

1.1 Giovanni Battista Chiodino's 'Loci communes musicales', as reprinted in Johann Andreas Herbst, *Musica poetica* (Nuremberg, 1643), p. 115   *page* 37

1.2 Johann Mattheson's assembly of a melody from commonplace fragments. Mattheson, *Der vollkommene Capellmeister* (Hamburg, 1739), p. 122   41

2.1 (a) Giovanni Gabrieli, *Beati omnes*, opening (from *Sacrae symphoniae* [Venice, 1587], no. 16); (b) Heinrich Schütz, *Wohl dem, der den Herren fürchtet*, SWV30, opening with continuo part omitted (from *Psalmen Davids* [Dresden, 1619], no. 9)   55

2.2 Heinrich Schütz, *Ich danke dem Herrn*, SWV34, quotation of Giovanni Gabrieli, 'Lieto godea', with continuo part omitted (from *Psalmen Davids* [Dresden, 1619], no. 13, bars 148–52)   57

2.3 Johann Kuhnau, *Frische Clavier-Früchte* (Leipzig, 1696), Suonata prima, bar 43. '!' denotes unresolved compound sevenths   60

2.4 Johann Kuhnau, *Frische Clavier-Früchte* (Leipzig, 1696), Suonata quinta, bar 3, with consecutive compound sevenths indicated   60

2.5 Heinrich Schütz, *Alleluja! Lobet den Herren in seinem Heiligtum* SWV38 as arranged by Andreas Oehme, opening   72

2.6 (a) Johann Caspar Kerll, *Missa superba*, Osanna, Canto primo concertato, bars 388–90; (b) Johann Sebastian Bach, *Sanctus* (after Kerll) BWV241, Soprano 1, bars 21–23   79

3.1 Johann Beer, different settings of 'Kyrie eleison'. From 'Schola phonologica', Leipzig, Stadtbibliothek, Musikbibliothek, I.4° 37, fol. 131v   112

3.2 Johann Adam Reincken, *An Wasserflüssen Babylon*, bars 16–23. Cantus firmus denoted by 'x'; initial motif indicated by 'y'   114

List of Music Examples

5.1 Josquin (attrib.), *De profundis*, initial bass entry (from
*Tomus secundus psalmorum selectorum quatuor et quinque
vocum* [Nuremberg, 1539], no. 31)   167

5.2 Hubert Waelrant, *Pater Abraham, miserere mei*, bars
48–55 (from *Sacrarum cantionum . . . liber sextus*
[Antwerp, 1558], no. 1)   168

Acknowledgements

I am grateful to the British Academy for a Mid-Career Fellowship that enabled me to undertake most of the research for this book, and I extend my thanks to the Music Department of Royal Holloway, University of London, for sabbatical leave that enabled me to finish writing it.

I would like to thank the staff of the following libraries and archives which have assisted me in this project: Staatsbibliothek zu Berlin; Bibliothèque du Conservatoire royal de Bruxelles; Bibliothèque Royale, Brussels; Cambridge University Library; Sächsische Landesbibliothek – Staats- und Universitätsbibliothek Dresden; Sächsisches Hauptstaatsarchiv, Dresden; Edinburgh University Library; National Library of Scotland, Edinburgh; Forschungsbibliothek, Gotha; Deutsches Musikgeschichtliches Archiv, Kassel; Stadtgeschichtliches Museum, Leipzig; British Library, London; Thüringisches Staatsarchiv, Meiningen; Bayerische Staatsbibliothek, Munich; Universitetsbiblioteket, Uppsala; Österreichisches Staatsarchiv, Vienna; Herzog August Bibliothek, Wolfenbüttel.

Rupert Ridgewell and his colleagues in the Music Department of the British Library kindly hosted a study day in June 2016 in connection with this project, and have continued to give constant support. I am grateful to Christa Maria Richter for her help in searching and scanning material at the Sächsisches Hauptstaatsarchiv, Dresden; to Gregory Johnston for his advice on using this archive; and to Frau Richter, Bernd Koska and Matthew Laube for checking my transcriptions of archival sources. I am grateful to Ester Lebedinski for transcribing the musical sources discussed in Chapter 2.

For comments and suggestions, I would like to thank Lars Berglund, John Butt, Tim Carter, Iain Fenlon, Mary Frandsen, Elisabeth Giselbrecht, Inga Mai Groote, Rebecca Herissone, Peter Holman, Tobias Klein, Matthew Laube, David Lee, Grantley McDonald, Noel O'Regan, Samantha Owens, Rudolf Rasch, Maria Schildt, Nigel Springthorpe, Tim Shephard, Peter van Tour, Sandra Tuppen, the staff and students at Royal Holloway, and any others who I may have overlooked. I am especially grateful to the anonymous referees and to Ester Lebedinski,

xii

Acknowledgements xiii

Michael Marissen, Bettina Varwig and Peter Wollny for commenting on draft chapters. Particular thanks go to Kate Brett and Eilidh Burrett at Cambridge University Press for their enthusiasm for this project. Finally I would like to thank Lucy, Imogen and Oliver for their patience and support.

Author's Note

All translations are the author's own except where indicated. Primary sources are quoted from the originals except where indicated. Transcriptions of archival sources follow the principles in Walter Heinemeyer (ed.), *Richtlinien für die Edition landesgeschichtlicher Quellen*, 2nd edn (Marburg, 2000). Original orthography is preserved. In transcriptions of German manuscript sources, nouns are capitalised only for proper names. Resolutions of contractions are indicated with ‹ ›; other editorial additions are marked with square brackets. Music examples are newly edited from the primary sources. Original time signatures and note values are maintained, clefs are modernised, and regular barring has been added according to modern convention.

Abbreviations

ASD	Desiderius Erasmus, *Opera omnia* (Amsterdam: North-Holland Publishing / Leiden: Brill, 1969 onwards)
BDok	*Bach-Dokumente* (Kassel: Bärenreiter, 1963 onwards)
CWE	Desiderius Erasmus, *Collected Works of Erasmus* (Toronto: University of Toronto Press, 1974 onwards)
HSR	*A Heinrich Schütz Reader: Letters and Documents*, ed. Gregory S. Johnston (New York: Oxford University Press, 2013)
NBR	*The New Bach Reader: A Life of Johann Sebastian Bach in Letters and Documents*, ed. Hans T. David and Arthur Mendel, revised by Christoph Wolff (New York: Norton, 1998)
RISM	Répertoire International des Sources Musicales, http://opac.rism.info
SDok	*Schütz-Dokumente* (Cologne: Dohr, 2010 onwards)
WA	*D. Martin Luthers Werke: kritische Gesamtausgabe* (Weimar: Böhlau, 1883–2009)

The following library sigla are used:

A-GÖ	Göttweig, Benediktinerstift Göttweig, Musikarchiv
A-Whh	Vienna, Österreichisches Staatsarchiv, Haus-, Hof- und Staatsarchiv
A-Wm	Vienna, Minoritenkonvent, Klosterbibliothek und Archiv
A-Wn	Vienna, Österreichische Nationalbibliothek, Musiksammlung
D-B	Berlin, Staatsbibliothek zu Berlin – Preußischer Kulturbesitz
D-Bhm	Berlin, Universität der Künste, Universitätsbibliothek
D-Bsa	Berlin, Sing-Akademie, Notenarchiv
D-Cv	Coburg, Kunstsammlungen der Veste Coburg, Bibliothek
D-Dl	Dresden, Sächsische Landesbibliothek – Staats- und Universitätsbibliothek
D-Dla	Dresden, Sächsisches Hauptstaatsarchiv
D-GOl	Gotha, Forschungsbibliothek
D-Kl	Kassel, Landesbibliothek und Murhardsche Bibliothek
D-LEm	Leipzig, Leipziger Stadtbibliothek - Musikbibliothek
D-LEsa	Leipzig, Stadtarchiv

D-LEsm	Leipzig, Stadtgeschichtliches Museum
D-Lr	Lüneburg, Ratsbücherei
D-Mbs	Munich, Bayerische Staatsbibliothek
D-W	Wolfenbüttel, Herzog August Bibliothek
D-WRz	Weimar, Herzogin-Anna-Amalia-Bibliothek
D-Z	Zwickau, Ratsschulbibliothek
F-Pn	Paris, Bibliothèque Nationale
GB-Lbl	London, British Library
GB-Eu	Edinburgh, University Library
GB-Och	Oxford, Christ Church
I-Bc	Bologna, Museo internazionale e biblioteca della musica
PL-GD	Gdańsk, Biblioteka Gdańska Polskiej Akademii Nauk
RUS-SPsc	St Petersburg, Rossijskaja nacional'naja biblioteka
S-N	Norrköping, Stadsbiblioteket
S-Uu	Uppsala, Universitetsbiblioteket
US-NH	New Haven, Yale University, Music Library

Introduction

In 1664 the aged Heinrich Schütz presented copies of almost all his printed music to Duke August of Brunswick-Lüneburg. He included items from every stage of his career, ranging from his Italian madrigals published in Venice in 1611, to the simple settings of metrical psalms in his revised Becker Psalter of 1661. Schütz accompanied the gift with a handwritten catalogue of his published works, listing them as his opus 1 to 14.[1] Writing to Duke August, he stated that the gifts were 'in consideration of the many and great princely kindnesses I have received from Your Princely Highness',[2] for whom he had acted as musical advisor and non-resident capellmeister since the 1640s. Schütz's presentation copies were placed in the ducal library in Wolfenbüttel, where they survive today, sometimes with the composer's manuscript corrections.[3] He annotated copiously the copy of the first part of the *Kleine geistliche Concerte* (1636), correcting misprints, and supplementing the texts of several settings of chorales with Latin versions.[4] Figure I.1 shows the title page of the Prima Vox partbook of this collection, where he wrote in red ink: 'Sum Henrici Sagittarii Autoris' (I am [the hand] of Heinrich Schütz, the author).

Schütz's inscription gave authority to the corrections, showing that this copy had been through his hands. Schütz likewise described himself as the 'author' in most of his printed editions, signing dedications and prefaces thus rather than with his proper name.[5] Occasionally he clarified his intentions as author: for the echo chorus in the *Musicalische Exequien* (1636),

---

[1] D-W, Cod. Guelf 54 Extrav., fols. 225r–226v. *SDok* 1, 412–15 (no. 188); *HSR*, 238–9.

[2] Letter from Schütz to Duke August dated 10 January 1664. D-W, Cod. Guelf. 376 Nov., fol. 322r. *SDok* 1, 417 (no. 189); *HSR*, 240–1.

[3] D-W, shelfmarks 9.2–9.9 Musica 2°; 11.1–11.7 Musica 2°; 12.1–12.7 Musica 2°; 12.8–12.12 Musica 2°; 13.1–5 Musica 2°; 14.1–6 Musica 2°; 1.2.3 Musica 2°; 2.7.15–19 Musica; 170.1–13 Musica div. 2°; 14.8–12 Musica 2°.

[4] The additional Latin texts are 'Christe Deus adjuva' (for *O hilf, Christe, Gottes Sohn*, SWV295); 'Veni redemptor gentium' (for *Nun komm, der Heiden Heiland*, SW301); and 'Meas dicavi res Deo' (for *Ich hab mein Sach Gott*, SWV305). Some of Schütz's corrections are listed in Heinrich Schütz, *Sämmtliche Werke*, ed. Philipp Spitta, vol. 6, *Kleine geistliche Concerte* (Leipzig: Breitkopf & Härtel, 1887), xiii–xxii.

[5] Schütz signed himself as 'author' in the *Historia ... der Aufferstehung* (Dresden, 1623), preface; *Musicalische Exequien* (Dresden, 1636), dedication; and *Geistliche Chor-Music* (Dresden, 1648), preface. RISM A/I S2277, 2289, 2294.

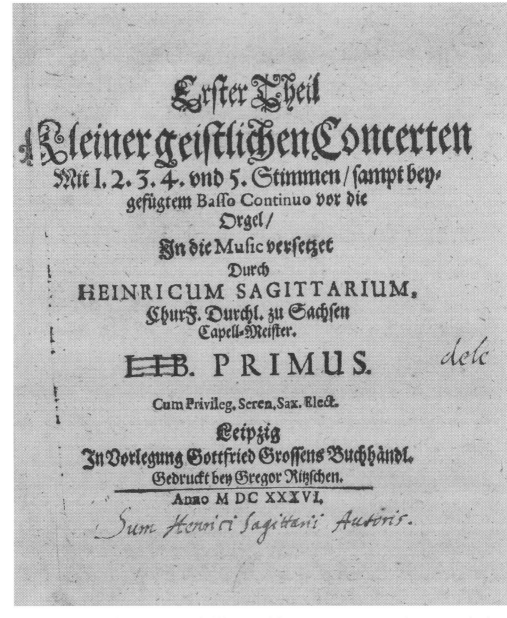

Figure I.1 Heinrich Schütz, *Erster Theil kleiner geistlichen Concerten* (Leipzig, 1636), Primus partbook, title page with composer's annotations. Wolfenbüttel, Herzog August Bibliothek, 13.1 Musica 2° (1).

Introduction

he explained: 'With this invention the author wishes ... to introduce and signify the joy of the disembodied blessed soul in heaven'.[6] Other composers of the early seventeenth century similarly called themselves 'author' in their printed music, including Johann Hermann Schein and Andreas Hammerschmidt. Even in the early eighteenth century, Johann Sebastian Bach used this term in some of his collections of music; for instance, to sign the title page of his *Orgel-Büchlein* manuscript, or to signal his role as self-publisher of his first engraved book of keyboard music, *Clavier-Übung I*.[7]

What did musicians between the late sixteenth and early eighteenth centuries understand by the term 'author'? A starting-point can be found in a Latin/German dictionary of 1536, which defined *autor* as: 'An originator of something, who makes a start or gives advice. Authors are said to be those who have made books'.[8] The reference to making books accords with how Schütz and Bach used the term, in connection with assembling a manuscript or printed book and submitting it to public judgement. The notion of 'an originator', however, is more problematic, for the author's role in creating texts and their meanings has varied greatly across different cultures, and was thoroughly deconstructed in the mid-twentieth century. In 1954 W. K. Wimsatt Jr. and Monroe C. Beardsley argued that a literary work 'is detached from the author at birth', and should be interpreted independently of claims about the author's intentions.[9] In 1968 Roland Barthes went further, declaring that the Author is dead and that meaning in a text is created by readers, not by a God-like originator: 'Writing is the destruction of every voice, of every point of origin'.[10]

Such extreme statements were nuanced by Michel Foucault in a 1969 lecture, 'Qu'est-ce qu'un auteur?', where he argued that the author's name is a function of discourse, and a means for texts to be classified and given cultural significance. According to Foucault, the term 'author' cannot be given to any writer, but 'is a variable that accompanies only certain texts to the exclusion of others: a private letter may have a signatory, but it does not have an author'.[11] He showed how the discursive function attached to

---

[6] 'Mit welcher *invention* ... der *Autor* die Freude der abgeleibten Sehligen Seelen im Himmel ... einführen vnd andeuten wollen'. Schütz, *Musicalische Exequien*, Bassus Continuus partbook, preface.

[7] D-B, Mus.ms. Bach P283; *BDok* 1, 214 (no. 148); *BDok* 1, 232 (no. 165).

[8] 'Ein vrheber eins dings/ d‹er› den Anfang thuet/ oder radt gibt. Vnde *Autores dictunt‹ur›*, die da bücher habe‹n› gemacht'. Petrus Dasypodius, *Dictionarium Latinogermanicum* (Strasbourg, 1536), sig. D3v.

[9] W. K. Wimsatt Jr. and Monroe C. Beardsley, 'The Intentional Fallacy', in W. K. Wimsatt Jr. (ed.), *The Verbal Icon: Studies in the Meaning of Poetry* (Lexington, KY: University of Kentucky Press, 1954), 3–18 (p. 5).

[10] Roland Barthes, 'The Death of the Author', in *Image – Music – Text*, trans. and ed. Stephen Heath (London: Fontana, 1977), 142–48 (p. 142); originally published as 'La mort de l'auteur' (1968).

[11] Michel Foucault, 'What Is an Author?' in *Language, Counter-Memory, Practice*, ed. Donald F. Bouchard (Ithaca, NY: Cornell University Press, 1977), 113–38 (pp. 123–24).

an author's name varies with time and place, for instance with shifting definitions of legal responsibility for texts or with notions of literary property. As for Schütz and Bach, their statements of authorial identity need to be understood within the discourses of authorship and authority current at the time.

Following Foucault's foundational study, many scholars of literature and book history have argued that authorship is best understood relationally, shaped by the interconnections between writers, texts, concepts and communities. Research has focused on the legal, economic, material and social negotiations surrounding authors between the sixteenth and eighteenth centuries. Joseph Loewenstein, Mark Rose and Martha Woodmansee examine the legal wranglings through which authors or booksellers asserted proprietary feelings over their products.[12] Rather than tracing a teleological progression towards modern copyright law, they show how concepts of authorial property arose from the specific circumstances of the book trade. Book historians show how material aspects of surviving copies (such as layout and typography), as well as the rhetorical strategies in prefaces and dedications, can project the figure of the author.[13] Acknowledging the collaborative nature of book production and use, such scholarship highlights how the author's presence was controlled by scribes, typesetters, publishers and the other trades involved in making a book. Other studies interrogate the notions of creativity, originality and individuality associated with the term 'author': Jeffrey Masten has investigated collective authorship in English drama around 1600, while historians of the visual arts have exposed workshop practices whereby a master sketched a painting but its execution was carried out by assistants.[14] Current research thus emphasises how the meanings of authorship arose through collaboration, in contrast to Romantic stereotypes of the creative artist as an isolated, singular genius.

An investigation of musical authorship is complicated by music's dual existence in writing and in performance. The identification of a musical author usually presupposes the preservation of compositions in notation. Reinhard Strohm shows how humanist traditions from the fifteenth

---

[12] Joseph Loewenstein, *Ben Jonson and Possessive Authorship* (Cambridge: Cambridge University Press, 2002); Mark Rose, *Authors and Owners: The Invention of Copyright* (Cambridge, MA: Harvard University Press, 1993); Martha Woodmansee, 'The Genius and the Copyright: Economic and Legal Conditions of the Emergence of the "Author"', *Eighteenth-Century Studies* 17 (1984), 425–48.

[13] On the role of layout in projecting authorial presence or an authorial notion of the text, see Loewenstein, *Ben Jonson and Possessive Authorship*, 134–60; D. F. McKenzie, 'Typography and Meaning: The Case of William Congreve', in Giles Barber and Bernhard Fabian (eds.), *Buch und Buchhandel im Europa in achtzehnten Jahrhundert: The Book and the Book Trade in Eighteenth-Century Europe* (Hamburg: Hauswedell, 1981), 81–126.

[14] Jeffrey Masten, *Textual Intercourse: Collaboration, Authorship and Sexualities in Renaissance Drama* (Cambridge: Cambridge University Press, 1997); Andrew Ladis and Carolyn Wood (eds.), *The Craft of Art: Originality and Industry in the Italian Renaissance and Baroque Workshop* (Athens, GA: University of Georgia Press, 1995).

Introduction

century onwards encouraged the idea of the musical opus – a composition or set of compositions fixed in writing, attributed to an author and remembered for posterity.[15] That Schütz subscribed to such an idea is evident in his use of opus numbers, and his eagerness for his set of printed works to be placed in the Wolfenbüttel court library. The opus is one component in the network of ideas comprising the musical work concept, which in later centuries gave aesthetic significance to compositions that became canonised and gained their own existence in the minds of musicians and audiences.[16] For studies of the musical opus in the seventeenth century, methods of book history can show how material characteristics of notated sources shaped perceptions of the durability of compositions and the presence of the composer. But because these notated sources represent only one facet of musical life, it is also necessary to ask how they were used in performance.

Previous studies of musical authorship have focused on historical periods when the figure of the composer apparently strengthened. Rob Wegman argues that until the late fifteenth century musicians rarely distinguished between composition and performance; the practice of improvised counterpoint meant that the activities of making and sounding music happened simultaneously and collaboratively. Around 1500, however, musicians increasingly perceived compositions as notated objects independent of performance, and some select musicians were employed specifically as composers.[17] In 1497 Heinrich Isaac was appointed as 'componist' at the Innsbruck court of Emperor Maximilian I, and in 1504 Jacob Obrecht was hired as 'compositore de canto' in Ferrara. Epitomising this new emphasis on the composer was Josquin, who was celebrated in anecdotes showing his concern for artistic freedom and the textual integrity of his compositions.[18] Complementing Wegman's approach, Michele Calella has explored the humanist discourse that praised composers such as Josquin and their compositions.[19] Yet this narrative perpetuates the emphasis on Flemish-trained polyphonists who already dominate histories of fifteenth- and early sixteenth-century music; it does not address the continuing importance of oral practices such as improvised counterpoint.

---

[15] Reinhard Strohm, '*Opus*: An Aspect of the Early History of the Musical Work-Concept', in Rainer Kleinertz, Christoph Flamm and Wolf Frobenius (eds.), *Musik des Mittelalters und der Renaissance. Festschrift Klaus-Jürgen Sachs zum 80. Geburtstag* (Hildesheim: Olms, 2010), 205–17.

[16] The standard introduction to debates about the musical work concept is Lydia Goehr, *The Imaginary Museum of Musical Works: An Essay in the Philosophy of Music* (Oxford: Clarendon Press, 1992).

[17] Rob C. Wegman, 'From Maker to Composer: Improvisation and Musical Authorship in the Low Countries, 1450–500', *Journal of the American Musicological Society* 49 (1996), 409–79.

[18] Ibid., 466–69.

[19] Michele Calella, *Musikalische Autorschaft. Der Komponist zwischen Mittelalter und Neuzeit* (Kassel: Bärenreiter, 2014), 182–242.

Another narrative highlights how music printing promoted 'composer-centred' genres in the sixteenth century. Initially the initiative in the printing of polyphony was taken by publishers assembling anthologies with music by a range of composers; but the names of composers rapidly became valuable marketing tools, and from the 1550s onwards more single-composer collections appeared than anthologies.[20] According to Strohm: 'Petrucci's idea of printing single-author musical editions had a sweeping success in the sixteenth century and brought composer-centredness into the homes of patrons, connoisseurs and amateurs alike'.[21] Such processes of composer-centring and canonisation are exemplified by Orlande de Lassus's posthumous *Magnum opus musicum* (1604), containing his collected motets with a title page that frames his name in a ceremonial arch. Kate van Orden takes a less triumphalist view, highlighting the performerly aspects of musical culture in the sixteenth century, and also the collaborative nature of book production: 'One could say that it was not composers who authored printed books, but printers, printer-booksellers, and editors'.[22] She nonetheless identifies folio choirbooks as a prestigious printed format which increasingly contained music by a single composer, including published collections by Carpentras (1532–*c*.1536), Cristóbal de Morales (1544–51) and Palestrina (1554 onwards).[23] Such sumptuous books reinforced the composer's name and status within a system of musical patronage.[24]

In contrast with these grand narratives about printing and the rise of musical authorship, other scholars have scrutinised extant manuscripts to uncover the working practices of composers in the period. Such research seeks historically informed concepts to replace the emphasis on originality and inspiration typical in studies of compositional process in Beethoven or later composers. Jessie Ann Owens investigates how the working methods of sixteenth-century polyphonists were shaped by writing technologies (such as erasable tablets) and their use of formulaic material.[25] In her study of late-seventeenth-century England, Rebecca Herissone shows the collaborative or serial nature of much compositional activity, whereby one musician reworked another's ode, or several composers contributed incidental music to a play. Acknowledging the blurred boundaries between

---

[20] For a statistical demonstration of the rise of single-composer collections, see Stephen Rose, Sandra Tuppen and Loukia Drosopoulou, 'Writing a Big Data History of Music', *Early Music* 43 (2015), 649–60 (pp. 651–52).

[21] Reinhard Strohm, 'Looking Back at Ourselves: The Problem with the Musical Work-Concept', in Michael Talbot (ed.), *The Musical Work: Reality or Invention?* (Liverpool: Liverpool University Press, 2000), 128–52 (p. 150).

[22] Kate van Orden, *Music, Authorship, and the Book in the First Century of Print* (Berkeley: University of California Press, 2014), 30.

[23] Ibid., 55–68.   [24] Calella, *Musikalische Autorschaft*, 103–16.

[25] Jessie Ann Owens, *Composers at Work: The Craft of Musical Composition, 1450–600* (New York: Oxford University Press, 1997).

Introduction

literate and oral transmission, she argues that musicians drew on memorised formulae and their own ingenuity to realise incompletely notated compositions (such as dance tunes lacking bass lines).[26] These studies show the relational nature of the musical author, shaped by collaborations with the composing, performing and copying activities of other musicians; they also destabilise the status of the musical work, itself closely linked with notions of authorship.

The present study complements previous work by probing the discourses and economic practices surrounding musical authorship in the seventeenth century. How did society conceptualise the ability of musicians to make compositions? What importance was given to individuality of style and technique in the making and reception of music? What reasons were given by composers when they attempted to control the circulation of their works? How were the activities of individual composers regulated by the authority of church and princely rulers? Such questions are addressed in relation to music in German-speaking Lutheran lands from the end of the sixteenth century to the start of the eighteenth century, a period conveniently demarcated by the lifespans of the two composers named in the title: Schütz (1585–672) and Bach (1685–750).

The history of Lutheran music in the long seventeenth century resists any attempt to impose a narrative of strengthening musical authorship. Indeed there are few continuities between the compositional concerns of Schütz and Bach, apart from a common Lutheran outlook that regarded God as the ultimate creator of music. Schütz and his contemporaries, for all their experimentation with Italianate concertos for solo voices and obbligato instruments, valued the contrapuntal craft exemplified in sixteenth-century polyphony. As Schütz advised in his *Geistliche Chor-Music* (1648): 'nobody can rightly embark on other types of composition and properly deal with or manage them, unless he is already sufficiently practised in the style without basso continuo'.[27] Composers aspired to publish their music in collections that could be used regularly in the liturgy or in recreation. The first half of the seventeenth century therefore witnessed a continuation of compositional and publishing practices established in the previous century, whereby composers presented themselves as authors of their printed works.

After the disruption of the Thirty Years War (1618–48), however, there were abrupt changes in musical life, so much so that Werner Braun and Peter Wollny have suggested that the 1650s should be interpreted as a

---

[26] Rebecca Herissone, *Musical Creativity in Restoration England* (Cambridge: Cambridge University Press, 2013).

[27] 'niemand andere Arten der *Composition* in guter Ordnung angehen/ und dieselbigen gebührlich handeln oder *tractiren* könne/ er habe sich dann vorhero in dem *Stylo* ohne den *Bassum Continuum* genugsam geübet'. Schütz, *Geistliche Chor-Music*, Bassus Continuus partbook, preface. Translation adapted from *HSR*, 164.

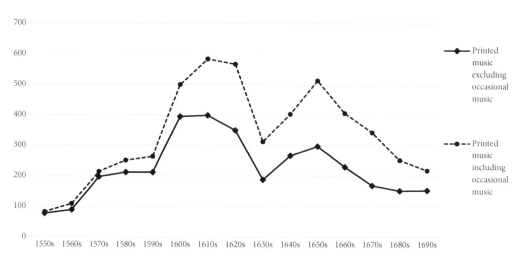

Figure I.2   Output of printed music from German-speaking lands by decade, 1550–699, using data from RISM A/I and B/I.

break between epochs of music history.[28] Musical life increasingly focused on courts, which often favoured styles that prioritised theatricality and the performer rather than contrapuntal craft. At the Dresden court, the music of Schütz was wholly replaced with the vocal concertos of the Italian capellmeisters Vincenzo Albrici and Marco Giuseppe Peranda.[29] Although there was a proliferation of musical genres in the period, a tendency towards the ephemeral is evident in the rise of the church cantata around 1700. Applying the theatrical style to sacred venues, musicians wrote their cantatas for specific Sundays, often with little prospect of repeat performance. For all Bach's interest and ability in counterpoint, his output is dominated by church cantatas, an ephemeral form of musical production that would have been alien to Schütz. Thus the decades around 1700 constitute a period that challenged notions of musical authorship, moving to a new emphasis on the event and the performer.

The weakening sense of musical authorship was associated with a decline of music printing in German-speaking lands across the seventeenth century. Figure I.2 shows the output of printed music per decade in German-speaking lands from 1550 to 1699, using bibliographical data from the A/I and B/I catalogues of Répertoire International des Sources

---

[28] Werner Braun, 'Die Mitte des 17. Jahrhunderts als musikgeschichtliche Zäsur', *Schütz-Jahrbuch* 21 (1999), 39–48; Peter Wollny, *Studien zum Stilwandel in der protestantischen Figuralmusik des mittleren 17. Jahrhunderts* (Beeskow: Ortus, 2016), 7–41.

[29] Mary Frandsen, *Crossing Confessional Boundaries: The Patronage of Italian Sacred Music in Seventeenth-Century Dresden* (New York: Oxford University Press, 2006), 172.

Introduction

Musicales (RISM).[30] (RISM A/I lists the printed works of single composers; RISM B/I lists printed anthologies with music by more than one composer.) The dashed line shows the total printed output including occasional music (single pieces for events such as weddings and funerals); the solid line excludes occasional pamphlets and therefore is a better guide to the health of the music trade. Figure I.2 indicates that the amount of music printing increased greatly in the last decades of the sixteenth century, reaching a peak in the 1610s. Many of these publications contained the works of a single composer, demonstrating their skill and preserving their works for posterity. Such was the dominance of print that relatively few compositions from the generation of Schütz and Schein survive solely in manuscript; extant handwritten sources tend to be copied from printed originals, and composers' autographs are extremely rare (see Chapter 1, p. 21).

The output of printed music halved in the 1630s, the decade when the Thirty Years War had its most devastating effect. In the 1640s and 1650s, there was a modest recovery, as publishers and musicians sought to return to pre-war forms of dissemination. Thereafter the amount of music printing declined steadily, so that by the 1690s fewer items of music were being printed than in the crisis-hit 1630s. By the end of the century, keyboard and instrumental ensemble music formed a greater proportion of the printed output, and publications generally contained fewer compositions than earlier in the century. My analysis stops at 1700, because after this date most printed editions are undated, and only rarely does RISM supply conjectural dates. However, a preference for manuscript dissemination remained the norm for most German composers of the early eighteenth century, with the exception of Georg Philipp Telemann, who had his own publishing business.[31] Autograph scores survive relatively often from this period and generally are working documents; a few show the composer trying to preserve and perfect a composition (as with Bach's autograph score of the St Matthew Passion).[32] The usual format, however, comprised sets of performing parts, prepared for a specific occasion and then possibly shared with other musicians for subsequent performances.

The reasons for the decline of music printing were complex and can only be summarised here.[33] The printing formats and technologies suitable for sixteenth-century repertories were increasingly inadequate for the

---

[30] RISM's data include about 80% of surviving copies. This analysis was done as part of A Big Data History of Music, a collaboration between the British Library and Royal Holloway, University of London, funded by the Arts & Humanities Research Council. See Rose, Tuppen and Drosopoulou, 'Writing a Big Data History of Music'.

[31] Steven Zohn, 'Telemann in the Marketplace: The Composer as Self-Publisher', *Journal of the American Musicological Society* 58 (2005), 275–356.

[32] D-B, Mus.ms. Bach P25.

[33] On the decline of printing in Lutheran church music of the late seventeenth century, see Friedhelm Krummacher, *Die Überlieferung der Choralbearbeitungen in der frühen evangelischen Kantate.*

newer genres of the seventeenth century. Schütz's generation used part-book format, with a separate book for each voice-part. This was ideal for polyphonic genres such as the motet, where each performing part had an equal quantity of notated music; it was less suitable for genres with heterogeneous scorings such as vocal concertos and theatrical music, where each performing part could have widely differing quantities of music. Furthermore, movable type (with a separate symbol for each note) could not readily represent the ornamentation or virtuosic fast passages in many newer repertories. In 1682 the heirs of the Nuremberg publisher Christoph Endter claimed: 'The deficiencies of previously printed music have become so serious for the advancing art that music-lovers would prefer to copy pieces with their own hands than submit to such annoyance'.[34] The preface noted that engraved music did not suffer from these difficulties, but it was extremely expensive and therefore 'very awkward' (*sehr mißlich*) for the publisher.

In addition to the technological difficulties faced by music printers, the market for sheet music fragmented in German-speaking lands, with niche repertories developing for specific locations or ensembles. By the start of the eighteenth century, it had become uneconomically unviable to print repertories such as church music, dramatic music and many genres of keyboard music. Where music publishing survived, it mainly served local markets; there were neither the major cities nor strong international trade links that fostered the music trade in London and Amsterdam. The decline of music printing is a backdrop to the developments discussed in this book, shaping the material forms through which purchasers and performers met the work of musical authors. It accompanied larger shifts in intellectual, cultural and economic life that also provide interpretive frameworks for this book.

This monograph explores authorship as an interplay between notions of authority and individuality. Etymologically the word *auctor* is derived from *auctoritas* (authority), which in classical and medieval times denoted the texts and symbolic devices carrying power or allowing it to be exercised. Larry Scanlon defines authority in medieval literature as involving 'not just deference to the past but a claim of identification with it and a representation of that identity made by one part of the present to another ... Authority, then, is an enabling past reproduced in the present'.[35] In the

---

Untersuchungen zum Handschriftenrepertoire evangelischer Figuralmusik im späten 17. und beginnenden 18. Jahrhundert (Berlin: Merseburger, 1965), 45–87.

[34] 'Die Mängel der bishero gedruckten *Musicalien*/ sind bey gestiegener Kunst/ endlich so groß worden/ daß die Liebhabere/ ihre Sachen lieber mit eigener Hand haben abschreiben/ als dero Verdruß unterworffen seyn wollen'. Johann Rosenmüller, *Sonate a 2. 3. 4. e 5. stromenti* (Nuremberg, 1682), Violin 1 part, preface (in D-LEm exemplar, shelfmark II.2.48). RISM A/I R2567.

[35] Larry Scanlon, *Narrative, Authority and Power: The Medieval Exemplum and the Chaucerian Tradition* (Cambridge: Cambridge University Press, 1994), 38.

Introduction   11

seventeenth century, the 'enabling past' included the Biblical stories that formed the basis of church doctrine, the princely ancestry that gave authority to rulers, and the intellectual lineage of venerated authors. Typically the past's authority was transmitted via patriarchal relationships, emphasising the duty of fathers to educate and discipline younger generations. Such an understanding of authorship required composers to secure recognition by aligning their work with external authorities such as the church, princely rulers or canonised authors. These relationships with authority might appear similar to those analysed by Stephen Greenblatt, who argued that self-fashioning in sixteenth-century England involved 'submission to an absolute power or authority situated at least partially outside the self'.[36] Greenblatt's formulation, however, shows the influence of Foucault in assuming that individual subjects are controlled by the hegemonic power of church and state, and any human self-assertion is an illusion created by these religious and political forces.[37] I prefer to understand power as decentralised, with constant negotiations between authors, authorities and the enabling past.

Alongside these evocations of external authority, authorship was also shaped by ideas of individuality and autonomy. Classical and humanist traditions already recognised that each person had a distinct character, and the autonomy of individual subjects gained further prominence via seventeenth-century developments often associated with the rise of modernity. War and political upheaval in England, France and German-speaking lands eroded faith in religious and princely authority. New modes of spirituality such as Pietism promoted the mystical experience of individuals, rather than the doctrine and corporate worship of the official church. Adherence to authority was further undermined by new developments in science, including the priority given to eyewitness observation by organisations such as the Royal Society of London (founded 1660). In Lutheran lands, Christian Thomasius (who lectured at Leipzig until 1689 and thereafter at Halle) popularised the view that the senses were the true path to knowledge. Instead of dogmatic obedience to authority, Thomasius advocated an 'eclectic philosophy', where the individual 'tests for himself whether this or that point of learning is well founded or might add to his own, and therefore sees more with his own eyes rather than those of others'.[38] In the arts such an approach was taken by the Hamburg musician and theorist Johann Mattheson, who rejected those musicians

---

[36] Stephen Greenblatt, *Renaissance Self-Fashioning: From More to Shakespeare* (Chicago: University of Chicago Press, 1980), 9.

[37] John Martin, 'Inventing Sincerity, Refashioning Prudence: The Discovery of the Individual in Renaissance Europe', *The American Historical Review* 102 (1997), 1309–42 (p. 1315).

[38] 'ob dieser und jener Lehr-Punct wohl gegründet sey/ selbst untersuche/ auch von dem Seinigen etwas hinzu thue/ und also vielmehr mit seinen eigenen Augen als mit anderen sehe'. Christian Thomasius, *Einleitung zur Hof-Philosophie* (Frankfurt am Main and Leipzig, 1710), 50.

who followed past authorities and instead argued that the ear should be the ultimate arbiter in musical disputes. Invoking Thomasius's pragmatic eclecticism, Mattheson declared: 'I am an eclectic musician, and I defer to no authority which is contrary to sense and reason'.[39] Individual experience and taste thus became the basis for the act of authoring a composition.

Another interpretive framework used in this book comprises the changing economic systems through which music was made and traded. During the sixteenth and seventeenth centuries, pre-capitalist practices of gift-giving existed alongside elements of a market economy. In a gift exchange, musicians offered their works to patrons in a chain of reciprocal relationships; compositions were not commodities but circulated within a network of social obligations. Exchange was also encouraged by the theological belief in music as a gift from God, a gift which musicians reciprocated by putting their talents to public use. Yet aspects of early capitalism can also be detected in the European economy of the period, in such features as the supply of distant rather than local markets, the production of commodities for sale at maximum profit, and a division between entrepreneurs who hold capital and labourers who work for a wage.[40] The trade in printed music encompassed aspects of gift exchange and of early capitalism: some music books served symbolic functions, enhancing the prestige of patron or author; but printing also allowed composers and publishers to reach markets of performers and readers beyond their immediate environment.

Some scholars argue that early capitalism encouraged self-assertion, enabling individuals to sell their skills or products for the highest price possible. Surveying political thought of the seventeenth century (including writers such as Thomas Hobbes and John Locke), the political scientist C. B. Macpherson formulated the notion of 'possessive individualism'. According to Macpherson, this entailed a 'conception of the individual as essentially the proprietor of his own person or capacities, owing nothing to society for them', and promoted social practices of consumption and acquisition.[41] Subsequent historians have criticised Macpherson's broad-brush approach, noting that aspects of early capitalism (such as labourers

---

[39] 'Ich bin ein *Musicus ecclecticus*, und kehre mich an keine *autorité* … wenns wieder Sinnen und Vernunfft streitet'. Johann Mattheson, *Critica musica* 1 (1722), 48. See also Wolfgang Hirschmann, '"Musicus ecclecticus". Überlegungen zu Nachahmung, Norm und Individualisierung um 1700', in Rainer Bayreuther (ed.), *Musicalische Norm um 1700* (Berlin: De Gruyter, 2010), 97–107.

[40] Robert S. DuPlessis, *Transitions to Capitalism in Early Modern Europe* (Cambridge: Cambridge University Press, 1997), 1–12.

[41] C. B. Macpherson, *The Political Theory of Possessive Individualism* (Oxford: Clarendon Press, 1962), 3.

Introduction

who work for a wage) could negate individual freedom.[42] Yet Locke's emphasis on the individual as proprietor appealed to Mattheson, who compared a composer's ideas to an individual's wealth (see Chapter 2). Capitalist notions of consumption may also explain the emphasis on constant production in church music around 1700, with church musicians obliged to supply weekly cantatas for congregations who prioritised novelty and fashion (see Chapter 5). Such changing economic models help explain the different ways in which musical authorship was understood and valued by patrons, purchasers and performers.

Chapter 1 of this book probes the models of creativity that underpinned Lutheran musical authorship in the seventeenth century. It identifies three intertwined viewpoints: the theological mindset that only God can create; the humanist notion of creativity as springing from individuals' innate talent, honed through art; and the craftworkers' concern with physical objects made through manual skill. Whereas the theological outlook viewed writers and musicians as instruments of God's will, humanist and artisanal notions of creativity acknowledged humans' capacity to shape the world around them. To expose the tensions between these differing concepts of creativity, this chapter explores debates about whether the invention of musical ideas was an innate talent or could be taught via techniques such as the arts of memory.

The dialogue between individuality and authority is uncovered in Chapter 2's examination of notions of musical borrowing in seventeenth-century Lutheran lands. Musicians believed that compositional production was possible only through the creative reception of existing music. Compositional borrowing was often conceived as *imitatio*, an act which claimed the authority of an 'enabling past' by following the models of respected teachers and exemplary musicians. An alternative approach was *aemulatio*, where musicians sought to surpass their models, as suggested by Georg Quitschreiber's 1611 interpretation of borrowing as a type of playing with art. The importance of individual labour is evident in discussions of plagiarism, which was distinguished from acts of 'honest theft', where the borrower was open about the model used or transformed it in significant ways. The chapter also considers Johann Mattheson's notion of reworking as increasing the musical wealth of individuals, a capitalist view shaped by his mercantile environment in Hamburg.

Notions of individuality and economic models intersect in Chapter 3, on how buyers and readers of sheet music sought to recognise signs of the composer's presence. Early capitalism caused anxieties about the authentication of material goods, which increasingly circulated at a distance from

---

[42] James Tully, 'The Possessive Individualism Thesis: A Reconsideration in the Light of Recent Scholarship', in Joseph H. Carens (ed.), *Democracy and Possessive Individualism: The Intellectual Legacy of C. B. Macpherson* (Albany: State University of New York Press, 1993), 19–44.

their makers; artisans responded with distinctive marks to indicate the provenance of their products. Chapter 3 shows how composers, scribes and publishers used similar techniques to verify their sheet music, along with devices such as portraits which simulated the author's presence and individuality. It also examines discussions about the personal styles of composers, in relation to humanist concepts of character and artisanal notions of distinctive craftsmanship.

Chapter 4 examines debates about who owned music, including whether composers could control the circulation of their works or had any right to be recognised as the authors of their music. The theological model of creativity was closely linked with the Lutheran doctrine that individuals should share their God-given talents for the benefit of their neighbours. Only princes were exempt from the prevalent belief of sharing for the common good. Composers and publishers, however, could petition a prince for a printing privilege to give them the exclusive right to publish a specified work for a limited period. The privilege system thus enabled authors to gain a modicum of individual recognition by submitting to princely authority. By Bach's day, the decline in music printing meant that composers no longer sought privileges, but some were concerned about misattributions in scribal transmission. Musicians again called on princely authority to uphold their claims to be recognised as authors of their works, as shown by the example of Johann Caspar Kerll.

The changing role of authority in musical life is examined in Chapter 5, which shows how practices for regulating church compositions altered in Saxony in the era between Schütz and Bach. In the early seventeenth century, the musical repertory in Saxon town churches was regulated by a 1580 edict that forbade musicians from performing their own compositions in worship. The edict regarded musical novelty as detrimental to social order, and instead promoted an authorised polyphonic repertory by composers such as Josquin and Lassus, whose music was available in printed editions. Attitudes changed rapidly after 1650, with increased demand for innovation and individuality in church music. By the early eighteenth century, cantors were expected to compose regularly for their church, and Bach wrote a cantata almost every week during his first two years in Leipzig. Church music was now regarded as a fashionable commodity, to be produced and discarded regularly in accordance with capitalist notions of production and consumption.

Chapter 6 asks how the displays of musical authorship outlined in the previous chapters related to the experience of music in performance. Rhetorical theory conceived of invention, elaboration and performance as connected stages of creativity, while allowing for separate individuals to take responsibility for each stage. Some composers such as Johann Hermann Schein and Tobias Michael welcomed the addition of ornamentation and distinctive vocal styles by performers; others, such as Johann

Introduction

Jacob Froberger, elevated themselves as the ideal performer of their music because of their distinctive technique or embodied knowledge. A few composers commanded performers to follow their intentions, and this chapter relates such claims to the humanist and artisanal notions of creativity. By exploring different historical versions of the relationship between author and performer, the chapter offers fresh perspectives on the discipline of performance studies.

The seventeenth century was a period of complex change in German musical culture, and in social, economic and intellectual life more broadly. Such constant shifts add interest to a study of musical authorship in this period, but this book seeks to avoid interpretations that impose unidirectional or teleological change. Although many of the same developments in philosophical thought and economic practice occurred in England and the Dutch Republic, the Lutheran territories of German-speaking lands showed a distinctive mix of older and newer attitudes. In Leipzig around 1690, the empiricist philosophy of Christian Thomasius and the capitalist practices of the city's merchants were juxtaposed with a strong loyalty to Lutheran theocentric beliefs promoted by church, school and university. A parallel mix of old and new can be seen in the lives and writings of musicians. Mattheson justified his empiricism by citing Locke's writings and also Biblical authority.[43] He described music as a divine gift, intended for the praise of God,[44] yet also celebrated the mercantile environment that supported Hamburg's musical life: 'It is indeed true, that where the best banks are, so are there the best operas'.[45] John Butt has identified a similar dialogue as crucial to the ongoing appeal of Bach's sacred vocal music: '[A] counterpoint between religious and subjective-autonomous elements in Bach's Passions means that neither automatically predominates, and this sort of balance – or productive tension – is perhaps part of the durable quality of these works'.[46] Whereas Butt traces this 'productive tension' via close musical analyses and wider philosophical discussion, the current study focuses on the debates about authorship as found in a range of musical, theological and philosophical writings of the period, and on the attempts at regulating music as documented by previously unknown archival sources. Such debates about authority and individuality expose the contested nature of Lutheran musical life in the long seventeenth century, an era in which musicians forged notions of authorship against a backdrop of musical, intellectual and social change.

---

[43] Mattheson quoted extracts from John Locke's *Essay on Human Understanding*, and also Romans 10.17 in a version based on the English translation ('So then faith cometh by hearing, and hearing by the word of God'). Johann Mattheson, *Das forschende Orchester* (Hamburg, 1721), 121–22, 126, 132–33.

[44] Johann Mattheson, *Der musicalische Patriot* (Hamburg, 1728), 9.

[45] 'Es trifft auch fast ein, daß, wo die besten Bancken, auch die besten Opern sind'. Ibid., 176.

[46] John Butt, *Bach's Dialogue with Modernity: Perspectives on the Passions* (Cambridge: Cambridge University Press, 2010), 20.

CHAPTER I

God, Talent, Craft: Concepts of Musical Creativity

In 1700 the Leipzig organist Johann Kuhnau singled out composers and music directors as holding power within and beyond their profession: 'Among musicians they are to be regarded as kings who, so to speak, wield the sceptre and prescribe other laws. ... The more a person is experienced in composition and is successful in invention ... the more will his virtue flourish and be respected by the world'.[1] This statement appeared in a code of conduct for virtuous musicians, printed at the end of Kuhnau's novel *Der musicalische Quack-Salber* and reprinted or paraphrased in several treatises.[2] For Kuhnau, compositional skill gave musicians agency – the power to shape musical materials, and through that to control their place in the wider world. This chapter explores how Lutherans conceptualised those skills and attributes that gave agency to composers. It is concerned with what Rebecca Herissone has termed 'creativity' in her studies of seventeenth-century England,[3] although in Lutheran lands of this period the ability 'to create' (*schöpfen*) was thought to reside in God alone. The act of composing music was instead described with such words as *machen*, *einführen*, *setzen*, *fingieren* and *hinzutun*, to take a sample found in Johann Andreas Herbst's 1643 treatise on composition.[4]

Lutherans understood the abilities and attributes of composers via three intertwined strands of thinking. Firstly, there was the theological view that only God can create, and that the composer is the instrument of God's will, producing music solely through divine grace. Secondly, there was the humanist view of authors as autonomous individuals, able to shape their

---

[1] 'so sind etliche gleichsam unter denen *Musicis* wie die Könige zu achten/ die/so zu reden /den Scepter führen / und andern Gesetze vorschreiben. ... Je mehr aber einer in der *Composition* erfahren/ über dieses auch in der *Invention* glücklich ist ... desto mehr wird seine *Virtù floriren* und von der geschickten Welt *aestimiret* werden'. Johann Kuhnau, *Der musicalische Quack-Salber* (Dresden, 1700), 503–4, 509–10.

[2] Kuhnau's 64 articles for 'the true virtuoso and happy musician' ('der wahre *virtuose* und glückselige *Musicus*') were reprinted in Andreas Werckmeister, *Cribrum musicum* (Quedlinburg and Leipzig, 1700), 42–60, paraphrased in the prefatory poem to Friedrich Erhardt Niedt's *Handleitung zur Variation* (Hamburg, 1706), and extensively excerpted in Johann Mattheson's treatises.

[3] Rebecca Herissone, *Musical Creativity in Restoration England* (Cambridge: Cambridge University Press, 2013); Rebecca Herissone and Alan Howard (eds.), *Concepts of Creativity in Seventeenth-Century England* (Woodbridge: Boydell, 2013).

[4] Johann Andreas Herbst, *Musica poetica* (Nuremberg, 1643), 32.

Theological Concepts of Creativity   17

works via their innate talent and rhetorical skill. Thirdly, there was the mindset of artisans, who recognised human agency in the creation of physical objects via the labour of their hands. These three traditions were not mutually exclusive, but existed in varying degrees of tension in German-speaking lands between the late sixteenth and early eighteenth centuries. Musicians argued about whether compositional ability was a divine gift or human attribute, and about the role of nature versus art in composers' achievements.

This chapter introduces the theological, humanist and artisanal notions of musical creativity, relating them to wider debates about the nature of human autonomy and agency in the period. By tracing the intellectual lineage of these different concepts of creativity, my discussion complements the paleographic case-studies offered by Herissone in her work on Restoration England. The chapter then examines how these contending views shaped discussions about musical invention (the ability to find musical ideas), including whether this ability was an innate gift or could be taught via such techniques as the arts of memory or systematic variation. Here I offer a historical counterweight to the notion of 'invention' used by Laurence Dreyfus in his analytical method for Bach's music.[5] By outlining the theological, humanist and artisanal concepts of creativity, the present chapter also establishes a framework for subsequent sections of this book.

THEOLOGICAL CONCEPTS OF CREATIVITY

According to Lutheran theology of the sixteenth to eighteenth centuries, human creativity was a gift from God. Such beliefs partly stemmed from the doctrine, transmitted by church fathers such as Augustine, that everything in the world is created by God.[6] Humans can create only in the image of God; they commit blasphemy by claiming to devise anything that does not already exist.[7] Such beliefs fitted closely with Luther's teaching in *De servo arbitrio* (*Bondage of the Will*, 1525) that God has complete power and responsibility for all things, and that humans' sinful nature prevents them achieving anything via willpower.[8]

To convey his understanding of God's grace as the source of everything, Luther used the concept of the gift.[9] He emphasised the utter unworthiness of humans, who receive salvation and other blessings only through God's favour. For Luther, the world of tangible objects and human

---

[5] Laurence Dreyfus, *Bach and the Patterns of Invention* (Cambridge, MA: Harvard University Press, 1996).
[6] G. R. Evans, *Getting It Wrong: The Medieval Epistemology of Error* (Leiden: Brill, 1998), 84–87.
[7] Augustine, *De quantitate animi* 18.31; Evans, *Getting It Wrong*, 87–88.   [8] *WA* 18, 750.
[9] Risto Saarinen, *Luther and the Gift* (Tübingen: Mohr Siebeck, 2017).

God, Talent, Craft: Concepts of Musical Creativity

achievements was a product of God's omniscient creation, a divine gift that never ceases. In his small catechism (1529), Luther glossed the first sentence of the Creed ('I believe in God the Father Almighty, Maker of heaven and earth'[10]) to explain that God's creative powers continue constantly in everyday life: 'God has given me my body and soul ... my reason and all my senses, and still preserves them. ... He provides me richly and daily with all that I need to support this body and life'.[11] Such provision occurs 'purely from fatherly, divine goodness and mercy without any merit and worthiness in me';[12] here Luther again indicated that humans lacked autonomy and agency.

Luther recognised music likewise as a product of God's bounty, stating in a 1530 draft treatise that 'music is a gift of God, not of man'.[13] He regarded even a polyphonic composition, with its artful combination of separate voice-parts, as a revelation of God's work rather than a human achievement. As he commented in 1538: 'When the natural music is strengthened and polished through art, one firstly beholds and recognises (yet cannot comprehend) with great admiration the great and complete wisdom of God in his wondrous work of music'.[14] Elsewhere, however, Luther recognised the agency of a few celebrated composers, anecdotally saying: 'Josquin is the master of the notes, which must do as he wishes'.[15]

Many Lutheran musicians echoed this theocentric notion of God as the true author of music, although sometimes their statements might be viewed as pious platitudes. In 1625 Schütz spoke of giving back to 'God, the most generous author and bestower of this art, what he had imparted to me'.[16] At the start of the eighteenth century, the Quedlinburg organist Andreas Werckmeister proclaimed: 'God the almighty creator is the author himself of music, for he in the act of creation ordered the stars and

---

[10] 'Ich gleube an Gott den Vater almechtigen Schepffer hymels und der erden'. *WA* 30/i, 292.

[11] 'Got ... mir leib unnd seel ... vernunfft und alle synne gegeben hat und noch erhelt. ... [Er] mit aller notturfft und narung dis leibs und lebens reichlich unnd teglich versorget'. Ibid.

[12] 'das alles aus lauter Veterlicher, Göttlicher güte und barmhertzickeit on alle mein verdienst und wirdickeit'. Ibid. 292, 294.

[13] 'donum Dei non hominum est', *WA* 30/ii, 696. On the notion of the gift in Luther's theology of music, see Miikka E. Anttila, *Luther's Theology of Music: Spiritual Beauty and Pleasure* (Berlin: De Gruyter, 2013), 71–97.

[14] 'Wo ... die natürliche Musica/ durch die Kunst gescherfft vnd polirt wird/ da sihet vnd erkennet man erst zum teil (denn gentzlich kans nicht begrieffen noch verstanden werden) mit grosser verwunderung/ die grosse vnd volkomene weisheit Gottes/ in seinem wunderbarlichen werck der Musica'. Luther's preface to Johann Walter, *Lob vnd Preis/ der himlischen Kunst Musica* (Wittenberg, 1564), sig. B1r; originally published in Latin as the preface to *Symphoniae jucundae* (Wittenberg, 1538).

[15] 'Josquin ... ist der noten meister/ die habens müssen machen wie er wolt.' Cited in Johann Mathesius, *Historien von des ehrwirdigen ... Martini Luthers Anfang, Lehr, Leben und Sterben* (Nuremberg, 1566), 152r–v.

[16] 'DEO benignissimo artis hujus autori largitoriq‹ue› quod impertiiset referrem'. Heinrich Schütz, *Cantiones sacrae* (Freiberg, 1625), tenor partbook, sig.):(1v. RISM A/I S2279.

Theological Concepts of Creativity

their paths according to musical proportions, as Holy Scripture reports (Job 38.7)'.[17] For Werckmeister, 'man is not actually the inventor [of compositions] but only the tool used by God for his purposes'.[18] The act of composition thus consisted of disclosing a God-given order, a task in which human autonomy was severely restricted.

Lutherans recognised the role of human labour through the doctrine of vocation (*Beruf*). In his *Von der Freiheit eines Christenmenschen (Freedom of a Christian*, 1520) Luther explained that the believer's spiritual freedom went hand-in-hand with a duty to serve God in the world. In later writings he argued that humans are called by God to fulfil a vocation for the benefit of others.[19] Many Lutheran musicians accordingly described their career as a divine calling, and attributed their achievements to God rather than any capability of their own. Such claims often occurred in autobiographical statements and job applications. When petitioning the Elector of Saxony in 1651 for permission to retire, Schütz included a brief account of his career, ascribing events such as his move to Dresden to divine command: 'It was ordained by God the Almighty, who undoubtedly had chosen me in the womb for the profession of music'.[20] In 1730 Bach narrated his recent career in a letter to his old friend Georg Erdmann, explaining that 'it pleased God that I should be called to be director of music and cantor at the Thomasschule'.[21] Bach's annotations of his Calov Bible also indicate a strong sense of fulfilling God's calling, as John Butt has analysed.[22] Other musicians gave thanks for divine assistance with specific projects. In a 1617 letter to the Elector of Saxony, Schein described publishing his works 'with God's help' and his aim to improve music in Leipzig 'by means of Godly assistance'.[23] In 1619 Michael Praetorius spoke of compositions 'which I finished through the grace loaned by God'.[24] Believing they were the recipients of a divine gift, Lutheran composers felt obliged to reciprocate this gift by sharing their talents for the benefit of the common good, as will be explored in Chapter 4.

---

[17] 'Wie GOtt der Allmächtige Schöpffer der *Music* Autor selber ist/ da Er in der Erschöpffung/ die Sternen/ und dero Lauf in die *Music*alischen *Proportiones* geordnet/ wie die Heil. Schrifft meldet *Job. 38.7*'. Andreas Werckmeister, *Musicalische Paradoxal-Discourse* (Quedlinburg, 1707), 4.

[18] 'der Mensch ist nicht eigentlich der *Inventor* sondern nur das Werckzeug/ so GOtt darzu gebrauchet'. Ibid., 26.

[19] *WA* 36, 201–6; see also Gustaf Wingren, *Luther on Vocation*, trans. Carl C. Rasmussen (Philadelphia: Muhlenberg, 1957).

[20] D-Dla, Loc. 8687/1, fols. 291v–292r. *SDok* 1, 322; *HSR*, 183.

[21] *BDok* 1, 67 (no. 23); *NBR*, 151.

[22] John Butt, *Bach's Dialogue with Modernity* (Cambridge: Cambridge University Press, 2010), 55.

[23] 'durch Göttliche verleÿhung'; 'vermittelst Göttlichen beÿstandes'. D-Dla, Loc. 10757/2, fols. 60r–v; transcribed and translated in Stephen Rose, 'Protected Publications: The Imperial and Saxon Privileges for Printed Music, 1550–700', *Early Music History* 37 (2018), 247–313 (pp. 304–6).

[24] 'so Ich durch GOttes verliehene Gnade . . . verfasset'. Michael Praetorius, *Polyhymnia caduceatrix et panegyrica* (Wolfenbüttel, 1619), dedication. RISM A/I P5370.

Despite commanding Christians to share their talents with the world, Luther urged believers to retain the humility characteristic of monasticism. In his 1520 treatise on good works, he instructed his followers to prioritise faith rather than seek fame through external achievements:

> Those men must be few and most spiritual, who, when honoured and praised, remain indifferent and unchanged, so that they do not care for it, nor feel pride and pleasure in it, but remain entirely free, ascribe all their honour and fame to God, offering it to Him alone, and using it only to the glory of God, to the edification of their neighbours, and in no way to their own benefit or advantage.[25]

Similarly in a 1537 sermon he told the congregation to renounce ambition and false pride.[26] Because all earthly talent came from God, humans should not claim credit for it.

Devout Lutheran musicians of the seventeenth century upheld these calls for modesty. In 1691 Werckmeister explained that because music is God's noblest gift, it should honour nobody but God.[27] Citing the polymath Erasmus Francisci, he castigated church musicians concerned solely for their own glory: 'He who sings or plays such artful songs must take care that he seeks not his own fame but that of God'.[28] In his code of conduct for virtuous musicians, Kuhnau advised that someone who excels in his profession should avoid 'boastful words' or 'haughty gestures'; rather 'he should consider that all these gifts of the intellect, as well as those of the body and good fortune, originate in God, and that each person in the world cannot show more skill than was allotted to him in the bosom of God's grace'.[29] As discussed below, this doctrine of modesty clashed with the quest for fame and commemoration encouraged by humanist views of authorship.

In the decades around 1700, many composers acknowledged the theological notion of authorship via inscriptions on their manuscripts. The markings 'JJ' ('Jesu juva' – Jesus help) or 'INJ' ('In nomine Jesu' – In the name of Jesus), found at the start of many manuscripts, signalled the inadequacy of humans and prayed for divine help in the act of

---

[25] 'Wenig unnd gantz hochgeistliche menschen mussen das sein, die in ehre unnd lob blos, gelassen und gleich bleiben, das sie sich der selben nit annehmen, gutdunckel und gefallen drinnen haben, sondern gantz frey unnd ledig bleyben, alle yhr ehre und namen allein got zurechnen, yhm allein aufftragen, unnd der selben nit anders gebrauchen, dan got zu ehre und dem nehsten zur besserung, unnd yhn selbs gar nichtz zu eygenem nutz odder vorteil'. *WA* 6, 221.

[26] *WA* 47, 402–3.

[27] Andreas Werckmeister, *Der edlen Music-Kunst Würde/ Gebrauch und Mißbrauch* (Frankfurt am Main and Leipzig, 1691), sig. :)(3r.

[28] 'Der solche künstliche Lieder singet oder spielet/ hat sich in acht zu nehmen/ daß er nicht vielmehr seinen eigenen/ als GOttes Ruhm hierunter suche'. Ibid., 13. Werckmeister cites a treatise by Erasmus Francisci, *Heilige Nachtigall*, which cannot now be located.

[29] 'erwege er doch hauptsächlich/ daß alle diese Gaben des Gemüthes/ eben so wohl/ wie die andern des Leibes und Glückes/ von GOtt den Ursprung haben/ und daß ein jeder in der Welt von Geschicklichkeit nicht mehr auffweisen könne/ als was ihm aus dem Schooße der Göttlichen Gnade zugemessen werden.' Kuhnau, *Der musicalische Quack-Salber*, 521–22.

Theological Concepts of Creativity 21

composition. The mottos 'SDG' ('Soli Deo Gloria' – To God alone be the glory) and 'Laus Deo' (Praise God), at the end of many manuscripts, indicated that the composition was written to honour not the author but God alone.

These inscriptions are best known in the manuscripts of J. S. Bach, where their significance has been a flashpoint in disputes between theological and secular interpretations of the composer. After 1945 a Marxist view developed in East Germany of Bach as a secular, proto-bourgeoisie figure. Such a view may have influenced Friedrich Blume, whose article on Bach for *Musik in Geschichte und Gegenwart* dismissed the 'JJ' and 'SDG' inscriptions as an 'artisan's custom' (*Handwerksbrauch*) found in many other music manuscripts of the period.[30] By contrast, theological Bach scholars argue these markings give insights into not only the composer's faith but also how his works should be interpreted. Robin Leaver, referring to Bach's extensive library of Lutheran theological books, stated that the inscriptions were 'no empty formality', but rather show that Bach had 'a specifically Christian understanding of human creativity under the grace of God'.[31] Walter Blankenburg claimed that the 'SDG' motto 'stands explicitly or implicitly under all [Bach's] creations'.[32] Eric Chafe has used the 'JJ' and 'SDG' mottos to justify his detailed readings of Bach cantatas as showing the 'dualism of God in His majesty and the human condition in need of aid from Jesus'.[33]

The debates about the significance of 'JJ' and 'SDG' can be partly defused by investigating the hitherto neglected question of how composers other than Bach used such mottos. The pious inscriptions are rarely found in musical sources before 1650, but this may be because few composers' autographs survive from this period (see p. 9). No such inscriptions are found in the few extant autographs of Schein and Schütz;[34] nor in the vast majority of printed editions before 1650. From 1650 onwards, the wording 'Soli Deo Gloria' appears occasionally at the end of printed collections, including Schütz's *Symphoniarum sacrarum tertia pars* (1650), Dietrich Becker's *Sonaten und Suiten* (1674), and the two volumes of Johann Kuhnau's *Neue Clavier Ubung* (1689, 1692).[35] Inscriptions are

---

[30] Friedrich Blume, 'Bach, Johann Sebastian', *Die Musik in Geschichte und Gegenwart*, vol. 1 (Kassel: Bärenreiter, 1949–51), 962–1047 (col. 1032).

[31] Robin A. Leaver, *J. S. Bach and Scripture: Glosses from the Calov Bible Commentary* (St. Louis: Concordia Publishing House, 1985), 53, 107.

[32] Walter Blankenburg, 'Bach', *Theologische Realenzyklopädie*, vol. 5 (Berlin: De Gruyter, 1979–80), 90–94 (p. 92).

[33] Eric Chafe, *Analyzing Bach Cantatas* (New York: Oxford University Press, 2000), 26.

[34] Schein's only extant musical autograph is the score and parts of the 'Madrigale', *Lobet den Herrn*, presented in 1615 to Friedrich von Sachsen-Weimar (D-GOl, Phil. 2⁰ 270/1 [75]). For Schütz, the score of *Weib, was weinest du* (SWV443) has text in the composer's hand (D-Kl, Ms.49x/2); moreover, there are a few performing parts of other compositions partly in the composer's hand (see works-list in Joshua Rifkin et al., 'Schütz, Heinrich', *Oxford Music Online*).

[35] RISM A/I S2295, B1527, K2982, 2986.

also found in autograph scores or tablatures prepared to a high calligraphic standard. Matthias Weckmann's autograph score of his four vocal concertos written in 1663, the plague year in Hamburg, is carefully presented, with the composer's name stated in full and also abbreviated as monograms. Each piece bears the date of copying, and the composer added occasional 'NB' annotations clarifying that the notated dissonances are correct.[36] The inscription 'Soli Deo Gloria' after each piece is like a calligraphic flourish indicating that each composition is complete, while dispelling any hint of pride on the part of the composer.

That pious inscriptions were relatively common on presentation autographs in the late seventeenth century is suggested by an analysis of the manuscripts of Dieterich Buxtehude's music in the Düben Collection, the collection of the Swedish court capellmeisters and now held in Uppsala University Library. The inscriptions do not appear on the performing parts of Buxtehude's music copied by various scribes including Gustav Düben himself; nor do they appear on the tablatures of Buxtehude's vocal compositions in Düben's hand. But the collection contains eight autograph manuscripts by Buxtehude, including presentation copies such as the Passiontide cycle *Membra Jesu nostri*.[37] Six of these autographs are in tablature or score, and start with 'INJ' and/or end with 'Soli Deo Gloria'.[38] The single set of parts in Buxtehude's hand, for *Herr, ich lasse dich nicht* BuxWV36, lacks any such markings, apart from a 'Laus Deo' at the end of the Organum part.[39] Parts mainly served a pragmatic purpose for performance and rarely bore pious inscriptions. Tablature or score, by contrast, allowed compositions to be appraised by a musically literate reader, and therefore were better formats for displaying the skill of the composer.[40] Here the 'INJ' and 'SDG' markings deflected any suspicion that composers wished to glorify themselves in their presentation autographs.

Surviving sources suggest that the use of these pious inscriptions intensified in the early eighteenth century. They appear on some printed music of the period, such as Philipp Heinrich Erlebach's *Gott-geheiligte Sing-Stunde* (1704),[41] but not in J. S. Bach's printed editions. The Darmstadt

---

[36] D-Lr, Mus. ant. pract. KN207/6.

[37] On these autographs, see Peter Wollny, 'From Lübeck to Sweden: Thoughts and Observations on the Buxtehude Sources in the Düben Collection', *Early Music* 35 (2007), 371–83.

[38] 'INJ' and 'Soli Deo Gloria' inscriptions are found on the following Buxtehude autographs in S-Uu: *Fürwahr, er trug unsere Krankheit*, BuxWV31 (score, vmhs 006:009); *Membra Jesu nostri*, BuxWV75 (tablature, vmhs 050:012); *Nimm von uns, Herr, du treuer Gott*, BuxWV78 (tablature, vmhs 082:038); and *Nun danket alle Gott*, BuxWV79 (tablature, vmhs 082:039). 'INJ' appears on *O Jesu mi dulcissime*, BuxWV88 (tablature, vmhs 082:040), and 'Deo Soli Gloria' on *O fröhliche Stunden, o herrliche Zeit*, BuxWV85 (tablature, vmhs 051:013a).

[39] S-Uu, vmhs 051:002.

[40] On the use of tablature for assessing compositions, see Andreas Werckmeister, *Harmonologia musica* (Frankfurt am Main and Leipzig, 1702), 68.

[41] Philipp Heinrich Erlebach, *Gott-geheiligte Sing-Stunde* (Rudolstadt, 1704). RISM A/I E763. The preface begins with 'INJ' and the two continuo partbooks end with 'Soli Deo Gloria'.

Theological Concepts of Creativity 23

court musician Christoph Graupner habitually used these markings in autograph scores of his cantatas, combining the 'INJ' with a date at the head of the score.[42] Many of J. S. Bach's autograph scores of the 1720s include 'JJ' and 'SDG' markings; Michael Marissen has constructed a chronology of Bach's use of these markings, showing that their incidence peaks in 1724–5, during the composer's second year in Leipzig.[43] Handel also inscribed 'SDG' on autographs of many of his sacred works, possibly as a legacy of his Lutheran upbringing.[44] In addition to autograph scores, the pious inscriptions were increasingly used by scribes when they copied music. Thus Bach marked 'JJ' and 'SDG' in most of his scores of cantatas by his second cousin Johann Ludwig Bach.[45] Bach's pupil Johann Ludwig Krebs, who concluded many of his autographs with 'SDG', added this or similar markings to some of his copies of Bach's works.[46] Although the early eighteenth century is often described as a period of growing secularisation, these inscriptions suggest that composers upheld theological notions of authorship (perhaps in response to the high levels of productivity demanded of them, as explored in Chapter 5).

The many 'JJ' and 'SDG' inscriptions in autograph manuscripts of the late seventeenth and early eighteenth centuries indicate the pervasiveness of the Lutheran view of musical creativity as a gift from God. My study shows that these markings occur in sources with specific formats and functions – namely score and tablature, which gave an overview of the composer's work and were used for composing or presentation. Such sources showcased the achievements of composers, obliging them to acknowledge the divine source of their talent. As Kuhnau advised in his 1700 code of conduct, the virtuous musician 'should thank God and attribute the honour to Him if he notices something in himself that elevates him above others. Otherwise God might take the loaned talent from him, and make him one of the unluckiest and most confused creatures'.[47] Kuhnau's advice suggests that musicians may have included the 'JJ' and SDG' markings as an insurance policy to ensure the continuation

---

[42] See digitized scores of Graupner's autographs, linked from https://christoph-graupner-gesellschaft .de/index.php/forschung/gwv-online.

[43] Michael Marissen, 'Bach against Modernity', unpublished typescript.

[44] For a list of these annotations in Handel manuscripts, see Donald Burrows, 'What's in a Name? Handel's Autograph Annotations', in Nicole Ristow, Wolfgang Sandberger and Dorothea Schröder (eds.), *'Critica musica'. Studien zum 17. und 18. Jahrhundert. Festschrift Hans Joachim Marx zum 65. Geburtstag* (Stuttgart: Metzler, 2001), 25–47.

[45] D-B, Mus.ms. Bach P397.

[46] 'Soli Deo Gloria' appears at the end of most of Krebs's autographs of his sacred vocal works and organ works; see Felix Friedrich, *Krebs-Werkeverzeichnis (Krebs-WV). Thematisch-systematisches Verzeichnis der musikalischen Werke von Johann Ludwig Krebs* (Altenburg: Kamprad, 2009). Krebs added 'Soli Deo Gloria' at the end of his copy of Bach's organ chorale *Christ lag in Todesbanden* BWV718 (D-B, Mus.ms.autogr. Krebs, J. L. 2 N), and on his copy (made jointly with his father) of Bach's Fantasia and Fugue in C minor BWV537, D-B, Mus.ms. Bach P803, Faszikel 15.

[47] 'Er dancke vielmehr seinem GOtt/ und schreibe ihm die Ehre zu/ wo er etwas an sich mercket/ das ihn über andere erhebet. Sonsten kan ihm dieser Herr das geliehene Pfund bald wieder nehmen/

of their God-given talent. Whereas Blankenburg and Chafe use the inscriptions to support their theological interpretations of Bach's works, my perspective from material culture suggests these markings indicate how musicians conceived their role in society, in accordance with Luther's treatise on good works. Moreover, the pious inscriptions do not unequivocally denote theological meanings in music of this period. As the following sections show, the view of creativity as God's gift mingled with attitudes more open to notions of human agency, by emphasising inborn talent or manual skill.

HUMANIST NOTIONS OF AUTHORSHIP

In contrast with the Lutheran doctrine of an all-powerful God as sole creator, humanist traditions asserted that man was an independent being, capable of free will and agency. Humanist notions of authorship drew on classical poetics to understand how poets and musicians held creative power through a combination of innate talent and rhetorical skill. The inborn abilities of authors were described with the term *ingenium*, which invoked a cluster of meanings including humans' natural dispositions and their powers of intelligence and invention.[48] Whereas theological traditions viewed human callings as commanded by God, humanists believed that vocation was determined by innate aptitudes.[49] They argued that poetic or musical works should be durable, preserved to immortalise the name of the author.

The importance of *ingenium* in poetry and oratory was stressed by a succession of Roman writers. Quintilian defined *ingenium* as an innate quality that is among the most important attributes in an orator.[50] Horace, following Greek pre-Socratics such as Democritus, argued that natural talent was essential in poets, but had to be refined by training and skill: 'Often it is asked whether a praiseworthy poem be due to nature or to art. For my part, I do not see of what avail is either study, when not enriched by Nature's vein, or native wit, if untrained.'[51] The significance of innate talent was summarised by a saying found in an AD 200 commentary on Horace: 'Poeta nascitur non fit' (A poet is born not made).[52]

---

und ihn zur aller unglückseligsten/ und im Verstande gantz verwirreten Creatur machen'. Kuhnau, *Der musicalische Quack-Salber*, 522.

[48] Alain Pons, 'Ingenium', in Barbara Cassin (ed.), *Dictionary of Untranslatables: A Philosophical Lexicon* (Princeton: Princeton University Press, 2014), 485–89.

[49] Richard M. Douglas, 'Talent and Vocation in Humanist and Protestant Thought', in Theodore K. Rabb and Jerrold E. Seigel (eds.), *Action and Conviction in Early Modern Europe: Essays in Honor of E. H. Harbison* (Princeton: Princeton University Press, 1969), 261–98.

[50] Quintilian, *Institutio oratoria* 10.2.12.

[51] Horace, *Ars poetica* 408–10, trans. H. Rushton Fairclough, Loeb Classical Library 194 (Cambridge, MA: Harvard University Press, 1961).

[52] On this proverb, see William Ringler, 'Poeta nascitur non fit. Some Notes on the History of an Aphorism', *Journal of the History of Ideas* 2 (1941), 497–504.

Humanist Notions of Authorship

A subcategory of classical conceptions of authorship viewed the poet as gripped by a divine muse. In Plato's *Ion*, Socrates described (perhaps ironically) the state of ἐνθουσιασμός (*enthousiasmos*; in later Latin, the *furor poeticus*), a divine frenzy that supplied the poet's invention.[53] In his *Fasti*, Ovid mused: 'There is a god within us. ... / It is his impulse that sows the seeds of inspiration.'[54] Although the divine origin of such inspiration might suggest a link with theological views of authorship, Plato and Ovid conceived it not as a God-given vocation but rather as an attribute separating the poet from the rest of society.

In the sixteenth century, classical notions of authorship were promoted by humanists in German-speaking lands, including those who applied aspects of ancient poetics to music. Heinrich Glarean used the term *ingenium* in his *Dodekachordon* (1547) to praise the qualities of composers such as Josquin, whose '*ingenium* is indescribable and we can be amazed at it more than we can treat it adequately'.[55] Glarean also admired the *ingenium* shown by Obrecht, Isaac and Ockeghem.[56] With regard to the invention of melodies, he asserted that this 'is to be ascribed more to the workings of *ingenium* and to some natural and inborn talent than to craftsmanship'.[57] In 1964 Edward Lowinsky translated *ingenium* in Glarean's treatise as 'genius', comparing it to nineteenth-century notions of musical genius as voiced by E. T. A. Hoffmann.[58] More recently Paula Higgins has critiqued Lowinsky for giving Josquin the quasi-mythological status of a 'musical genius'.[59] Glarean's use of *ingenium* can be better interpreted as upholding the classical belief that innate talent (*natura*) is more important than skill (*ars*).[60]

Classical ideas also shaped the development of the discipline of *musica poetica* (the study of composition) in German grammar schools of the sixteenth century. The term *musica poetica* was first used by the Wittenberg cantor Nikolaus Listenius in the 1530s. Influenced by the Aristotelian classification of science into three branches (speculative, practical and productive), Listenius divided musical study into the realms of *theoretica*,

---

[53] Plato, *Ion* 533d–535a.

[54] Ovid, *Fasti* 6.5–6, trans. James G. Frazer, Loeb Classical Library 253 (Cambridge, MA: Harvard University Press, 1931).

[55] 'Porro cum ingenium eius inenarrabile sit, magisque mirari possimus, quam digne explicare'. Heinrich Glarean, *Dodekachordon* (Basel, 1547), 363.

[56] Ibid., 454, 456, 460.

[57] 'utrique id viribus ingenii accidere, et naturali quadam ac ingenita virtute, magis quam arte'. Ibid., 174.

[58] Edward Lowinsky, 'Musical Genius: Evolution and Origins of a Concept', in Bonnie J. Blackburn (ed.), *Music in the Culture of the Renaissance and Other Essays*, 2 vols. (Chicago: University of Chicago Press, 1989), vol. 1, 40–66 (pp. 50–51). Originally published in *The Musical Quarterly* 50 (1964), 321–40 and 476–95.

[59] Paula Higgins, 'The Apotheosis of Josquin des Prez and Other Mythologies of Musical Genius', *Journal of the American Musicological Society* 57 (2004), 443–510.

[60] Heinz von Loesch, *Der Werkbegriff in der protestantischen Musiktheorie des 16. und 17. Jahrhunderts: Ein Mißverständnis* (Hildesheim: Olms, 2001), 44–50.

practica and *poetica*.[61] For Listenius, *musica poetica* was the productive branch of music, which is 'content neither with an understanding of the subject nor with practice alone, but rather leaves an opus behind after the labour'.[62] Subsequent theorists outlined the skills involved in this art of 'combining melodic lines into a harmony adorned with various affections of periods, in order to incline men's minds and hearts to various emotions' (to quote Joachim Burmeister's 1606 treatise).[63] Such a goal of moving the hearts of listeners emphasised the agency of composers, similar to that of orators. Writers on *musica poetica* also maintained the classical emphasis on *ingenium*. Gallus Dressler, cantor in Magdeburg until 1574, described his composition lessons as intended for 'those who are led by a natural inclination to this art'.[64]

In the seventeenth century a vernacular poetics emerged in German-speaking lands, with ramifications for how musicians regarded the discipline of composition. The notion of innate talent (*Naturell* or *Geist*) still played a major role. Martin Opitz in his *Buch von der deutschen Poeterey* (1624) explained that poetic writings 'stem from a godly impulse and from nature, as Plato says in various places'.[65] Referring to Ovid, he declared: 'There is a spirit in us, and all that is written, thought and said by us, is impelled by it'.[66] Poets acknowledged the importance of rhetorical skills, but asserted that innate talent was the ultimate prerequisite for their profession. Georg Philipp Harsdörffer adapted a simile used by Quintilian, declaring: 'Art without the help of nature is weak, and can achieve as little as a farmer without seeds and fields.'[67] By the early eighteenth century, this emphasis on innate talent converged with the preference for a literary style that imitates nature.[68] In 1724 Johann Georg Neukirch declared that 'natural talent gives good ideas and achieves more than a thousand rules'.[69]

---

[61] On the Aristotelian basis, see ibid., 87–94.

[62] 'quæ neque rei cognitione, neque solo exercitio contenta, sed aliquid post laborem relinquit operis'. Nikolaus Listenius, *Musica* (Wittenberg, 1537), sig. A4v.

[63] 'conjungendo sonos Melodiarum in Harmoniam, varijs periodorum affectionibus exornatam, ad animos hominum cordaque in varios motus flectenda'. Joachim Burmeister, *Musica poetica* (Rostock, 1606), 1; modern edn as *Musical Poetics*, trans. Benito V. Rivera (New Haven: Yale University Press, 1993), 17.

[64] 'qui naturali inclinatione ducuntur ad hanc artem'. *Gallus Dressler's* Præcepta musicæ poëticæ, ed. Robert Forgács (Urbana: University of Illinois Press, 2007), 190–91.

[65] 'welcher schrifften auß einem Göttlichen antriebe vnd von natur herkommen/ wie Plato hin vnd wieder hiervon redet'. Martin Opitz, *Buch von der deutschen Poeterey* (Breslau, 1624), sig. B1r.

[66] 'Es ist ein Geist in vns/ vnd was von vns geschrieben/ Gedacht wird vnd gesagt/ das wird durch ihn getrieben'. Ibid., sig. I4v.

[67] 'Die Kunst ist sonder Behuff der Natur ohnmächtig/ und kan so wenig ausrichten/ als ein Ackermann sonder Samen und Feld'. Georg Philipp Harsdörffer, *Deß poetischen Trichters Dritter Theil* (Nuremberg, 1653), preface, sig.)(1r, alluding to Quintilian, *Institutio oratoria* 1.pr.27.

[68] Hans Peter Herrmann, *Naturnachahmung und Einbildungskraft: zur Entwicklung der deutschen Poetik von 1670 bis 1740* (Bad Homburg: Gehlen, 1970), 52–80.

[69] 'Das *Ingenium* giebet gute Einfälle und verrichtet mehr als tausend Regeln'. Johann Georg Neukirch, *Anfangs-Gründe zur reinen teutschen Poesie itziger Zeit* (Halle, 1724), 230.

Humanist Notions of Authorship

Musicians likewise argued that natural ability was crucial in shaping a composer's vocation. In the same 1651 autobiographical statement where he attributed his calling to God's command, Schütz stated: 'I was destined by nature for music'.[70] From the late seventeenth century onwards, musicians echoed vernacular poetics by emphasising the priority of innate talent, albeit refined by art and skill. In 1677 the Sorau cantor Wolfgang Caspar Printz specified the first prerequisite of a composer as 'a good and skilled nature which has a desire and love for music'.[71] He added, however, that such nature needed to be tempered by judgement as fostered by experience.[72] Similarly Johann David Heinichen listed in 1728 the first requisite of a composer as natural talent (*Talent*), followed by knowledge (*Wissenschaft*) and experience (*Erfahrung*).[73] In 1739 Mattheson claimed that a composer required 'natural ability' (*Naturell*), 'enthusiasm' (*Lust*, redolent of Platonic *furor*), and 'diligence' (*Fleiß*).[74]

Highlighting the importance of innate talent, several musicians adapted the motto 'Poeta nascitur non fit'. In 1677 the Weissenfels musician Johann Beer included in his satirical novel *Der simplicianische Welt-Kucker* a scene where court musicians discuss entering the profession. A castrato declares: 'You can easily become a cobbler or tailor, but music requires a heaven-sent spirit.' Such a statement distanced music from the world of artisans, aligning it instead with the divine *furor* described by Plato and Ovid. The castrato continues: 'Poets are born not made, and I also think that musicians are likewise born not made. I speak only of artists; just as a hack can't be a poet, a beerfiddler can't be a *musicus*'.[75] Versions of Beer's maxim were later quoted by Martin Heinrich Fuhrmann and Mattheson;[76] even Werckmeister cited it, albeit within a theocentric perspective that understood a composer's gifts as divinely ordained.[77] The most artful advocate of the view that nature alone determined musical ability was Georg Philipp Telemann, who portrayed himself as a self-taught musician. In a letter to Johann Gottfried Walther, he claimed:

---

[70] D-Dla, Loc. 8687/1, fol. 291r; *SDok* 1, 321; *HSR*, 182.

[71] 'eine gute und geschickte Natur/ welche zur *Music* Lust und Beliebung träget'. Wolfgang Caspar Printz, *Phrynis oder satyrischer Componist*, 2 vols. (Quedlinburg, 1676–77), vol. 2, sig. E1v.

[72] Ibid., sig. E2r, E2v.

[73] Johann David Heinichen, *Der General-Bass in der Composition* (Dresden, 1728), 21

[74] Mattheson, *Der vollkommene Capellmeister* (Hamburg, 1739), 108.

[75] 'Ein Schuster und Schneider kan man leichtlich werden/ zu der *Music* gehört ein Himmlischer Geist/ man sagt die Poeten werden gebohren/ ich lasse es zu/ aber ich sage auch die *Musici* werden gebohren/ ich rede aber von Künstlern/ dann gleich wie ein Pritschmeister kein *Poët* kan genennet werden/ also kan auch nicht ieder Bierfiedler/ oder Brätel und Schertzel-Geiger ein *Musicus* seyn'. Johann Beer, *Der simplicianische Welt-Kucker*, book 1 (n.p., 1677), 34.

[76] Martin Heinrich Fuhrmann, *Musicalischer Trichter* (Frankfurt an der Spree, 1706), 29; *Friederich Erhard Niedtens Musicalischer Handleitung Anderer Theil Von der Variation*, ed. Johann Mattheson (Hamburg, 1721), 8.

[77] Werckmeister, *Harmonologia musica*, 55.

'In every aspect, nature alone is my teacher'.[78] In his first published autobiography (1718), Telemann attributed his talent to God and nature, using the motto 'Quod Musici nascuntur, non fiant' (Musicians are born, not made), and quoting Horace to explain why his natural inclinations could not be eradicated by his disapproving parents.[79]

In contrast to the Lutheran insistence that all human endeavour should glorify God, classical and humanist poetics recognised that authors might be motivated by a desire for glory and immortality.[80] At the end of his third book of odes, Horace described his achievement in rendering lyric poetry in Latin: 'I have raised a monument more permanent than bronze'.[81] In his treatise on poetry, Horace contrasted the different ways in which authors could achieve success: 'That is the book to make money for the Sosii [booksellers]; this is the one to cross the sea and extend to a distant day its author's fame'.[82] Such an approach was anathema to Luther, who declared in his 1520 sermon on good works that 'all pagan books are suffused with this poison of seeking praise and honour'.[83]

Yet treatises in the *musica poetica* tradition – embedded in the teaching practices of Lutheran schools – recognised the durable products of compositional activity. Listenius defined the goal of *musica poetica* as 'making or constructing, that is, in such labour that even after itself, when the artificer is dead, leaves a perfect and absolute opus'.[84] Much scholarly ink has been spilled over how Listenius's definition might relate to the work-concept of subsequent centuries.[85] For our purposes, the emphasis on the durability of the notated opus reinforced a sense of the musical author. Subsequent writers on *musica poetica* commented how notated compositions could preserve the composer's name in perpetuity: in 1643 Johann Andreas Herbst declared that 'a composer assembles a little musical work with great diligence, effort and labour in this art, to leave behind an

---

[78] 'Bey allem dem ist die bloße Natur meine Lehr-Meisterin'. Letter of 20 December 1729, in Georg Philipp Telemann, *Briefwechsel. Sämtliche erreichbare Briefe von und an Telemann*, ed. Hans Grosse and Hans Rudolf Jung (Leipzig: Deutscher Verlag für Musik, 1972), 33.

[79] Telemann's 1718 autobiography, printed in Johann Mattheson, *Grosse General-Bass-Schule* (Hamburg, 1731), 161. On p.163 he quoted 'Naturam expellas furca, tamen usque recurret' (You may drive out Nature with a pitchfork yet she will always return) from Horace, *Epistles* 1.10.24.

[80] Stephen Murphy, *The Gift of Immortality: Myths of Power and Humanist Poetics* (Madison: Associated University Presses, 1997).

[81] 'Exegi monumentum aere perennius'. Horace, *Odes* [*Carmina*], 3.30.1.

[82] Horace, *Ars poetica* 345–46, trans. Fairclough.

[83] 'alle heidenische bucher seind mit diser gifft des lob und ehre suchens gantz durchmachet'. *WA* 6, 220.

[84] 'Consistit enim in faciendo siue fabricando, hoc est, in labore tali, qui post se etiam, artifice mortuo, opus perfectum et absolutum relinquat'. Listenius, *Musica*, sig. A4v.

[85] Lydia Goehr, *The Imaginary Museum of Musical Works. An Essay in the Philosophy of Music* (Oxford: Clarendon Press, 1992), 115–19; Loesch, *Der Werkbegriff*.

enduring memory of his name to his descendants'.[86] Christoph Bernhard began his treatise of counterpoint by noting how specific qualities in a composition might ensure fame for its author: 'from the diverse use [of the rules of counterpoint] and the influence of [a composer's] nature it results that one composition is good, another however even better, pleasing [audiences] either less or more and making the author famous'.[87] As Keith Chapin notes, this formulation recalled Horace's opinion on the power of poetry to immortalise the author.[88] Through the influence of classical poetics, Lutherans thus celebrated the agency and durability of the musical author.

The humanist notion of authorship recognised composers as having the nature and skill to create lasting musical works with power over human emotions. Although writers in this tradition might recognise human talents as initially endowed by God, they argued that subsequently those talents could be used by individuals independent of God's will. Thus humanism acknowledged the importance of self-assertion, even before the empiricism of the seventeenth century promoted an individuality fostered by human observation and judgement.

THE ARTISANAL VIEW OF PRODUCTION

A third set of beliefs about musical composition viewed it as an artisan's craft. In the ancient world, manual crafts such as carpentry, painting, sculpting and metalwork were regarded as *artes mechanicae*. These had a lower status than the *artes liberales*, which were intellectual pursuits practised by freemen and not used for financial gain. In German towns during the sixteenth and seventeenth centuries, however, manual crafts gained status and prestige from the attitudes of artisans. Artisans focused on creating objects with their hands, prizing the manual skills involved in examining and shaping materials.[89] As Pamela Smith explains, artisanal culture 'operated from an understanding of the human relationship to the material world and the power of human art',[90] and consequently

---

[86] 'ein *Musicus Poëticus* oder *Compon*ist/ ein dergleiche‹n› *Musicali*sches Wercklein/ welches er mit grossem fleiß/ müh vnd arbeit/ durch diese Kunst zusammen gebracht/ zu seines Namens im‹m›erwärendem Gedächtnuß den Nachkömlingen hinderlassen'. Herbst, *Musica poetica*, 1.

[87] 'aus deren unterschiedlichen Brauch und natürlichen *Influentz* es herrühret, daß eine *Composition* gut, die andere aber besser ist, die [Zuhörer] minder oder mehr vergnüget und den *Authorem* berühmt macht'. Joseph Müller-Blattau, *Die Kompositionslehre Heinrich Schützens in der Fassung seines Schülers Christoph Bernhard* (Leipzig: Breitkopf & Härtel, 1926), 40.

[88] Keith Chapin, '"A Harmony or Concord of Several and Diverse Voices": Autonomy in Seventeenth-Century German Music Theory and Practice', *International Review of the Aesthetics and Sociology of Music* 42 (2011), 219–55 (p. 227).

[89] Pamela H. Smith, *The Body of the Artisan: Art and Experience in the Scientific Revolution* (Chicago: University of Chicago Press, 2004), 6–8.

[90] Pamela H. Smith, *The Business of Alchemy: Science and Culture in the Holy Roman Empire* (Princeton: Princeton University Press, 1994), 8.

had some overlaps with early scientific investigation of the properties of natural objects. Generally such crafts were regulated by guilds and their skills were transmitted not in writing but via apprenticeships, in which trainees imitated a master's handiwork in order to develop their own expertise.

Artisans valued skill (*Kunst*), a term with dual meanings in the period. When derived from *können*, the term *Kunst* indicated the human ability to make objects and carry out specific tasks; when derived from *kennen*, by contrast, it denoted theoretical knowledge unrelated to practical application (as in the term *freie Künste*, liberal arts).[91] Artisans favoured the first meaning of *Kunst*, to indicate the skill involved in crafts as disparate as sculpture, painting, or the making of musical instruments. However, some individuals rooted in artisanal culture, including the artist Albrecht Dürer, used the word *Brauch* to denote their practical abilities, reserving the term *Kunst* to describe their individual knowledge.[92] The artisanal emphasis on *Kunst* contrasted with the humanist belief that skill (*ars*) is only meaningful when combined with innate talent (*natura*).

A further characteristic of artisanal culture was its glorification of hard work. Still circulating in the sixteenth century was a poem by the Nuremberg blacksmith Hans Rosenplüt (*c.*1400–*c.*60), contrasting the productivity of artisans with the sinful behaviour of the idle. Hard work could cleanse the soul, he claimed:

> A worker who washes his brow
> With the sweat of his hard work
> This is like a lime and a brine
> That in his soul will be purified
> So he will soon reach heaven.[93]

Following the Reformation, Lutherans abandoned any suggestion that salvation could be obtained through good works, but craftworkers still idealised hard labour. In a 1576 poem praising a group of artisans who rowed from Zurich to Strasbourg, Johann Fischart celebrated how their industry overcame obstacles in their journey. 'Work and diligence are the

---

[91] *Deutsches Wörterbuch von Jacob Grimm und Wilhelm Grimm*, http://dwb.uni-trier.de/de/, q.v. 'Kunst'.

[92] Jeffrey Ashcroft, 'Zum Wort und Begriff "Kunst" in Dürers Schriften', in Alan Robertshaw and Gerhard Wolf (eds.), *Natur und Kultur in der deutschen Literatur des Mittelalters: Colloquium Exeter 1997* (Tübingen: Niemeyer, 1999), 19–28.

[93]
> 'Welcher arbaitter sein antlitz netzt
> Mit herter arbeit in seinem sweiß
> Das ist ein zyment vnd ein beiß
> Dar in sein sel wirt so gepleicht
> Das yr schon uff in himel reicht . . .'

Quoted in Jörn Reichel, 'Handwerk und Arbeit im literarischen Werk des Nürnbergers Hans Rosenplüt', in Rainer S. Elkar (ed.), *Deutsches Handwerk in Spätmittelalter und früher Neuzeit. Sozialgeschichte – Volkskunde – Literaturgeschichte* (Göttingen: Schwartz, 1983), 245–63 (p. 256).

The Artisanal View of Production

wings/ That carry us against the current and past the hill.'[94] He further declared that: 'Nothing is so hard or tough / That work can't overcome it.'[95] This glorification of hard work predated the radical Protestant sects that Max Weber associated with a work ethic.[96] Rather, as Josef Ehmer notes, the pre-modern attitudes towards labour in German towns gave a strong sense of self-worth to manual workers, while reinforcing their place within the social hierarchy.[97] When applied to crafts that required a mix of physical labour and intellectual skill, the belief in hard work suggested that individuals could excel through their diligence regardless of talent.

The artisanal viewpoint pervaded only selected parts of musical life. Since antiquity, music had been classified as belonging both to the *artes liberales* and the *artes mechanicae*. Music's status as a liberal art stemmed partly from theoretical discussions of its numerical basis and its power to move the emotions. This categorisation persisted into the seventeenth century and was used by Lutheran musicians to defend their status against other professions, for instance by Fuhrmann in his *Musicalischer Trichter* (1706),[98] or in a dispute between musicians and painters narrated in Printz's satirical novel *Pancalus* (1691).[99] The discipline of composition was also usually classified as a liberal art. Herbst explained that *musica poetica* was an art allowing the composer to move the hearts and feelings of listeners.[100] In his composition treatise, Beer described *Harmonie* as the greatest of the liberal arts, as its proportions were the basis of all other arts and sciences.[101]

Other aspects of musical practice, however, were closer to the *artes mechanicae*. The manual skill required by instrumentalists was similar to that of craftworkers, requiring dexterity gained via practice and insights into the properties of materials. Instrumentalists produced and shaped sound through the skill of their fingers on gut strings, wood and metal. Reinforcing the parallel with manual crafts, instrumental musicians learned their trade via apprenticeships, copying the techniques displayed

---

[94] 'Arbeit vnd fleis/ das sind die flügel | so füren vber Stram vnd hügel'. Johann Fischart, *Das glückhafft Schiff von Zürich* [Strasbourg, 1576], sig. A2v.

[95] 'Dann nichts ist also schwer vnd scharff/ | Das nicht die arbeit vnderwarff.' Ibid., sig A2r.

[96] Max Weber, *Die protestantische Ethik und der 'Geist' des Kapitalismus* (1904/5), modern English edition as *The Protestant Ethic and the Spirit of Capitalism*, trans. and updated by Stephen Kalberg (New York: Oxford University Press, 2011).

[97] Josef Ehmer, 'Discourses on Work and Labour in Fifteenth- and Sixteenth-Century Germany', in Jürgen Kocka (ed.), *Work in a Modern Society: The German Historical Experience* (Oxford: Berghahn, 2010), 17–36.

[98] Fuhrmann, *Musicalischer Trichter*, 16.

[99] Wolfgang Caspar Printz, *Musicus magnanimus oder Pancalus* (n.p., 1691), chapter 41; see Stephen Rose, *The Musician in Literature in the Age of Bach* (Cambridge: Cambridge University Press, 2011), 91–93.

[100] Herbst, *Musica poetica*, 4.

[101] Johann Beer, 'Schola phonologia', D-LEm I.4° 37, fol. 2v; modern edition in Johann Beer, *Sämtliche Werke*, vol. 12/ii, ed. Michael Heinemann (Bern: Peter Lang, 2005), 9.

by their master – a system of education celebrated in Printz's novels.[102] The materiality of notated compositions could also suggest similarities with the objects crafted by artisans. In his definition of *musica poetica*, Herbst reported that some people described the finished musical opus as a building (*Aedificium, Baw*); and in his discussion of posterity, he likened the composer to a workman or carpenter who is outlived by the products of their handiwork.[103] Some musicians regarded their compositions as akin to the masterworks with which artisans demonstrated the skill that allowed them to join a guild, gain the status of a master, and get married.[104] Schütz claimed that in the mid-1610s he kept his compositional skills 'out of sight, as it were, until I had refined them somewhat more and could then make my mark with the publication of a worthy work'.[105] This 'worthy work' was his *Psalmen Davids* (1619), with its lavish polychoral settings of German psalms; like an artisan who had delivered his masterwork, Schütz got married shortly after this collection was published.[106] Chapter 3 explores further how musicians portrayed their skill in notated works, with reference to Johann Adam Reincken's setting of *An Wasserflüssen Babylon*.

Furthermore, some compositional techniques could be compared with artisanal methods. Herbst's analogy with construction implies that the rules of counterpoint were like the structural principles that kept a building square and sound. Musicians following an artisanal outlook might think of composition as an act of assembly (*Zusammensetzung*), combining different voice-parts or contrapuntal formulae in a similar way to how a blacksmith or carpenter might join different components. An awareness of manual skill was shown in the compositions and notated improvisations by solo instrumentalists. Such musicians exploited their tactile knowledge of their instrument, for instance by using idiomatic hand-positions. The prevalence of arpeggiated tonic chords in the first 15 preludes of book 1 of Bach's *Wohltemperirte Clavier* has been interpreted by David Ledbetter as a systematic exploration of the hand-positions required for different tonalities.[107]

The artisanal viewpoint is most evident in those musicians who insisted that hard work was crucial to compositional success. Such views added a distinctive contribution to the debate about the relationship of natural

---

[102] Rose, *The Musician in Literature*, 75–112. Fuhrmann even suggested that civic instrumentalists should learn and practise another manual craft such as painting, in order to diversify their income; see Fuhrmann, *Musicalischer Trichter*, 9.

[103] Herbst, *Musica poetica*, 1.

[104] On the connection between an artisan's master status and marriage, see Merry Wiesner, *Gender, Church and State in Early Modern Germany* (London: Longman, 1998), 169–70, 180.

[105] D-Dla, Loc. 8687/1, fol. 291v; *SDok* 1, 322; *HSR*, 183.

[106] On 1 June 1619, Schütz married Magdalena Wildeck; the same date is given on the printed dedication of his *Psalmen Davids* (Dresden, 1619), RISM A/I S2275.

[107] David Ledbetter, *Bach's* Well-Tempered Clavier: *The 48 Preludes and Fugues* (New Haven: Yale University Press, 2002), 56.

talent (*natura*) and art (*ars*). Printz's 1677 list of the necessary attributes of a composer mentioned the importance of natural ability (see above), but added: 'Considerable and long-lasting practice is required in anyone who wants to become a good composer. ... No art can be learned without practice, even in someone who has natural ability and a good teacher'.[108] The best-known statement in this vein is that ascribed to Bach (as reported by Johann Abraham Birnbaum, in his defence of the composer against Johann Adolph Scheibe): 'That which I have achieved by industry and practice, anyone else with tolerable natural talent and skill can also achieve. ... One can do anything if only one really wishes to, and if one industriously strives to convert natural abilities, by untiring diligence, into finished skills'.[109] Birnbaum quoted this statement in a discussion about the difficulty of playing Bach's keyboard music, but it could be interpreted as applying more widely to the composer's work ethic. Bach's reported statement acknowledged the role of natural talent (*Naturell*), in line with humanist traditions; but by claiming hard work can achieve anything, he aligned himself with the mindset of craftworkers. This viewpoint was in keeping with Bach's upbringing: as the son of town instrumentalist, he grew up in an environment that regarded music as an artisan's trade.[110]

The artisanal values of skill and industry have subsequently acquired heavy ideological baggage. In 1737 Scheibe claimed that the compositional style of Germans was characterized by 'laborious work' (*mühsame Arbeit*) and a 'far more thorough' (*weit gründlicher*) approach.[111] Alongside notions such as depth and profundity, these artisan-inspired attributes were central to the ideal types of the German in music, as analysed by the musicologist Bernd Sponheuer.[112] After 1945 artisanal ideals of craftsmanship were celebrated by East Germans who sought to align Bach with the experience of workers, and who interpreted his compositions as concerned not with spiritual matters but with exploiting the basic materials of music.[113] This book, by contrast, seeks to understand the artisanal view of authorship via approaches from the study of material culture. Such approaches permit an investigation of how musicians drew on craftworkers' practices to

---

[108] 'wird von einem guten *Componist*en eine emsige/ stete und langwierige Ubung erfordert. ... keine Kunst ohne Ubung gelernet werden kan/ ob einem schon weder die natürliche Fähigkeit noch guter Unterricht mangelt'. Printz, *Phrynis*, vol. 2, sig. E2v.

[109] *BDok* 2, 303 (no. 409); *NBR*, 346.

[110] Ulrich Siegele, '"I Had to be Industrious ... ": Thoughts about the Relationship Between Bach's Social and Musical Character', *Bach* 22 (1991), 5–12.

[111] Johann Adolph Scheibe, *Der critische Musicus*, no. 15 (17 September 1737), 118.

[112] Bernd Sponheuer, 'Reconstructing Ideal Types of the "German" in Music', in Celia Applegate and Pamela Potter (eds.), *Music and German National Identity* (Chicago: University of Chicago Press, 2002), 36–58.

[113] Walther Vetter, for instance, attributed Bach's *Materialtreue* (use of materials for their inherent characteristics) to the artisanal basis of his art. Walther Vetter, *Der Kapellmeister Bach* (Potsdam: Athenaion, 1950), 10.

34 · *God, Talent, Craft: Concepts of Musical Creativity*

authenticate their products (Chapter 3), and how artisanal secrecy shaped attitudes to musical ownership (Chapter 4).

DEBATES ABOUT INVENTION

The tensions between theological, humanist and artisanal notions of creativity are exposed by German discussions of musical *inventio*. In Ciceronian rhetoric, *inventio* was the first stage in the composition of a speech and involved the discovery of arguments. Subsequent stages involved the arrangement of material (*dispositio*), the choice of appropriate language (*elocutio*), and the memorisation (*memoria*) and delivery (*pronuntiatio*) of the speech (see Chapter 6).[114] The German term for invention (*Findekunst*) clarified that the technique did not involve creating something new (which would be God's prerogative) but rather uncovering that which already existed (for instance, the retrieval of ideas from the author's memory).[115]

Applied to music, the term 'invention' referred to the devising of initial ideas such as a contrapuntal subject or concerto ritornello. Musicians regarded this as a mental process undertaken before anything was written down. As Johann Gottfried Walther explained, *musica poetica* involved 'how one firstly should invent a sweet and pure combination of sounds, and thereafter should set and bring it onto paper, so it can subsequently be sung or played'.[116] In recent musicology the term 'invention' is associated with Laurence Dreyfus's analyses of Bach's music. He defines an 'invention' as 'the essential thematic idea underlying a musical composition', arguing that Bach encoded in every idea the 'mechanisms that ensure its elaboration'.[117] Through a study of such elaborations, Dreyfus seeks to show what is exceptional about Bach's music; but he says less about how Bach devised a workable idea in the first place. The following paragraphs probe historical debates on the nature of invention, to complement Dreyfus's study with an understanding of the agency attributed to composers in the period.

Around 1700 the emphasis on natural talent in German poetics led many musicians to claim that an ability to invent compositional ideas depended on innate gifts. The Göppingen teacher and instrumentalist Daniel Speer stated that there is no formula for invention, but 'a man

---

[114] Cicero, *De inventione* 1.7.9; Cicero, *Rhetorica ad Herennium* 1.2.3.

[115] Herrmann, *Naturnachahmung*, 52.

[116] 'wie man eine liebliche und reine Zusammenstimmung der Klänge erstlich *inventir*en, und hernach aufsetzen und zu Papier bringen soll, damit selbige hernachmahls kann gesungen oder gespielet werden'. Johann Gottfried Walther, *Praecepta der musicalischen Composition*, ed. Peter Benary (Leipzig: Breitkopf & Härtel, 1955), 15.

[117] Dreyfus, *Bach and the Patterns of Invention*, 1, 10.

must be specially endowed by God and nature with this quality'.[118]
Echoing the Platonic notion of *furor*, he asserted that the prerequisites
for invention were 'passion and an innate love for this noble art'.[119]
A similar attitude was displayed by Mattheson, who in 1713 claimed that
'one cannot find a teacher who will instruct in *inventio*, because this is
an innate quality that cannot be acquired'.[120] By 1739 Mattheson had
retreated from this extreme position, although he still declared that invention 'depends on an inborn quality of the mind and the fortuitous disposition of cells in the brain'.[121] In his opinion, the best way to test an
individual's 'natural gifts for music' was to see 'if he could undertake to
grasp something new from his brain, or whether he would be satisfied with
mere patchwork and pieces from diverse sources which were laboriously
collected by begging'.[122] Johann David Heinichen likewise argued that
'innate talent gives natural, good ideas for the art of composition. ...
Anyone to whom Nature denies musical talent had better leave composing alone'.[123] J. S. Bach concurred with such views, according to
C. P. E. Bach's account of his father's teaching: 'As for the invention of
ideas, he required this skill from the very beginning, and anyone who had
none he advised to stay away from composition altogether'.[124] If this
report can be trusted, Bach's belief in innate ability would have clashed
with his artisanal viewpoint that hard work can overcome every obstacle
(see above).

Yet there were methods for stimulating invention, often involving
rhetorical arts for memorisation and fluency. Other techniques involved
variation, whether via an artisanal approach of manipulating physical
materials or quasi-scientific methods for systematically exploring all possibilities. As Wulf Arlt has argued, the diversity of notions of musical *ars
inveniendi* shows there was no unified system of musical rhetoric in the
period.[125] Instead musicians adapted an assortment of techniques they

---

[118] 'Mit dieser *Quali*tät muß ein Mensch von GOtt und der Natur absonderlich darzu begabet seyn'. Daniel Speer, *Grund-richtiger ... Unterricht der musicalischen Kunst oder vierfaches musicalisches Kleeblatt* (Ulm, 1697), 262.

[119] 'der Eyfer und tragende Liebe zu dieser edlen Kunst'. Ibid.

[120] 'Daß sich aber kein *Maitre* findet/ einem die *Invention* beyzubringen/ solches kommet daher/ weil sie *qualitatem innatam non vero acquisitam*'. Johann Mattheson, *Das neu-eröffnete Orchestre* (Hamburg, 1713), 104.

[121] 'kömmt auf eine angebohrne Gemüths-Beschaffenheit und glückliche Einrichtung der Fächer im Gehirne an'. Mattheson, *Der vollkommene Capellmeister* (Hamburg, 1739), 121.

[122] 'ob er sich wol unterstehen könne, was neues aus seinem Gehirn zu ersinnen; oder ob er sich mit lauterm Flicken und Stücken, mit lauter bald hie bald da aufgerafften, und mühsam zusammengebettelten Lappen behelffen wolle'. Ibid., 106.

[123] 'Das *musicali*sche *Talent*, oder *Naturell* ... giebet ihnen auch natürliche gute Einfälle zur *arte Compositoria* ... Wem aber die Natur selbst ein *Musicali*sches *Talent* versaget, der lasse die *Composition* ja mit frieden'. Heinichen, *Der General-Bass*, 21.

[124] *BDok* 3, 289 (no. 803); *NBR*, 399.

[125] Wulf Arlt, 'Zur Handhabung der "inventio" in der deutschen Musiklehre des frühen achtzehnten Jahrhunderts', in George J. Buelow and Hans Joachim Marx (eds.), *New Mattheson Studies* (Cambridge: Cambridge University Press, 1983), 371–92.

would have encountered in school lessons in rhetoric, with even Heinichen and Mattheson outlining ways in which invention could be stimulated.

Fundamental to most methods for invention were memory systems based on *loci* (places). Since ancient times, writers and orators had described the mind as a storehouse which could be navigated via a spatial ordering of material.[126] Systems of *loci communes* (commonplaces) were intended to aid the classification, memorisation and retrieval of material. Philipp Melanchthon advised the novice to collect quotations from authoritative writers and group them under commonplaces, in order to accumulate material for speeches and to foster critical judgement.[127] Similar recommendations were given by the Lutheran pedagogue David Chytraeus.[128]

Within music, the term *loci communes* usually referred to contrapuntal and harmonic formulae, and a framework for their memorisation and recollection. In 1610 the Italian theologian and orator Giovanni Battista Chiodino published a set of thirty *loci communes musicales* in his *Arte pratica latina et volgare di far contrappunto à mente, et à penna*. These commonplaces are short formulae of two-part counterpoint, either the approaches to cadences or sequential patterns (Example 1.1). Chiodino's *loci* were influential in German-speaking lands: they were twice reprinted by Johann Andreas Herbst, and appear in at least one manuscript miscellany.[129] Stefano Lorenzetti has argued that Chiodino's *loci* were intended for memorisation by musicians, enabling 'spatially organized storage and subsequent logically ordered reminiscence'.[130] Lorenzetti shows how contrapuntal formulae similar to Chiodino's were used in improvisations and also notated keyboard compositions such as the toccatas of Giovanni Gabrieli.[131]

Some rare survivals of musical commonplace books offer insights into how musicians collected and assimilated harmonic and contrapuntal formulae. Such commonplace books can be recognised from their classification of the extracts under headings (*loci*). The Vatican library in Rome

---

[126] Mary Carruthers, *The Book of Memory. A Study of Memory in Medieval Culture* (Cambridge: Cambridge University Press, 1990), 33–45.

[127] Philipp Melanchthon, *Elementorum rhetorices libri duo* (Wittenberg, 1532), sig. E3v–E6v; Ann Moss, *Printed Commonplace-Books and the Structuring of Renaissance Thought* (Oxford: Clarendon Press, 1996), 119–30.

[128] Moss, *Printed Commonplace-Books*, 160–64.

[129] Herbst, *Musica poetica*, 115–19; Herbst, *Arte prattica et pöetica* (Nuremberg, 1653), 26–32; 'Instrumentalischer Bettlermantl', GB-Eu, Ms. Dc.6.100, fols. 110v–112r.

[130] Stefano Lorenzetti, 'Musical *Inventio*, Rhetorical *Loci*, and the Art of Memory', in Massimiliano Guido (ed.), *Studies in Historical Improvisation: From* Cantare super librum *to* Partimenti (Abingdon: Routledge, 2017), 25–40.

[131] Stefano Lorenzetti, '"Scritte nella mente"? Giovanni Gabrieli's Keyboard Music and the Art of Improvised Composition', in Rodolfo Baroncini, David Bryant and Luigi Collarile (eds.), *Giovanni Gabrieli: Transmission and Reception of a Venetian Musical Tradition* (Turnhout: Brepols, 2016), 135–48.

Example 1.1   Giovanni Battista Chiodino's 'Loci communes musicales', as reprinted in Johann Andreas Herbst, *Musica poetica* (Nuremberg, 1643), p. 115.

holds 41 volumes assembled by Giuseppe Ottavio Pitoni (1657–743), containing noteworthy contrapuntal or harmonic passages from exemplary composers, grouped according to the type of intervallic progression.[132] Christ Church library in Oxford holds the commonplace book of the singer Francis Withy (c.1645–727), containing samples of cadences and contrapuntal progressions classified according to key.[133] A likely example from German-speaking lands was the *Themata, clausulae atque formulae virtuosorum musicorum* (1698) assembled by the organist Johann Christoph Graff (c.1670–709) but now lost.[134] Such albums were used by musicians as a storehouse of contrapuntal or harmonic progressions, to assimilate into their personal vocabulary or for use in teaching.

The most comprehensive example of how German musicians memorised and manipulated commonplace material is provided by the Bamberg organist Spiridion (Johann Nenning, 1615–85). He claimed that his *Nova instructio pro pulsandis organis* (published in four volumes, 1670–c.675/77) showed

> how one may fully attain in a short time not only complete skills in organ and keyboard playing but also in the craft of composition; so easy and clear that anyone

---

[132] Rome, Biblioteca Apostolica Vaticana, Cappella Giulia I,4–I,44; the first volume was printed as *Guida armonica . . . libro primo* (Rome, c.1690). See Siegfried Gmeinwieser, 'Die *Guida armonica* von G. O. Pitoni. Eine historisch-kritische Kompositionslehre in Beispielen', in Marcel Dobberstein (ed.), *Artes liberales: Karl-Heinz Schlager zum 60. Geburtstag* (Tutzing: Schneider, 1998), 245–81.
[133] GB-Och, Mus. 337. See Robert Thompson, '"Francis Withie of Oxon" and His Commonplace Book, Christ Church, Oxford, MS 337', *Chelys* 20 (1991), 3–27.
[134] Graff's album contained motifs from works by Böhm, Buxtehude, Corelli, Froberger, Kuhnau, Pachelbel and Reincken among others. See August Gottfried Ritter, *Zur Geschichte des Orgelspiels, vornehmlich des deutschen, im 14. bis zum Anfange des 18. Jahrhunderts*, 2 vols. (Leipzig, 1884), vol. 1, 173.

who understands music and the keyboard, and understands the first lesson (which can be grasped in a bar or beat) can thereafter play, in a few months without any kind of difficulty, all kinds of preludes, canzonas or fugues, toccatas and figured bass, and can fully accomplish and practise the craft of composition.[135]

Making no mention of innate talent, Spiridion presented keyboard improvisation and composition as a craft learnable through practice, where invention stems from the manipulation of existing material.

Spiridion's method offers a storehouse of vocabulary for the novice keyboard improviser. He supplied many examples of formulaic harmonic progressions (which he dubbed *cadentiae*), including schema such as perfect and imperfect cadences, and longer patterns derived from rising or falling bass scales of a sixth.[136] Further *cadentiae* adorn these scales, for instance with leaps of thirds, fourths or fifths added on each tone, to give the effect of a sequence. For each *cadentia*, Spiridion supplied up to 72 examples of variations; Figure 1.1 shows some of his variations upon his first *cadentia* (a perfect cadence). He also included 64 samples of *passaggi*, freely improvisatory passages which he told the keyboardist to intersperse between the *cadentiae*.

In the preface to his treatise, Spiridion emphasised the importance of memorisation and manual skill. Novice keyboardists should learn the *cadentiae*, incorporating them in their mental inventory. The *cadentiae* 'must be transposed through all keys ... for in this transposing is the principal part of the work'.[137] Such an exercise would allow the player to learn the feel of the *cadentiae* in different keys, gaining a tactile memory of hand-patterns similar to an artisan's awareness of the manual skills involved in manipulating physical materials. The modular method of construction required close attention to questions of connection (*zusammensetzen*). Spiridion instructed that: 'The *cadentiae* must be joined together so that the last note of the previous one is always the first note of the next one'.[138] Rhythmic motion should be maintained: 'In connecting the *cadentiae*, one must pay attention to those which are proportional

---

[135] 'Wie man in kurtzer Zeit nicht allein zu vollkommenem Orgel- und Instrument-Schlagen/ sondern auch zu der Kunst der *Composition* gäntzlich erlangen mag/ also leicht und klar/ daß wer die *Music*, und das *Clavier* verstehen/ und die erste *Lection* (so nur in einem *Tact* oder *Battuta* begriffen) wol fassen thut/ nachmahls von sich selbsten/ ohne einigen *difficultet*, in wenig Monaten/ allerhand *Praeludia, Canzonen* oder Fügen/ *Toccaten*, den *General Bass* spielen/ und zu der Kunst der *Composition* völlig gelangen und *practiciren* kan'. Spiridion, *Nova instructio pro pulsandis organis*, vol. 1 (Bamberg, 1670), title page. RISM A/I S4119. Spiridion's title page and preface are bilingual Latin/German; I quote the German here.

[136] On the term *cadentiae*, see Bruce Alan Lamott, 'Keyboard Improvisation according to *Nova instructio pro pulsandis organis* (1670–ca.75) by Spiridion a Monte Carmelo' (PhD thesis, Stanford University, 1980), 41.

[137] 'müssen durch alle *Claves* hinauss *transponirt* werden ... Dann in diesem *transponi*ren bestehet das fürnembste dieses Wercks'. Spiridion, *Nova instructio*, vol. 1, preface.

[138] 'Die *Cadenzen* müssen dergestalt zusammen gehenckt werden/ daß allzeit die letztere *Nota* der vorhergehende/ sey zugleich die Erste der darauff folgende *Cadenzen*'. Ibid.

Figure 1.1 Spiridion (Johann Nenning), *Nova instructio pro pulsandis organis*, vol. 1 (Bamberg, 1670), p. 3. Brussels, Bibliothèque royale de Belgique, Fétis 2.940 C (RP). Copyright Bibliothèque royale de Belgique

to each other in the quantity or length of notes'.[139] Through this artisanal attention to assembly, keyboardists would avoid their prefabricated pieces sounding like the proverbial beggar's cloak, patched out of many fragments.

Spiridion was criticised by the anonymous author of another keyboard treatise, the *Wegweiser*, for acting 'as if this wonderful science and one of the most difficult arts were only a secret or riddle to be immediately solved'.[140] Yet his method suggests how a store of harmonic formulae could be manipulated in order to fashion an individualised composition. Spiridion took many of his extracts unacknowledged from the toccatas of Frescobaldi: for instance, variant 42 in Figure 1.1 is the close of the third toccata from Frescobaldi's *ll secondo libro di toccate* (1627), transposed up a fourth.[141] Frescobaldi was lionised for his exceptional talent and individuality: Lorenzo Penna described him as 'il Mostro de suoi tempi', the term 'mostro' suggesting a prodigy or marvel, and this epithet was repeated by Johann Gottfried Walther.[142] Spiridion's manual, however, identifies the harmonic commonplaces underpinning Frescobaldi's apparently singular compositions. As Christine Jeanneret has shown in her analysis of Bibliothèque nationale de France Rés. Vmc. ms.64, Frescobaldi used similarly formulaic modules as the starting-point for notated keyboard compositions.[143] Keyboardists who memorised Spiridion's *cadentiae* would therefore gain the fluency to use them in improvisations, and the ability to transform them into something new.

Towards the end of the seventeenth century, scepticism developed about the value of commonplace books in general. Descartes decried the disjointed thinking promoted by such excerpts, as well as the reliance on authoritative quotations rather than empirical observation.[144] Christian Thomasius advised that: 'Commonplace books, poetic treasure chests,

---

[139] 'In zusammen Henckung der *Cadenzen*, muß man achtung geben auff solche/ welche ein andern in der *Quantitet* oder Grösse der *Noten proportionirt* seyn'. Ibid.

[140] 'als wäre diese so herrliche Wissenschafft/ und eine von den schwersten Künsten/ nur ein *Secretrum*, oder Rätzel/ so sich stehends Fuß auflösen laßt'. *Kurtzer jedoch gründlicher Wegweiser/ vermittelst welches man aus dem Grund die Kunst die Orgel recht zu schlagen* (Augsburg, 1689), 4.

[141] For a list of Spiridion's borrowings from Frescobaldi, see Lamott, 'Keyboard Improvisation', 202–5.

[142] Lorenzo Penna, *Li primi albori musicali per li principianti della musica figurata*, 3 vols. (Bologna, 1672), vol. 3, 6; Johann Gottfried Walther, *Musicalisches Lexicon* (Leipzig, 1732), 261. On such descriptions of Frescobaldi, see Christine Jeanneret, 'La construction d'un monstre: la figure de Frescobaldi, virtuose génial et gribouilleur', in Caroline Giron-Panel and Anne-Madeleine Goulet (eds.), *La musique à Rome au XVIIᵉ siècle: études et perspectives de recherche* (Rome: École Française, 2012), 321–39.

[143] Christine Jeanneret, 'Places of Memory and Invention: The Compositional Process in Frescobaldi's Manuscripts', in Andrew Woolley and John Kitchen (eds.), *Interpreting Historical Keyboard Music: Sources, Contexts and Performance* (Farnham: Ashgate, 2013), 65–81.

[144] Moss, *Printed Commonplace-Books*, 272–74.

Example 1.2 Johann Mattheson's assembly of a melody from commonplace fragments. Mattheson, *Der vollkommene Capellmeister* (Hamburg, 1739), p. 122.

poetic guides and those handbooks which help imitation will take those who lack poetic talent no further than being hacks. But someone with a natural talent for poetry needs no such miserable supplies'.[145]

Such attitudes shaped Mattheson's discussion of musical commonplaces in *Der vollkommene Capellmeister* (1739). Indicative of changing musical priorities, he applied the technique to melodic invention rather than harmonic or contrapuntal formulae. Modifying his earlier view that invention could not be taught, Mattheson explained that a melody could be assembled from figures and motives collected by the composer 'through much experience and attentive listening to good works'.[146] As Example 1.2 shows, he gave a demonstration involving three melodic cells: a 6/8 undulating figure; a question-like motif in duple time; and a 3/8 motif evocative of a passepied. His new phrase began with the 3/8 motif adapted for common time and repeated in a modified form; its middle comprised the questioning motif, and it ended with a version of the 6/8 undulating figure. Echoing his contemporaries' suspicion of codified systems of invention, Mattheson warned:

These particulars must not be taken as if one should write down an index of similar fragments and, as in school, make an orderly invention box out of them; but one would do it in the same way as we stock up a provision of words and expressions for speaking, not necessarily on paper nor in a book, but in one's head and memory.[147]

---

[145] '*Loci communes*, Poetische Schatzkasten/ Poetische Trichter und dergleichen Bücher mehr/ ingleichen die *Imitationes* helffen denenjenigen die kein Poetisch *Ingenium* haben zu weiter nichts/ als daß sie Pritschmeister daraus werden. Wer aber ein *Naturell* zur *Poesie* hat/ braucht dergleichen armseligen Vorrath nicht ...' Christian Thomasius, *Höchstnöthige Cauteln ... zu Erlernung der Rechts-Gelahrtheit* (Halle, 1713), 153.
[146] 'durch viele Erfahrung und aufmercksames Anhören guter Arbeit'. Mattheson, *Der vollkommene Capellmeister*, 122.
[147] 'Diese Specialien müssen aber nicht so genommen werden, daß man sich etwa ein Verzeichniß von dergleichen Brocken aufschreiben, und, nach guter Schulweise, daraus einen ordentlichen Erfindungs-Kasten machen müste; sondern auf dieselbe Art, wie wir uns einen Vorrath an Wörtern und Ausdrückungen bey dem Reden, nicht eben nothwendig auf dem Papier oder in einem Buche, sondern im Kopffe und Gedächtniß zulegen ...'. Ibid., 123.

Thus Mattheson reinterpreted the ancient arts of memory as analogous to the natural process of language acquisition. Despite its simplicity, Mattheson's example was the latest in a long line of methods showing musicians how to accumulate a storehouse of material that they could then make their own. These systems of *loci communes* offer a historical basis for understanding how composers manipulated formulaic material and its connotations (or in Dreyfus's words, 'composed against the grain').[148]

A second set of methods of musical invention involved techniques of variation and elaboration, as explored by Printz in the second volume of his composition treatise *Phrynis* (1677, republished 1696). He demonstrated how a plain crotchet can be divided up into many patterns of semiquavers and quavers, with varying placements of melodic steps and leaps. He calculated that a crotchet beat could be varied in 2897 ways with various permutations of quavers and semiquavers.[149] Printz claimed his method would allow a musician lacking talent to 'achieve all inventions with a little diligence and be assured that he has copied nothing, still less stolen something'.[150] His treatise is written in the guise of a travel narrative, and he presented his method of variation as a 'Tractat' supplied by a composer 'who had considerable knowledge about how to write a strict musical piece, but he was lacking inventions, on account of which he previously had made many parodies and merely imitated the works of other composers'.[151] By exhaustively demonstrating how a single note can be varied, Printz's treatise provides a historical starting-point for the more complex variation techniques that Dreyfus analyses with quasi-structuralist terminology in his study of Bach's 'patterns of invention'. As Printz explained, 'from the principle of variation flows each and every invention of a composer'.[152]

Some methods of variation drew on the artisanal approach to composition. Friedrich Erhardt Niedt's *Handleitung zur Variation* (1706) showed how keyboardists could decorate a bass-line with quaver or semiquaver figuration, a technique shaped by the dexterity of the players' fingers. He also showed how movements in a dance suite could be generated from a common bass-line, a procedure discernible in keyboard suites by Johann Adam Reincken.[153] Niedt voiced the craftworkers' belief in hard work,

---

[148] Dreyfus, *Bach and the Patterns of Invention*, 37.

[149] Printz, *Phrynis* (1677 edition), vol. 2, sig. I2v

[150] 'er ... durch einen wenigen Fleiß allerhand Erfindungen zu wegen zu bringen/ geschickt macht/ und dadurch versichert wird/ daß er keinem etwas ausgeschrieben/ viel weniger abgestohlen'. Ibid., sig. K1v.

[151] 'Dieser hätte zwar eine sattsame Wissenschafft ein *Musicali*sches Stück rein zu setzen; Es fehleten ihm aber *Inventiones*; weßwegen er denn bis dahin mehrentheils *Parodien* gemacht/ und andere *Componisten* nur *imitiret*'. Ibid., sig. F4v.

[152] '*de Variatione* aus welcher alle und jede Erfindungen eines *Componis*ten fliessen'. Ibid., sig. G1v.

[153] See Reincken's Suite no. 2 in C major (S-N, Samling Finspong Ms.1136:2, no. 4) where all four movements are built on the same descending bass-line. For further examples, see Robert S. Hill, 'Stilanalyse und Überlieferungsproblematik: das Variationssuiten-Repertoire J. A. Reinckens', in

Debates about Invention 43

stating that 'through assiduous industry you can achieve a thousand-fold inventions'.[154] In a prefatory poem to the treatise, he asserted that manual facility at the keyboard could overcome a lack of talent in invention:

> And someone who is complained about by musicians
> That he has a great lack of invention
> He is to be consoled and undeterred
> Because among those remaining many are composing.[155]

Such a musician should learn 'the correct hand positions' (*die rechten Griffe*) and have everything at their fingertips, 'so that one can separate invention from composition'.[156] For Niedt, an artisanal grasp of keyboard dexterity could obviate the need for any other type of musical invention.

Mattheson saw enough value in Niedt's method to oversee a second, enlarged edition of the *Handleitung zur Variation* in 1721. But he modified Niedt's emphasis on manual skill as a substitute for invention, instead noting that numerous variations could be achieved 'particularly when there occurs a good *ingenium*, skilled by nature'.[157] In his *Kleine General-Bass-Schule* (1735), Mattheson was sceptical of Niedt's method, comparing it to the French *bouts rimes* (a puzzle where a list of rhyming words has to be fashioned into a full poem). Niedt's focus on manual skill did not suit the increasing emphasis on melody and the imitation of nature. Starting with the melody rather than the bass, Mattheson argued, 'is the most natural way: for nobody can say what flower a root will bear, unless he has previously seen the flower'.[158] Thus Niedt's artisanal methods for invention clashed with approaches that prioritised natural talent.

Around 1700 some musicians linked variation techniques with current developments in mathematical logic. Earlier in the century, Gottfried Wilhelm Leibniz had built on Ramon Llull's work to develop an *ars combinatoria* that could systematically display all the possible permutations of ideas, words or other entities (represented by numbers). It promised a

---

Arnfried Edler and Friedhelm Krummacher (eds.), *Dietrich Buxtehude und die europäische Musik seiner Zeit. Bericht über das Lübecker Symposion 1987* (Kassel: Bärenreiter, 1990), 204–14.

[154] 'du ... könntest ... durch embsigen Fleiß tausenderley *Inventiones* dardurch erlangen'. Friedrich Erhardt Niedt, *Handleitung zur Variation* (Hamburg, 1706), sig. X2r.

[155]
> 'Und wann auch mancher sich von *Musicis* beklagt;
> Daß an *Invention* er grossen Mangel findt/
> Er sey deswegen nur getrost und unverzaget
> Weil deren übrig viel beym *Componiren* sind'. Ibid, sig. A4v.

[156] 'Da man Erfindung wolt vom *Componiren* trennen'. Ibid.

[157] 'absonderlich wann ein gutes/ von Natur dazu geschicktes *Ingenium* darüber kömmt'. *Friederich Erhard Niedtens Musicalischer Handleitung Anderer Theil*, 8.

[158] 'Das ist der natürlichste Weg: denn niemand kann sagen, was die Wurzel für eine Blume tragen werde; er habe denn die Blume vorher gesehen'. Johann Mattheson, *Kleine General-Bass-Schule* (Hamburg, 1735), 45.

mechanised discovery of all aspects of an argument, as required by the *ars inveniendi* in dialectics. Leibniz's system, published in his Leipzig University dissertation of 1666, was applied to music by Kuhnau, whose interests as a polymath were fostered by his place in Leipzig's academic milieu. In 1700 Kuhnau promised to publish a treatise on composition, showing the value of mathematical procedures (*matheseos*) and 'especially the *ars combinatoria* so useful for invention'.[159] Although this treatise never appeared in print and does not survive in manuscript, Kuhnau alluded to its likely contents in 1709, when he mentioned that a set of four notes can be arranged in 24 ways, and a set of five notes can be arranged in 120 different permutations. This was a direct adaptation of Leibniz's dissertation, which showed how the first four letters of the alphabet can be arranged in 24 different permutations;[160] Kuhnau claimed 'that each combination has a different effect on the emotions of the listener'.[161] His precedent was followed by other musicians immersed in academic traditions. The organist Johann Heinrich Buttstett praised the *ars combinatoria* in response to Mattheson's 1713 claim that invention could not be taught.[162] The mathematician Lorenz Christoph Mizler, founder of Leipzig's Correspondierende Sozietät der Musicalischen Wissenschaften, declared that 'when you understand [Leibniz's *ars combinatoria*], you can invent something new in composition every minute of your whole life, even if you are deficient in invention'.[163]

Other musicians, however, disagreed that invention could be stimulated by mathematical operations. In 1711 Heinichen dismissed the *ars combinatoria* 'because it is impossible to find the tenderness or soul of music in such wooden notes, and so one must seek other, sometimes harder modes of invention that chiefly presuppose a good natural imagination in the composer'.[164] Heinichen's attack on the *ars combinatoria* may have

---

[159] 'sonderlich der ... zur *Invention* vortrefflich dienenden *Artis combinatoriae*'. Johann Kuhnau, *Musicalische Vorstellung einiger Biblische Historien* (Leipzig, 1700), sig. B2v. RISM A/I K2997.

[160] Gottfried Wilhelm Leibniz, *Dissertatio de arte combinatoria* (Leipzig, 1666), 58.

[161] 'dass bald jede Combination einen andern Effect in dem Gemüthe der Zuhörer operire'. Bernhard Friedrich Richter, 'Eine Abhandlung Joh. Kuhnaus', *Monatshefte für Musikgeschichte* 34 (1902), 147–54 (p. 150). Trans. by Ruben Weltsch as 'A Treatise on Liturgical Text Settings (1710)', in Carol K. Baron (ed.), *Bach's Changing World: Voices in the Community* (Rochester, NY: University of Rochester Press, 2006), 219–26.

[162] Johann Heinrich Buttstett, *Ut, mi, sol, re, fa, la, tota musica et harmonia aeterna* (Erfurt, n. d.), 57–58.

[163] 'Wenn ihr diese verstehet, so könnet ihr in der Composition, wenn es euch an der Erfindung fehlen solte, alle Minuten eure ganze Lebens-Zeit hindurch was neues erfinden'. Lorenz Christoph Mizler, *Anfängs-Gründe des General Basses* (Leipzig, 1739), 115.

[164] 'weil die *Tendresse* oder Seele der *Music* unmöglich bey solchen höltzern *Noten* zu finden ist/ so muß man dabey auff andere/ wiewohl etwas schwerere *Modos Invention* zu suchen/ bedacht seyn/ da hauptsächlich/ nebst der *Combinatoria* eine gute natürliche *Fantasie* bey dem *Componist*en *praesupponir*et wird'. Johann David Heinichen, *Neu erfundene und gründliche Anweisung ... zu vollkommener Erlernung des General-Basses* (Hamburg, 1711), 13.

stemmed from his conflict with his former teacher Kuhnau,[165] but also indicated his preference for innate talent (*Naturell*) over learned art.

As an alternative, Heinichen outlined a system of *loci topici* for invention, whereby the composer analysed an operatic libretto to find an affection that could be expressed in an aria. Such systematic examination of texts recalled how the *ars inveniendi* was used in dialectic to analyse and develop different elements of an argument. He showed how the aria text 'Non è sola, non è straniera' could be set in three different ways, representing three different affections derived from the surrounding libretto.[166] By searching for invention in a text, Heinichen countered the artisanal tradition that drew on harmonic and contrapuntal formulae. His method was followed by Mattheson, who in 1739 advised that the portrayal of affections (or *locus descriptionis*, to use his term) was 'the richest source' and 'the most reliable and most fundamental guide to invention'.[167]

Techniques for musical invention were fundamental to the art and craft of composition in Lutheran lands during the long seventeenth century. The debates discussed here provide a historical foundation for Dreyfus's study of Bach's 'patterns of invention', showing the ongoing importance of the arts of memory and of artisanal methods for manipulating the materials of music. Spiridion and Niedt claimed their methods allowed any musician with manual skill and a strong work ethic to compose. Mattheson and Heinichen preferred methods to strengthen the innate powers of imagination in musicians. The debates about invention thus reveal how notions of musical creativity continued to be contested throughout the period studied by this book.

EPILOGUE

The theological, humanist and artisanal notions of creativity all implied different viewpoints on whether musicians held agency, and therefore had ramifications for the place of musicians in society and how they should be rewarded for their work. In 1657 Adam Krieger applied for the vacant post of cantor at the Thomasschule in Leipzig. He was the favoured candidate for the post, having been recommended for it by the Elector and Electress of Saxony, and having already worked as organist at the city's Nicolaikirche for the previous two years.[168] Krieger wanted to reshape the cantor's role

---

[165] Michael Maul, 'Johann David Heinichen und der "Musicalische Horribilicribrifax". Überlegungen zur Vorrede von Heinichens *Gründlicher Anweisung*', in Rainer Bayreuther (ed.), *Musikalische Norm um 1700* (Berlin: De Gruyter, 2010), 145–65.

[166] Heinichen, *Der General-Bass*, 31–41.

[167] 'die reicheste Quelle ... die sicherste und wesentlichste Handleitung zur Invention'. Mattheson, *Der vollkommene Capellmeister*, 127.

[168] Michael Maul, *"Dero berühmbter Chor". Die Leipziger Thomasschule und ihre Kantoren (1212–804)* (Leipzig: Lehmstedt Verlag, 2012), 112–13.

into a directorship for the city's music, by abandoning the teaching duties that were usually central to the job. To support his request, he argued:

The pursuit of musical composition is today very refined and does not consist of one being able to string together one, two, three or more pieces, but one must see how they are set, from what kind of intellect [*Geist*] they flow, how the fundamental and famed artists achieve this science, otherwise one will never produce what is competent.[169]

Krieger did not acknowledge the theological view of creativity as God's gift, and he distanced himself from an artisanal notion of composition whereby pre-existing formulae were assembled together. Instead his emphasis on the underlying *Geist* asserted the humanist view of the importance of natural talent, specifically Opitz's description of a spirit that impels poetic creation.

Strengthening his case to be exempted from teaching, Krieger explained:

this effort [of teaching] would be too burdensome to combine with the pursuit of composition, to the extent that someone who slaves away in school subsequently has little inclination to write a vocal concerto, and without any desire to compose he will turn out poor things.[170]

By arguing that inclination (*Lust*) was essential for composition, Krieger invoked the Platonic notion of a fiery impulse underpinning creative work, a trope also used by Opitz and subsequently by musicians such as Speer and Mattheson (see above).

Krieger's arguments were not accepted by the Leipzig council, which rejected his application. Possibly the council was wary of the strong self-assertion in his letter. It undoubtedly preferred candidates who viewed compositional ability as a divine calling or as akin to a craftworker's skill; such musicians would be more likely to accept their place in the hierarchy of school staff and in the city's regimented social order. Yet as the following chapters will show, the differing notions of creativity shaped the production and reception of music in Lutheran lands throughout the seventeenth century. Theological beliefs in human talents as divine gifts led many to argue that all music should be freely shared (see Chapter 4). Humanist programmes of studying the classics influenced the technique of composing in imitation of models (discussed in Chapter 2), while the humanist preoccupation with innate character led some musicians to explore how their individuality might be represented in printed music or compositional

---

[169] 'Das studium musicum compositionis ist heutzutage sehr schlipfrich und bestehet nicht hierinnen, daß man endlich, ein, zwey, drey oder mehr stücke zusammensetzen könne, sondern man muß sehen, wie sie gesetzet seyn, aus was vor einem geist sie fließen, bey welchen fundamentirten und berühmten künstler diese wißenschaft erlangt worden, denn für sich selbst wird keiner was tüchtigs fürbringen können'. D-LEsa, Tit.VII.B.116, fol. 147v.

[170] 'diese mühe neben dem studio compositionis alzuschwer fallen würde, maßen derjenige, der sich in der schule abarbeitet, nachmals schlechte lust hat ein musicalisch concert aufzusetzen, und ohne lust zu componiren pflegt schlecht zugerathen'. Ibid.

style (see Chapter 3). Artisans' techniques for authenticating their products were followed by musicians seeking to verify their printed or manuscript sources (see Chapter 3), and the artisanal preference for embodied knowledge shaped the reluctance of some instrumentalists to disclose their music (see Chapters 4 and 6). The status of musical authors in seventeenth-century Lutheran society reflected this mix of concepts of creativity, whereby individual achievements could be attributed to a vocation commanded by God, a talent implanted by nature, or a craft honed through practice.

CHAPTER 2

Between Imitatio *and Plagiarism*

Visiting Berlin in the 1690s, the Saxon capellmeister Nicolaus Adam Strungk (1640–700) joked about his use of musical borrowing: 'I am one of the greatest musical rogues, because I must steal all my ornaments from envious artists. But one hangs such art-thieves not in irons, but in golden chains.'[1] By 'golden chains', Strungk referred to his visit to the imperial court in Vienna in 1661–62, when he performed before Emperor Leopold I and was rewarded with a portrait miniature suspended from a golden chain.[2] Strungk's statement was reported by Martin Heinrich Fuhrmann in a discussion of how composers could set pre-existing melodies in varied ways. Fuhrmann commented: 'In such a way one can gain many lovely tunes and so forth from mere listening, and so to speak steal one of them. But this is an honourable theft, as it is called: Steal what you have, and leave to each his own.'[3]

Strungk's tale encapsulates the issues central to this chapter. The discussion of invention in the previous chapter showed how seventeenth-century Lutherans doubted whether humans could create *ex nihilo*. Instead creativity was viewed as an act of reception, involving the adaptation of what already existed. Such practices of reworking raise questions about the relationship between individuality and models. To what extent were individuality and originality expected in a musical culture guided by authoritative models? To what extent was there a sense of plagiarism, and could it be distinguished from legitimate borrowing?

One difficulty in discussing musical borrowing is that it was used in many varied ways in this period. It was a pedagogical technique, enabling novice composers to learn from established models; it was used by experienced composers to explore new techniques or to show their mastery

---

[1] 'Ich bin solchergestalt auch einer von den grössesten Musicalischen Mäuse-Köpffen/ weil ich alle meine Manieren denen neidischen Künstlern recht abstehlen müssen; Aber man hängt solche Kunst-Diebe deßhalb nicht in eiserne/ sondern zuweilen noch in güldene Ketten'. Martin Heinrich Fuhrmann, *Musicalische Strigel* ([Leipzig], *c*.1719–21), 20–21.

[2] Reported in Johann Mattheson, *Grundlage einer Ehren-Pforte* (Hamburg, 1740), 353.

[3] 'Auf solche Art kan man manche schöne Arie & c. vom blossen Zuhören bekommen, und so zu reden einem abstehlen. Dis ist aberein ehrlicher Diebstahl, da es heist: Stihl was, so hast du was, und laß einem jeden das Seine'. Fuhrmann, *Musicalische Strigel*, 20.

Between Imitatio *and Plagiarism*

relative to rivals; it was also used pragmatically, to arrange an existing composition for different performing forces or to supply a vocal work with different words.[4] A similar range of purposes was recognised in literary theories for the imitation of models, a technique used by apprentice and accomplished poets alike.[5] Further challenges arise in finding suitable nomenclature to discuss compositional reworkings. Terms such as 'allusion' or 'emulation' make assumptions about the composer's intention; even 'borrowing' may not fully capture the acts of citation, repurposing and transformation typically involved in polyphonic reworkings. Musing on this inadequate terminology, John Milsom has coined the term 'T-Mass' for Masses built on borrowed material, the 'T' denoting the processes of transfer, transformation and transfusion when composers used pre-existing material for new polyphonic works.[6] As yet, however, there has been little investigation of how musicians at the time described such transformations.

Cases of musical borrowing have been extensively studied for several composers within the chronological scope of this monograph. A tradition of polyphonic reworkings, including Masses derived from motets, persisted from the sixteenth into the early seventeenth centuries.[7] Techniques of musical borrowing continued with the advent of the concerted style in the early seventeenth century: many of Samuel Scheidt's few-voiced vocal concertos of the 1630s and 1640s are adaptations of his own fuller scored pieces, or of chorale settings from the previous century.[8] From the 1640s onwards, German composers often reworked vocal concertos by Italian composers: Schütz and Rosenmüller chose Venetian models such as Monteverdi and Grandi, while subsequent generations (including Dieterich Buxtehude, Kaspar Förster and Christian Geist) made heavy use of models from Roman composers.[9] At the start of the eighteenth century, Handel's

---

[4] On the range of types of musical borrowing in England, see Rebecca Herissone, *Musical Creativity in Restoration England* (Cambridge: Cambridge University Press, 2013), 3–41.

[5] Thomas Greene, *The Light in Troy: Imitation and Discovery in Renaissance Poetry* (New Haven: Yale University Press, 1982), 54.

[6] John Milsom, 'The T-Mass: *quis scrutatur?*', *Early Music* 45 (2018), 319–31.

[7] For Masses based on Josquin motets, see Milsom, 'The T-Mass'; for parody Masses in the early seventeenth century, see Andreas Waczkat, *'Ein ehrenhaftes Spielen mit Musik': Deutsche Parodiemessen des 17. Jahrhunderts* (Kassel: Bärenreiter, 2000).

[8] Werner Braun, 'Samuel Scheidts Bearbeitungen alter Motetten', *Archiv für Musikwissenschaft* 19–20 (1962–63), 56–74; Andreas Waczkat, 'Samuel Scheidt und die neue Parodietechnik des 17. Jahrhunderts', in Konstanze Musketa and Wolfgang Ruf (eds.), *Samuel Scheidt (1587–1654). Werk und Wirkung. Bericht über die Internationale wissenschaftliche Konferenz am 5. und 6. November 2004 . . . in der Stadt Halle und über das Symposium in Creuzburg zum 350. Todesjahr, 25.–27. März 2004* (Halle: Händel-Haus, 2006), 57–68.

[9] Peter Wollny's studies in this area, initially published in separate articles, are brought together in his *Studien zum Stilwandel in der protestantischen Figuralmusik des mittleren 17. Jahrhunderts* (Beeskow: Ortus, 2016), 329–98; see also Lars Berglund, *Studier i Christian Geists vokalmusik* (Uppsala: Uppsala Universitet, 2002), 148–56.

borrowings are well known and have been mapped by John Roberts;[10] Bach also reused material from other composers, as well as parodying his own works (by changing the text underlay). However, the significance of these examples of borrowing is often unclear, as evident in the extensive scholarly disagreement on why Bach parodied his music.[11]

The aim of this chapter is not to detect further examples of musical reworking, but instead to analyse the debates surrounding this practice in Lutheran lands during the long seventeenth century. As a counterpart to studies by G. W. Pigman and Thomas Greene on theories of literary imitation,[12] it focuses on how musicians described the process of borrowing. These descriptions often invoked rhetorical concepts such as *imitatio* and *aemulatio*, reflecting how deeply such humanist techniques permeated systems of knowledge and education in the period. The first part of the chapter examines *imitatio*, the imitation of authoritative models; this technique was associated with a patriarchal transmission of knowledge. By contrast, *aemulatio* involved a competitive attempt to surpass the model: as Erasmus explained in his *Ciceronianus* (1528), 'imitation aims at similarity, emulation at victory'.[13] Such emulation indicated confidence in historical progress and human self-assertion; it could lead to playful allusions as described in a short treatise, *De παρῳδία* [*De parodia*] (1611), by the Jena musician Georg Quitschreiber. The chapter then examines the shifting boundary between legitimate and illegitimate borrowing in the period, discussing how musicians used the term 'plagiarism' and probing the concept of 'honest theft'. After 1700, shifting economic models led musicians such as Johann David Heinichen and Johann Mattheson to develop new attitudes towards borrowing, whereby musical ideas were understood as the personal capital of a musician. The discourses of *imitatio* and plagiarism examined here not only offer a historically informed vocabulary with which to assess musical reworking; they also clarify the value placed on individual authorship in the period.

IMITATIO AND AUTHORITY

The rhetorical technique of *imitatio* was a way to learn from authority, namely those authors who had been canonised as having value. Such learning could be done in proximity to the model, with the pupil imitating

---

[10] John Roberts (ed.), *Handel Sources: Materials for the Study of Handel's Borrowing*, 9 vols. (New York: Garland, 1986).

[11] Hans-Joachim Schulze, 'The Parody Process in Bach's Music: An Old Problem Reconsidered', *Bach: The Quarterly Journal of the Riemenschneider Bach Institute* 20 (1989), 7–21.

[12] G. W. Pigman III, 'Versions of Imitation in the Renaissance', *Renaissance Quarterly* 33 (1980), 1–32; Greene, *The Light in Troy*.

[13] 'Siquidem imitatio spectat similitudinem, aemulatio victoriam'. *ASD* I-2, 634; *CWE* 28, 379.

Imitatio *and Authority*

a teacher, or with models that were chronologically or geographically distant. Involving a 'patriarchal pattern of transmission through kinship and legacy' (as Rita Copeland has stated),[14] this type of imitation was described with metaphors of genealogical descent or following a guide's footsteps. Authoritative models remained important outside didactic situations, being used by established composers to justify innovation.

Imitation was central to the educational methods of the ancient Greeks and Romans. Aristotle and Quintilian noted that imitation was a universal human behaviour, shown by children copying their parents and teachers; Cicero instructed novice orators to select and imitate the best aspects of others' works.[15] Humanist pedagogues revived such advice on *imitatio*, now with a chronological gap between imitators and their models from pagan times. Melanchthon recommended that Lutheran schoolboys imitate the speeches of Cicero, Terence, Livy and other writers, paying attention to the subject, structure and choice of words.[16] An abridged version of Melanchthon's advice on *imitatio* circulated in Lucas Lossius's textbook, written in the question-and-answer style of a catechism.[17] School ordinances prescribed *imitatio* for advanced schoolboys: at the electoral schools in Saxony, according to the 1580 edict discussed in more detail in Chapter 5, pupils were to study Cicero, gather useful words and phrases, and write their own imitations.[18]

Lutheran musicians recommended similar techniques for novice composers. The Magdeburg cantor Gallus Dressler instructed in his manuscript *Praecepta musicae poeticae* (1563–64) that 'beginners must choose for themselves some polyphonist to be imitated'.[19] More detailed advice was offered by the Rostock cantor Joachim Burmeister, who defined *imitatio* as 'the study and endeavour to pattern and model our musical compositions after the works of master composers, which are skilfully examined through analysis'.[20] Burmeister borrowed several elements from the rhetoric textbook of his teacher Lossius, for instance distinguishing between imitation of general style and imitation of specific authors.[21]

---

[14] Rita Copeland, *Rhetoric, Hermeneutics and Translation in the Middle Ages: Academic Traditions and Vernacular Texts* (Cambridge: Cambridge University Press, 1991), 27.

[15] Greene, *The Light in Troy*, 54–66.

[16] Philipp Melanchthon, *Elementorum rhetorices libri duo* (Wittenberg, 1531), sig. K4v–L2r.

[17] Lucas Lossius, *Erotemata dialecticae et rhetoricae Philippi Melanthonis* (Frankfurt an der Oder, 1554), 201–4.

[18] Reinhold Vormbaum, *Die evangelischen Schulordnungen des 16. Jahrhunderts* (Gütersloh, 1860), 283–85.

[19] 'elegant sibi tyrones aliquem symphonistam imitandum quorum'. *Gallus Dressler's* Præcepta musicæ poëticæ, ed. Robert Forgács (Urbana: University of Illinois Press, 2007), 190–91.

[20] Joachim Burmeister, *Musica poetica* (Rostock, 1606), 74; modern edn as *Musical Poetics*, trans. Benito V. Rivera (New Haven: Yale University Press, 1993), 207–9.

[21] Martin Ruhnke, *Joachim Burmeister. Ein Beitrag zur Musiklehre um 1600* (Kassel: Bärenreiter, 1955), 166–67.

Instructions on imitating praiseworthy authors were subsequently issued by the Berlin cantor Johannes Crüger in the 1630 and 1654 editions of his *Synopsis musica* and by Christoph Bernhard in his manuscript *Tractatus compositionis augmentatus* (*c*.1657). The practice of *imitatio* was also implied by Schütz's 1648 advice that novice composers train themselves in counterpoint by studying 'the Italian and other classic authors, old and new, canonised by all the most distinguished composers'.[22] Similar techniques persisted into the early eighteenth century. In a manuscript treatise from *c*.1702, Christian Demelius (1643–711), cantor in Nordhausen, advised the novice musician to study and emulate the works of older and newer composers, comparing such a process to the classicist imitating authors of the Golden Age such as Cicero and Terence.[23] The young Bach studied the works of authoritative keyboardists such as Johann Jacob Froberger and Johann Caspar Kerll, in addition to 'some old and good Frenchmen', according to C. P. E. Bach.[24]

The notion of learning by imitation was also central to artisanal methods, where an apprentice gained embodied knowledge by copying the activities of a master. In 1556 the Wittenberg organist Hermann Finck commented: 'He who is fired by nature with the love of music should have the benefit of an experienced teacher in whose imitation he may fashion himself completely.'[25] Unlike humanist notions of *imitatio*, in an apprenticeship there was no chronological or geographical distance between pupil and model. Apprenticeships were organised along patriarchal lines, with the apprentice acting as a surrogate son, to be moulded by the master. Paula Higgins argues such ways of learning encouraged a '"discourse of creative patriarchy" – a patrilineal system in which male teachers passed down musical knowledge and skill as if by inheritance to their male students'.[26] Novice musicians could claim this patriarchal authority by imitating or simply naming their teacher.

A prerequisite of humanist *imitatio* was the existence of a canon of exemplary authors whose works could be taken as models by the novice.

---

[22] 'die von allen vornehmsten Componisten gleichsam *Canonisierte* Italianische und andere/ Alte und Newe *Classicos Autores*'. Heinrich Schütz, *Geistliche Chor-Music* (Dresden, 1648), Bassus Continuus partbook, preface. RISM A/I S2294.

[23] GB-Lbl, Add. Ms. 4910, fol. 38v [pencilled foliation]. Another copy exists at D-B, Mus. ms. theor. 1595, fols. 1r–33v. Both manuscript copies are anonymous and are attributed to Demelius on the basis of a reference in chapter 9 to the author's *Sacrum tirocinium musicum* (Nordhausen, *c*.1680), which although published anonymously was ascribed to Demelius by Johann Gottfried Walther (*Musicalisches Lexicon* [Leipzig, 1732], 201). See Werner Braun, *Die Kompositionslehre des Christian Demelius (Nordhausen um 1702)* (Nordhausen: Friedrich-Christian-Lesser-Stiftung, 2000).

[24] *BDok* 3, 288 (no. 803); *NBR*, 398.

[25] 'ut a natura amore Musicae flagrans praeceptore utatur perito, ad cuius imitationem totum se componat.' Hermann Finck, *Practica musica* (Wittenberg, 1556), sig. SS1r.

[26] Paula Higgins, 'Musical "Parents" and Their "Progeny": The Discourse of Creative Patriarchy in Early Modern Europe', in Anthony M. Cummings and Jessie Ann Owens (eds.), *Music in Renaissance Cities and Courts: Studies in Honor of Lewis Lockwood* (Warren, MI: Harmonie Park Press, 1997), 169–86 (p. 171).

Imitatio *and Authority*

Honey Meconi, discussing musical borrowings in the fifteenth and sixteenth centuries, observed that 'at no time ... was there an acknowledged set of "antichi" as far as borrowing from "classical" models was concerned, nor was there any consistent attempt to preserve or maintain the music of earlier generations'; consequently she questions the relevance of the term *imitatio* for music of this period.[27] By the seventeenth century, however, there was usually a chronological or geographical gap between the novice musician and the recommended model, giving a greater sense of a canon. Several theorists advised the imitation of sixteenth-century polyphonists epitomising the *prima prattica*: Lassus was mentioned as a model by Burmeister, Crüger (1630) and Demelius; and Palestrina was identified as a paragon by Bernhard and Demelius. Theorists also recommended Italian models: Bernhard listed Monteverdi, Rovetta, Cavalli and Carissimi as exemplars of the *stylus luxurians communis* and *theatralis*, while Crüger's 1654 treatise mainly listed Italians such as Monteverdi, Gasparo Casati, Rovetta, Rigatti, Grandi and Merula.[28] Although Lutheran musicians did not agree over exactly which composers to imitate, their canonisation of these models is suggested by Schütz's use of the term 'classic authors'.[29]

Regardless of which composers were chosen as models, the process of *imitatio* required careful study of their works. Novices imitating their teacher's style or technique would usually start by making manuscript copies of compositions shared with them. Bach's pupil Philipp David Kräuter noted that his teacher 'shares with me all the music I ask for'.[30] Dressler, Schütz, Bernhard and Demelius advised transcribing compositions from parts into score or tablature, so that contrapuntal and harmonic features could be fully appreciated.[31] Novices might use a commonplace book to copy noteworthy excerpts from the model works. The Quedlinburg cantor Henricus Baryphonus chastised those composers 'who have never transcribed the work of canonised composers into score, performed them well, and recorded and memorised what is notable, or digested it in *loci communes*'.[32] Crüger used the words ἀνάλυσις (analysis) and σύνθεσις (synthesis) to describe how novices should assimilate their musical models.[33] Analysing praiseworthy compositions was analogous to

---

[27] Honey Meconi, 'Does *Imitatio* Exist?', *Journal of Musicology* 12 (1994), 152–78 (p. 159).

[28] Burmeister, *Musica poetica*, 74; Johannes Crüger, *Synopsis musica* (Berlin, 1630), 125; Crüger, *Synopsis musica*, 2nd edn (Berlin, 1654), 185–86; Joseph Müller-Blattau (ed.), *Die Kompositionslehre Heinrich Schützens in der Fassung seines Schülers Christoph Bernhard* (Leipzig: Breitkopf & Härtel, 1926), 90; GB-Lbl, Add. Ms. 4910, fol. 38v.

[29] Schütz, *Geistliche Chor-Music*, preface; GB-Lbl, Add. Ms. 4910, fol. 38v. [30] *NBR*, 318.

[31] Dressler advised that the 'songs of approved composers' should 'be unravelled onto ten lines' ('cantiones probatorum autorum ... resolvantur in decem lineas'); *Gallus Dressler's* Præcepta musicæ poëticæ, ed. Forgács, 188–89.

[32] 'denn sie haben niemahls *Canonisi*rter *Componi*sten Arbeit in die *Partitur* gebracht/ dieselbe wohl *excuti*ret/ und was darinn *notab*el/ auffgezeichnet/ und zu Gedächtniß gefasset/ oder *in Locos communes digeri*ret'. Quoted in Andreas Werckmeister, *Cribrum musicum* (Quedlinburg, 1700), 39.

[33] Crüger, *Synopsis musica* (1630 edn), 125.

the exegetical contemplation recommended for the *imitatio* of literary works. By assimilating the praiseworthy features of a model, novices could take some of its authority for themselves, thereby fostering their own judgement and style.

The next stage of *imitatio* required pupils to write in the style of recommended models. For musicians, this stage is not described in treatises, but it can be inferred from apprentice-like pieces written early in the career of composers and clearly modelled on the works of their teachers or other models. A case in point from the early seventeenth century comprises the 'opus 1' collections of madrigals published in Venice, including those by northern pupils of Giovanni Gabrieli such as Schütz, Johann Grabbe and Hans Nielsen.[34] Although these published collections were the fruits of the pupils' study in Venice, they stand in an indirect relationship with the music of Gabrieli, who did not publish any books of his own madrigals. Schütz's *Il primo libro de madrigali* (1611) shows him practising techniques of the polyphonic madrigal, such as the simultaneous presentation of two contrasting themes and the evocation of poetic content through the character of themes; here he followed the example of madrigalists such as Andrea Gabrieli and Giaches de Wert.

Beyond their madrigal collections, Giovanni Gabrieli's pupils sought to annex some of their teacher's authority by quoting excerpts from his compositions.[35] Through such allusions, pupils could create a family resemblance between Gabrieli's and their own compositions, thereby presenting him as their musical father. Creating such a filial relationship with models had long been an ideal of literary *imitatio*, as Seneca the Younger indicated in his Epistle 84, a staple of educational manuals in the sixteenth century: 'Even if there shall appear in you a likeness to him who, by reason of your admiration, has left a deep impress upon you, I would have you resemble him as a child resembles his father.'[36]

Schütz artfully fashioned his genealogical relationship with Gabrieli in his *Psalmen Davids* (1619), which he described as 'various German psalms in the Italian style in which I was diligently instructed by my dear and world-famous teacher, Giovanni Gabrieli, while I stayed with him in Italy'.[37] Many aspects of the *Psalmen* are modelled on Gabrieli: the double-choir

---

[34] For an overview of these collections, see Konrad Küster, *Opus primum in Venedig. Traditionen des Vokalsatzes 1590–650* (Laaber: Laaber Verlag, 1995).

[35] Rodolfo Baroncini, '"Et per tale confirmato dall'auttorità del signor Giovanni Gabrieli". The Reception of Gabrieli as a Model by Venetian and Non-Venetian Composers of the New Generation (1600–20)', in Rodolfo Baroncini, David Bryant and Luigi Collarile (eds.), *Giovanni Gabrieli: Transmission and Reception of a Venetian Musical Tradition* (Turnhout: Brepols, 2016), 5–31 (p. 6).

[36] Seneca, *Epistles* 84, 7–8, trans. Richard M. Gummere, Loeb Classical Library 76 (Cambridge, MA: Harvard University Press, 1920).

[37] 'etzliche Teutsche Psalmen auff Italienische Manier/ zu welcher ich von meinem lieben vnd in aller Welt hochberühmten *Praeceptore* Herrn Johan Gabrieln/ so lange in *Italia* ich mich bey jhme auffgehalten/ mit fleiß angeführet worden'. Schütz, *Psalmen Davids* (Dresden, 1619), Cantus 1 Chori partbook, dedication, sig.):(2r. RISM A/I S2275).

Example 2.1 (a) Giovanni Gabrieli, *Beati omnes*, opening (from *Sacrae symphoniae* [Venice, 1587], no. 16); (b) Heinrich Schütz, *Wohl dem, der den Herren fürchtet*, SWV30, opening with continuo part omitted (from *Psalmen Davids* [Dresden, 1619], no. 9).

scoring; the mingling of homophonic and contrapuntal sections; the grand climaxes at final cadences; the handling of dissonance (where the leading note sounds simultaneously against its resolution in another part); and the triple-time refrains on 'Alleluja' and 'Lobe den Herren'. Some harmonic devices also recall Gabrieli, such as the chordal shift by an upward third at the opening of *Wie lieblich sind die Wohnungen* SWV29.

Furthermore, Schütz alluded in the *Psalmen Davids* to various compositions by his teacher. As Example 2.1 shows, he started his setting of Psalm 128, *Wohl dem, der den Herren fürchtet* SWV30, with the same chordal succession that opens Gabrieli's setting of that psalm, *Beati omnes*. To use the anachronistic language of common-practice tonality, this is a tonic to dominant progression that is anticipated and decorated by the tenor part. Schütz repeats this progression, to reiterate the initial syntactic unit of the German text, before the voice-parts move outwards in an expanded version of Gabrieli's opening.[38]

Even clearer is the citation in *Ich danke dem Herrn* SWV34 of Gabrieli's madrigal *Lieto godea*. This madrigal was one of Gabrieli's most widely disseminated works: it appeared in the Nuremberg anthology *Gemma musicalis*, in Latin and German sacred contrafacta, and in lute arrangements.[39] In Italy it was the basis for parodies such as two Magnificat settings by Adriano Banchieri.[40] With its catchy canzona rhythms and prominent Phrygian cadences made by the downward semitone steps in the bass, Gabrieli's opening would have been recognised by at least some of Schütz's listeners. But as Example 2.2 demonstrates, Schütz assimilated it within his musical language, adapting it to the speech rhythms of the German doxology 'Ehre sei dem Vater'. He also recomposed the homophony on 'godea sedendo' as syncopated counterpoint on 'und dem Sohn'. Through such quotations, Schütz advertised his lineage with his teacher, as well as his command of the Italian style that was highly valued at German courts. Yet the *Psalmen* also asserted Schütz's independence from his teacher, partly because their German texts require more rapid and consonant-rich declamation than the Latin and Italian used by Gabrieli.

Schütz claimed his teacher's authority in other ways. In his 1651 autobiographical memorial, he claimed that Gabrieli 'on his deathbed bequeathed to me out of singular affection, in memory of him, one of his rings left behind, which after his death was presented and delivered to me by his father confessor'.[41] The ring was a material symbol of the eternal filial bond between Gabrieli and Schütz, proof that the teacher reciprocated the respect that his pupil showed him. Along with his musical allusions to Gabrieli, Schütz thereby presented himself as the chosen pupil carrying Gabrieli's authority forward to future generations.

Beyond pedagogical situations, musicians imitated authority to justify innovations such as the irregular treatment of dissonance. In his treatises *Tractatus compositionis augmentatus* and *Ausführlicher Bericht vom Gebrauche der Con- und Dissonantien* (*c.*1670), Bernhard explained the

---

[38] For a comparison of Schütz's and Gabrieli's settings of Psalm 128, see Victor Ravizza, 'Schütz und die Venezianische Tradition der Mehrchörigkeit', in Dietrich Berke and Dorothee Hanemann (eds.), *Alte Musik als ästhetische Gegenwart: Bach, Händel, Schütz: Bericht über den internationalen musikwissenschaftlichen Kongress, Stuttgart 1985*, 2 vols. (Kassel: Bärenreiter, 1987), vol. 1, 53–65.

[39] David Bryant, 'Gabrieli, Giovanni', *Oxford Music Online*, works-list.

[40] Adriano Banchieri, *Canzoni alla francese* (Venice, 1596). RISM A/I B835. See Baroncini, '"Et per tale confirmato dall'auttorità del signor Giovanni Gabrieli"', 26.

[41] D-Dla Loc. 8687/1, fol. 291v; *SDok* 1, 322; *HSR*, 183.

Example 2.2   Heinrich Schütz, *Ich danke dem Herrn*, SWV34, quotation of Giovanni Gabrieli, 'Lieto godea', with continuo part omitted (from *Psalmen Davids* [Dresden, 1619], no. 13, bars 148–52).

contrapuntal licences of modern composers as figures embellishing a consonant foundation. Both treatises include reductive analyses showing the *prima prattica* framework underpinning such figures. Joshua Rifkin argued that Bernhard's approach clarifies the contrapuntal foundations of Schütz's compositional technique, and John Butt interpreted Bernhard's treatises as showing how composers drew on performers' ornamental figures to change 'the norms of the compositional language itself'.[42] But Bernhard's approach also exemplifies the use of past authority to legitimise

---

[42] Joshua Rifkin, 'Schütz and Musical Logic', *The Musical Times* 113 (1972), 1067–70; John Butt, *Music Education and the Art of Performance in the German Baroque* (Cambridge: Cambridge University Press, 1994), 160.

change. As Nancy Struever comments: '[R]hetorical *imitatio*, with its concept of virtuosity as both a command of past techniques which possess continuous sanctions and a sensitivity to the unique demands of the present situation, provides a model of continuity in change'.[43] In his *Ausführlicher Bericht*, Bernhard advised: 'Such [irregular] figures and themes, however, have the old composers as their basis, and what cannot be thereby excused should be justly removed from the composition as a monstrosity'.[44] Novelty therefore had to be reconciled with the imitation of past authority.

In the *Tractatus*, Bernhard combined his list of irregular dissonance figures with comments on the relationship between theoretical rules and authoritative examples. He explained:

Should the diligent student of composition find another [dissonant figure] in the works of good authors, it can either be reduced to one of the aforementioned figures, or it will be left to his judgement whether he should imitate it or not. For the imitation of the most distinguished composers is no less profitable – indeed necessary – in this profession than in any other art, as a part of one's practice, without which all precepts are useless.[45]

For Bernhard, contrapuntal rules in isolation were meaningless; rather, they had to be considered in conjunction with the practices of canonised authors.

The justification of current practices with reference to authority was exemplified by the Württemberg capellmeister Samuel Capricornus in a 1659–60 dispute.[46] Capricornus defended compositions in his *Opus musicum* (1655) against allegations by his rival Philipp Friedrich Böddecker that they were composed 'not according to the foundations and rules of music but according to my own imagined charms'.[47] Böddecker censured Capricornus on the basis of rules, disregarding the qualities of imagination associated with *ingenium*. Specifically, he complained about irregular voice-leading such as consecutive fifths or the resolution of a minor sixth onto a fifth via a downward step in the bass. Capricornus used theoretical

---

[43] Nancy Struever, *The Language of History in the Renaissance: Rhetoric and Historical Consciousness in Florentine Humanism* (Princeton: Princeton University Press, 1970), 193.

[44] 'Solche Figuren und Sätze aber, haben die alten *Componisten* zu ihrem Grunde, und was durch solche nicht kann *excusiret* werden, dasselbige soll billich aus der *Composition* als ein Ungeheuer außgemustert werden'. Müller-Blattau, *Die Kompositionslehre Heinrich Schützens*, 147.

[45] 'Solte ein fleißiger *Discipel* der *Composition* über angeführtes etwas mehreres bey guten *Authoribus* antreffen, so wird solches entweder leicht zu besagten *Figuris* können *reduciret* werden, oder dem *Judicio* anheimgestellet, ob er solches *imitiren* wolle oder nicht. Denn doch die *Imitation* der vornehmsten *Authorum* dieser Profession nicht weniger als in allen andern Künsten nützlich ja nöthig ist, als ein Theil der *Praxeos*, ohne welche alle *Praecepta* ohne Nutzen sind'. Ibid., 90.

[46] Hauptstaatsarchiv Stuttgart, A202 Büschel 1919; transcribed in Josef Sittard, 'Samuel Capricornus contra Philipp Friedrich Böddecker', *Sammelbände der internationalen Musikgesellschaft* 3 (1901–02), 87–128.

[47] As Capricornus reported: 'meine *musicali*sche Stücke ... daß sie nicht *secundum fundamenta et regulas musicales*, sondern nach meiner selbst eingebildeten Lieblichkeit *componirt* seyen'. Ibid., 96.

Imitatio *and Authority*

and practical authorities to justify these passages. He referred to the views of respected theorists such as Seth Calvisius and Athanasius Kircher (who noted in *Musurgia* that consecutive consonances could occasionally be used to move the affections).[48]

Capricornus bolstered his argument by referring to Giovanni Valentini and Antonio Bertali as 'those two outstanding composers, who I myself sometimes imitate in compositions, and hold in high respect'.[49] Valentini and Bertali served as imperial capellmeisters in Vienna, and not only would have been formative figures for Capricornus during his previous employment in nearby Pressburg (present-day Bratislava); they were also the highest-ranking musicians to serve the Holy Roman Emperor and therefore carried additional authority. Capricornus showed how they used the same voice-leading for which he had been criticised, quoting excerpts from Valentini's *Cantate gentes*,[50] an unidentified sonata *a 8* by Bertali, and various unidentified Mass movements by Valentini. Another of Capricornus's models was the 'outstanding and famed composer Giacomo Carissimi, who most hold as the foremost musician of our age',[51] specifically the closing chorus 'Plorate filii Israel' of *Jephte* for its resolution of a minor sixth onto a fifth via a downward step in the bass. Echoing Bernhard's viewpoint on the relationship of precepts and examples, Capricornus declared: 'My opinion is sufficiently affirmed as much by rules as by the examples and authority of the most esteemed authors'.[52] He further explained: 'As an experienced practitioner I am not bound to the rules that a novice must observe, but instead I walk with the example of the most outstanding practitioners ... by my side'.[53] Modifying the rhetoricians' metaphor of following the footsteps of predecessors, Capricornus's notion of walking beside authority gave him an element of greater independence, yet showed he could not justify innovation solely by himself.

Even at the end of the seventeenth century, some musicians still invoked external authorities to justify stylistic change. In his third published collection of keyboard music, *Frische Clavier-Früchte* (1696), Johann Kuhnau explained how he weighed up the differing authorities of older and newer composers with regard to unorthodox voice-leading.

---

[48] Ibid., 97–98, 103; the reference is to Athanasius Kircher, *Musurgia universalis sive ars magna consoni et dissoni*, 2 vols. (Rome, 1650), vol. 1, 620–24.

[49] 'denen beyden vortrefflichen *Componi*sten, die ich selbsten in theils Sachen *imitire* und sehr hoch halte'. Ibid., 98.

[50] Bars 154–63 of the critical edition by Andrew Weaver, available in the Web Library of Seventeenth-Century Music.

[51] 'der vortreffliche und berühmte Jacobus Carissimi (welcher von den meisten für einen *Principem Musicorum nostri seculi* gehalten wird)'. Sittard, 'Samuel Capricornus', 110.

[52] 'ist also meine *Opinion* ... *tam Regulis quam Exemplis et autoritate probatissimorum autorum* nach Genüge bekräfftiget worden'. Ibid., 101.

[53] 'ich, alß ... ein *exercitatus Practicus* mich so genawe an die *Leges*, die ein *Tyro* zu *observir*en, nicht binden, sondern nach dem *Exempel* der vornehmsten *Practicorum* ... in etwas bey Seite gehen'. Ibid, 102.

Example 2.3   Johann Kuhnau, *Frische Clavier-Früchte* (Leipzig, 1696), Suonata prima, bar 43. '!' denotes unresolved compound sevenths.

Example 2.4   Johann Kuhnau, *Frische Clavier-Früchte* (Leipzig, 1696), Suonata quinta, bar 3, with consecutive compound sevenths indicated.

In these sonatas, he wrote, 'there will now and again appear things that scarcely agree with the rules of the old composers. For I have included many passages that in previous years I myself would not have approved in the works of famed authors, and which often appeared to me like sour grapes or other unripe fruit.'[54] The 'unripe' passages probably included unresolved dissonances (such as the compound sevenths marked in Example 2.3) and unconventional voice-leading (such as the consecutive compound sevenths in Example 2.4). Ultimately, however, Kuhnau reported that 'the authority of the same virtuosos brought me to change my mind, and realise that such things are similar to green pears: in appearance they seem unripe, yet though these fruits are rejected on account of their colour, they can be ripe and tasty.'[55] Kuhnau neither named the authoritative virtuosos who had led him to alter his opinion, nor commented on how these musicians had gained their stature. However, like Bernhard, he rationalised the dissonant passages as decorating a

---

[54] 'Es lässet sich zwar hin und wieder etwas blicken/ welches mit denen *Regul*en der alten *Componist*en wenig übereinzukommen scheinet. Denn ich habe manche Sätze oder Gänge gemachet/ die ich vor etlicher Jahren in anderer/ wiewohl berühmter *Autorum* Wercken selbst nicht *approbir*en wollen/ und sind sie mir öffters wie Herlinge/ oder ander unzeitiges Obst vorgekommen'. Kuhnau, *Frische Clavier-Früchte* (Leipzig, 1696), preface. RISM A/I K2991.

[55] 'Allein die *Autor*ität selbiger *exercir*ten *Virtuo*sen hätte mich damahls sollen auff andere Gedancken bringen/ und erwegen lassen/ daß es mit ihren Wercken fast die Beschaffenheit habe/ wie mit denen so genandten Ritter- oder grünen Birnen: Diese sind dem Ansehen nach fast niemahls reiff; Doch so verdächtig als dieses Obst wegen seiner Farbe ist/ so reiff und wohlgeschmack kan es hingegen seyn'. Ibid.

prima prattica foundation: 'I realised that they did not transgress the rules of the ancients, but merely sought to conceal the simple and natural blending of consonances and dissonances under rhetorical figures.'[56] Further indicating his desire for historical continuity, Kuhnau reverted to the trope of following in the footsteps of authority: 'I am not to be taken amiss in these piece when I follow the good modern authors.'[57]

Thus *imitatio* was used to claim musical authority, by pupils establishing their musical parentage, and by experienced composers such as Capricornus and Kuhnau showing the historical continuity underpinning their stylistic innovations. *Imitatio* was an act of creative reception, strengthening the status of those composers canonised as worthy models. Such practices show how authorship was partly constituted through external authority: musicians felt obliged to invoke the enabling power of a patriarchal model as they devised their own compositional works.

EMULATION AND ALLUSION

A second type of borrowing aimed to go beyond the footsteps of esteemed authors, instead seeking to surpass them. Such emulation was advocated by Roman poets who promoted a competitive relationship between imitators and models, particularly to clarify their relationship with Greek predecessors. Horace railed against servile imitators, advising poets not to linger on easy or open pathways.[58] Quintilian urged poets to compete with their predecessors:

The man whose aim is to prove himself better than another, even if he does not surpass him, may hope to equal him. But he can never hope to equal him, if he thinks it his duty merely to tread in his footsteps: for the mere follower must always lag behind.[59]

Similar views were voiced in the sixteenth century. Erasmus attacked those poets who imitated faithfully the style of Cicero, noting that 'one cannot walk properly if one is always placing one's foot in someone else's footprints'.[60] He also asserted that borrowing should not suppress the distinctive style stemming from each poet's nature: 'I welcome imitation with open arms – but imitation which assists nature and does not violate it, which turns its gifts in the right direction and does not destroy them.

---

[56] '[ich] bekenne/ daß sie wider die *Regul*en der Alten durchaus nicht gesündiget/ sondern bloß gesuchet haben/ die schlechte und natürliche Vermischung der *Consonanti*en und *Dissonanti*en gleichsam unter denen *Oratori*schen *Figur*en vermunfftmäßig zu verstrecken'. Ibid.

[57] 'Dannenhero werde ich nicht zuverdencken seyn/ wenn ich numehro in diesem Stücke denen guten neüen *Autoribus* auch nachgegangen bin'. Ibid.

[58] Horace, *Epistles* 1.19.19; *Ars poetica* 132.

[59] Quintilian, *Institutio oratoria* 10.2.10; trans. H. E. Butler, Loeb Classical Library 127 (Cambridge, MA: Harvard University Press, 1922).

[60] *ASD* I-2, 708; *CWE* 28, 445–46.

62   *Between* Imitatio *and Plagiarism*

I approve of imitation – but imitation of a model that is in accord with, or at least not contrary to, your own native genius'.[61]

Compared to the practice of imitating patriarchal models, techniques of emulation showed a greater confidence in human agency, including the capacity of individuals to act without depending on the authorities around them. Such confidence can be seen in Erasmus's insistence that borrowing should not suppress an individual's *ingenium* or personal style. It can also be seen in attitudes to historical progress, with emulators regarding the past as a source of inspiration rather than legitimation. Quintilian advised that 'it is generally easier to make some advance than to repeat what has been done by others'.[62] Erasmus argued that a poet or orator must write in ways suitable for his own day, for instance by modifying elements of Greek or Roman style to reflect the Christian environment.[63] Such self-assertion placed emulators closer to the mindset of human autonomy associated with modernity.

Notions of musical borrowing as playful emulation underpin Georg Quitschreiber's treatise *De* παρῳδία [*De parodia*] (1611). This Latin pamphlet, in the style of an academic disputation, is terse and enigmatic, and has been overlooked by scholars apart from brief treatments by Klaus Wolfgang Niemöller and Andreas Waczkat.[64] Quitschreiber defined *parodia* by quoting Quintilian's *Institutio oratoria*: 'a term derived from songs made with a likeness to others, and so misused to mean imitations in verse or prose'.[65] His treatise starts with the question 'Should musical parody be allowed?',[66] and refers to two antagonists, Thrason Terence and Marcus Taubmann, whose views do not survive but who presumably voiced the opposite argument in the disputation.[67] Much of the treatise lists examples of musical parodies, with Quitschreiber asking rhetorically whether such reworkings are permissible, and offering no comment on the relationship between model and imitation. Yet an exploration of the treatise's intellectual context and the music cited in it (hitherto not fully discussed by scholars) can illuminate Quitschreiber's understanding of borrowing as playful manipulation of art.

The intellectual framework for Quitschreiber's treatise is provided by those Roman poets who competitively emulated their predecessors. He

---

[61] *ASD* I-2, 704; *CWE* 28, 441.   [62] Quintilian, *Institutio oratoria* 10.2.10, trans. Butler.

[63] *ASD* I-2, 698–702; *CWE* 28, 436–39.

[64] Klaus Wolfgang Niemöller, 'Parodia–Imitatio: Zu Georg Quitschreibers Schrift von 1611', in Annegrit Laubenthal (ed.), *Studien zur Musikgeschichte: Eine Festschrift für Ludwig Finscher* (Kassel: Bärenreiter, 1995), 174–80; Waczkat, *'Ein ehrenhaftes Spielen'*, 33–37.

[65] 'quod nomen ductum a canticis ad aliorum similitudinem modulatis abusive etiam in versificationis ac sermonum imitatione servatur'. Quintilian, *Institutio oratoria* 9.2.35; partly quoted by Georg Quitschreiber, *De* παρῳδία (Jena, 1611), sig. A2v and A3r.

[66] 'An Parodia Musicalis concedatur?' Quitschreiber, *De* παρῳδία, sig. A2r.

[67] Ibid., sig. A2v. The format of the disputation suggests that Quitschreiber's treatise may have stemmed from scholarly discussions at Jena University, where he matriculated in 1588 (Georg Mentz, *Die Matrikel der Universität Jena. Band 1: 1548 bis 1652* [Jena: Gustav Fischer, 1944], 247). However, Terence and Taubmann are not listed in the Jena matriculation registers.

Emulation and Allusion

answered his initial question (on the permissibility of musical borrowing) indirectly, quoting the *Saturnalia* of the fifth-century Latin grammarian and philosopher Macrobius: 'We are ignorant of many things that would not lie hidden if we were accustomed to read the writings of ancients (and also moderns).'[68] *Saturnalia* itemises Virgil's borrowings from writers such as Homer, and may have inspired Quitschreiber's list of examples of musical reworkings. Macrobius urged his readers to understand the allusions in Latin poetry, including 'things fetched from the inner sanctum of Greek literature, things no Roman knows, save those who have earnestly drunk a full draught of Greek learning. For this poet here was as evasive and secretive in his learning as he was diligent and finicky: as a result, the sources of many of his borrowings are difficult to recognize.'[69] Such connoisseurship would encourage poets to outdo their literary heritage.[70] As Macrobius said: 'This is one of the benefits of reading, to emulate the things you approve in others and by a timely borrowing to turn to your own use the words of others that you most admire – a form of competition that our authors engaged in among themselves as much as with the Greeks'.[71]

Quitschreiber appreciated the learning involved in musical allusions: 'Our age is rich in famous and great inventions, so one can say that nowadays those with a good musical education can play with music (in an honest way).'[72] Like the poetic rivalry described by Macrobius, his notion of playing with art regarded the past not as a source of patriarchal authority but as raw material for the ingenuity of present-day musicians. Indeed Quitschreiber emphasised the historical progress achieved by his contemporaries. Following his initial extract from Macrobius, he quoted two sixteenth-century texts on scientific discovery: a 1590 treatise on the monochord by the Thuringian pastor Cyriacus Schneegass ('Until now is still unknown to many in the arts, what others have been unable to comprehend')[73] and an encyclopedia of natural philosophy by Girolamo Cardano ('There are new discoveries every day, and they are being uncovered without limits').[74] While retaining the prevalent notion of invention as discovering what already exists, these quotations implied that human knowledge was constantly advancing. To show how music had progressed to its present state, Quitschreiber listed innovations such

---

[68] 'Multa ignoramus, quae nos non laterent, si Veterum (imo et Neotericorum) lectio nobis esset familiaris'. Slightly modified (by the addition of 'imo et Neotericorum'), Macrobius, *Saturnalia* 6.9.9 (misattributed by Quitschreiber to book 1 of *Saturnalia*).

[69] Macrobius, *Saturnalia* 5.18.1, trans. Robert A. Kaster, Loeb Classical Library 511 (Cambridge, MA: Harvard University Press, 2011).

[70] Pigman, 'Versions of Imitation', 26.   [71] Macrobius, *Saturnalia* 6.1.2, trans. Kaster.

[72] 'nostra aetas illustribus inventis et maximis foecunda est, ut quasi hodie cum Musica ludere (at honeste) illi dicantur'. Quitschreiber, *De* παρῳδία, sig. A2r.

[73] 'Multa adhuc in artibus latere, quae illi non viderint'. Quoted from Cyriacus Schneegass, *Nova et exquisita monochordi dimensio* (Erfurt, 1590), sig. A4r.

[74] 'Sunt artium inventa in singulos dies nova, nec ullo fine comprehenduntur'. Girolamo Cardano, *De subtilitate* (Nuremberg, 1550), 315; quoted in Quitschreiber, *De* παρῳδία, sig. A2r.

as an eight-line staff used in the notation of Luca Marenzio's madrigal *Bianchi cigni e canori*, and the extended instrumental tessitura encouraged by Moritz of Hesse.[75]

Many of Quitschreiber's examples of musical borrowing likewise showed an advance upon their models. He listed composers who made contrapuntal elaborations of works, including Jacopo de Antiquis and Francesco Soriano, who added a bass part to unidentified duos by Rocco Rodio. He mentioned Sweelinck's version of the chanson *Susanne un jour*,[76] where the composer 'retained the descant part of Lassus's five-voice setting and added four further parts according to what is pleasing in music' (a somewhat convoluted description of a cantus firmus composition).[77] He summarised how Melchior Vulpius reworked the imitative opening of Hieronymus Praetorius's five-voice *Miserere mei Deus*, by adding an extra voice for his own motet on the same text.[78] Such instances involving the addition or substitution of contrapuntal voices might be associated with the technique described in 1783 by Johann Philipp Kirnberger but probably practised in earlier centuries, whereby a composer devised a piece by writing a new bass to an existing melody, then writing a new melody for that bass line.[79]

Quitschreiber made a passing reference to parody Masses, the polyphonic genre most closely associated by modern scholars with borrowing and intertextuality.[80] But he spent more time listing examples which showed the range of uses to which borrowing was put. These include contrapuntal reductions of pieces (Alessandro Striggio's 40-voice motet *Ecce beatam lucem* reduced to seven voices by Johannes Lippius; Lassus's eight-voice *Confitebor tibi Domine* reduced to four, five or six voices);[81] Seth Calvisius's simplified version of Josquin's motet *Praeter rerum seriem*; contrafacta (specifically Valentin Haussmann's German-texted versions of Italian songs);[82] and

---

[75] Quitschreiber, *De* παρῳδία, sig. A2r.

[76] Sweelinck, *Chansons a cinc parties* (Antwerp, 1594), no. 8. RISM B/I 1594⁵.

[77] 'Discantum Orlandi Susanna, se videns 5. voc. retinuit, et alias quatuor voces ipso ad placitum Musicum addidit'. Quitschreiber, *De* παρῳδία, sig. A2v.

[78] Hieronymus Praetorius, *Cantiones sacrae de praecipuis festis totius anni* (Hamburg, 1599), no. 44; Melchior Vulpius, *Pars prima. Cantionum sacrarum cum sex, septem, octo et pluribus vocibus* (Jena, 1602), no. 5. RISM A/I P5336, V2569. Quitschreiber, *De* παρῳδία, sig. A3r.

[79] W. S. Newman, 'Kirnberger's Method for *Tossing off Sonatas*', *Musical Quarterly* 47 (1961), 517–25.

[80] 'The majority of masses, one could say, are artfully assembled as imitations of motets'. ('Sic pleraeque Missae, ut vocant, ad imitationes Mutetarum concinnatae, decantantur'.) Quitschreiber, *De* παρῳδία, sig. A2v.

[81] These reductions cannot be now located. Striggio's motet survives in a 1587 manuscript in D-Z, Mu 566; Lassus's motet is one of his first published eight-voice motets, in *Thesaurus musicus ... tomi primi* (Nuremberg, 1564). RISM B/I 1564¹.

[82] Haussmann's editions of Italianate secular songs with German texts include *Ausszug aus Lucae Marentii ... Villanellen und Napolitanen* (Nuremberg, 1606), *Liebliche fröliche Ballette ... von Thoma Morlei gesetzt* (Nuremberg, 1609), and three volumes of *Vierstimmigen Canzonetten Horatii Vecchi* (Nuremberg, 1610). RISM A/I M611, M3700, V1035–37. For a study of these translations, see Susan Lewis Hammond, *Editing Music in Early Modern Germany* (Aldershot: Ashgate, 2007), 77–116.

citations (Gemignano Capilupi's canzonetta *Piu che mai vaga e bella*, whose refrain quotes Palestrina's well-known madrigal *Vestiva i colli*, reduced to three voices).[83] Some of these reworkings were probably made for pragmatic purposes, to suit a specific occasion or ensemble. For Quitschreiber, however, they demonstrated the artifice of composers: 'Are these not examples of skill and effort?'[84]

In the history of music theory, Quitschreiber's disputation is a one-off, with no other extant treatises articulating similar views. Yet he claimed his views on parody were endorsed by his contemporaries, including Michael Praetorius, Hans Leo Hassler and Johann Steuerlein.[85] The practices of elaboration and allusion he described can be detected in a much wider repertory from across the seventeenth century. Peter Wollny uses the term *aemulatio* to describe how Germans wrote vocal concertos on the same texts used by Roman composers – for instance, Dieterich Buxtehude's *O dulcis Jesu* BuxWV83 modelled on the setting by Bonifazio Graziani. As Wollny comments, Buxtehude's version cannot be regarded as an apprentice work. The resemblances between these two compositions (including similar vocal motifs, set with more repetition and elaboration by Buxtehude) instead suggest that 'Buxtehude's *O dulcis Jesu* is to be judged in its complex relationship with Graziani's prototype as a typical emulation, as an artistically independent construction on a preformed structure and a transformative appropriation of this model'.[86]

Such transformative appropriations were in the spirit envisaged by Quitschreiber, showing the artifice of composers and enabling music to reach new peaks of perfection. Contrapuntal elaboration was a particularly valuable technique for realising potential latent in the original composition. Quitschreiber expressed the importance of artifice with a poem based on Horace's proverb 'Tractent fabrilia fabri' (carpenters handle carpenters' tools):[87]

> The musician and the poet both praise the parody
> All that can be art, he says, he knows it well.
> I sing of such, but concede it is not known by every cowherd.
> The grammarian shall pursue his art, just like the musician.[88]

---

[83] Capilupi's canzonetta is no. 16 in *Canzonette a tre voci di Horatio Vecchi et di Gemignano Capi Lupi da Modena* (Nuremberg/Venice, 1597). RISM B/I 1597²¹, 1597²². Quitschreiber quotes the German contrafacta *Wenn ich gedenck der Stunden*, as edited by Valentin Haussmann with German texts in *Canzonette, mit dreyen Stimmen, Horatii Vecchi unnd Gemignani Capi Lupi* (Nuremberg, 1606). RISM B/I 1606¹³.

[84] 'An non artis et laboris est?' Quitschreiber, *De* παρῳδία, sig. A3r.   [85] Ibid., sig. A3v–A4r.

[86] Wollny, *Studien zum Stilwandel*, 397.   [87] Horace, *Epistles* 2.1, 115–16.

[88]
> 'Musicus atq‹ue› Poeta canunt nunc ambo παρῳδήν:
> Quanta sit ars, dicat, qui bene novit eam.
> Talia canto simul, licet haud sciat ille Bubulcus:
> Tractet Grammaticus, Musicus atq‹ue› sua.'

Quitschreiber, *De* παρῳδία, sig. A3r.

The poem advises individuals to respect the skills required for different arts and crafts. Through their contrapuntal artifice, musicians could build on and surpass the achievements of their predecessors. The concept of emulation thus recognised the power of musicians to position themselves relative to the past and to develop their discipline in new ways.

PLAGIARISM VERSUS HONEST THEFT

A further set of arguments discussed the legitimacy of musical borrowing, seeking to distinguish plagiarism from honest theft. Quitschreiber and other musicians of the early seventeenth century adhered to the humanist viewpoint that legitimate borrowing required imitators to be open about their models or to transform these models significantly. Musical reworkings that lacked such honesty or transformation might be described as acts of plagiarism.

The meaning of plagiarism (*plagium*) was discussed by several German scholars in the seventeenth century. The lawyer Johann von Felden traced the etymology of *plagium* to the act of theft, specifically the kidnapping of a person or child.[89] Another writer on this topic, Jacob Thomasius (headmaster of the Thomasschule in Leipzig), noted that the term 'plagiarism' had been applied to literature by the first-century poet Martial.[90] Martial regarded his poems as his metaphorical children, which were kidnapped when a rival claimed authorship of them.[91] Contrary to Martial, however, Thomasius argued that plagiarism in learned literature was not theft in a strict sense, but rather an act of dishonesty, disrupting the open exchange of information necessary for scholarly communication.[92]

Since classical times the usual symbol for a plagiarist was the crow or jackdaw. In one of Aesop's fables, the crow dressed himself in feathers stolen from other birds in order to claim the crown of the most handsome bird. But when these filched feathers fell out, the lowly crow was exposed as a vain cheat. In another version, the jackdaw used stolen feathers in a failed attempt to masquerade as a peacock.[93] In both stories the bird imitates surface features without transforming its underlying character, and becomes a social outcast when its deception is discovered. Horace

---

[89] Johann von Felden, *Elementa juris universi* (Frankfurt am Main and Leipzig, 1664), 195.
[90] Jacob Thomasius, *Dissertatio philosophica de plagio literario* (Leipzig, 1673), sig. E1r–E1v.
[91] Martial, *Epigrams* 1.52–53.
[92] Thomasius, *Dissertatio philosophica*, sig. F1r–F1v; on the implications of Thomasius's theory for notions of public criticism, see Herbert Jaumann, 'Öffentlichkeit und Verlegenheit. Frühe Spuren eines Konzepts öffentlicher Kritik in der Theorie des "plagium extrajudiciale" von Jakob Thomasius (1673)', *Scientia Poetica. Jahrbuch für Geschichte der Literatur und der Wissenschaften* 4 (2000), 62–82.
[93] Ben Edwin Perry, *Aesopica: A Series of Texts Relating to Aesop or Ascribed to Him or Closely Connected with the Literary Tradition That Bears His Name* (Urbana: University of Illinois Press, 1952), nos. 101, 472.

Plagiarism versus Honest Theft

used the crow as a symbol of literary misappropriation when he warned the novice poet Celsus

to search for home treasures, and to shrink from touching the writings which Apollo on the Palatine has admitted; lest, if some day perchance the flock of birds come to reclaim their plumage, the poor crow, stripped of his stolen colours, awake laughter.[94]

Rather than cultivating his own abilities, Celsus relied on borrowings from ancient authors preserved in the Bibliotheca Apollonis on Palatine Hill. Horace warned that should such dishonest borrowings be exposed, Celsus's reputation would be destroyed (as had happened with Greek poets whose literary thefts were uncovered by Aristophanes of Byzantium).[95]

Quitschreiber invoked this passage from Horace, cautioning: 'We must take care not to appropriate poems already circulating and placed in the library of Apollo on the Palatine hill, nor to sell them as our own, so we do not experience what happened to Aesop's crow'.[96] Other musicians, concerned to preserve their reputations, distanced their borrowings from the example of the deceitful crow. Acknowledging his reworkings of Monteverdi's *Armato il cor* and *Zefiro torna*, Schütz declared in 1647: 'I am not accustomed to adorn my work with others' feathers'.[97] In 1641 the Königsberg song-writer Heinrich Albert announced he had given correct attributions for nine melodies by other composers in the first four parts of his *Arien* because 'otherwise it would do ill, when one dresses oneself with false feathers'.[98]

Another metaphor for dishonest borrowing was the patchwork, in which source materials are insufficiently integrated into a new whole. As Chapter 1 showed (p. 35), this metaphor was associated with authors lacking sufficient *ingenium*. In 1528 Erasmus advised that an imitation should not resemble a mosaic.[99] A similar metaphor was used by Kuhnau to describe the efforts of the fradulent musician, Caraffa, the eponymous subject of his novel *Der musicalische Quack-Salber*. When devising a composition, Caraffa

---

[94] Horace, *Epistles* 1.3.15–20, trans. H. Rushton Fairclough, Loeb Classical Library 194 (Cambridge, MA: Harvard University Press, 1961).

[95] Andrea Cucchiarelli, 'Return to Sender: Horace's *Sermo* from the Epistles to the Satires', in Gregson Davis (ed.), *A Companion to Horace* (Oxford: Wiley-Blackwell, 2010), 291–318 (p. 296).

[96] 'caveamus sedulo ac diligenter, ne Poemata evulgata, et Apollini Palatino jam ante consecrata, attingamus, aut ea pro nostris venditemus, ne aliquando idem nobis accidat, quod Graculo Aesopico accidit'. Quitschreiber, *De* παρῳδία, sig. A3v.

[97] 'als der ich nicht gefliessen bin/ mit frembden Federn meine Arbeit zu schmücken'. Heinrich Schütz, *Symphoniarum sacrarum secunda pars* (Dresden, 1647), Bassus ad Organum partbook, preface. RISM A/I S2292.

[98] 'Were sonst gar übel gethan/ wenn man sich mit frembden Federn bestecken wolte'. Heinrich Albert, *Vierter Theil der Arien* (Königsberg, 1641), sig. A1v. RISM A/I A627.

[99] 'opus Musaicum'. *ASD* I-2, 704; *CWE* 28, 442.

picked up all his concertos and sonatas and spread them across the room so that ... the organ blower outside the open door thought he was seeing nothing other than a grocer's shop with scraps of paper lying around to be always at hand for the countless packets of pepper. This was Caraffa's habit when he was required to compose something: he gained all his invention from his copies of music. The concertos composed by him were like a beggar's coat patched together from many stolen patches, where not one patch agrees with the next in colour or quality.[100]

This is a parody of the methods of assembly that might result from superficial use of a commonplace book, without mental transformation of its contents.

In contrast to these examples of literary and musical theft, Quitschreiber explained that honest borrowing was characterised by moderation:

The republic of letters long ago acquired use of the precept, to use and enjoy sparingly and soberly the work of others; however, this should be in the manner of an honest head of household, not like a cheating overlord, so that it maintains a state of good repair and is not destructive. If it is plagiarism (which it is not), it is an honest plagiarism, which would imitate neither this nor that.[101]

The analogy of the honest *paterfamilias* asserted a patriarchal hierarchy that preserved order and kinship, as opposed to the unjust behaviour of a repressive feudal overlord. More specifically, poets and musicians believed that honest borrowers should be truthful about, or should significantly transform, their models.

Quitschreiber emphasised the importance of openness, explaining: 'Certainly we ought to give our work, namely our own labours and the results of our lucubrations, to be published, rather than being secretly copied from books.'[102] Such a recommendation followed those classical writers who advised that borrowings should be acknowledged to allow readers to evaluate the degree of transformation achieved. In the *Suasoriae* of Seneca the Elder, the interlocutor Gallio praised Ovid for borrowing phrases from Virgil with the intention that this candid borrowing be noticed.[103]

---

[100] 'Er nahm alle seine *Concerten* und *Sonaten* zur Hand/ breitet dieselben in der gantzen Stube aus/ also daß der *Calcant* ... aussen vor der Thüre/ als sie auffgemachet wurde/ nicht anders dachte/ als sähe er in ein Würz-Gewölbe/ da *Maculatur* so häuffig herumb läge/ damit er dasselbe zu den unzehlichen Pfeffer-Dieten immer bey der Hand haben könte. Also pflegte es *Caraffa* zumachen/ wenn er etwas *componi*ren solte/ nahm er alle seine *Invention* aus seinen geschriebenen *Musicali*en. Die von ihm gesetzten *Concerten* waren wie ein aus vielen gestohlnen Stücken/ zusammenge-flickter Bettel-Rock/ da kein einziger Fleck mit dem andern an der Farbe und Güte *accordi*ret'. Johann Kuhnau, *Der musicalische Quack-Salber* (Dresden, 1700), 76–77.

[101] 'Respublica enim literaria morem hunc diuturna jam praescriptione acquisivit, parce et sobrie alienis uti, frui: in modum tamen boni Patrisfamilias, non in fraudem Domini, ita ut sarta tecta habeat, non ut destruat: id quod, si plagium foret, quod non est, esset tamen honestum plagium, quod nec hic nec ille imitari posset.' Quitschreiber, *De* παρῳδία, sig. A3v.

[102] 'Certe operam dare debemus, ut proprios labores et a nobis elucabratos, non autem furtim ex aliorum libris exscriptos, in lucem edamus'. Ibid.

[103] Seneca the Elder, *Suasoriae* 4.7.

Plagiarism versus Honest Theft 69

Cicero's *Brutus* (a dialogue on oratory) implied that an acknowledged borrowing is a debt, but if the author denies such a borrowing, it becomes a theft.[104] Seventeenth-century German poets made similar recommendations. Georg Philipp Harsdörffer in his summary of poetic imitation advised that: 'Someone who trades honestly, and does not intend to take others' goods as his own, will add to [a poem], as [Martin] Opitz does: "from the Netherlandish", "after Ronsard's sonnet" etc.'[105]

Schütz took care to acknowledge borrowings in his published compositions. In the *Psalmen Davids* (1619) for the polychoral psalm *Ich danke dem Herrn* that cites Gabrieli's madrigal (see above), each of the partbooks contains the rubric 'Imitatione sopra: Lieto godea. Canzone di Gio. Gab.' on blank staves at the relevant point. The rubric highlights the filial relationship between Schütz and his teacher as mentioned in the dedication. In subsequent printed collections, Schütz identified the models for his compositions in the prefatory or paratextual material. In the *Geistliche Chor-Music* (1648) the list of contents (printed at the end of each partbook) notes that *Der Engel sprach zu den Hirten* is '*Super Angelus ad Pastores, Andreae Gabrielis*'; Schütz's version is a contrafactum of Gabrieli's original, a practical demonstration of his advice to young composers to score up and study the works of classic Italian contrapuntists (see above). In *Symphoniarum sacrarum secunda pars* (1647) Schütz revived the familiar metaphor of following the footsteps of an established author, explaining 'in the concerto *Es steh Gott*, I followed in some respects Claudio Monteverdi's madrigal *Armato il cor* and also his ciaccona with two tenors [*Zefiro torna*]'.[106] In *Symphoniaraum sacrarum tertia pars* (1650) an erratum explained that the concerto *O Jesu süss, wer dein gedenkt* should have the information '*Super Lilia Convallium, Alexandri Grandis*' printed above it. The Italian models in these two last examples are readily recognisable, perhaps because Schütz wanted to invoke their cultural prestige; his dutiful acknowledgements therefore deflected any accusations of dishonesty.[107]

A second requirement of 'honest plagiarism' was that the borrower should assimilate and transform the model. Seneca the Younger used the image of digestion, comparing the imitator to bees who digest the nectar from various flowers in order to make honey. He advised imitators to 'sift whatever we have gathered from a varied course of reading . . . then, by

---

[104] Cicero, *Brutus* 76.
[105] 'Wer nun redlich handeln/ und fremdes Gut nicht für sein eignes ausgeben will/ der setzet darzu wie Herr Opitz: fast aus dem Niederländischen/ nach Ronsards Sonnet &c.'. Georg Philipp Harsdörffer, *Deß poetischen Trichters Dritter Theil* (Nuremberg, 1653), 41.
[106] 'ich auch in dem Concert: Es steh GOtt auff/ &c. des Herrn *Claudii Monteuerdens Madrigal* einem *Armate il Cuor, & c.* so wohl auch einer seiner *Ciaccona*, mit zweyen Tenor-Stimmen/ in etwas weniges nachgangen bin'. Schütz, *Symphoniarum sacrarum secunda pars*, preface.
[107] Wollny, *Studien zum Stilwandel*, 332–37.

70 *Between* Imitatio *and Plagiarism*

applying the supervising care with which our nature has endowed us – in other words, our natural gifts – we should so blend those several flavours into one delicious compound that, even though it betrays its origin, yet it nevertheless is clearly a different thing from whence it came'.[108] The independent status of the imitation could also be indicated with genealogical metaphors, for instance Seneca's advice that the imitation should resemble the model as a child resembles its father (see above, p. 54).

Such views on transformative imitation were further developed by German poets of the seventeenth century. Harsdörffer offered a parable on why borrowers should supply elements of their own invention. Set in the quintessentially Teutonic location of a silver mine, his story reverses the patriarchal bias of many writings on rhetoric, describing the mine as run by a mother symbolising Invention (*Erfindung*). Imitating the mother were three daughters, with varying degrees of success:

> The eldest daughter found a rich vein (*inventio*), signifying other noteworthy thoughts and smelted gold. ... The second daughter worked over the silver already found, smelted it and made coins, signifying those who imitate the inventor in another manner, bringing other circumstances, figures and words to the work. ... But the youngest and least intelligent sister found tin instead of silver; in other words, she wanted to imitate her mother but a false likeness (as between silver and English tin) led her to something reprehensible rather than praiseworthy, which can only serve as a false coin.[109]

Borrowers who discover their own inventive vein can surpass their models, as opposed to those who imitate surface attributes or create a counterfeit with tin instead of silver.

The perils of dishonest borrowing are shown by the two-volume anthology *Geistliche wolklingende Concerte* published in Goslar in 1637–38. It includes several arrangements by the Nordhausen organist Andreas Oehme, reducing a full-voiced piece to a vocal duo or trio with continuo.[110] Three of these duos are attributed to Oehme, as compositions *ad imitatione* respectively of Hans Leo Hassler's *Verbum caro factum est* a 6,[111]

---

[108] Seneca, *Epistles* 84.5, trans. Gummere.

[109] 'die ältste Tochter eine reichere Fundgruben angetroffen/ (*Inventio*) (dardurch andre mehrwirdige Gedanken bedeutet) derselben Gold geschmeltzet. ... Die andre Tochter hat das gefundene Silber helffen ausarbeiten/ umschmeltzen und zu gäng- und geber Müntze zu fördern/ bedeutend die jenigen/ welche dem Erfundenen nachahmen/ und selbes auf eine andre Weise/ mit andern Umständen/ Figuren und Worten zu Werke bringen. ... Die jüngste und unverständigste Schwester aber hat an Statt deß Silbers Zinn gefunden/ das ist/ sie hat ihrer Mutter nachahmen wollen/ aber eine falsche Gleichheit/ wie unter Silber und Englischen Zinn ist/ geführt/ deßwegen sie auch vielmehr scheltbar/ als lobwirdig/ welches nur zu einer falschen Müntze dienen kan' Georg Philipp Harsdörffer, *Nathan und Jotham: das ist geistliche und weltliche Lehrgedichte* (Nuremberg, 1659), sig. B3v–B4r.

[110] On Oehme's role in the anthology, see Werner Braun, 'Bemerkungen zu den "Nordhäusischer Concerten" von 1637/38', *Schütz-Jahrbuch* 25 (2003), 85–104 (pp. 93–94).

[111] Hans Leo Hassler, *Cantiones sacrae de festis praecipuis totius anni* (Augsburg, 1591), no. 23. RISM A/I H2323. Arrangement in *Fasciculus primus geistlicher wolklingender Concerten* (Goslar, 1638) no. 34. RISM B/I 1638⁵. For further few-voiced arrangements of this motet and other Hassler

Plagiarism versus Honest Theft 71

Hassler's *Alleluja laudem dicite* a 5,[112] and Johann Hermann Schein's *Gott sei gelobet* a 3.[113] Here the term 'imitatio' indicates not an act of creative transformation, but a pragmatic reduction. Oehme's versions are usually the same length as the originals, reducing them to the two highest sounding voices plus continuo. According to the dedication, Oehme made these arrangements for music-lovers in Nordhausen, who felt few-voiced concertos moved listeners more effectively and had more intelligible text-setting than polyphonic motets.[114] As with Scheidt's 1630s arrangements of his large-scale concertos, these few-voiced versions were also easier to perform by the choirs depleted by the Thirty Years War.

More problematic are the anthology's two arrangements of compositions by Schütz. Whether by accident or design, these are not termed *imitatio*. One such piece, *Lobe den Herren, meine Seele* is attributed to Schütz, with no mention that it is a heavily reduced version of his double-choir psalm SWV39 for two voices and continuo.[115] More awkward still is the arrangement of Schütz's setting of Psalm 150, *Alleluja! Lobet den Herren in seinem Heiligtum* SWV38.[116] This is attributed to Andreas Oehme, with no mention of Schütz; yet Oehme did not sufficiently transform the original to claim authorship of it.

Schütz scored his setting of Psalm 150 for four choirs each with four vocal or instrumental parts. He used an array of textures, including vocal duos, rapid dialogue between choirs, and all-enveloping tuttis. Responding to the panoply of instruments mentioned in the psalm text, Schütz included obbligato lines for recorder and violin, and for pairs of cornetts, bassoons and trombones. Typically he introduced each line of the psalm with a vocal duo and solo instrumental writing, before the section culminates in a polychoral climax. The popularity of the piece is indicated by an anonymous parody mass, *Missa super Halleluja. Lobet den Herren H. Schützen*, which survives in a manuscript in Wrocław (formerly Breslau).[117]

Oehme, however, struggled to reduce this resplendent piece to a sparse scoring of three voices (tenor, two basses) and continuo.[118] Example 2.5 shows how, for the initial lilting 'Alleluja', he replaced the grand Venetian-style tutti with the dark sound of three low voices, their lines derived

---

compositions, see Bernhold Schmid, 'Hassler-Bearbeitungen des frühen 17. Jahrhunderts', in Paul Mai (ed.), *Im Dienst der Quellen zur Musik. Festschrift Gertraut Haberkamp zum 65. Geburtstag* (Tutzing: Schneider, 2002), 249–58.

[112] Hans Leo Hassler, *Sacri concentus* (Augsburg, 1601), no. 18. RISM A/I H2328. Arrangement in *Fasciculus primus*, no. 47.

[113] Johann Hermann Schein, *Opella nova Ander Theil* (Leipzig, 1626), nos. 13 and 14. RISM A/I S1388. Arrangement in *Fasciculus primus*, no. 37.

[114] *Fasciculus secundus geistlicher wolklingender Concerten* (Goslar, 1637), Prima Vox partbook, dedication. RISM B/I 1637³.

[115] *Fasciculus primus*, no. 52.   [116] *Fasciculus secundus*, no. 55.

[117] Waczkat, *'Ein ehrenhaftes Spielen'*, 173.

[118] I am grateful to Ester Lebedinski for transcribing Oehme's arrangement.

Example 2.5   Heinrich Schütz, *Alleluja! Lobet den Herren in seinem Heiligtum* SWV38 as arranged by Andreas Oehme, opening.

from the principal parts (*coro favorito*) of the original. Whereas Schütz often repeated a phrase several times while progressively increasing the scoring, Oehme shortened such sections or transposed the repeated phrase (as on 'Lobet ihn in seinen Thaten', bars 43–51). He tried to recreate Schütz's interplay of voices by notating echoes in a single voice-part with *forte* and *piano* markings (compare Schütz's bars 118–31 with Oehme's bars 61–67).

Oehme also added some sections of his own invention. Whereas Schütz's initial triple-time 'Alleluja' culminates with a repetition of its final strain, Oehme instead inserted a duple-time passage featuring an anapaest figure while the bass moves through part of the circle of fifths (bars 12–18 of Example 2.5). Instead of the concerted writing for solo voices, recorder and violin used by Schütz on 'Lobet ihn mit Pauken und Reigen' (Praise him with drums and dances, bars 167–84), Oehme inserted a war-like alternation of tonic and dominant chords on these words. But Oehme's additions are formulaic and are not integrated with the whole: the piece could be compared to the patchworks characteristic of failed *imitatio*, or (adapting Harsdörffer) to a silver ingot fused to tin. By not acknowledging Schütz's original and by insufficiently transforming the piece, Oehme's attempt at *imitatio* became an act of plagiarism.[119]

The anonymous editor of the Nordhausen anthology voiced apprehension about the arrangements, writing in the dedication: 'We have presumed to print and publish [these concertos] without incurring the displeasure of the authors themselves, to whose distinguished works we intend no damage.'[120] Schütz was evidently indignant about these unacknowledged and covert borrowings. As Chapters 3 and 4 show (pp. 96 and 141), the Nordhausen anthology provoked his efforts to authenticate and protect his publications, including his use of personalised paper and his acquisition of an imperial printing privilege.

Other authors transformed their model so much that there was no need to acknowledge the original. In 1554 the humanist Henri Estienne commented on Horace's borrowings from Anacreon and other poets: 'This material from elsewhere that he thus borrows, in order to make it nevertheless seem his own, he transmutes it into such a variety of forms that it could scarcely be recognized by its author, if he were present. And this is honest theft.'[121] A similar delight in manipulating others' material,

---

[119] A manuscript copy of Oehme's arrangement (copied in Sangerhausen before *c*.1675) reinstated the attribution to Schütz. D-Dl, Mus. 1/C/2, no. 157.

[120] 'Haben dieselbe wir ... zu öffentlichem Truck wie wir vermeinen/ ohne Vnwillen der Autoren selbst/ welcher vornehmen *Operibus* wir hiermit keinen Abbruch zuthun gemeinet'. *Fasciculus secundus*, Prima Vox, dedication (signed by 'etzliche der Music Liebhabere'), sig. A3r.

[121] 'quae autem aliunde ita mutuatur, vt sua tamen velit videri, ea ita in varias formas commutat, vt vix ab eo cuius sunt, si adsit, agnosci possint. Et hoc est honeste furari'. Quoted in John O'Brien, *Anacreon Redivivus: A Study of Anacreontic Translation in Mid-Sixteenth-Century France* (Ann Arbor: University of Michigan Press, 1995), 26.

as a playful sleight-of-hand, is evident in the works of composers such as Buxtehude who transformed Roman models, as studied by Wollny. By putting such importance on acknowledging or transforming their models, musicians upheld a boundary between the work of the imitated and the imitator.

EARLY CAPITALISM AND MUSICAL BORROWING

In the early eighteenth century, Johann Mattheson and Johann David Heinichen voiced new attitudes to musical borrowing, partly in response to altered economic models which regarded individuals as proprietors of their own talents. Possessive individualism, detected by C. B. Macpherson in the writings of Thomas Hobbes and John Locke, arguably encouraged an awareness that the results of an individual's mental labour could be protected and sold as property.[122] Another reason for changed views on borrowing was the increased demand for new music, particularly in the theatrical styles used in secular and sacred music. Chapter 5 discussses the expectation that church cantors write a new cantata each week, and similar productivity was expected of opera composers. Musicians accordingly had to devise a vast quantity of ritornello themes for arias, conveying the stylised emotion of each movement. The theatrical style did not suit the contrapuntal elaborations described by writers such as Quitschreiber, instead showing what Peter Wollny calls an 'astonishing simplicity' compared to works in earlier styles.[123] Musical borrowings in this style instead involved the overt re-use of ritornello themes, as with many examples in Handel's output.

The difficulty of contrapuntal transformation in the theatrical style may explain Johann David Heinichen's comments on musical borrowing. In 1711 Heinichen stated that 'the *stylus theatralis* requires a much greater amount of invention than most (I will not say all) styles of composition'.[124] Here he presumably referred to the requirement for each aria to have a distinct theme. He continued:

Today one must be careful, in many large theatrical works not to include a single aria, nor even a phrase of 14 or 15 notes which appears similar to an earlier phrase, even in the slightest points. For even if these similarities are approximate or at the

---

[122] C. B. Macpherson, *The Political Theory of Possessive Individualism* (Oxford: Clarendon Press, 1962).

[123] Peter Wollny, 'On Johann Sebastian Bach's Creative Process: Observations from His Drafts and Sketches', in Sean Gallagher and Thomas Forrest Kelly (eds.), *The Century of Bach and Mozart: Perspectives on Historiography, Composition, Theory, and Performance* (Cambridge, MA: Harvard University Department of Music, 2008), 217–38 (p. 237).

[124] '... findet der *Theatralische Stylus* in der *Invention* weit mehr zu thun/ als die Meisten/ ich will nicht sagen/ alle Arten der *Composition*'. Johann David Heinichen, *Neu erfundene und gründliche Anweisung ... zu vollkommener Erlernung des General-Basses* (Hamburg, 1711), 12.

Early Capitalism and Musical Borrowing

least contrary to the intention of the composer, the ignorant or passionate will take the opportunity to accuse the composer of being a plagiarist.[125]

Compared to the hidden allusions that Quitschreiber described, musical borrowing was easier to detect in theatrical music, because of the limited opportunities for contrapuntal elaboration of an aria ritornello. Heinichen had little patience with the contrapuntal techniques that he associated with the church style, dismissing those composers who could fill two or three sheets of paper with workings-out of a single theme.[126] (His belief in the superiority of the theatrical style was perhaps reinforced by his feud with his former teacher Kuhnau about the legitimacy of opera.[127]) Heinichen instead advised musicians to devise ritornellos for arias in accordance with the affections expressed in a libretto (see Chapter 1, p. 45).

Mattheson's views on musical borrowing were shaped by his belief in the importance of innate talent and his lack of enthuasiasm about counterpoint. In his journal *Critica musica*, he voiced scepticism about *imitatio* during published exchanges with the Wolfenbüttel capellmeister Heinrich Bokemeyer. In a letter defending the value of canonic writing, Bokemeyer noted that

those composers without instruction in [contrapuntal] imitation have followed the example of other famed masters (instead of rules), and from *imitatio* of these [masters] their practice has come into being. ... When diligence and a true grasp of advice are taken via *imitatio*, art (achieved through the example of excellent musicians) can offer a helping hand to natural talent.[128]

Such advice recalled the methods of learning from authority described at the start of this chapter. Echoing the esoteric traditions explored by Quitschreiber a century earlier, Bokemeyer quoted the proverb: 'Art has no haters but the ignorant'.[129]

Such arguments could not sway Mattheson from his conviction in the importance of talent. He declared: 'The example of famed masters,

---

[125] 'Ja heute zu Tage hat man dahin zu dencken/ daß man in so grossen und vielen *Theatrali*schen Wercken und Opern nicht eine eintzige *Aria*, oder nur eine *Clausul* von 14. oder 15. *Noten* noch einmal vorbringe/ welche etwan einer ehemahligen *Clasul*, auch nur in den geringsten Pünctgen ähnlich scheinet. Denn wenn solches gleich nur ohngefehr und zum wenigsten wieder die *Intention* der *Componis*ten also gerathen/ so wollen doch Unverständige oder *passionir*te gleich daher Geleghenheit nehmen/ den *Componis*ten vor einen *Plagiarium* zu schelten'. Ibid.; a similar statement is in Johann David Heinichen, *Der General-Bass in der Composition* (Dresden, 1728), 29.

[126] Heinichen, *Der General-Bass*, 29.

[127] On this feud, see Michael Maul, 'Johann David Heinichen und der "Musicalische Horribilicribrifax": Überlegungen zur Vorrede von Heinichens *Gründlicher Anweisung*', in Rainer Bayreuther (ed.), *Musikalische Norm um 1700* (Berlin: De Gruyter, 2010), 145–65.

[128] 'Die jenigen Componisten/ so ohne gehabte Anweisung geschickt imitiren/ haben anderer berühmte‹n› Meister Exempel/ statt der Reguln/ angenom‹m›en/ aus deren *imitation* hernach der *habitus* entstanden. ... Wenn bey der *imitation* der Fleiß und die rechten Griffe zu Rathe gezogen werden/ so leistet schon die Kunst/ vermöge der vor sich habenden Exempel *excellen*ter *Musicorum*, dem Naturell hülffliche Hand'. *Critica musica* 1 (1722), 303.

[129] '*Ars non habet osorem, nisi ignorantem*'. Ibid., 249.

who one emulates to thereby gain practice, does something but not everything'.[130] He then quoted 'O imitators, you servile herd',[131] from Horace's condemnation of poets who imitate faulty models and who drink water (symbolising art) rather than wine (denoting inspiration). In Mattheson's opinion, 'art can offer talent a helping hand, but talent is always the best thing'.[132] He rebuffed the idea that an individual voice could arise through *imitatio*: 'Each good composer must be an original; the copy will be less or not at all regarded'.[133] Contemptuous of the deference to authority required by *imitatio*, Mattheson voiced an attitude similar to Strungk's (as quoted at the start of this chapter): 'Stealing is worth more than emulating'.[134]

Earlier in his exchange with Mattheson, Bokemeyer made the mistake of comparing canonic writing to 'a Latin style controlled by common rules of syntax', and claiming that 'a galant Ciceronian cannot do without the rules of syntax'.[135] Bokemeyer thereby invoked the purists who insisted that Latin should be written in imitation of Cicero, with no additional vocabulary used. As a self-declared musical eclectic (see p. 12), Mattheson was disdainful of such restrictions: 'What could be more pedantic, forced and affected than a Ciceronian?'[136] Naming Renaissance revivers of Ciceronian Latin such as Paulus Manutius, Pietro Bembo and Marc Antoine Muret, Mattheson opined that these imitators lacked the crucial qualities of taste and judgement (*sapere, bon gout*). 'Therefore [taste] is a cold thing for a Ciceronian; but for a natural talent inclined towards music, it is a galant and great thing. It triumphs over all rules. ... A natural talent summons the rules and helps itself to them'.[137] Thus Mattheson combined Erasmus's suspicion of slavish imitation with an empiricist awareness of present-day taste.

For music written in the theatrical style, Mattheson conceptualised borrowing in capitalist terms, a view doubtless shaped by the mercantile environment of his home city of Hamburg. Writing in *Critica musica* on questions of voice-leading, he digressed onto the question of Handel's borrowings from Antonio Lotti and from Mattheson's aria 'Diese Wangen

---

[130] 'Exempel von berühmten Meistern/ die man nachahmet/ und etwa einen *habitum* darüber erlangt/ thun etwas; aber lange nicht alles'. Ibid., 304.

[131] '*O imitatores ... servum pecus!*' Horace, *Epistles* 1.19.19, quoted in *Critica musica* 1 (1722), 304.

[132] 'So leistet auch die Kunst dem Naturell hülffliche Hand; aber das Naturell thut doch immer das beste zur Sache'. Ibid.

[133] 'Jeder guter Componist muß ein Original seyn; die Copien werden wenig oders nichts geachtet'. Ibid.

[134] 'Das Stehlen gilt schon mehr/ als das nachahmen'. Ibid.

[135] 'Ein *Stilus Latinus*, so pur nach den gemeinen *regulis Syntacticis* eingerichtet ist ... gleichwohl kan‹n› ein galanter Ciceronianer der Syntactischen Regeln nicht entbehren'. Ibid., 249.

[136] 'Ob was pedantischer/ gezwungener und affectirter sey/ als eben ein Ciceronianer?' Ibid., 250.

[137] 'Also ist es ein kahles Ding um einen Ciceronianer; aber ein zur Music aufgelegtes Naturel/ das eine galante und grosse Sache. Das triumphirt über alle Regeln. ... Das Naturell *adhibi*rt Regeln/ und bedienet sich derselben'. Ibid., 250–51.

Early Capitalism and Musical Borrowing

will ich küssen' (in his opera *Porsenna*).[138] Mattheson's account was coloured by a mix of admiration and jealousy of Handel, a former friend whose success in London had distanced him from his Hamburg acquaintances.[139] Mattheson claimed he did not want to accuse Handel of plagiarism,[140] but inserted a snide footnote arguing that such borrowings enhanced the credit of the original composer. 'These things must infallibly please everyone, including those who first invented them and are their rightful owners: for nobody finds fault with his own handiwork'.[141] To have one's music borrowed is 'an uncommon honour, as when a famous man gets on the trail of [the original inventor] and borrows from him the true basis for his own ideas. Even if only three people know about it, this is already honour enough!'[142] Such belief in the supremacy of invention reinforced Mattheson's sense of superiority over Handel.

Mattheson then introduced his economic metaphor for musical borrowing:

But those people who interpret this as plagiarism and who as such would excuse it because of its felicitous development are on the wrong path and reason falsely. It is exactly as if someone pinched 1000 Reichsthaler from me and wanted me not to look disapprovingly, because he knew how to invest them to bring him a few per cent more than they did for me. All *elaboratio*, no matter how beautiful it may be, is only like interest; the original *inventio* should be compared with the capital itself.[143]

The term *Capital* was a recent borrowing in German-speaking lands from French and English (where it denoted the stock of a company or the assets of an individual).[144] Reflecting the ideology of possessive individualism and his attitude to invention, Mattheson argued that musical ideas are the property of the composer and the origin of his or her wealth; elaboration, by contrast, had little value.

---

[138] For an identification of the exact pieces borrowed, see Steffen Voss, 'Händels Entlehnungen aus Johann Matthesons Oper *Porsenna* (1702)', *Göttinger Händel-Beiträge* 10 (2004), 81–94.

[139] Alfred Mann, 'Mattheson as Biographer of Handel', in George J. Buelow and Hans Joachim Marx (eds.), *New Mattheson Studies* (Cambridge: Cambridge University Press, 1983), 345–52.

[140] 'nicht zwar/ als ob ich den Mann eines *plagii* beschuldigen wollte', *Critica musica* 1 (1722), 72.

[141] 'dergleichen Sachen … unausbleiblich allen/ auch so gar/ deren ersten Erfindern und rechten Eignern/ gefallen müssen: weil niemand sein eignes Machwerk zu tadeln pflegt'. Ibid.

[142] 'wohl aber eine ungemeine Ehre zuwächst/ wenn ein berühmter Mann ihm dann und wann auf die Spuhr geräth/ und gleichsam seiner Gedanken wahren Grund von ihm borget. Soltens auch nur drey wissen/ so ist es schon Ehre genug!' Ibid.

[143] 'Diejenigen Leute aber/ so ein *plagium* daraus machen/ und es/ *qua tale*, mit der glücklichen Ausarbeitung entschuldigen wollen/ sind auf dem unrechten Wege/ und *raisonni*ren falsch: denn es wäre eben so/ als wenn mir einer 1000. Rthlr. abzwackte/ und begehrte/ ich sollte nicht sauer dazu sehen/ weil er sie so zu belegen wüste/ daß sie ihm etwa ein paar *procent* mehr trügen/ als mir. Alle *elaboratio*, sie sey so schön wie sie wolle/ ist nur mit Zinsen; die *inventio* aber mit dem Capital selbst zu vergleichen'. Ibid.

[144] Robert S. DuPlessis, 'Capital Formations', in Henry S. Turner (ed.), *The Culture of Capital. Property, Cities, and Knowledge in Early Modern England* (New York: Routledge, 2002), 27–49 (p. 35).

Fourteen years later, Mattheson reworked his interpretation of musical borowing into a fully capitalist version that emphasised the accumulation of wealth. In *Der vollkommene Capellmeister*, he now admitted there was some value in musical borrowing, 'provided fine models are chosen, and the inventions are simply imitated, but not copied and stolen'.[145] He proceeded with his capitalist metaphor: 'Borrowing is a permitted thing, but one must return the thing borrowed with interest, i.e. one must so construct and develop imitations that are prettier and better than the pieces from which they are derived'.[146] Rather than giving priority to the original 'capital', he now argued that borrowers should accumulate wealth in the form of elaborations on that initial idea. Mattheson continued:

For whom this is not necessary and has sufficient resources, he should wish those borrowers well; yet I believe that there are very few of such people. Indeed even the greatest capitalists are given to borrowing money, when they see special advantage or convenience in it.[147]

By describing the necessity of paying interest on musical borrowings, Mattheson not only updated the classical notion that borrowers should transform their models. His capitalist terminology also indicated a new conception of musical invention as personal property, a mercantile view that clashed with the theological belief that human achievement belonged to God, and also with the humanist desire to manipulate the intellectual legacy of previous generations.

EPILOGUE

In the late 1740s, Johann Sebastian Bach reworked the Sanctus of Johann Caspar Kerll's *Missa superba*, a piece written approximately 75 years earlier. Although Kerll spent most of his career in Munich and Vienna, his mass was well known in the Lutheran heartland of Saxony. Copies were owned by the Dresden organist Emanuel Benisch and at the Thomasschule in Leipzig,[148] which Bach used as the basis for his reworking. Bach's version (BWV241) survives in his autograph score (which has no ascription of

---

[145] 'wenn nur feine Muster dazu erwehlet, und die Erfindungen bloß imitiret, nicht aber nachgeschrieben und entwendet würden'. Johann Mattheson, *Der vollkommene Capellmeister* (Hamburg, 1739), 131.

[146] 'Entlehnen ist eine erlaubte Sache; man muß aber das Entlehnte mit Zinsen erstatten, d. i. man muß die Nachahmung so einrichten und ausarbeiten, daß sie ein schöneres und besseres Ansehen gewinnen, als die Sätze, aus welchen sie entlehnet sind'. Ibid.

[147] 'Wer es nicht nöthig hat und von selbst Reichthum gnug besitzet, dem stehet solches sehr wol zu gönnen; doch glaube ich, daß deren sehr wenig sind; maassen auch die grössesten Capitalisten wol Gelder aufzunehmen pflegen, wenn sie ihre besondere Vortheile oder Bequemlichkeit dabey ersehen'. Ibid., 131–32.

[148] Emanuel Benisch's music collection is listed in the commonplace book of Johann Sigismund Kusser (US-NH, Osborn Music Ms.16, p. 265); see Samantha Owens, 'Music via Correspondence: A List of the Music Collection of Dresden Kreuzorganist Emanuel Benisch', *Understanding Bach* 11 (2016), 39–56 (p. 42). The Leipzig copy was acquired by the Thomasschule in *c.*1677 from the estate of the deceased cantor Sebastian Knüpfer; see D-LEsa, Stift. IX. A. 35, fol. 1r.

Example 2.6 (a) Johann Caspar Kerll, *Missa superba*, Osanna, Canto primo concertato, bars 388–90; (b) Johann Sebastian Bach, *Sanctus* (after Kerll) BWV241, Soprano 1, bars 21–23.

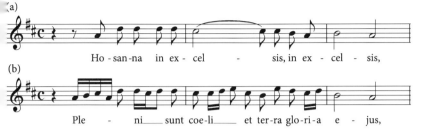

authorship) and in performing parts in his hand and that of his son Johann Christoph Friedrich.[149] Bach left the first two sections almost unchanged from Kerll's original – 'Sanctus' is set to upward scales moving like a wave through the voices, and 'Domine Deus Sabaoth' uses incisive quaver motifs – apart from some alterations to accidentals that may indicate he performed the piece at a slower tempo than seventeenth-century performers.[150] For the 'Pleni sunt coeli', Bach apparently 'abandoned his model entirely', to quote Hans T. David's account.[151] Instead of the grand Gabrielian chords of Kerll's setting, he used a lively semiquaver theme in imitation between strings and voices. Peter Wollny, however, has shown that Bach's semiquaver theme is a decorated version of the repeated-note fugato subject used by Kerll for 'Hosanna in excelsis' (Example 2.6).[152]

Unlike the musicians discussed in this chapter, Bach left no comments on his re-use of musical materials. But his reworking of Kerll's Sanctus can be linked with many of the attitudes and practices discussed in this chapter. Kerll was already regarded as a musical authority in his lifetime, with his *Litaniae sex vocum* gaining enthusiastic endorsements from Roman musicians such as Bernardo Pasquini.[153] In the 1700s, the young Bach took Kerll's music as a model, according to C. P. E. Bach's recollections.[154] And Kerll's pupil Franz Xaver Murschhauser upheld his teacher as a compositional authority in his treatise *Academia musico-poetica bipartita* (1721), based 'on the tradition of the world famous Johann

---

[149] D-Cv, Ms. A.V,1109,(1),1a and 1b.
[150] I am grateful to Peter Holman for this observation on changing performance practice.
[151] Hans T. David, 'A Lesser Secret of J. S. Bach Uncovered', *Journal of the American Musicological Society* 14 (1961), 199–223 (p. 220).
[152] Peter Wollny, 'Bachs Sanctus BWV 241 und Kerlls *Missa superba*', *Bach-Jahrbuch* 77 (1991), 173–76.
[153] Recorded in the manuscript formerly in A-Wm; described in Hugo Botstiber, 'Ein Beitrag zu J. K. Kerll's Biographie', *Sammelbände der Internationalen Musikgesellschaft* 7 (1906), 634–36.
[154] *BDok* 3, 288 (no. 803).

Caspar Kerll ... and other approved classics'.[155] Through the creative reception of Kerll's music, Bach positioned himself not as an apprentice but rather as an experienced composer aligning himself with canonised contrapuntists of the past.[156]

Bach's version of Kerll's Sanctus could also be interpreted as a pragmatic adaptation to suit the needs of a specific ensemble or location. This chapter has already encountered examples of pragmatic reworking, such as the contrafacta listed by Georg Quitschreiber in his treatise, or Andreas Oehme's reductions of polychoral psalms by Schütz and motets by Hassler. Bach updated Kerll's scoring, replacing the trombones with violas and bassoon. He modernised Kerll's continuo line by breaking the semibreves into repeated crotchets more characteristic of eighteenth-century writing. Possibly Bach may have rewritten the 'Pleni sunt coeli' section because Kerll's sustained chords and harmonic progressions by a descending third sounded antiquated to mid-eighteenth-century ears.

Finally Bach's reworking of Kerll's 'Hosanna in excelsis' for his 'Pleni sunt coeli' showed his ability to transform the original. The allusion would be hidden except to connoisseurs, perhaps members of the Thomasschule choirs who had previously sung or heard Kerll's piece. The thematic transformation showed that Bach could assume some of Kerll's musical authority but also surpass him, conjuring a distinctive theme from the commonplace quaver motif used by Kerll.

Musical borrowing had a mix of meanings and it can be hard to identify the significance of the relationship between a particular composition and its model. As Milsom has shown, there are also difficulties in finding appropriate terminology for the varieties of polyphonic adaptation.[157] This chapter has uncovered the metaphors used by musicians to describe the act of borrowing: disciples who follow the footsteps of authoritative masters or walk alongside them; emulators who outdo their models; plagiarists who construct an incoherent patchwork; and capitalists who borrow another's resources in order to accumulate further wealth. Such metaphors clarify attitudes to individuality and agency in a compositional culture that valued authority, and also supply today's scholars with a toolkit of concepts for analysing examples of musical reworking.

---

[155] 'nach des Welt-berühmten Herrn Johann Caspar Kerlls ... und anderer *approbir*ten *Classicorum Tradition*'. Franz Xaver Murschhauser, *Academia musico-poetica bipartita* (Nuremberg, 1721), title page.
[156] Bach also reworked Palestrina's *Missa sine nomine* in the 1740s; D-B, Mus.ms. 16695 and 16714.
[157] Milsom, 'The T-Mass'.

CHAPTER 3

Signs of Individuality

In his novel *Teutsche Winter-Nächte* (1682), the Weissenfels musician Johann Beer relayed an anecdote about the Saxon court musician Adam Krieger:

They say of the major musician Adam Krieger that he once played the organ while disguised as a sailor. The musicians looking on knew well that these were not sailor's chords. They took no notice of his rough outer appearance, instead showing him a respect one would never give to a sailor.[1]

Along with many other tales of disguise and unmasking in the novel, Beer here raised questions about how a person is recognised. Are individuals identified by their name, ancestry, physical appearance or temperament? Do aspects of a person's appearance indicate his or her inner nature? Or should, as Beer indicated here, individuals be recognised via their deeds – in the case of a musician, by their compositions and performances? Such questions not only arose in debates about the conception of character, but also influenced the techniques used in the sixteenth and seventeenth centuries to verify a person's identity.[2]

Two traditions for demonstrating and recognising individuality existed in seventeenth-century German lands, related to the humanist and artisanal notions of authorship discussed in Chapter 1. Humanist traditions drew on classical notions that every individual had a distinctive nature (Greek *phusis*, Roman *natura*), detectable via external attributes.[3] As Petrarch said: 'Each person has been endowed by nature with something distinctive and personal, in their face and gestures, in the sound of their

---

[1] 'Man erzehlet von dem hauptsächlichen Musico/ Adam Krüger/ daß er sich einsmals/ gleich einem Schiff-Knecht/ verkleidet/ und auf einer Orgel gespielet habe. Die umstehenden Musicanten merckten wol/ daß diese keine Schiffers-Griffe wären/ und unerachtet seine äusserliche Gestalt grob genung aussahe/ erwiesen sie ihme doch eine solche Reverentz/ die man billig keinem Schiff-Knecht erwiesen hätte'. Johann Beer, *Teutsche Winter-Nächte* ([Nuremberg], 1682), 243.

[2] Valentin Groebner, *Who Are You? Identification, Deception, and Surveillance in Early Modern Europe*, trans. Mark Kyburz and John Peck (Brooklyn: Zone Books, 2007).

[3] On the Greek notion of *phusis* (nature), see Stephen Halliwell, 'Traditional Greek Conceptions of Character', in Christopher B. R. Pelling (ed.), *Characterization and Individuality in Greek Literature* (Oxford: Clarendon Press, 1990), 32–59.

voice and the style of their speaking'.[4] Erasmus similarly believed that an individual's face and voice revealed his or her inner character.[5] The belief that outward signs indicated an inner nature was further developed in the neo-Platonic doctrine of signatures. In German lands such principles were espoused by the Görlitz mystic Jakob Böhme, who asserted: 'There is nothing in nature, whether created or born, which does not also reveal its inner form externally, because the inner things always work towards revelation'.[6] He continued: 'By the external form of all creatures, by their inclination and desire, and by their sound, voice and speech, one can recognise their hidden spirit'.[7] Yet this conviction that character could be read from a vocabulary of external signs might lead to stereotyping, and thereby undermine humanist beliefs in the unique nature of individuals.

A second set of identification practices comprised those used by artisans, who demonstrated their manual skills via the quality of their products. German craftworkers proved their worthiness to join a guild by completing a masterwork, an ambitious artefact that showed their full handiwork. Some artisans added their name, initials or distinctive sign to their products, either from pride in their achievements or for economic reasons. Masons marked the blocks they had hewn in order to get paid for their work; metalworkers used hallmarks or individual signs to indicate the quality of their products. In Italian law from the fourteenth century onwards, such marks were protected as the property of specific artisans, because they identified an individual's work and could boost demand for that person's products.[8] In specialist crafts, a maker's mark could command a premium price: the artist Pieter Paul Rubens charged a higher price for artworks bearing his signature, as opposed to those produced entirely by his workshop assistants.[9] Artisans thus recognised individuality via the distinctive handiwork displayed in their products.

This chapter shows how debates about identification shaped musical authorship in seventeenth-century German-speaking lands, examining ways in which composers were projected as distinct individuals via their

---

[4] 'Et est sane cuique naturaliter, ut in vultu et gestu, sic in voce et sermone quiddam suum ac proprium ... ' Petrarch, letter to Boccaccio *c*.1359, *Epistole familiares* 22.2.17, quoted from Francesco Petrarca, *Le familiari*, 4 vols., ed. Vittorio Rossi (Florence: G. C. Sansoni, n.d.), iv, 107.

[5] Erasmus, *De civilitate morum puerilium* (Basel, 1530), chapter 1; *ASD* I-8, 316; *CWE* 25, 274.

[6] 'Und ist kein Ding in der Natur, das geschaffen oder geboren ist, es offenbaret seine innerliche Gestalt auch äusserlich, denn das innerliche arbeitet stets zur Offenbarung'. Jakob Böhme, *Sämtliche Schriften*, vol. 6: *De signatoria rerum (1622)* (Stuttgart: Frommann, 1957), 7.

[7] 'dann an der äusserlichen Gestaltniß aller Creaturen, an ihrem Trieb und Begierde, item, an ihrem ausgehenden Hall, Stimme und Sprache, kennet man den verborgenen Geist ...' Ibid.

[8] Osvaldo Cavallar, Susanne Degenring and Julius Kirshner (eds.), *A Grammar of Signs: Bartolo da Sassoferrato's* Tract on Insignia and Coats of Arms *(1358)* (Berkeley: Robbins Collection, University of California at Berkeley, 1994), 147.

[9] Ilja van Damme, 'From a "Knowledgeable" Salesman Towards a "Recognizable" Product? Questioning Branding Strategies before Industrialization (Antwerp, Seventeenth to Nineteenth Centuries)', in Bert de Munck and Dries Lyna (eds.), *Concepts of Value in European Material Culture, 1500–900* (Farnham: Ashgate, 2015), 75–101 (p. 97).

Capitalism and the Crisis of Authentication 83

notated works. It begins with the uncertainties about identification caused by early capitalism, in particular the question of how to verify goods (including printed books) sold at a remove from their original maker. Turning to printed and manuscript music, the chapter explores the techniques used by scribes and printers to simulate the composer's presence in notated music. Another way to simulate authorial presence was via portraits, which this chapter investigates in relation to the humanist belief that inner character could be read from external appearance. Finally I analyse the debates about whether composers' works show a distinctive personal style. Signs of individuality such as signatures were not transhistorical universals, but must be understood via the material and economic practices that gave rise to identification techniques in the period.

CAPITALISM AND THE CRISIS OF AUTHENTICATION

The authentication practices analysed in this chapter developed partly in response to uncertainties caused by early capitalism. As discussed in the Introduction, one feature of early capitalism was trade with distant markets, involving economic transactions without a face-to-face relationship between seller and client. Fernand Braudel argued that these long-distance transactions lacked the 'transparence and regularity' involved in everyday exchanges between artisans and their consumers. Merchants and their clients might be uncertain whether goods would be supplied as ordered and whether credit agreements would be honoured.[10] Methods of payment involved substitutes for tangible currency such as bills of exchange (whereby an individual ordered a second person to make a payment to a third person), again raising concerns about trust and transparency.[11] Martha Howell's study of the Low Countries shows how merchants responded to this 'crisis of information' by cultivating their reputations and the social bonds on which economic relationships could flourish.[12]

Such uncertainties in early capitalism shaped consumers' attitudes to material goods. Savvy purchasers were wary of forgeries and engaged all their senses to verify the quality of products.[13] In 1516 Erasmus gave a vivid account of how to scrutinise products, in his preface to the second

[10] Fernand Braudel, *Civilization and Capitalism, 15th–18th Century*, vol. 2: *The Wheels of Commerce*, trans. Siân Reynolds (London: Fontana, 1982), 455–57.

[11] Ibid., 113, 142–48.

[12] Martha Howell, *Commerce before Capitalism in Europe, 1300–600* (Cambridge: Cambridge University Press, 2010), 22–29.

[13] Evelyn Welch, 'The Senses in the Marketplace: Sensory Knowledge in a Material World', in Herman Roodenburg (ed.), *A Cultural History of the Senses in the Renaissance* (London: Bloomsbury Academic, 2004), 61–86.

volume of his edition of the works of St Jerome (an author whose output was plagued by disputes about authentication):

You are not satisfied with the label on a physician's pillbox, but you sniff, handle and taste the contents; nor do you at once believe the unguent to be balsam if the unguent jar is so labelled. Instead you take every precaution not to be fooled by a label and receive poison in place of medicine and mud in place of ointment. Not content with the inscription, you test a coin. Not trusting the price-tag, you examine closely a piece of cloth. You rub gold on a touchstone when uneasy about its colour.[14]

Artisans' marks as described above were partly intended to reassure consumers – for instance, hallmarks attesting to the quality of precious metals.

Suspicions about provenance and quality also afflicted the German book trade. As a form of mechanical reproduction, printing distanced readers and consumers from the original text and its maker. This distancing effect can be understood via Walter Benjamin's 1936 insight that a reproduction lacks the original's 'presence in time and space, its unique existence at the place where it happens to be'.[15] Although Benjamin formulated these ideas with reference to photography and film, they resonate with sixteenth- and seventeenth-century anxieties about the untrustworthiness of printed products. Erasmus noted how many works circulated with attributions to the wrong author: 'If we accept sight unseen . . . any work that displays the name of an approved author, who would not find it easy to deceive the world, especially in these times when any writing is immediately multiplied in thousands of copies and circulated throughout the land?'[16] After the publication of his translation of the Bible, Luther became increasingly anxious about unauthorised copies, 'for I have previously experienced how much is printed falsely and carelessly among us'.[17] Jane Newman has shown how the difficulty of establishing authenticity among the profusion of printed texts led Luther increasingly to emphasise the role of faith in biblical interpretation.[18] Driven largely by financial motives, the printing industry exemplified how early modern capitalism caused concerns about authentication.

The market for printed music suffered too from these problems of trust and verification. A typical partbook edition lacked the presence not only of a manuscript made for a specific individual or purpose, but also of the music in performance. Much printed music was sold by bookdealers, away

---

[14] *CWE* 61, 75.

[15] Walter Benjamin, 'The Work of Art in the Age of Mechanical Reproduction', in *Illuminations*, trans. Harry Zohn, ed. Hannah Arendt (New York: Harcourt, 1968), 217–51 (p. 221).

[16] *CWE* 61, 75.

[17] 'Denn ich bisher wol erfaren, wie unvleissig und falsch uns andere nachdrucken'. *WA Deutsche Bibel* 6, 1.

[18] Jane O. Newman, 'The Word Made Print: Luther's 1522 New Testament in an Age of Mechanical Reproduction', *Representations* 11 (1985), 95–133.

Capitalism and the Crisis of Authentication 85

from the composer and without the opportunity for buyers to hear its contents. The partbook format used for almost all printed music until the late seventeenth century prevented purchasers and readers from gaining an overview of the compositions, unless they transcribed the music into tablature or score. Instead the title page and prefatory material of a part-book edition might heavily sway the decisions of casual browsers whether to buy it. Buyers also worried whether an edition was printed accurately, because misprints were difficult to spot until the music was performed. As Orlande de Lassus said in 1581 when applying for an imperial privilege to protect his publications (see Chapter 4): 'Particular care must be taken lest books of music appear corrupted or poorly corrected, for whereas with ordinary books it may be possible for anyone to correct the mistakes, it is not easy for anybody to succeed in acting as corrector for misprinted songs'.[19] Music publishers and composers therefore had to convince purchasers that their editions were accurate and reliable.

By the late sixteenth century, an array of techniques existed for authenticating scribal texts such as letters and legal documents. Generally these techniques linked the material text to the body of its writer or authoriser. Most basic was the signature, which as Peggy Kamuf puts it, 'is the mark of an articulation at the border between life and letters, body and language'.[20] Signatures, however, could be forged or supplied by a secretary; hence they were often supplemented by wax seals. As Brigitte Bedos-Rezak shows, the seal recorded the presence of the signatory via the imprint of a signet ring worn on the finger; sometimes it also carried fingerprints, toothmarks or the imprint of hair.[21] Signet rings bore either a generic symbol such as a cross, or something personal to the owner, such as a coat of arms or monogram; their wax imprint therefore could refer to the individual identity as well as the bodily presence of the scribe.

Techniques also developed to authenticate printed reproductions. From the late fifteenth century, the market for German art was transformed by the rise of woodcut and engraving technologies. Artists such as Albrecht Dürer increasingly reached a wider market by selling their work as printed reproductions, thereby supplementing or even abandoning the personal relationship when an artist produced work for a patron. Several artists used their stylized initials as a monogram to authenticate their woodcuts and

---

[19] 'tum vero maxime singulari cura cavendum, ne libri Musici corrupte incorrecteve in lucem prodeant. Nam ut in caeteris fortasse aliquis vitia emendare posse videatur, tamen in cantionibus depravatis correctorem agere non cuiusvis esse facile evincitur'. Musée royal de Mariemont, Inv. Aut. 1112/4; transcribed in Henri Vanhulst, 'Lasso et ses éditeurs: remarques à propos de deux lettres peu connues', *Revue belge de musicologie*, 39–40 (1985–86), 80–100 (p. 95).

[20] Peggy Kamuf, *Signature Pieces: On the Institution of Authorship* (Ithaca: Cornell University Press, 1988), 39.

[21] Brigitte A. Bedos-Rezak, 'Loci of Medieval Identity', in Franz-Josef Arlinghaus (ed.), *Forms of Individuality and Literacy in the Medieval and Early Modern Periods* (Turnhout: Brepols, 2015), 81–106 (p. 103).

engravings. In Lucas Cranach's woodcut *Venus and Cupid* (1506), his monogram (comprising his initials and a winged serpent) hangs prominently on a tree on the upper right, along with the coat of arms of his patron Friedrich III of Saxony. Dürer's 'AD' monogram is conspicuous in his woodcuts and engravings, for instance on a tablet propped against the wall when the Angel Gabriel appears to Mary, or carved on the frame of the Virgin's deathbed.[22] Although monograms were sometimes added by engravers when they copied others' images,[23] most of the known examples denote the designer of the image. Michael Liebmann suggested that monograms were mainly used by artists who published their works.[24] Joseph Koerner elaborated this argument, arguing that monograms (like signatures and seals) compensated for an absent presence: 'For in the medium of engraving, the artist is potentially absent both from the community of viewers who initially purchase and use the image, and from the actual process of production, which demands manual labor from the artist only in fashioning the original plate.'[25] The monograms authenticated the duplicated image, connecting each iteration with the name and presence of its originator.

Dürer's monogram was easy to replicate and was used in unauthorised copies of his works by engravers such as Marc'Antonio Raimondo of Venice. Dürer was unable to get legal protection of his images, which were regarded as common property. But in Venice and Nuremberg, he successfully gained edicts forbidding false use of his name and monogram. In 1512 the Nuremberg town council ordered a merchant selling unauthorised Dürer prints 'to remove all such signs and sell none of them here'.[26] Thus Dürer's monogram had a legal status similar to the artisan marks that were protected in Italian law. The monogram enhanced the economic value of Dürer's engravings, not only authenticating them but also connecting them to his name and his distinctive style as an artist.

Some authors and publishers likewise sought to authenticate printed books and give them an aura of presence. Cathy Shrank has shown how some English books of the sixteenth century imitate scribal formats (for

---

[22] Albrecht Dürer, 'Annunciation' and 'Death of the Virgin', in the 'Life of the Virgin' series. Rainer Schoch, Matthias Mende and Anna Scherbaum, *Albrecht Dürer, das druckgraphische Werk*, 3 vols. (Munich: Prestel, 2001–04), ii, nos. 173, 183.

[23] Martin Olmütz put his initials on his copy of a Death of the Virgin after Martin Schöngauer. See David Landau and Peter Parshall, *The Renaissance Print 1470–550* (New Haven: Yale University Press, 1994), 54.

[24] Michael J. Liebmann, 'Die Künstlersignatur im 15.–16. Jahrhundert als Gegenstand soziologischer Untersuchungen', in Peter H. Feist, Ernst Ullmann, Gerhard Brendler (eds.), *Lucas Cranach: Künstler und Gesellschaft. Referate des Colloquiums mit Internationaler Beteiligung zum 500. Geburtstag Lucas Cranachs d. Ä. Staatliche Lutherhalle Wittenberg 1.–3. Oktober 1972* (Halle: Staatliche Lutherhalle, 1973), 129–34 (p. 131).

[25] Joseph Koerner, *The Moment of Self-Portraiture in German Renaissance Art* (Chicago: University of Chicago Press, 1993), 204.

[26] 'dieselben zaichen alle abzethun und der kaine hie fail ze haben'; cited in ibid., 488 n. 35.

Composers and Authentication Marks 87

instance, the dedicatory letters use typography and layout similar to a manuscript letter), and argues that typesetters and editors thereby sought to recreate the intimacy of scribal communication.[27] Authenticity could also be denoted by the signature of the author or an approved inspector. A 1582 edition of Boccaccio's *Decameron* included an engraved facsimile of a handwritten testimony by the editor Lionardo Salviati, attesting he had checked the text personally.[28] In the German book trade, from 1524 onwards Luther marked his authorised editions with a woodcut of his monogram. The monogram depicts a rose whose petals enclose a heart bearing a cross, with the initials 'M. L.';[29] from 1530 Luther sealed his correspondence with a signet ring bearing this symbol.[30] In his printed editions, Luther's rose evoked the seals imprinted by signet rings, and thus simulated his bodily presence. As he explained in his 1524 edition of the Old Testament: 'This sign shall testify that such books as bear it have gone through my hands, for there is much illegal printing and corruption of books these days'.[31]

Thus signatures and other authentication marks were in part a response to the depersonalising effect of long-distance trade and mechanical reproduction. When objects such as printed books circulated away from the presence of their makers, these marks acted as signs of provenance, building trust among consumers and enhancing the value of the product. In certain contexts they could be compared to a brand or trademark, authenticating and advertising a producer's distinctive wares.[32] Additionally, those signs indicating an individual's name or place of origin might be believed to reveal something of the essence of the person thereby represented.

COMPOSERS AND AUTHENTICATION MARKS

In German lands from the late sixteenth to late seventeenth centuries, printed and manuscript music appeared with a variety of authentication marks. Some music books bear a printer's or publisher's mark: around 1600 the Leipzig publisher Abraham Lamberg used a winged Pegasus, and the Erfurt printer Georg Baumann used a woodcut of a building site as

---

[27] Cathy Shrank, '"These Fewe Scribbled Rules": Representing Scribal Intimacy in Early Modern Print', *Huntington Library Quarterly* 67 (2004), 295–314.

[28] Marco Bernardi and Carlo Pulsoni, 'Primi appunti sulle rassettature del Salviati', *Filologia italiana* 8 (2011), 167–201 (pp. 170, 197).

[29] Hans Volz, 'Das Lutherwappen als "Schutzmarke"', *Libri* 4 (1954), 216–25.

[30] Luther described the signet ring in a letter to Melanchthon, 15 September 1530; *WA Briefwechsel* 5, 620. The ring is preserved in the Staatliche Kunstsammlungen, Dresden, inventory number VIII 97.

[31] 'Dis zeichen sey zeuge, das solche bucher durch meine hand gangen sind, denn des falschen druckes vnd bucher verderbens, vleyssigen sich ytzt viel'. *WA Deutsche Bibel* 2, 273.

[32] Van Damme, 'From a "Knowledgeable" Salesman', 98.

a punning reference to his name.[33] Many music books carry the coats of arms of a patron or the ruler whose privilege protected the edition (see Chapter 4). This section focuses on authentication marks that referred to the name or physical presence of the composer. In a phenomenon not hitherto analysed by scholars, some composers such as Schein and Schütz used their monograms to authenticate the music they published themselves. Such signs added value to their publications, reassuring consumers that these books could be trusted, and giving an aura of personal presence when these editions were offered to potential patrons. This section also considers the markings used to verify some music manuscripts as autographs. Authentication signs were a niche practice, found on only a minority of printed and manuscript sources, but they nonetheless show how the practice of signing music was rooted in economic and material conventions.

Johann Hermann Schein, cantor at Leipzig's Thomasschule from 1616 until his death in 1630, embarked in 1617 on a major project to publish his own music. Previously he had used local bookdealers to publish his collections of student songs, sacred music and consort music.[34] He thereafter published all his music himself, including two volumes of sacred concertos, two books of madrigals, three sets of villanellas, a collection of drinking songs, and a hymnal.[35] That he had commercial motives for self-publishing is suggested by his 1617 petition for a Saxon printing privilege, in which he described booksellers as 'unreasonable' and 'self-interested' as publishers;[36] if this can be taken at face value, it implies that he wished to receive all the profit from his books himself. To develop a market for his publications, Schein had to differentiate them from the products of commercial booksellers. From 1621 he included engraved title pages in all his publications, with designs complementing the poetico-musical meanings. His first book of villanellas, *Musica boscareccia* (1621), has a multi-panel title page showing various sylvan characters singing, dancing and playing instruments; his set of spiritual madrigals, *Israelis Brünlein*

---

[33] For an example of Lamberg's mark, see the colophon of Erhard Bodenschatz, *Harmoniae angelicae cantionum* (Leipzig, 1608) (D-W, 1164.102 Theol.); for Baumann's mark, see the colophon of Seth Calvisius, *Hymni sacri latini et germanici* (Erfurt, 1594) (D-GOl, Druck 8° 01229 [02]). RISM A/I B3242, C257. See also Heinrich Grimm, *Deutsche Buchdruckersignete des XVI. Jahrhunderts. Geschichte, Sinngehalt und Gestaltung kleiner Kulturdokumente* (Wiesbaden: Guido Pressler, 1965), 201, 295.

[34] Johann Hermann Schein, *Venus Kräntzlein* (Wittenberg, 1609) published by Thomas Schürer; and *Cymbalum sionium* (Leipzig, 1615) and *Banchetto musicale* (Leipzig, 1617), both published by Abraham Lamberg. RISM A/I S1374–76.

[35] On Schein as self-publisher, see Stephen Rose, 'The Composer as Self-Publisher in Seventeenth-Century Germany', in Erik Kjellberg (ed.), *The Dissemination of Music in Seventeenth-Century Europe. Celebrating the Düben Collection* (Bern: Peter Lang, 2010), 239–60 (pp. 243–45).

[36] D-Dla, Loc. 10757/2, fol. 60v; transcribed in Rose, 'Protected Publications: The Imperial and Saxon Privileges for Printed Music, 1550–700', *Early Music History* 37 (2018), 247–313 (pp. 304–5).

(1623), has a similar multi-panel design showing musicians around an organ, plus allegorical figures pointing heavenwards.[37] Such eye-catching iconography would draw the attention of buyers. As Georg Philipp Harsdörffer explained a few decades later: 'Nowadays no book can be sold without an engraved title page, which represents to the reader the book's content not only in words but also with an image'.[38]

Further distinguishing Schein's publications, his engraved title pages feature his monogram that comprised his initials IHS and a rose. As with Luther's monogram, this sign evoked the imprint of the author's signet ring. In the *Musica boscareccia* series and *Israelis Brünlein*, Schein's monogram appears in a small panel in the centre of the multi-panel engraving. For other books he incorporated his monogram or initials into a larger scene. In his set of secular madrigals *Diletti pastorali*, the title page represents its pastoral theme via a rustic landscape including a bagpiper and mythological figures, with a city in the background; Schein's intertwined initials IHSG (G denoting his birthplace of Grünhain) are carved on a stone in the foreground right. Figure 3.1 shows the title page of his sacred concertos *Opella nova Ander Theil* (1626), where a small engraved panel depicts a decorated altar bearing a lyre whose laurel wreath is being blessed by a cherub. Schein's initials appear on the altar frontal, where the IHS of Christ would usually be found, underlining that his initials were the same as Christ's.[39]

By including his monogram on title pages, Schein evoked the practices of graphic printmakers such as Cranach and Dürer. Of course, Schein did not make the engravings himself, and on some of his title pages the initials of the engraver are also visible.[40] Yet he probably drafted the design for the engraver to execute, as poets did later in the century.[41] Schein's monogram therefore marks him as responsible for the creative conception of the printed book. It also signals that he was publisher and wished to authenticate the duplicated copies. Significantly, the monogram did not appear on unauthorised editions of his music, such as the three volumes of *Musica boscareccia* published by Paul Ledertz in Strasbourg in 1628:[42] these

---

[37] RISM A/I S1379, 1385.

[38] 'Bey dieser Zeit/ ist fast kein Buch verkäufflich/ ohne einen Kupfertitel/ welcher dem Leser desselben Jnhalt nicht nur mit Worten/ sondern auch mit einem Gemähl vorbildet'. Georg Philipp Harsdörffer, *Frauenzimmer Gesprechspiele, so bey Ehr- und Tugendliebenden Gesellschaften . . . beliebet und geübet werden mögen*, vol. 6 (Nuremberg, 1646), sig. A6r.

[39] Schein's parents presumably chose his forenames to bear the auspicious initials of Christ, in the belief that a name can foretell an individual's life. On this tradition of *Nomen est omen*, see Ernst R. Curtius, *European Literature and the Latin Middle Ages*, trans. Willard R. Trask (London: Routledge, 1979), 495.

[40] The engraved title page for the tenor partbook of *Diletti pastorali* (Leipzig, 1624), RISM A/I S1387, bears the engraver's initials 'CC'.

[41] John Roger Paas, 'Inseparable Muses: German Baroque Poets as Graphic Artists', *Colloquia Germanica* 29 (1996), 13–38 (p. 14).

[42] RISM A/I S1381, 1391, 1401.

OPELLA NOVA,

Ander Theil/

Geistlicher Concerten/

mit 3. 4. 5. vnd 6. Stimmen zu-
sampt dem General-Bass,

Auff jetzo gebreuchliche Italiänische Invention

Componirt

Von

Johan-Herman Schein/Grünhain

Directore Music. Chori zu Leipzig.

Mit Churfürstl. Sächs. Befreyung.

TENORE.

In Verlegung des Autoris, vnd bey demselben auff der
Schulen zu S. Thomas daselbst zu finden.

M. DC. XXVI.

Figure 3.1 Johann Hermann Schein, *Opella nova Ander Theil* (Leipzig, 1626), Tenore partbook, title page. Munich, Bayerische Staatsbibliothek, 4 Mus.pr. 2696, urn:nbn:de:bvb:12-bsb00091037–6

Composers and Authentication Marks   91

reproduce every element of Schein's editions apart from the engraved title pages and the mention of the composer's Saxon privilege (see Chapter 4). Ledertz would have been unable to replicate Schein's engraved title pages, and the legal judgement secured by Dürer indicated that it was a crime to affix a monogram falsely to unauthorised products. Like the reference to a privilege on a title page, Schein's monogram showed customers that his editions were authorised.

The monogram arguably enhanced the value of Schein's publications, akin to a trademark that indicated provenance and quality. He was keen for his title pages to be visible to prospective buyers, so that their visual impact might encourage sales. In 1626 and again in 1628, he complained about booksellers who did not stock his music, stating it was hard to sell his editions without a shop in which to display them.[43] Yet Schein's publications sold well by the standards of the day, with most of them appearing in repeat editions during his lifetime, and in further editions published by Jakob Schuster after the composer's death in 1630.[44] Schuster set such store on the monogrammed title pages that he purchased the copperplates for them from Schein's widow,[45] and used them in many of his editions of Schein's music.[46] Along with the quality of Schein's compositions, the consistent branding of his title pages may have contributed to sales and to the composer's subsequent reputation. As early as 1638, he was celebrated as one of the three 'S's of German music (along with Schütz and Scheidt), an accolade repeated by Wolfgang Caspar Printz in 1690.[47]

In other circumstances, however, composers' monograms provoked a mixed response from musicians and purchasers. Later in the seventeenth century, publication in print had become the exception rather than the norm for German musicians (see Introduction). The Hamburg organist Johann Adam Reincken, however, entered print for his *Hortus musicus* (*c.*1688), a collection of trio sonatas. Like Schein with his printed music, Reincken named himself as publisher on the title page; but his inclusion of his monogram seems to be motivated less by economic factors and more by his high self-regard. The engraved title page (Figure 3.2) depicts an

---

[43] Johann Hermann Schein, *Opella nova Ander Theil* (Leipzig, 1626), Basso Continuo partbook, Auvertimento. RISM A/I S1388. D-Dla, Loc. 10757/3, fol. 77v; transcribed in Rose, 'Protected Publications', 306–8.

[44] On repeat and posthumous editions of Schein's music, see Rose, 'Protected Publications', 286–88.

[45] D-Dla, Loc. 10758/01, fol. 44r; transcribed in Rose, 'Protected Publications', 309–10.

[46] For instance, the 1650 edition of *Studenten-Schmauß*. D-W, L 294.4° Helmst. (24–28), tenor partbook.

[47] In 1638 Rudolf von Dieskau singled out Schütz, Schein and Scheidt as among the most skilful composers included in Apollo's library on Parnassus. See Klaus Conermann (ed.), *Die Deutsche Akademie des 17. Jahrhunderts: Fruchtbringende Gesellschaft*, Reihe I, Abteilung A: Köthen, Band 5: *Briefe der Fruchtbringenden Gesellschaft und Beilagen: Die Zeit Fürst Ludwigs von Anhalt-Köthen 1617–50* (Berlin: De Gruyter, 2010), 124; Wolfgang Caspar Printz, *Historische Beschreibung der edelen Sing- und Kling-Kunst* (Dresden, 1690), 136.

Figure 3.2 Johann Adam Reincken, *Hortus musicus* (Hamburg, *c.*1688), title page. Staatsbibliothek zu Berlin, Preußischer Kulturbesitz, Mus.ant.pract. R283, http://resolver.staatsbibliothek-berlin.de/SBB0001CB5A00000000

Composers and Authentication Marks

arcaded structure resembling a triumphal arch, beyond which is a formal garden. The garden refers to the title of the collection and also to Reincken's belief, expressed in the preface, that incompetent musicians 'should therefore be sent to plough and to hoe, and to be expelled in disgrace from the sweet garden of holy music (as its most harmful members)'.[48] The scene is dominated, however, by the triumphal arch, whose plan has been interpreted by Christine Defant and Ulf Grapenthin as representing the immutable harmonic ratios that Reincken sought to encapsulate in his music.[49] The upper panel describes Reincken as the 'director of the celebrated organ at the Katharinenkirche in Hamburg',[50] while the front two columns are decorated with 'JAR' monograms at their base. The arch thus monumentalises Reincken as worthy of praise and as the gatekeeper of the garden of harmonious music.

Whereas Schein's editions served a strong commercial demand, Reincken's *Hortus musicus* was a lavish engraved edition aimed at a smaller audience. Consequently Reincken's monograms on the title page appear less as authentication marks and more as a symbol of the composer's professional status, complementing his social prestige as one of the leading north German organists. Even the prominent 'Soli Deo Gloria', a nod to the theological model of creativity (see Chapter 1), cannot temper this sense of Reincken's pride. Indeed Johann Mattheson interpreted the title page as indicating Reincken's overbearing personality. He acerbically described Reincken's monograms as ensuring 'that one does not forget his name ... This example is not for emulation, but to be avoided'.[51] Mattheson instead advocated modesty: 'Honour where it is due, but not claimed by oneself'.[52] Such comments reflect Mattheson's recurring resentment at Reincken, a resentment that apparently originated when he was not named as Reincken's successor after an audition at the Katharinenkirche in 1705.[53] Given the cantankerous and exclusionary rhetoric in the preface of *Hortus musicus*, Reincken's monograms could be interpreted as an excess of authorial signature.

---

[48] 'qui ad stivam et rastra ablegentur, atque ex amoenissimo divinae Musices horto, tanquam membra nocentissima, cum infamia expellantur'. Johann Adam Reincken, *Hortus musicus* (Hamburg, [1688]), Violino Primo partbook, preface. RISM A/I R1072.

[49] Christine Defant, 'Johann Adam Reinckens *Hortus musicus*: Versuch einer Deutung als Metapher für die hochbarocke Musikauffassung in Deutschland', *Die Musikforschung* 42 (1989), 128–48; Ulf Grapenthin, 'Beziehungen zwischen Frontispiz und Werkaufbau in Johann Adam Reinckens *Hortus musicus* von 1688', in Sverker Jullander (ed.), *Proceedings of the Weckmann Symposium. Göteborg, 30 August–3 September 1991* (Göteborg: Department of Musicology, 1993), 199–210.

[50] 'Organi Hamburgensis ad D. Cathar. celebratissimi Directore'.

[51] 'damit man seines Nahmens nicht vergesse ... Diese Exempel werden nicht zur Nachahmung, sondern zur Vermeidung angeführet'. Johann Mattheson, *Grundlage einer Ehren-Pforte* (Hamburg, 1740), 293.

[52] 'Ehre dem Ehre gebühret; nur nicht von sich selbst'. Ibid.   [53] Ibid., 194.

Figure 3.3   Watermark in Heinrich Schütz, *Symphoniarum sacrarum secunda pars* (Dresden, 1647), Prima Vox, leaf after p. 62. British Library, F.21. By permission of the British Library Board

By contrast with external signs such as monograms, books could be authenticated in ways that penetrated deeper into their material structure – for instance, via watermarks. In this period, paper was made by dipping a wire mould in a vat of pulp; the wires of the mould contained shapes that became embedded in the fibres of the paper as watermarks and other features such as chainlines. Purchasers or inspectors could scrutinise the watermark by holding the sheet of paper up to the light. Already from the fourteenth century, Italian law protected watermarks as the property of particular paper mills, guaranteeing the origin and quality of the paper.[54] Watermarks were also used to authenticate legal documents, acting as a proof against counterfeits.[55]

From 1639 Heinrich Schütz issued copies of his music on a private supply of paper with a personalised watermark (Figure 3.3). The watermark shows a drawn bow and arrow (the coat of arms of the Schütz family, whose name means 'archer'[56]) and the initials 'HSC' (usually assumed to denote Heinrich Schütz Capellmeister, though the 'C' might indicate his place of birth at Bad Köstritz). Scholars have detected Schütz's private paper in most of his printed editions from the second half of his career, including the *Anderer Theil kleiner geistlichen Concerten* (1639), the second

---

[54] Cavallar, Degenring and Kirshner (eds.), *A Grammar of Signs*, 149.
[55] Groebner, *Who are You?*, 158–59.
[56] Eberhard Stimmel, 'Die Familie Schütz. Ein Beitrag zur Familiengeschichte des Georgius Agricola', *Abhandlungen des staatlichen Museums für Mineralogie und Geologie zu Dresden* 11 (1962), 377–417 (pp. 379–80).

Composers and Authentication Marks

nd third parts of *Symphoniae sacrae* (1647, 1650), the *Geistliche Chor-Music* (1648), the *Zwölff geistliche Gesänge* (1657) and the printed portion of the *Historia der Geburt Jesu Christi* (1664).[57] All these collections were published by Schütz or his associates. The paper was also used for author-sed manuscripts from the scriptorium evidently operated by Schütz, such is the copy of his setting of Psalm 119 known as the *Schwanengesang*.[58] It does not appear in the 1661 edition of Schütz's metrical psalms, the revised Becker Psalter, which was sponsored by Johann Georg II of Saxony rather than the composer himself.[59] As yet, however, scholars have not commented on the significance of Schütz's watermark in economic terms or in relation to authentication practices.

Schütz started using his private paper as part of a systematic project to publish his own music, in collaboration with associates and pupils such as Johann Klemm.[60] The start of this publishing business is documented by Schütz's 1637 imperial printing privilege (see Chapter 4, p. 129), which mentions his plan to publish works in Latin and in German, sacred and secular, with and without texts.[61] Publishers were responsible for supply-ng paper for a print-run, and Schütz may have had to invest in his own stock because of the difficulty of obtaining paper of sufficient quality during the Thirty Years War. He may have been assisted in this task by the Elector of Saxony, whom he thanked in 1650 for 'the most gracious means granted to me some time ago … through which the dissemina-tion of my musical work can be further promoted and its publication facilitated'.[62] Possibly the Elector provided Schütz with a special mould at the Dresden paper mill or funded the paper supply in its entirety.

Self-publication, however, does not explain why Schütz chose to use his distinctive watermark; he is the only seventeenth-century composer known to have incorporated his monogram into a watermark. Normally only

---

[7] RISM A/I S2291–2, 2294–5, 2297, 2299. Editions using the private paper were initially identified by Wolfram Steude, 'Das wiederaufgefundene *Opus ultimum* von Heinrich Schütz. Bemerkungen zur Quelle und zum Werk', *Schütz-Jahrbuch* 4–5 (1982–83), 9–18 (p. 11) and his edition of *Der Schwanengesang* for Heinrich Schütz, *Neue Ausgabe sämtlicher Werke*, vol. 39 (Kassel: Bärenreiter, 1984), 275. For the private paper in the *Historia der Geburt Jesu Christ*, see Bettina Varwig's edition in Heinrich Schütz, *Neue Ausgabe sämtlicher Werke*, vol. 1 (Kassel: Bärenreiter, 2017), 109. Schütz's private paper is used for some gatherings of Rosenmüller's *Kern-Sprüche Ander Theil* (1652–53), suggesting that he supported the publication of a younger composer; see Peter Wollny, 'Heinrich Schütz, Johann Rosenmüller und die *Kern-Sprüche* I und II', *Schütz-Jahrbuch* 28 (2006), 35–47 (pp. 39–40).

[8] D-Dl, Mus. 1479-E-504; GB-Lbl, Zweig Ms.84.

[9] Heinrich Schütz, *Psalmen Davids, Hiebevor in deutsche Reime gebracht Durch D. Cornelium Beckern* (Dresden, 1661). RISM A/I S2284. Copy examined: GB-Lbl, G.483.b. The title page and dedication indicate Johann Georg II's sponsorship of this edition.

[0] On Schütz as self-publisher, see Rose, 'The Composer as Self-Publisher', 245–47.

[1] A-Whh, Impressoria, Karton 61, Konvolut 1, no. 3, fols. 5r–6r; *HSR*, 108–9.

[2] 'die jenige … vor etlicher Zeit/ mir bewilligte gnädigste Mittel/ wordurch die *Publici*rung oder Auslassung meiner Musicalischen Arbeit hinfüro auch weiter befördert/ und derer Verlag erleichtert werden kan'. Heinrich Schütz, *Symphoniarum sacrarum tertia pars* (Dresden, 1650), dedication. RISM A/I S2295.

members of the nobility had paper with a personalised watermark, and Schütz's supply therefore indicates his high social status. More specifically, Schütz may have introduced the watermark in response to the unauthorised reprints and reductions of his sacred concertos that appeared a year or two earlier in the Nordhausen anthologies *Geistliche wolklingende Concerte* (1637–38). Chapter 2 examined these unauthorised reductions as an example of plagiarism, and Chapter 4 shows how Schütz sought legal protection against such illicit publications via his 1637 imperial privilege. His watermark was another way to counteract unauthorised editions, allowing purchasers to authenticate a copy by holding its pages up to the light. The watermark also differentiated manuscripts produced by the composer's scriptorium from the 'many pieces of my compositions carelessly and defectively copied', as Schütz complained about in 1647.[63] Much remains to be researched about Schütz's paper supply. A systematic analysis of the watermarks and paper chainlines in surviving copies of his publications might reveal the gradual degradation of the mould through successive batches of his paper, permitting study of the chronology of his paper supply. For now, though, Schütz's watermark can be interpreted as a unique way to authenticate copies of his notated compositions. Redolent of the composer's signet ring and using an artisanal technique of verification, the watermark embedded Schütz's identity in the fibres of the paper on which his music was disseminated.

Some music manuscripts contain authentication marks attesting to the presence of the composer and enhancing the value of the source. Because manuscripts were usually tailored for their intended recipient, they were more likely than printed copies to have a sense of unique existence. Yet manuscripts could have different degrees of aura, depending on their scribe and the style of their presentation. In 1528 Erasmus declared: 'A letter written by a third party hardly deserves to be called a letter at all. Secretaries often make their own changes. Even if you dictate rigidly, intimacy will still be missing'.[64] He warned that a signature could be easily forged. By contrast, an entirely autograph document could evoke the writer's voice and through that his or her character. Erasmus explained: 'When we get letters in their own hand from friends and fellow-scholars, how we welcome them and seem to be listening to their very voices and to be looking at them face to face'.[65] To enhance the aura of a document, a signatory often added authentication marks such as monograms, the words *manu propria [scripsi]* (with my own hand I wrote this) and the paraph

---

[63] 'wie viel Stücken solcher meiner *Composition* ... unfleissig und mangelhafft abgeschrieben'. Heinrich Schütz, *Symphoniarum sacrarum secunda pars* (Dresden, 1647), Bassus ad Organum, preface. RISM A/I S2292.

[64] *CWE* 26, 391; *ASD* I-4, 34.   [65] Ibid.

Composers and Authentication Marks

(an ornamental flourish consisting of repeated pen strokes).[66] Such features recording the physical presence of the scribe appear in some music manuscripts, including a few that are not autographs.

As mentioned above, Schütz operated a scriptorium in the later decades of his life, producing authorised manuscripts of those compositions that were uneconomic to print. Some of these, such as the *Historia der Geburt Jesu Christi* (1664) or the *Schwanengesang* (1671), circulated in a hybrid form whereby elements such as the title page were printed, and some or all of the music was available in manuscript. The surviving parts for the *Schwanengesang* were copied by one of Schütz's scribes in a calligraphic style usually associated with autograph manuscripts. At the end of each vocal partbook, the scribe added Schütz's initials HSC, written across the stave after the final double barline flourish (Figure 3.4).[67] These markings exemplify the collaborative nature of authorship. The monogram is not written by the composer, but still serves to authenticate the work and strengthen the author's presence. It is a visible counterpart to Schütz's crest lodged within the paper as the watermark.

The keyboardist Johann Jacob Froberger presents a stronger example of how musicians incorporated authentication marks into handwritten notation. As Chapter 6 shows, the value of Froberger's keyboard music lay in its exclusivity, especially its association with his idiosyncratic performance style. This music could be fully understood only by those who had heard the composer play it. The principal manuscript sources of Froberger's music – including three autograph volumes presented to the Holy Roman Emperor and now preserved in the Österreichische Nationalbibliothek – reinforce this exclusivity with references to the composer's presence.[68] The dedication to one of these volumes alludes to the biographical meanings encoded in the allemandes, including bodily experiences such as a dangerous crossing of the Rhine: Froberger explained that he had composed 'several works according to the various feelings that have been occasioned in me by various vicissitudes of the times'.[69]

The calligraphy of the Froberger manuscripts also acted as a material trace of the composer's body. Figure 3.5 shows how, at the end of each piece, the scribe connected the distinctive eye-shaped fermatas into a paraph that functions as a double-bar marking. The zig-zags of this paraph

---

[56] On such authentication practices in English letter-writing, see James Daybell, *The Material Letter in Early Modern England: Manuscript Letters and the Culture and Practices of Letter-Writing, 1512–635* (Basingstoke: Macmillan, 2012), 97–102.

[57] Heinrich Schütz, *Königs und Propheten Davids Hundert und Neunzehender Psalm* [*Der Schwanengesang*] (Dresden, 1671), D-Dl, Mus. 1479-E-504. The initials are not found in the continuo partbook preserved in GB-Lbl, Zweig Ms.84.

[58] A-Wn, Mus. Hs. 18706 (dedicated to Ferdinand III, dated 1649); Mus. Hs. 18707 (dedicated to Ferdinand III, dated 1656); Mus. Hs. 16560 (dedicated to Leopold I, *c*.1658).

[59] 'alla composit^ne d'alcune opere, secondate per il più dall'humore, che hà cagionato in me la varietà degl'accidenti del tempo'. A-Wn, Mus. Hs. 18707, fol. 4r.

Figure 3.4   Heinrich Schütz, *Königs und Propheten Davids Hundert und Neunzehender Psalm* [*Der Schwanengesang*] (Dresden, 1671). Sächsische Landesbibliothek – Staats- und Universitätsbibliothek Dresden, Digitale Sammlungen, Mus. 1479-E-504, p. 37

also serve as the 'm' in an abbreviated *manu propria* sign, connecting in a single pen-stroke to the inscription '[pro]pria s[cripsi]'.[70] This flourish finishes each piece with a signature of authority, canonising it with the mark of the composer's hand. In addition, the 'Fine' decoration at the end of one volume incorporates Froberger's initials JJF.[71]

Although the Vienna volumes are likely to be autographs, this cannot be proved, owing to the absence of any autograph letters in a comparable

---

[70] Similar marks appear in the Froberger autograph sold at Sotheby's in 2006 and now privately owned. Bob van Asperen, 'A New Froberger Manuscript', *Journal of Seventeenth-Century Music*, 13/i (2007), https://sscm-jscm.org/v13/no1/vanasperen.html

[71] A-Wn, Mus. Hs. 18707, fol. 166r.

Figure 3.5   Johann Jacob Froberger, *manu propria scripsi* sign. Vienna, Österreichische Nationalbibliothek, Mus. Hs. 18706, fol. 12r

script by Froberger.[72] The paraph and *manu propria* signs are not infallible indicators of an autograph document. Recent studies of sixteenth-century letter-writing have exposed the complex relationship between scribes and signatories, showing the collaborative way in which most manuscripts were produced.[73] Indeed, demonstrably non-autograph manuscripts of Froberger's music replicate some of the authentication marks found in the Vienna manuscripts. The Froberger manuscript held by the Berlin Sing-Akademie reproduces the zig-zag double barlines that allude to the paraph. Probably copied by the Hamburg organist Johann Kortkamp, this manuscript may have had a pedagogical function, to inform north German students about Froberger's distinctive performance style;[74] accordingly the scribe sought to convey the composer's presence by mimicking features of the autograph that presumably was the copy-text. Further examples occur in the Bauyn manuscript in the Bibliothèque Nationale, Paris, an anthology of keyboard music assembled by an unknown French scribe around 1690 and containing music by a range of French, Italian and central European composers.

---

[72] *Seventeenth-Century Keyboard Music*, vol. 3: *Vienna, Österreichische Nationalbibliothek, Musiksammlung, Mus. Hs. 18706 (Froberger Autographs)*, introduction by Robert Hill (New York: Garland, 1988), ix.

[73] Giacomo Giudici, 'The Writing of Renaissance Politics: Sharing, Appropriating, and Asserting Authorship in the Letters of Francesco II Sforza, Duke of Milan (1522–35)', *Renaissance Studies* 32 (2018), 253–81.

[74] D-Bsa, SA4450. See David Schulenberg, 'Crossing the Rhine with Froberger: Suites, Symbols, and Seventeenth-Century Musical Autobiography', in Claire Fontijn and Susan Parisi (eds.), *Fiori musicali: Liber amicorum Alexander Silbiger* (Sterling Heights, MI: Harmonie Park Press, 2010), 271–302 (p. 301).

Some of its Froberger pieces end with the rubric 'propria', perhaps a remnant of the authentication marks found in the scribe's exemplar.[75] Yet the Berlin Sing-Akademie and Bauyn manuscripts are not autographs; their use of these markings confirms that (as Erasmus warned) features of autograph manuscripts could be copied by other scribes. The making of manuscripts was a collaborative undertaking, and signs of autograph presence must be read with care.

The monograms and other verification signs discussed here are found in only a small minority of surviving musical sources from the seventeenth century. Musicians who aligned themselves with a theological view of creativity preferred to sign their notated works with the pious inscriptions of 'JJ' and 'SDG' (see Chapter 1, p. 20). Composers rarely added their signature when copying parts for performers. The authentication marks used by Schein, Schütz and Froberger added authority to their notated music and linked it with their name (which was believed to indicate inner attributes such as character). To modern eyes, these authentication marks may seem somewhat superficial indicators of identity; yet Dürer's successful defence of his monogram shows that they held legal status. Such markings enhanced the value of printed and manuscript music, increasing the aura of these material objects and thereby eliciting the trust of buyers and users.

COMPOSER PORTRAITS IN PRINTED MUSIC

A portrait in printed music offered a strong mark of the composer's identity, simulating the author's presence. Previous scholarship has focussed on painted portraits of cantors and court musicians in this period, analysing them for symbols of professional office such as rolled-up music paper for beating time, notated canons as symbols of contrapuntal ingenuity, quill pens for writing down compositions, and medals bestowed by grateful patrons.[76] Here I investigate how portraits within printed music boosted the value of the publications by attracting buyers and guiding readers. Because printed music was likely to circulate away from the composer's presence, a portrait displayed the facial features from which buyers and users might infer the mental attributes and moral character of the author. The inscriptions on portraits elaborate on the identity of the musical author, including the role of body and mind in defining their individuality.

---

[75] F-Pn, Ms. Rés. Vm⁷ 674–675, vol. 2, fols. 94r–v; for recent research on its likely purpose, see *Paris, Bibliothèque nationale de France, Rés. Vm⁷ 674–675: The Bauyn Manuscript*, ed. Bruce Gustafson, 4 vols. (New York: The Broude Trust, 2014), iv, 3–38.

[76] Werner Braun, 'Arten des Komponistenporträts', in Ludwig Finscher and Christoph-Hellmut Mahling (eds.), *Festschrift für Walter Wiora zum 30. Dezember 1966* (Kassel: Bärenreiter, 1967), 86–94; Karoline Czerwenka-Papadopoulos, *Typologie des Musikerporträts in Malerei und Graphik: das Bildnis des Musikers ab der Renaissance bis zum Klassizismus*, 2 vols. (Vienna: Verlag der Österreichischen Akademie der Wissenschaften, 2007).

In sixteenth-century Italy, author portraits in printed and manuscript books followed one of several conventions. They might represent the author as a scholar-saint (in accordance with Christian traditions), as a heroic figure crowned with laurels (following classical precedent), or as a donor to a patron.[77] Music theorists were regularly portrayed in their treatises, as scholars lecturing to pupils (as with Franchinus Gaffurius and Pietro Aaron) or working alone in their study (as with Johannes Tinctoris).[78] Portraits of composers, by contrast, rarely appeared in music books in sixteenth-century Italy.[79] One possible reason for this absence is that Italian music publishing in the first half of the century was mainly driven by commercial publishers and few composers wished to assert their presence in print.[80] Another likely reason is technological, for publishers such as Gardano and Scotto lacked the facilities to produce woodcut or engraved portraits without significantly adding to the cost of their books.[81] The well-known woodcuts of Cristóbal de Morales and Giovanni Pierluigi da Palestrina presenting their Mass collections to the pope are versions of a standard donor portrait used by Andrea Antico in his *Liber quindecim missarum* (1516).[82] Otherwise one of the earliest composer portraits in Italian printed music is the woodcut of Adrian Willaert in his *Musica nova* (1559), a retrospective collection containing music that the composer had written several decades earlier.[83] A commemorative purpose was again served by the 1604 woodcut of Claudio Merulo found in several posthumous editions of his music.[84] In the early seventeenth century, portraits also appeared of instrumentalists such as Girolamo Frescobaldi and the lutenist Bellerofonte Castaldi, marking the increasing status of these virtuosi and facilitated by the use of engraving technology in their books.[85]

---

[77] Ruth Mortimer, 'The Author's Image: Italian Sixteenth-Century Printed Portraits', *Harvard Library Bulletin* new series 7/ii (summer 1996), 7–87.

[78] Franchinus Gaffurius, *Angelicum ac divinum opus musice* (Milan, 1508), sig. A2r; Pietro Aaron, *Toscanello in musica*, 3rd edn (Venice, 1539), frontispiece; for Tinctoris, see Universitat de València. Biblioteca Històrica, Ms. 835, fol. 2r.

[79] Tim Shephard, Sanna Raninen, Serenella Sessini and Laura Ştefănescu, *Music in the Art of Renaissance Italy c.1420–540* (London: Harvey Miller, 2019), chapter 5.3. Shephard observes that many printed poetry anthologies from early-sixteenth-century Italy picture the poet with a lyre, indicating the recitation of verse to music; but these images are a separate category from those of composers of sacred polyphony. I am grateful to Tim Shephard for sharing his team's work prior to publication.

[80] On the limited interest of Italian musicians in print as a 'locus for authorial identity' before 1550, see Kate van Orden, *Music, Authorship, and the Book in the First Century of Print* (Berkeley: University of California Press, 2014), 42–51.

[81] I am grateful to Tim Carter for this observation.

[82] Cristóbal de Morales, *Missarum liber secundus* (Rome, 1544), title page. RISM A/I M3582. Giovanni Pierluigi da Palestrina, *Missarum liber primus* (Rome, 1554), title page. RISM A/I P655.

[83] RISM A/I W1126.

[84] Claudio Merulo, *Ricercari da cantare libro secondo* (Venice, 1607), *Ricercari da cantare libro terzo* (Venice, 1608), *Misse Due* (Venice, 1609). RISM A/I M2367, 2380–1.

[85] Girolamo Frescobaldi, *Il secondo libro di toccate* (Rome, 1627). RISM A/I F1866. Bellerofonte Castaldi, *Capricci a 2 stromenti* (Modena, 1622). RISM A/I C1452.

102   *Signs of Individuality*

In German-speaking lands, there was arguably a stronger appetite for composer portraits in printed music. Such images satisfied a Lutheran desire to revere figures of religious and cultural authority, as Ulinka Rublack has discussed with reference to depictions of reformers such as Luther.[86] A cluster of composers in Saxon lands included portraits in their printed music. Giovanni Battista Pinello, capellmeister at the Dresden court, had a woodcut of his portrait in his *Deutsche Magnificat* (1583).[87] The Meiningen court secretary and poet Johann Steuerlein included a woodcut of his portrait in his *Sieben und zwentzigk newe geistliche Gesenge* (1588), on the reverse of the title page. This portrait is even more prominent in Steuerlein's *Psalmus CL Laudate Dominum* (1588) and *Octo cantiones sacrae* (1589), appearing in the middle of the title page of each partbook.[88] Steuerlein is known to have contributed to the cost of his publications, perhaps explaining the element of vanity implied by these prominent portraits.[89] (Indeed, the Englishman Fynes Moryson, who visited Leipzig and Wittenberg in 1591–92, commented on how Germans tended to publish books 'for the desyre of vayne glory'.)[90] Some German instrumentalists also incorporated portraits of themselves in their printed tablatures, possibly to reinforce their reputation as players and teachers. A woodcut of the Heidelberg lutenist Sebastian Ochsenkun holding his instrument appears at the end of his *Tabulaturbuch auff die Lauten* (1558). The lutenist Melchior Neusidler (with his instrument and a scroll of tablature) is depicted in his *Teutsch Lautenbuch* (1574).[91]

A significant number of German music books of the early seventeenth century contain portraits of the composer as an authoritative figure, resplendent in official church or court costume. The woodcut of Michael Praetorius in his *Musae Sioniae* series (Figure 3.6) shows him in his robes as capellmeister to the Wolfenbüttel court, with a cape and lavishly hemmed doublet. He wears three medals, each bearing a head that may represent his employer Heinrich Julius of Brunswick-Wolfenbüttel. Prominent on his hands are signet rings which probably carried monograms or heraldic symbols similar to those in Schein's and Schütz's authentication devices (see above). In addition to these trappings of courtly authority, Praetorius's portrait represented his compositional activities with the pen and ink by his right elbow, and the canon 'In Deo speravit cor meum' in his right hand. A similar display of authority occurs in the portrait of

---

[86] Ulinka Rublack, 'Grapho-Relics: Lutheranism and the Materialization of the Word', *Past & Present* 206, suppl. 5 (2010), 144–66.

[87] RISM A/I P2388.   [88] RISM A/I S6035–7.   [89] Rose, 'Protected Publications', 282.

[90] Graham David Kew, 'Shakespeare's Europe Revisited. The Unpublished *Itinerary* of Fynes Moryson (1566–630)', 4 vols. (PhD dissertation, University of Birmingham, 1995), iv, 1227.

[91] RISM B/I 1558[20], 1574[13].

Composer Portraits in Printed Music

Figure 3.6 Michael Praetorius, portrait in prefatory insertion bound with *Musae Sioniae* (Regensburg / Wolfenbüttel, 1605–10). Herzog August Bibliothek Wolfenbüttel, 2.5 Musica (1), fol. 1v

Samuel Scheidt in the first volume of his collection of keyboard music *Tabulatura nova* (1624).[92] Signalling his status as capellmeister to Margrave Christian Wilhelm of Brandenburg, he wears an elaborate starched ruff, a decorated doublet, and a medal (presumably a gift from a patron or the recipient of a presentation copy). The inscription describes him as a prince among musicians and compares him to the winged horse Pegasus, a symbol of wisdom and fame. Such portraits celebrated the social prestige of the composers, enhancing the value of their books when given as presentation copies, and commanding the trust of buyers and readers who would never meet them in person.

Some portraits invoked classical tropes to give authority to the composer. The inscriptions might liken the sitter to mythological musicians such as Orpheus, as with a 1676 portrait of the Darmstadt capellmeister Wolfgang Carl Briegel or a 1688 engraving of Johann Caspar Kerll.[93] Even without an inscription, the iconography of a portrait could allude to classical traditions. For his first published collection of music (the *Neue Clavier Ubung* of 1689), Johann Kuhnau (who then held the position of organist at the Thomaskirche in Leipzig) presented himself as monumentalised above his harpsichord. Figure 3.7 shows a hand-coloured version of this title page where the symbolism is vividly brought to life.[94] The engraving is presented as a stage scene, with a curtain pulled back on the right-hand side to reveal a background of hills with red-roofed houses and towers. This background evokes the Erzgebirge (Ore Mountains) of southern Saxony, a territory which included Kuhnau's birthplace in Geising. On the centre of the stage, a pedestal is formed by the harpsichord and a panel containing the title; at the head of this pedestal is Kuhnau's portrait, wreathed by laurels (a symbol of Apollo, but also used to crown poets laureate in the Holy Roman Empire).[95] Aged 29 when this engraving was made, Kuhnau identified himself via his birthplace and his keyboard skill, and gave himself the authority of a laureate.

Whereas many portraits showed composers as authoritative figures, a few purported to represent their inner character. That an individual's attributes could be read from his or her facial appearance was popularized by advocates of physiognomy. In a 1504 treatise published in Italy and reprinted in German-speaking lands, the poet Pomponio Gaurico defined physiognomy as 'a certain kind of observation by which we deduce the

---

[92] Samuel Scheidt, *Tabulatura nova, cantinens variationes aliquot Psalmorum fantasiarum, cantilenarum, passamezo, et canones aliquot* (Hamburg, 1624). RISM A/I S1352. Portrait found on the verso of the title page in some copies such as F-Pn, Vm[7] 1808 (1).

[93] Walter Salmen, *Musiker im Porträt*, vol. 2: *Das 17. Jahrhundert* (Munich: Beck, 1983), 102, 106.

[94] RISM A/I K2982; Bach-Archiv Leipzig, Rara II, 727-D.

[95] On laurel crowns in images of seventeenth-century poets, see Susanne Skowronek, *Autorenbilder. Wort und Bild in den Porträtkupferstichen von Dichtern und Schriftstellern des Barock* (Würzburg: Königshausen & Neumann, 2000), Abbildung 40.

Composer Portraits in Printed Music

Figure 3.7 Johann Kuhnau, *Neue Clavier Ubung* (Leipzig, 1689), title page. Leipzig, Bach-Archiv, Rara II, 727-D. Heritage Image Partnership Ltd / Alamy Stock Photo

qualities of minds from the signs that are on bodies'.[96] Many humanists believed that the face offered a window on the soul, showing qualities such as virtue.[97]

Such attitudes underlie the woodcut of Schein found in his first published collection, *Venus Kräntzlein* (1609), shown in Figure 3.8. Issued when the composer was aged 23 and studying at Leipzig University, this set of partbooks contains student songs on the themes of love and companionship.[98] The woodcut is an unusual example of a portrait showing a musician who lacked an official position and therefore did not wear formal clothes such as a ruff. Instead Schein's appearance signals his status as a student: his hair flares fashionably outwards, and he wears a knight's tunic with a sword. Leipzig students fiercely defended their right

---

[96] 'Ea autem est certa queda‹m› obseruatio, qua ex iis quae corpori insunt signis, animorum etiam qualitates denotamus'. Pomponio Gaurico, *De sculptura* (Nuremberg, 1542), sig. E3v.
[97] Martin Porter, *'Windows of the Soul'. Physiognomy in European Culture 1470–780* (Oxford: Oxford University Press, 2005).
[98] Schein described himself on the title page of *Venus Kräntzlein* as 'In Acad. pro temp: L. L. Studioso'. After matriculating at Leipzig University in 1603, he studied for several years at the electoral school at Schulpforta, before re-joining the university in 1608. See Georg Erler, *Die jüngere Matrikel der Universität Leipzig, 1559–809*, 3 vols. (Leipzig, 1909), i, 393; Arthur Prüfer, *Johan Herman Schein* (Leipzig: Breitkopf & Härtel, 1895), 7, 10.

Figure 3.8 Johann Hermann Schein, *Venus Kräntzlein* (Wittenberg, 1609), portrait in Tenor partbook, sig.):(3v. Wolfenbüttel, Herzog August Bibliothek, 46.3 Musica

Composer Portraits in Printed Music

to carry a sword, which indicated their freedom from servitude, and their willingness to defend their honour in a duel.[99] Schein's secular attire suits the student songs within *Venus Kräntzlein*; indeed, he holds a rolled-up piece of music quoting the start of the Quinta Vox for the last piece in the collection ('Laßt uns freuen und fröhlich sein', a quodlibet where this voice has the tavern cries 'Post Martinum, bonum vinum'). Thus Schein fashioned himself for his portrait via the rituals of student masculinity rather than as an authoritative figure.

Yet the inscription by Johannes Hahn interprets Schein's portrait in physiognomic terms, reading the composer's face for signs of his inner nature:

> In Hermann's face shine a bright mind, virtue,
> music; there's no evil here, you do not seek the satyr.
> Or if you are Apollo, speak the truth: for are
> Virtue and even music able to carry falsehoods?[100]

The poem counters the image of the rowdy student and the earthy nature of the song texts in *Venus Kräntzlein*, instead scrutinising Schein's face for signs of mental lucidity and virtue.[101] For the ambitious young composer, introducing himself to readers who had not met him in person, the portrait showcased his social status and inner virtues.

For some portraits, however, the inscriptions abandoned the claims of physiognomy and instead directed attention to the products of the composer's mind. A 1635 engraving of Johann Andreas Herbst bears a couplet by Hieronymus Ammon that seeks evidence of the composer's mental abilities not in his face but in his works:

> The face of the very famous Herbst, musician, stands here in copper.
> The songs he has written prove the gifts of his mind.[102]

That a composer's works should speak for themselves was also asserted by the commendatory poem in posthumous editions of Adam Krieger's *Neue Arien*:

---

[99] On students' right to bear a sword, see Christoph August Heumann, 'Historia de gladio academico', in Johann Volkmar Bechmann, *Tractatus historico-juridicus de privilegiis ac juribus studiosorum* (Jena, 1741), 3–12.

[100]
> 'Fulget in Hermani vultu mens candida, virtus,
> Musica, ne niger hunc, ne Satyrusve petas.
> Aut si quis Phoebus fueris, dic vera: sed anne
> Falsa etiam virtus Musica ferre potest?'

[101] On virtue as an attribute in panegyrics of the learned, see Skowronek, *Autorenbilder*, 229.

[102]
> 'Praeclari Autumni facies hic Musici in aere
> Stat, dona ingenii cantica scripta probant.' Inscription on 1635 portrait of author
> in Johann Andreas Herbst, *Musica poetica* (Nuremberg, 1643),
> inserted before sig. A2r.

If Herr Krieger was not crowned by us
His beautiful works still crown him.[103]

The portrait of Krieger shows him in courtly costume including a wig and laced ruff; yet the poem indicates that such worldly recognition was secondary to the accolades that his works paid him.

Portraits of seventeenth-century poets commonly had inscriptions contrasting their mortal bodies with the everlasting spirit preserved in their works.[104] Invoking the humanist concern for posterity, this trope was apt for composers too, because their music could live on in performance. In 1664 the Stralsund organist Johann Martin Rubert included his portrait in his self-published book of sacred concertos, *Musicalische Seelen-Erquickung*. The inscription drew attention to Rubert's forehead, indicative of mental power according to physiognomy; but then noted that the products of his intellect grant him immortality:

Behold the forehead and mouth of Herr Rubert, whose compositions
Are made from sweet loveliness and singing skill
That when he dies, he does not die; he shows
What works his skilled mind can make.[105]

A similar sentiment is found in posthumous editions of Adam Krieger's *Neue Arien*, where the commendatory poem emphasises the enduring power of his songs:

How beautifully sounds a truly inspired song
That stays in the world after the [author's] death.[106]

Although the portraits of Rubert and Krieger recorded their facial appearance for posterity, the abiding reputation of these musicians rested on their compositions existing in print and also in performance.

Composer portraits were a prominent feature of German printed music of the first half of the seventeenth century, occurring less frequently after 1650 with the decline of music printing. This section has complemented the customary iconographical studies of such portraits by interpreting

---

[103] 'War gleich bey uns Herr Kriger nicht gekrönt
So krönen ihn doch seine schöne Sachen.' Poem by David Schirmer in Adam Krieger, *Neue Arien* (Dresden, 1676), sig.):(2v. RISM A/I K2438.

[104] Skowronek, *Autorenbilder*, 188–92.

[105] 'So sihet Stirn und Mundt Herr Ruberts, dessen Sachen
Von süsser Lieblichkeidt und Sing-ahrt werden machen
Daß, wan er stirbt, nicht stirbt, Er zeiget damidt an,
Waß sein geschickter Geist vor Wercke machen kan.' Johann Martin Rubert, *Musicalische Seelen-Erquickung* (Stralsund, 1664), Bassus Generalis partbook. RISM A/I R3031.

[106] 'Wie schöne klingt ein wohlbeseeltes Lied
Das in der Welt / auch nach dem Tode bleibet.' Krieger, *Neue Arien*, sig.):(2v.

Individuality and Compositional Style

them in relation to material culture and debates about identity. By representing the composer as an authoritative or virtuous figure, such portraits encouraged readers who had no personal contact with the composer to trust the music book. Seeking to monumentalise the author, portraits also drew attention to the musical works that were the basis for a composer's ongoing reputation.

INDIVIDUALITY AND COMPOSITIONAL STYLE

Such questions of individuation and character lead to the final section of this chapter, on whether musicians could be recognised from the style of their compositions. That individual poets or musicians could be judged on the basis of their work was fundamental to the humanist and artisanal notions of production discussed in Chapter 1. Humanists searched for evidence of an author's mental prowess in his or her output. Artisans judged an individual's skill on the basis of the products of his or her hands. The following section discusses the debates about personal style in music, then analyses how Reincken represented his individual character and skill in a notated composition.

For most of the period discussed in this book, notions of musical style were shaped by the rhetorical code of decorum – whereby an orator chose a manner of communication suitable for the audience – and thus were closely related to the social function of compositions. Marco Scacchi's *c.*1646 classification of styles divided music into three branches (church, chamber, theatre) according to its venue. This taxonomy could be nuanced according to the compositional techniques used in each location. Christoph Bernhard's *Tractatus compositionis augmentatus* (*c.*1657) differentiated the types of counterpoint (*stylus gravis, stylus luxurians communis, stylus luxurians comicus*) associated with church, chamber and theatre, respectively.[107] In addition, Ciceronian rhetoric supplied the notion of different stylistic registers, whereby 'high style' included figurative language and grand effects, whereas 'low style' involved plain language and comic effects.[108] These different genera were applied to music in 1606 by Joachim Burmeister, who listed composers as examples of each style. Presumably he had specific works in mind when he identified Leonhard Lechner and Alexander Utendal as typifying the elevated style, Clemens

---

[107] Bernhard's terminology varies slightly in different parts of his treatise; see Joseph Müller-Blattau, *Die Kompositionslehre Heinrich Schützens in der Fassung seines Schülers Christoph Bernhard* (Leipzig: Breitkopf & Härtel, 1926), 42–43, 71, 82. On seventeenth-century taxonomies of styles, see Lorenzo Bianconi, *Music in the Seventeenth Century* (Cambridge: Cambridge University Press, 1987), 45–51; Claude V. Palisca, 'The Genesis of Mattheson's Style Classification', in George J. Buelow and Hans Joachim Marx (eds.), *New Mattheson Studies* (Cambridge: Cambridge University Press, 1983), 409–23.

[108] Cicero, *Orator* 21–27.

non Papa and Luca Marenzio as epitomising the middle style, and Gallus Dressler and Antonio Scandello as representing the low style.[109] Mattheson too spoke of high, medium and low styles, recognising these as subdivisions of the church, theatre and chamber styles.[110]

Such classifications indicated the importance of composing in a variety of styles to suit different occasions. Consequently musical discourse in the seventeenth century rarely emphasised the personal style of a composer. Johann Staden, evaluating a copy of Schein's *Opella nova Ander Theil* (1626) presented to the Nuremberg town council, confirmed that the pieces were 'set according to the current Italian style' (as was claimed on the title page of this collection).[111] Early in the eighteenth century, Johann Krieger emphasised the need for musicians to respect the boundaries between church, chamber and theatrical styles.[112] A composer who rigidly adhered to a fixed personal style would not show the sensitivity to an audience as required by the rhetorical code of decorum.

Yet a connection between musical style and personal idiom was recognised in Mattheson's 1717 definition of style (which he borrowed from the French lexicographer Sébastien de Brossard): 'Musical style is the manner and way that each person uses to compose, to perform and to communicate; and all these are to be greatly differentiated according to the genius of the author, of the country and of the people'.[113] Such a definition drew on humanist traditions which regarded style as a manifestation of an individual's nature. In his 1516 preface to his edition of St Jerome's works, Erasmus defined style in a wide-ranging manner, without reference to the social function of texts: 'The term style comprehends all at once a multiplicity of things – manner in language and diction, texture, so to speak, and further, thought and judgement, line of argumentation, inventive power, control of material, emotion, and what the Greeks call ethos'.[114] Following humanist ideas of how a person's character manifested itself in external signs, Erasmus argued: 'As each individual has his own appearance, his own voice, his own character and disposition, so each has his own style of writing'. Reinforcing the humanist emphasis on *ingenium*, he regarded style as 'an imaging of the mind in its every facet . . . whenever

---

[109] Joachim Burmeister, *Musica poetica* (Rostock, 1606), 75.

[110] Mattheson, *Der vollkommene Capellmeister* (Hamburg, 1739), 69.

[111] 'dem yetzigen Italienischen stylo . . . nicht vngemäß gesetzet'. Heinz Zirnbauer, *Der Notenbestand der Reichsstädtisch Nürnbergischen Ratsmusik: Eine bibliographische Rekonstruktion* (Nuremberg: Stadtbibliothek, 1959), 33.

[112] Letter from Johann Krieger, published in Johann Mattheson, *Critica musica* 2 (1725), 221.

[113] '*Stylus* in der Music wird von der Art und Weise verstanden/ welche eine jede Person vor sich zu *compon*iren/ zu *execut*iren und zu *inform*iren hat; und alles dieses ist sehr unterschieden nach Maßgebung des *Genii* der Verfasser/ des Landes und des Volckes'. Johann Mattheson, *Das beschützte Orchestre* (Hamburg, 1717), 115; trans. from Sébastien de Brossard, *Dictionaire de musique, contenant une explication des termes Grecs, Latins, Italiens, & François les plus usitez dans la musique* (Paris, 1703), s.v. 'Stilo'.

[114] *CWE* 61, 78.

Individuality and Compositional Style

the inner faculty exercises its power to produce something, all the peculiarities of the mind may be recognised in it, especially by a knowledgeable observer'.[115] Humanists valued personal style as an outward expression of mental attributes. As Petrarch said: 'I would much prefer my style to be my own, however rough and unrefined, but well fitted like a robe, made to measure for my *ingenium*'.[116]

Humanist notions of personal style occasionally appeared in the writings of musicians, even those who subscribed to the taxonomies of styles outlined above. In listing specific composers as examples of high, middle or low styles, Burmeister acknowledged that 'each of these has an individual disposition and style'.[117] Notions of individual style were elaborated by Johann Beer, concertmaster at the Weissenfels court from 1676/77 until his death in 1701. Beer's writings are so satirical and multi-voiced that it is hard to extract a consistent view towards musical authorship from them. Nonetheless he subscribed to elements of humanist notions of creativity, as indicated by his use of the proverb that musicians are born not made (see Chapter 1, p. 27). In his undated treatise 'Schola phonologica', Beer initially classified style in terms of compositional features. Recalling Bernhard's categories of *stylus gravis* and *stylus luxurians communis*, he coined the terms *kurtze stylus* and *lange stylus* to describe the short or long note-values used in different idioms.

Beer then digressed onto questions of personal style, declaring that 'another style is the *stylus genii* or the inborn musical nature that separates one composer from another ... What book is big enough to recount the differences in these styles?'[118] Alluding to the belief that physical appearance revealed individuality, Beer explained: 'Just as a composer resembles nobody else in the external lineaments of his face, therefore his new [composition] differs from most pieces by others'.[119] To support this claim, Beer quoted two settings of the words 'Kyrie eleison': both descend by a fifth to a D-Dorian final, but the long notes of the first version create a different character from the shorter notes and upper neighbour-note decoration in the second version (Example 3.1). Beer thus welcomed the

---

[115] Ibid., 79.

[116] 'multo malim meus michi stilus sit, incultus licet atque horridus, sed in morem toge habilis, ad mensuram ingenii mei factus'. Petrarch, *Epistole familiares* 22.2.16; quoted from Petrarca, *Le familiari*, iv, 106.

[117] 'unicuique horum propria est vena et stylus'. Burmeister, *Musica poetica*, 75.

[118] 'ein anders ist aber der *Stylus Genii* oder die angebohrne *Musicalische Natur* Vermittelst ein *Componist* von den andern ... Und welches Buch wäre groß genung, die *Differentien* des *Styli* zu erzehlen?' Musikbibliothek der Stadt Leipzig, Ms. I. 4° 37, fol. 131v; quoted from Johann Beer, *Sämtliche Werke*, vol. 12/ii: *Musikalische Schriften. Schola-Phonologica*, ed. Michael Heinemann (Bern: Peter Lang, 2005), 192–93.

[119] 'Wie der *Componist* dem andern nicht gleich siehet in den äuserl: *Liniamenten* des Gesichts, also *differiret* seine neul. *Form* von eben denselben in den meisten Stüken und zwar so sehr, daß wie man einen von den andern nach dem Gesicht unterscheiden kan ... ' Beer, *Sämtliche Werke*, vol. 12/ii, 193.

Example 3.1 Johann Beer, different settings of 'Kyrie eleison'. From 'Schola phonologica', Leipzig, Stadtbibliothek, Musikbibliothek, I.4° 37, fol. 131v.

differences in invention stemming from the temperaments of specific composers. Recalling humanist debates about whether *imitatio* should erase or encourage individuality, he added: 'I advise the pupil not to confine himself to absorbing another's style, because a forced nature rarely bakes straight pretzels. He keeps himself with good judgement to the fundamental rules and follows his *ingenium*'.[120]

Beer's musings on the importance of individual style led him to conclude that: 'by listening one can precisely distinguish whether a piece is by this or that author, provided one is already familiar with their work'.[121] He here echoed the humanist belief that individual style was an identifying feature of authors, composers and other artists. As Erasmus wrote in 1516: 'It is the sculptor who immediately recognises the work of a sculptor, the painter the work of a painter. The master musician knows the composer of a song from its harmonies. ... [But] some ploughman is not likely to see the difference between the work of Fulvius or Rutuba from that of Apelles or Zeuxis'.[122] Indeed, by the end of the seventeenth century, some composers' styles were so recognisable that their names became eponymous with specific idioms. Palestrina's name became a shorthand for strict counterpoint;[123] in central German lands, the name of Andreas Hammerschmidt denoted a simple and accessible style of church music.[124] Yet when a style becomes so familiar it can be imitated, it may no longer be a secure indicator of authorship. As with physiognomy and other efforts to discern individuals' natures from external signs, notions of personal style could lead to stereotyping rather than insights into individuality.

Nonetheless, notated compositions remained important indicators of the skill and talent of individual musicians, as is shown by contemporary discussion of Reincken's organ fantasia on the chorale *An Wasserflüssen Babylon*. Very little notated organ music by Reincken survives, possibly because he guarded his skills as secrets to be disclosed primarily in the

---

[120] 'Rathe Demnach dem *Scholar* durch aus nicht, was vor einen *Stÿlum* er an sich soll nehmen, weil die gezwungene *Natur* selten gerade Pretzeln bäckt. Er halte sich nur mit guthen *Judicio* an die Grund Regeln und folge seinen *genio* ... '. Ibid.
[121] 'also kan man sie nach dem Ohr genau *distingvir*en, wer nehml: zu diesen od. jenen *Author* seÿ, im fall ihre Arbeit zuvor etwas bekand ist'. Ibid.
[122] *CWE* 61, 78.
[123] For comments on composers such as Bernhard writing in 'the Palestrina style', see Mattheson, *Grundlage einer Ehren-Pforte*, 18.
[124] Johann Beer, *Musicalische Discurse* (Nuremberg, 1719), 70–73.

Individuality and Compositional Style

moment of improvisation. In 1732, however, Johann Gottfried Walther printed an anecdote suggesting that Reincken wrote down his setting of *An Wasserflüssen Babylon* to demonstrate his abilities. The anecdote appears in Walther's article on the Hamburg organist Heinrich Scheidemann:

> Scheidemann died in 1654 and was so famed for his composition and his playing that a great musician in Amsterdam, on hearing that Adam Reincken had taken Scheidemann's place, said: 'It must be an impertinent person who has taken upon himself to take the place of such a famed man, and [I] would be curious to see this person'. Reincken sent him his keyboard setting of the chorale *An Wasserflüssen Babylon* with the following statement: 'Here you may see a portrait of the impertinent person'. The Amsterdam musician then came to Hamburg, heard Reincken on the organ, and afterwards spoke to him, and in veneration kissed his hands.[125]

Although this anecdote cannot be verified, Reincken's description of the composition as a portrait suggests how it represented his bodily presence and mental character to someone unable to witness his improvisations in person. At 327 bars in length, Reincken's fantasia is one of the most ambitious pieces in the north German organ repertory; it can be related to artisanal and also humanist practices of identification.

Just as artisans showed their manual skill in their products, so too does Reincken's setting of *An Wasserflüssen Babylon* display how his hands and feet could shape sound from the keys and pipes of the organ. At the start, his right hand glosses the notes of the chorale (marked with crosses in Example 3.2) on the solo stops of the Rückpositiv, creating a monodic setting in the manner of his predecessor Scheidemann. Later his left hand and right hand show their propensity for virtuosic figuration, leading to hand-crossing as the momentum of the figuration pushes beyond the normal tessitura of each hand (bars 87–97, 101–7). Finally there are two sections involving double pedalling, showing how Reincken's technical control extends to using both feet simultaneously (bars 223–28, 322–27). Like the masterworks used by artisans to show their technical prowess, Reincken's musical 'portrait' demonstrates what he could craft with his embodied skills.

Reincken's 'portrait' also exemplified humanist notions of discerning an individual's mental virtues from external signs. Although the surviving

---

[125] 'Scheidemann ... ist an. 1654 gestorben, und so wohl wegen seiner Composition, als seines Spielens dergestalt berühmt gewesen, daß ein grosser *Musicus* zu Amsterdam, als er gehöret, daß Adam Reincke an des Scheidemanns Stelle gekommen, gesprochen: "es müsse dieser ein verwegener Mensch seyn, weil er sich verstanden, in eines so sehr berühmten Mannes Stelle zutreten, und wäre er wohl so *curieux*, denselben zu sehen." Reincke hat ihm hierauf den aufs Clavier gesetzten Kirchen-Gesang: An Wasser-Flüssen Babylon, mit folgender Beyschrifft zugesandt: Hieraus könne er des verwegenen Menschen *Portrait* ersehen. Der Amsterdammische *Musicus* ist hierauf selbst nach Hamburg gekommen, hat Reincken auf der Orgel gehöret, nachher gesprochen, und ihm, aus *veneration*, die Hände geküsset'. Johann Gottfried Walther, *Musicalisches Lexicon* (Leipzig, 1732), 547–48.

Example 3.2 Johann Adam Reincken, *An Wasserflüssen Babylon*, bars 16–23. Cantus firmus denoted by 'x'; initial motif indicated by 'y'.

sources of *An Wasserflüssen Babylon* do not bear any genre designation,[126] Reincken's contemporaries would have recognised it as evoking the fantasia. The fantasia style (*stylus phantasticus*) was defined by Athanasius Kircher as 'the most free and unrestrained method of composing … it was instituted to display *ingenium*'.[127] Kircher might have quibbled at Reincken's chorale setting being described as a fantasia, because his definition of the *stylus phantasticus* ('bound to nothing, neither to words nor to a melodic subject'[128]) excluded works based on existing tunes. Yet as Stefano Lorenzetti has shown, 'fantasia' carried Aristotelian associations as the prerequisite for thought and memory, transforming sensual perceptions into intellectual elaboration.[129] A musical fantasia hence might reveal the qualities nowadays described with the term 'imagination'.

---

[126] Reincken's *An Wasserflüssen Babylon* survives in manuscripts copied by the young Johann Sebastian Bach (D-WRz, Theol. Fol. 49/11) and by Bach's pupil Johann Christoph Altnickol (D-Bhm, H9364).

[127] 'est liberrima, & solutissima componendi methodus … ad ostentandum ingenium … institutus'. Athanasius Kircher, *Musurgia universalis sive ars magna consoni et dissoni*, 2 vols. (Rome, 1650), i, 585. On definitions of the *stylus phantasticus*, particularly Mattheson's modification of the term to indicate improvisatory freedom, see Kerala J. Snyder, *Dieterich Buxtehude: Organist in Lübeck*, 2nd edn (Rochester, NY: University of Rochester Press, 2007), 250–60.

[128] 'nullis, nec verbis, nec subiecto harmonico adstrictus'. Kircher, *Musurgia universalis*, i, 585.

[129] Stefano Lorenzetti, '"Scritte nella mente"? Giovanni Gabrieli's Keyboard Music and the Art of Improvised Composition', in Rodolfo Baroncini, David Bryant and Luigi Collarile (eds.), *Giovanni Gabrieli. Transmission and Reception of a Venetian Musical Tradition* (Turnhout: Brepols, 2016), pp. 135–48 (pp. 137–38).

Individuality and Compositional Style 115

Reincken's fantasia on *An Wasserflüssen Babylon* amply demonstrates his ability to generate and elaborate upon musical materials. At the start, the notes of the chorale (marked with crosses in Example 3.2) are hidden within a melody of his own devising, in which each phrase starts with a distinctive initial motif jumping down and up an octave (motif *y* in Example 3.2). The more contrapuntal sections also show his ingenuity, for instance when he sets the second line of the chorale against an imitative counter-subject that recalls motif *y* (bars 42–81). Later passages juxtapose strongly contrasting material and again display his capacity to generate new ideas (bars 264–71). As Chapter 1 explained, a talent for musical invention was regarded as indicating the prized quality of *ingenium* in a composer. Just as proponents of physiognomy argued that facial appearance could reveal inner attributes such as virtue, so did Reincken's use of the term 'portrait' imply that his chorale fantasia reveals his mental powers of *ingenium*. The notated composition simulates his presence at the keyboard for those unable to witness his improvisations, justifying his status before the sceptical organist of Amsterdam.

At the start of this chapter, Beer's anecdote about Adam Krieger suggested that an individual's identity could be recognised from his or her actions. Artisans believed that craftworkers could be identified via the products crafted by their hands. Humanists believed that the character and morals of individuals could be discerned from their deeds. This chapter has offered the first account of how seventeenth-century musicians engaged with debates about identification, especially via techniques for authenticating their notated works. Because the sound of their music could be only imperfectly captured in printed or manuscript notation, composers felt the necessity to assert their presence in these written sources. Reincken's fantasia on *An Wasserflüssen Babylon* shows how one musician projected his distinctive character in a notated composition, displaying the physical and mental attributes that gave him his professional and social status.

CHAPTER 4

Rites of Musical Ownership

Many Lutherans of the sixteenth and seventeenth centuries would have been bemused by the claim that music can be owned. As an auditory phenomenon, music was recognised as transient, decaying as soon as it sounds, yet able to cross barriers. Philipp Melanchthon noted the mysterious power of molecules vibrating in the air to penetrate human minds and imprint themselves on the memory.[1] Accounts of the early Reformation celebrated how individuals were converted to Protestantism by the power of musical sound, for instance by a song carried on the wind across a field.[2] Yet, as already remarked, music also existed as material objects, and this chapter is concerned with the attempts of musicians to control the ownership of their notated works. Besides the control of the circulation of physical copies, did composers have any sense of intangible property in their works? Did they have a right to have their name associated with copies of their compositions? Did they have a right to profit from the sale of copies of their compositions?

Modern notions of intellectual property emphasise economic rights and moral rights. Economic rights entitle authors to profit financially from their works. As Mark Rose has shown, the concept of economic rights partly derives from the possessive individualism of John Locke.[3] Locke argued that individuals make objects their own by adding their own manual or intellectual labour: 'Whatsoever then he removes out of the State that Nature hath provided, and left it in, he hath mixed his Labour with it, and joined to it something that is his own, and thereby makes it his Property.'[4] In 1759 Edward Young developed this argument in respect of authorship, telling writers that originality ('to prefer the native growth of thy own mind to the richest import from abroad') allowed them to claim

---

[1] Philipp Melanchthon's preface to Lucas Lossius, *Psalmodia, hoc est cantica sacra veteris ecclesiae selecta* (Nuremberg, 1553), sig. A3v. RISM A/I L2874.
[2] Matthew Laube, 'Materializing Music in the Lutheran Home', *Past & Present* 234, suppl. 12 (2017), 114–38 (p. 120).
[3] Mark Rose, *Authors and Owners: The Invention of Copyright* (Cambridge, MA: Harvard University Press, 1993), 4–5.
[4] John Locke, *Two Treatises on Government* (London, 1690), 245–46.

Rites of Musical Ownership

their works as their 'sole property'.[5] According to modern copyright law, economic rights are earned via an author's originality, usually defined as the result of individual skill, labour, effort and judgement.[6] Additionally there is the notion of moral rights, whereby authors are entitled to have their names associated with their works, and to object to distorted forms of their works that might detract from their reputation.

In 1962 the legal historian Hansjörg Pohlmann claimed that German composers of the sixteenth and seventeenth centuries were pioneers in asserting economic and moral rights over their works.[7] Pohlmann based his claim partly on a study of musicians who complained at the corrupt transmission of their compositions, but mainly on a study of imperial and Saxon printing privileges held by musicians. These privileges granted an author or bookseller an exclusive right to publish specified works for a limited period (usually ten years); they threatened confiscation of any unauthorised copies and fines for anyone caught printing or selling them. Pohlmann interpreted the privileges as an early system of copyright, describing them as 'rights of protection for creators, a formal confirmation of the exclusive publication rights of authors already won by virtue of their creative work, for the purpose of faster, more effective enforcement against copyright infringements'.[8] He even compared the 'Cum gratia et privilegio' rubric on a title page with the © sign.[9] Yet, as this chapter will show, such teleological interpretations are highly problematic: they assume an attitude of self-assertion among composers, ignoring the religious and political realities that subjugated musicians to the dual authority of God and earthly rulers.

This chapter offers a historically nuanced account of ideas of musical ownership in German-speaking lands during the long seventeenth century. It begins by referring to the models of musical creativity discussed in Chapter 1, showing how Lutheran theology required musicians to follow an ideology of sharing for the common good. Only princes could legitimately defy the imperative to share the musical products of God's gifts. Princely authority also underpinned the privileges that in exceptional cases gave composers an exclusive right to publish their works for a limited period. Using a wealth of newly unearthed archival documentation, I reconstruct the workings of the privilege system and ask whether these legal instruments provided composers with effective defence against pirate

---

[5] Edward Young, *Conjectures on Original Composition* (London, 1759), 53–54.

[6] Andreas Rahmatian, 'The Elements of Music Relevant for Copyright Protection', in Andreas Rahmatian (ed.), *Concepts of Music and Copyright: How Music Perceives Itself and How Copyright Perceives Music* (Cheltenham: Edward Elgar Publishing, 2015), 78–122 (p. 105).

[7] Hansjörg Pohlmann, *Die Frühgeschichte des musikalischen Urheberrechts (ca.1400–800). Neue Materialien zur Entwicklung des Urheberrechtsbewußtseins der Komponisten* (Kassel: Bärenreiter, 1962), 259.

[8] Ibid., 189.   [9] Ibid., 190.

publishers. The chapter then discusses how notions of musical ownership changed with the decline of music printing after 1650, including how musicians such as Johann Caspar Kerll sought to control the scribal transmission of their compositions. By examining debates about musical ownership in conjunction with evidence of how the music trade was regulated, this chapter aims to understand better the relationship between individual musicians and wider society in the period.

COMMON GOOD VERSUS PRINCELY SECRECY

In German-speaking lands during the sixteenth century and for much of the seventeenth century, the ideology of the common good (*Gemeinnutz*) regulated individuals' attempts to profit from their own labour. *Gemein* denoted the collective, whether comprising the citizens of a town or the subjects in a prince's territory; *Gemeinnutz* was used in sixteenth-century ordinances and legal cases to indicate how individuals should regulate their behaviour in the interests of the community.[10] *Gemeinnutz* was often contrasted with *Eigennutz* (self-interest), in which individuals pursued their interests to the disadvantage (*Schaden*, *Nachteil*) of others. The notion of *Gemeinnutz* had classical antecedents (for instance, Aristotle's concept of *utilitas communis*), and its importance was reinforced by Lutheran theology.[11] The following section shows how the theological doctrine of serving the community clashed with artisanal and princely attempts to control the circulation of knowledge.

As explained in Chapter 1, the theological model of creativity regarded human abilities as gifts of God. Luther taught that Christians should use their talents to help their neighbours, rather than pursuing introspective practices such as monasticism or the Catholic doctrine of 'good works'. In his *Von der Freiheit eines Christenmenschen* (1520), he declared: 'See, according to this rule God's gifts should flow from one to another and be common to all, so that everyone should treat his neighbour as though he were himself. From Christ flow to us the things that he has undertaken in his life, as if he had been that which we are.'[12] Lutheran theology thus recognised the distinct abilities of each individual, while imposing an obligation to serve the wider community.

Many musicians adhered to the Lutheran doctrine of service, arguing that they should reciprocate God's gifts by sharing the fruits of their talents

---

[10] Winfried Schulze, 'Vom Gemeinnutz zum Eigennutz. Über den Normenwandel in der ständischen Gesellschaft der frühen Neuzeit', *Historische Zeitschrift* 243 (1986), 591–626.

[11] Ernst-Wilhelm Kohls, *Die Schule bei Martin Bucer in ihrem Verhältnis zu Kirche und Obrigkeit* (Heidelberg: Quelle & Meyer, 1963), 121–28.

[12] 'Sihe also mussen gottis gutter fliessen auß eynem yn den andern und gemeyn werden, das ein yglicher sich seynis nehsten also annehm, als were erß selb. Auß Christo fliessen sie yn uns, der sich unser hatt angenommen ynn seynem lebenn, als were er das gewesen, das wir sein'. *WA* 7, 37.

Common Good versus Princely Secrecy   119

for the common good. In his first published collection, *Venus Kräntzlein* (1609), Johann Hermann Schein explained: 'That which is good should itself be communicated, and this and other gifts of God should not be hidden under a bushel, but should be dispersed for the use of one's neighbour'.[13] Similar comments were made by Johann Rosenmüller and Andreas Hammerschmidt in the prefaces to their printed music.[14] In the code of conduct appended to his novel *Der musicalische Quack-Salber* (1700), Kuhnau advised: 'Because each and every person must have learned his profession to the end of serving God and the world, a musician has to display the products of his skills.'[15] Alluding to the Parable of the Talents (Luke 19:12–27), he warned that a musician who hides God-given talents 'would be suspected of laziness for not having taken the effort to profit properly from the investment made in him'.[16] Even in the 1710s, Bach upheld this Lutheran doctrine of service, as shown by his couplet on the title page of the *Orgel-Büchlein*: 'To the highest God in his honour/ To my neighbour, that he may instruct himself from it.'[17]

The Lutheran emphasis on serving the common good clashed with the practices of early capitalism. In a 1524 sermon on trade and usury, Luther condemned merchants who subscribed to the view that: 'I sell my wares for as much as I can get.'[18] Such self-interest, he alleged, was tantamount to saying: 'So long as I have my profit and satisfy my greed, what does it matter to me, if I harm my neighbour in ten ways at once?'[19] Luther also criticised greed (*Geitz*) in the book trade, attacking in 1545 the publishers who issued his writings and Bible translations without his permission: 'Seeking their own profit, they do not care for the accuracy of what they print ... They just print it quickly, to make money.'[20] Luther clarified that he was not financially motivated himself, but rather concerned that the Word of God be disseminated as widely and as accurately as possible. 'It is not for my own sake, though, that I am concerned, since freely have

---

[3] 'quod bonum sit suit communicativum, Vnd das solche vnd andere Gaben Gottes nicht vnterm Scheiffel verborgen gehalten/ Sondern zum nutz des Nehesten außgebreitet werden solten'. Schein, *Venus Kräntzlein … Newe Weltliche Lieder* (Leipzig, 1609), tenor partbook, sig. A2r. RISM A/I S1374.

[4] Johann Rosenmüller, *Andere Kern-Sprüche* (Leipzig, 1652–3), Prima Vox partbook, sig. A3v; Andreas Hammerschmidt, *Geistliche Gespräche über die Evangelia* (Dresden, 1655), Sechste Stimme partbook, sig. Aaaaaa2v–Aaaaaa3r. RISM A/I R2549, H1948.

[5] 'Denn/ weil doch ein jeder Mensch seine *Profession* zu dem Ende muß gelernet haben/ daß er GOtt und der Welt damit dienen soll; So wird freylich auch ein *Musicus* … die Waaren seiner Künste auspacken'. Johann Kuhnau, *Der musicalische Quack-Salber* (Dresden, 1700), 517.

[6] '[E]r würde wegen der Faulheit verdächtig werden/ daß er sich nicht die Mühe nehmen/ und mit dem ihm anvertraueten Pfunde recht wuchern wolte'. Ibid., 518.

[7] 'Dem Höchsten Gott allein' zu Ehren/ Dem Nechsten, draus sich zu belehren'. *BDok* 1, 214 (no. 148).

[8] 'Ich mag meyne wahr so thewr geben alls ich kan'. *WA* 15, 294.

[9] 'Hette ich nur meynen gewynn und geytz vol, was gehet michs an, das es zehen schaden meynem nehisten thet auff eyn mal?' Ibid.

[20] 'Denn weil sie allein yhren geitz suchen fragen sie wenig darnach, wie recht oder falsch sie es hin nach drucken … Sie machens hin, rips raps. Es gilt gelt'. *WA Deutsche Bibel* 8, 8.

I received, freely have I given, and I desire nothing in return. Christ my Lord has repaid me many hundred and thousand times over.'[21]

Such disquiet at self-interest in the book trade was echoed by Michael Praetorius, who denied any desire to profit from his many publications of sacred music. His *Musae Sioniae Achter Teil* (1610) included the following remarks, purportedly an address by the printer to the reader (*Typographus lectori candido s[alve]*) but possibly an example of the composer writing in the third person:

The favourable reader and music-lover shall know that the author has never sought money in mercenary fashion, seeking private profit through remuneration and counter-rewards. But, because the work has become somewhat extensive and because the cantors in all towns do not always have the wealth to buy this work, the author has many times … given out his *Musae Sioniae* German and Latin … in good intentions with the right hand, to good friends and music-lovers from a willing heart, without any concern for being sent remuneration. For him it is sufficient reward that his modest work is accepted and welcomed not by everyone (that would be impossible) but by some.[22]

The metaphor of giving music away 'with the right hand' is later clarified by a variant of a proverb: 'What he gives charitably with the right hand, he does not take away with the evil left hand, but would leave as his favourable desire.'[23] With these claims of disinterested donations, Praetorius placed his publications within the system of gift exchange sanctioned by Luther.

Praetorius similarly disavowed any desire for remuneration when presenting copies of his printed music to institutions. In 1608 he sent copies of his *Musarum Sioniarum motectae et psalmi latini* and *Musae Sioniae Fünffter Theil* to the town council of Mühlhausen. In his covering letter he wrote: 'I ask nothing more than my desire that [the music] be understood and accepted for the best, and I do not want to be imputed with pursuing a reward'.[24] Yet in early modern society, to accept a gift carried an obligation

---

[21] 'Wiewol meinet halben daran nichts gelegen, Denn ich habs vmb sonst empfangen, vmb sonst hab ichs gegeben, vnd begere auch dafur nichts, Christus mein HErr hat mirs viel hundert tausentfeltig vergolten'. Ibid., 7.

[22] 'So wolle der günstige Leser vnd Liebhaber der *Music* wissen/ das der *Autor* durchauß keinen Geltkram darmit auffgeschlagen/ seinen *privat* Nutz vnd Gewinn durch *remunerationes* vnnd gegenvorehrungen zu suchen/ sondern weil das Werck etwas weitleufftig werden wollen/ vnd alle *Cantores* in Städten offt des vermügens nicht seyn/ solch Werck einzukeuffen: Er der *Autor* … solche seine *Musas Sionias* Teutsche vnd Lateinische … wolmeinent mit rechter Handt herfür zugeben/ guten Freunden vnd *Musices amatoribus* von Hertzen willig vnd gerne/ ohne einige entgeltnuß mitzutheilen/ kein bedencken getragen: vnd sich alleine darmit *contentiret*, das sein geringes Wercklin/ wo nicht bey allen (welches vnmüglich) jedoch bey etlichen angenehm vnd willkommen seyn möchte'. Praetorius, *Musae Sioniae* … *Achter Theil* (Wolfenbüttel, 1610), Cantus partbook, sig. A3r. RISM A/I P5357.

[23] 'was er mit der RECHTEN mildiglich gegeben/ nicht mit der LINKEN vbel deutendt auffnehmen/ sondern sich günstiger massen mit belieben lassen wolle'. Ibid.

[24] 'Nichts mehr bittend noch begehrend, denn daß es im besten Verstanden vnndt uffgenommen, vnnd mir nicht einigem recompens dadurch nachzustellen, imputieret werden möchte …' Quoted

Common Good versus Princely Secrecy 121

to reciprocate it. The Mühlhausen council did reward Praetorius, to judge from a letter two years later in which he thanked them.[25] By claiming not to be interested in a reward, Praetorius paid at least lip service to the Lutheran belief that individuals should serve their neighbours.

The Lutheran doctrine of service was resisted by singers and instrumentalists who adhered to rival notions of music's social function. The artisanal view of musical workmanship discussed in Chapter 1 encouraged guild-like secrecy among some instrumentalists. Just as artisans protected their economic status by disclosing skills only to their apprentices, so too did instrumentalists guard the expertise and repertory that were the source of their income as performers and teachers. While there was a clear economic basis for such behaviour, it gave rise to the stereotype of secretive instrumentalists obstructing the common good. In 1571 the organist at the Thomaskirche in Leipzig, Elias Nikolaus Ammerbach, justified the publication of his *Orgel und Instrument Tabulatur* by criticising self-interested keyboardists: 'Many teachers keep this art completely hidden and secret, and do not honestly and thoroughly instruct their pupils, thereby causing many of them to think that this art cannot be learned thoroughly or correctly understood, and often the pupils abandon it altogether'.[26] By providing a guide to tablature notation and keyboard fingering (along with 90 intabulations of popular songs, dances and sacred polyphony), Ammerbach offered a way to learn keyboard playing outside an apprenticeship.

Jealous keyboardists were also attacked by Michael Praetorius in 1612. He claimed that a few years earlier, when he announced his intention to publish a book of organ music,[27] he was criticised by keyboardists wanting to keep their repertory secret:

They presumed I would make this [repertory] completely public, and that all organists and others, even half-musicians, would stuff their mouths with it, so that each and every organist should and could perform their duty with fame and status. Accordingly, if I should carry nothing more than criticism, hatred, envy and ingratitude (which are not unfamiliar to me), I can easily spare the effort, labour and expense. But it is nothing less than shameful envy and resentment, which

---

in Markus Rathey, 'Ein unbekanntes Mühlhäuser Musikalienverzeichnis aus dem Jahre 1617', *Die Musikforschung* 51 (1998), 63–69 (pp. 68–69).

[25] Ibid.

[26] 'viel Meister solche Kunst gantz verborgen vnd heimlich halten/ vnd ihren Discipulis nicht trewlich vnd gründlich mittheilen/ dadurch ihrer viel verursacht werden/ das sie meinen/ als könne diese kunst nicht gründlich vnd richtig gelehret vnd gefasset werden/ vnd offtmals dieselben gantz vnd gar fahren lassen'. Elias Nikolaus Ammerbach, *Orgel oder Instrument Tabulatur* (Leipzig, 1571), sig.)(3v–)(4r. RISM B/I 1571[17].

[27] In 1609 Praetorius announced that he would publish '*Tocaten ... Fugen, Phantasien* vnd *Concerten,* auff zwo *Claviren,* &c in der deutschen Orgel*Tabulatur*'; see his *Musae Sioniae ... Siebender Theil* (Wolfenbüttel, 1609), cantus partbook, sig.):(3v. RISM A/I P5355.

begrudges other good journeymen (who lack the necessary means, yet give great money for a little ornamented piece and similar things).[28]

Praetorius's reference to journeymen (those travelling craftworkers who had not yet gained the status of master) confirms that his criticism was aimed at artisanal attitudes. For Praetorius, such protectionism was contrary to the Lutheran doctrine of service. He instead appealed to Teutonic patriotism to support his ideal of sharing for the common good: 'For it befits us Germans ... to live as brothers and more in common than other peoples, who have advanced their nation by letting their things be published'.[29]

The persistence of artisanal attitudes partly explains why so little solo instrumental music was published in German lands during the seventeenth century. It also accounts for the behaviour of organists such as Johann Heinrich Buttstett, who refused to share all his manuscripts with his pupils.[30] Kuhnau, however, satirised the attitude that 'if someone has a beautiful piece, he would rather let himself be stripped of his jacket and trousers, than communicate one note to another musician'.[31] He then recounted: 'I know that once an excellent organist in the presence of an attentive devotee played as if his fingers were weighted with lead and as if his main studies had been intabulations of Hammerschmidt's motets, even though he knew there was another person present who could recommend him to a great prince and thus help him gain an imposing salary'.[32] As mentioned in Chapter 3, Hammerschmidt's name was a byword for the

---

[28] 'Sintemahl sie vermeynen/ ich würde dergestaldt alles gar zugemeyn machen/ vnd jedem Organisten vnd andern/ auch *Semimusicis*, gleichsamb ins Maul streichen/ wie eins vnd anders solle vnd könne der gebür/ mit ruhm vnd bestandt/ gemacht vnd angeordnet werden/ Wohero ich denn auch solcher Mühe/ Arbeit vnd Vnkosten/ wenn ich nicht mehr als Klügeln/ Haß/ Neyd vnd Vndanck/ welches mir zwar nichts newes/ darvon haben vnd tragen solte/ gar wol kan vberhoben seyn. Es ist aber nichts anders als der leidige Neydhart vnd Abgunst/ vnd daß man andern guten Gesellen (so das vermögen vnd die *Sumptus* nicht haben/ groß Geldt vnd Verehrung vor ein klein *colorirtes* oder *diminuirtes* Stücklein/ vnd dergleichen Sachen/ zugeben) nichts gönnet'. Michael Praetorius, *Terpsichore* (Wolfenbüttel, 1612), Cantus partbook, sig. (:)3v. RISM A/I P5366.
[29] 'Welchs dann vns Deutschen (die wir daher *Germani* heissen/ daß wir als Brüder miteinander leben/ vnd solche Vnahrt von vns nicht hören lassen solten) vmb soviel mehr in gemein geziemet/ Alldieweil je andere Völcker/ ihrer *Nation* zum besten/ ihre Sachen *publiciren* zulassen/ kein bedencken tragen'. Ibid.
[30] Johann Gottfried Walther, *Briefe*, ed. Klaus Beckmann and Hans-Joachim Schulze (Leipzig: Deutscher Verlag für Musik, 1987), 68–69.
[31] 'Wenn einer etwa ein schönes Stücke hat/ so ließ er sich wohl eher Wamst und Hosen ausziehen/ ehe er dem andern eine *Note communicir*te'. Kuhnau, *Der musicalische Quack-Salber*, 518–19.
[32] 'Ich weiß/ daß ehmahls ein *excellent*er Organist in eines andern auffmercksamen Liebhabers Gegenwart so spielte/ als wenn ihm Bley an den Fingern hienge/ und als wenn er sich die Hammerschmiedischen *Motetten* zu seinem grösten *Studio* in die *Tabulatur* gesetzet hätte; ungeachtet er wuste/ daß ein anderer sich in der Gesellschafft befand/ welcher ihn an einen grossen Fürsten *recommendir*en/ und ihm also zu einem stattlichen jährlichen *Salario* helffen konte'. Ibid., 519.

Common Good versus Princely Secrecy 123

unsophisticated music of village churches. The anecdote demonstrated how the organist's self-interest prevented him gaining credit for his true skill, and therefore reinforced Kuhnau's advice that musicians should use their God-given talents to serve their neighbours.

Princes, however, could legitimately resist the notion of sharing music for the common good. As feudal overlords, princes had a proprietorial claim over their servants including musicians. This sense of ownership was intensified by models of absolutism arriving in the late sixteenth century from Italy, which emphasised the mystique and opacity of princely life. According to one of the interlocutors in the 1599 German translation of Stefano Guazzo's *La civil conversatione*, 'it is not for us to speak of [princes'] doings, which remain irreprehensible and beyond comprehension'.[33] To maintain their social distinction, aristocrats deemed certain musical repertories to be exclusive to the court, as cultural trophies to be experienced only by favoured guests.

From the late sixteenth century onwards, the contracts of German court musicians often forbade them from circulating music beyond the court. At the Saxon court in Dresden, this stipulation first appeared in the 1568 Kantoreiordnung made on the occasion of the appointment of Antonio Scandello as capellmeister. The ordinance instructed him to write 'Latin, German and Italian-texted songs' to be performed by the choirboys as table music, but then specified:

[We] will not permit these and other songs composed for us (which we allowed to be registered and written down) to be made public. We also herewith command that our capellmeister forbid and prevent the copyists from copying motets and sending them elsewhere[34].

This clause was maintained in the 1592 Kantoreiordnung during the tenure of Rogier Michael as capellmeister;[35] and although no Kantoreiordnung exists from Schütz's time in Dresden, he probably had a similar prohibition placed on him. The same ban on circulating court music was imposed on other German capellmeisters (at Stuttgart, for instance, in Leonhard Lechner's 1595 contract and Basilius Froberger's 1621 certificate

---

[33] 'es vns nicht anstehet/ von ihren Handtlungen zuredeⸯn/ welche vnsträfflich/ vnd gleichsam vnerforschlich seyn.' Stefano Guazzo, *De civili conversatione, das ist von dem Bürgerlichen Wandel vnd zierlichen Sitten*, German edn (Frankfurt am Main, 1599), 188.

[34] '[Wir] wollen nicht gestattenn das solche vnd anndere gesenge so vns componirt werdenn vnd [die] wir ingrossiren vnd notiren lassenn, gemein werdenn, befelen auch hiemit vnserm capelmeister das ehr solches verhutte, vnnd denn notistenn nicht gestatte, einige muteten abtzuschreiben vnd andⸯerⸯs wohin zuschicken'. D-Dla, Loc. 32435, Rep. 28, Cantorey Ordnung nr. 2, fol. 8v.

[35] The 1568 ordinance (see note above) survives in a version with deletions and additions to adapt it for the 1592 edict. Partial transcription of 1592 edict in Reinhard Kade, 'Der Dresdener Kapellmeister Rogier Michael', *Vierteljahresschrift für Musikwissenschaft* 5 (1889), 272–89 (p. 280).

of appointment);[36] it continued to be a feature of courtly contracts until the late eighteenth century.[37]

Because of these stipulations of secrecy, court musicians required the consent of their patron before publishing compositions. The 1604 contract of Michael Praetorius as capellmeister at the Wolfenbüttel court specified that he could not publish his compositions written for courtly use without his prince's prior knowledge.[38] Glimpses of the procedure for requesting permission can be found in correspondence at the Dresden court. On 26 August 1575, Elector August wrote to the court printer Gimel Berg, explaining that 'our capellmeister, Antonio Scandello, has humbly desired of us with the enclosed supplication, that you be permitted to print the songs which he has composed. We have graciously agreed to this'.[39] The publication in question was Scandello's 1575 book of German partsongs, whose official status is shown by the large electoral coat of arms in the prefatory material, and the dedication thanking the Elector for his 'most gracious permission'.[40]

Schütz likewise had to gain the Elector's consent to publish music originally written for the Dresden court. In a letter of 15 April 1618, he thanked Johann Georg I for granting permission for the publication of the *Psalmen Davids*, which eventually appeared in print the following year: 'Your Electoral Grace will most graciously remember that some time ago I most humbly informed you about the planned publication of some of my slight compositions. At that time my intention met with Your Electoral Grace's most gracious favour'.[41] It is not surprising that Johann Georg allowed the *Psalmen Davids* to be published: this collection showcased the Italianate polychoral writing that put the Dresden court at the vanguard of musical fashion, yet its use of German Biblical texts proclaimed the

---

[36] Josef Sittard, *Zur Geschichte der Musik und des Theaters am württembergischen Hof*, 2 vols. (Stuttgart: Kohlhammer, 1890), i, 29, 44–45.

[37] Samantha Owens, '"Zum Fürstl: Hoff Staat gehörige Musicalien": The Ownership and Dissemination of German Court Music, 1665–c.750', in Konstanze Musketa and Barbara Reul (eds.), *Musik an der Zerbster Residenz: Bericht über die internationale Wissenschaftliche Konferenz vom 10. bis 12. April 2008 im Rahmen der 10. Internationalen Fasch-Festtage in Zerbst*, Fasch-Studien 10 (Beeskow: Ortus, 2008), 103–15 (p. 109).

[38] 'die [Gesänge] komponierte ohn Unser Vorwissen in öffentlichen Druck nicht geben'. Walter Deeters, 'Alte und neue Aktenfunde über Michael Praetorius', *Braunschweigisches Jahrbuch* 52 (1971), 102–20 (p. 103).

[39] 'Uns hat unser cappelmeister Antonius Scandellus mit inliegender supplication unterthänigst angelangt, dir zu vergönnen, dass du ihm etzliche gesenge so er componirt in druck verfertigen möchtest. Darauf haben wir gnädigst bewilligt . . . ' D-Dla, Kopiale 407 (1575), fol. 12v.

[40] Antonio Scandello, *Nawe schöne außerlesene geistliche Deudsche Lieder* (Dresden, 1575), tenor partbook, sig. Aa2v. RISM A/I S1155.

[41] 'Eur‹e› Churf‹ürstlichen› G‹naden› werden sich noch gnedigst zuerrinnern wißen, wie deroselben vor dieser zeitt, ich wegen vorhabender publication etlicher meiner wenigen composition vnderthenigst zu vorstehen geben habe, welche meine intention Eur‹en› Churf‹ürstlichen› G‹naden› Ihr damals . . . gantz gnedigst gefallen'. D-Dla, Loc. 10757/2, fol. 85r; see also *SDok* 1, 65; *HSR*, 21.

Elector's status as a defender of Lutheranism. The reputations of both Schütz and the Elector were enhanced by the publication of these polychoral psalms.

The value of other court repertories, however, depended on their exclusivity. Such was the case with certain pieces that Orlande de Lassus wrote for Duke Albrecht V of Bavaria. As Samuel Quickelberg, the Munich court librarian, wrote in 1565: 'Although compositions by Lassus are indeed to be found in great abundance everywhere in the world, there are nonetheless many more which are at present held apart by his prince, who does not in the least want to share them with the vulgar crowd'.[42] Chief among these withheld pieces were Lassus's *Prophetiae Sibyllarum*, Penitential Psalms and *Sacrae Lectiones ex Propheta Job*. The rarefied style of these pieces is exemplified by the chromatic opening of the *Prophetiae Sibyllarum* and the intense text-expression of the Penitential Psalms. Quickelberg commended the Psalms for 'expressing the force of the individual affections and in placing the object almost alive before the eyes',[43] and described them as 'musica reservata', the term commonly used for repertories solely for courtly cognoscenti.[44] Albrecht sought to keep both the Penitential Psalms and *Prophetiae Sibyllarum* for his exclusive use. In 1563 he asked Johann Jakob Fugger to apprehend the copyist Jan Pollet, who had stolen a manuscript of the Penitential Psalms and reportedly fled to the Low Countries.[45] The Penitential Psalms were printed only in 1584, five years after Albrecht's death, while the *Prophetiae Sibyllarum* remained relatively inaccessible until a posthumous edition appeared in 1600. Even though Lassus made heavy use of printed publication to disseminate his music and increase his fame, Albrecht's princely power required parts of his output to be kept exclusive to the Munich court. A similar desire to maintain the prestige of rarefied repertories may explain why the Italian musicians at the Dresden court in the 1650s, such as Vincenzo Albrici and Marco Giuseppe Peranda, never put their compositions into print.

Throughout the long seventeenth century, many Lutheran musicians believed that their compositions were a gift from God that should be shared for the common good. Solo instrumentalists who followed artisanal

---

[42] 'Tametsi vero Orlandinae cantiones ubique terrarum extent maxima copia, sunt tamen adhuc plura, quae subinde principi suo separatim custodiunt, quae is vulgari minime permittit'. Heinrich Pantaleon, *Prosopographiae heroum atque illustrium virorum totius Germaniae*, 3 vols. (Basel, 1565–66), iii, 542.

[43] 'singularum affectuum vim exprimendo, rem quasi actam ante oculos ponendo, expressit'. Quoted in Orlande de Lassus, *Sämtliche Werke*, Neue Reihe, vol. 26: *Sieben Busspsalmen*, ed. Horst Leuchtmann (Kassel: Bärenreiter, 1995), xvi.

[44] 'Hoc quidem musicae genus MUSICAM RESERVATAM vocant'. Ibid., xvii.

[45] Ignace Bossuyt, 'The Copyist Jan Pollet and the Theft in 1563 of Orlandus Lassus's "Secret" Penitential Psalms', in Albert Clement and Eric Jas (eds.), *From Ciconia to Sweelinck: Donum natalicium Willem Elders* (Amsterdam: Rodopi, 1994), 261–67.

126 *Rites of Musical Ownership*

traditions of secrecy might be condemned as self-interested and jealous. Only princes, on account of their divinely ordained status, could defy the ideal of *Gemeinnutz* and withhold music for themselves. The following section examines how musicians could assume some of this princely authority by applying for printing privileges.

PRIVILEGES AS PRINCELY PROTECTION

Printing privileges offered authors or publishers time-limited rights of protection for specific books. Hundred of music books from the decades around 1600 indicate a privilege on their title page with statements such as 'Cum gratia et privilegio', but these rubrics reveal little about how the privilege system functioned. More informative are the archival records of privilege applications in the Österreichisches Staatsarchiv, Vienna, and the Hauptsächsisches Staatsarchiv, Dresden. Elsewhere I have reported in detail on my systematic research into these records and the insights they offer into the music trade in the period.[46] This section summarises that research in order to gain a more nuanced understanding of privileges than Pohlmann's teleological interpretation of them as forerunners of copyright. A privilege was a 'special favour and liberty'[47] granted to an individual, a form of recognition gained when that individual subjected himself or herself to the authority of a prince. Here I examine the application process to illuminate the negotiations involved in granting a privilege. I also investigate the rhetoric used in privileges and applications, showing how individual recognition was reconciled with the ideal of the common good, and which kinds of labour were protected by privileges.

In the mosaic of jurisdictions over German-speaking lands in the early seventeenth century, printing privileges were most frequently granted by the Holy Roman Emperor or the Elector of Saxony.[48] An imperial privilege was valid throughout the Holy Roman Empire, but had particular relevance to the twice-yearly book fair at Frankfurt am Main, which was regulated by the imperial book commission. The commission could confiscate any book sold at the Frankfurt fair that infringed an imperial privilege, and it required booksellers at the fair to display any imperial

---

[46] Stephen Rose, 'Protected Publications: The Imperial and Saxon Privileges for Printed Music, 1550–700', *Early Music History* 37 (2018), 247–313.

[47] 'besondere gnade gethan, vnd freyheit gegeben'. From the imperial printing privilege granted to Schütz on 3 April 1637, A-Whh, Impressoria, Karton 61, Konvolut 1, no. 3, fol. 5r.

[48] Overviews of printing privileges include Ian Maclean, *Scholarship, Commerce, Religion: The Learned Book in the Age of Confessions, 1560–630* (Cambridge, MA: Harvard University Press, 2012), 134–51; Ludwig Gieseke, *Vom Privileg zum Urheberrecht: die Entwicklung des Urheberrechts in Deutschland bis 1845* (Göttingen: Schwartz 1995); Hans-Joachim Koppitz, 'Die Privilegia impressoria des Haus-, Hof- und Staatsarchivs in Wien', *Gutenberg-Jahrbuch* 69 (1994), 187–207.

privileges they held.[49] A Saxon privilege was valid solely within Electoral Saxony, but gave protection against unauthorised copies at the Leipzig book fair, which was regulated by the Saxon book commission under the command of the Elector.[50] Privileges could be obtained in other territories such as Electoral Brandenburg, but these were generally less sought after because they did not hold jurisdiction over the book fairs.

Table 4.1 shows musicians active in German-speaking lands between 1550 and 1700 who held imperial or Saxon printing privileges, as documented by records in the Österreichisches Staatsarchiv and the Sächsisches Hauptstaatsarchiv; Table 4.2 shows publishers who held imperial or Saxon printing privileges specifically for music. Of the composers with imperial privileges, some were internationally famous and their publications circulated across and beyond the Empire – notably Lassus, who had the unusual honour of a perpetual privilege.[51] Other imperial privileges were granted for compositions by imperial court musicians such as Pietro Andrea Ziani or Franz Sales. Saxon privileges, by contrast, were mostly held by musicians from that territory, including Leipzig cantors such as Seth Calvisius and Johann Hermann Schein, and musicians connected to the Dresden court such as Heinrich Schütz and Michael Praetorius. Occasionally Saxon privileges were acquired by composers working further afield (as with Johannes Schultz, organist at the Brunswick-Lüneburg court in Dannenberg); such musicians may have wanted to protect their publications at the Leipzig book fair or draw the Elector of Saxony's attention to their work. However, none of the musicians with Saxon privileges also held imperial privileges, with the exception of Schütz, who gained an imperial privilege in 1637 (as discussed below). This may indicate how Saxon composers and publishers served mainly a regional market for printed music.

Privileges usually belonged to one of two types: the *privilegium speciale* (for one or more designated books, as listed in the application and the privilege itself) and the *privilegium generale* (for all the past, present and future works by a named author or publisher).[52] Rulers were reluctant to grant general privileges, because these could dilute their control over the book trade. Privileges were usually granted for ten years; their limited duration signalled they were favours awarded by the prince, liable to be revoked at any time. Most privileges stipulated a standard set of penalties for those who printed or sold unauthorised copies, threatening to confiscate infringers' stock and impose a fine (paid half to the ruler, half to the

---

[49] Maclean, *Scholarship, Commerce, Religion*, 137–39.

[50] See electoral rescripts of 13 May 1620 and 7 November 1636 in *Codex Augusteus oder neuvermehrtes Corpus Juris Saxonici* (Leipzig, 1724), vol. 1, cols. 409–12.

[51] James Haar, 'Orlando di Lasso, Composer and Print Entrepreneur', in Kate van Orden (ed.), *Music and the Cultures of Print* (New York: Garland, 2000), 125–62.

[52] Friedrich Lehne, 'Zur Rechtsgeschichte der kaiserlichen Privilegien', *Mitteilungen des österreichischen Instituts für Geschichtsforschung* 53 (1939), 323–409 (p. 341).

128   Rites of Musical Ownership

Table 4.1   *Composers who held imperial or Saxon printing privileges 1550–1700, as documented by archival evidence.*

Asterisk denotes self-publisher (or works published by musical associates). For details of archival sources and publications protected by privileges, see Rose, 'Protected Publications'.

Date	Composer	Type	Duration	Genres protected by privilege
1559	NEUSIDLER, Melchior	Imperial	10 years	Lute book
1562	HEIDE, Tobias von der	Imperial	10 years	No printed compositions survive
1565	BAKFARK, Valentin	Imperial	12 years	Lute book
1565	JOANELLUS, Petrus (Giovanelli, Pietro)	Imperial	10 years	Sacred polyphony
1581	LASSUS, Orlande de	Imperial	Perpetual	Sacred and secular polyphony
1588	HANDL [Gallus], Jacobus	Imperial	6 years	Sacred polyphony
1591	HASSLER, Hans Leo	Imperial	10 years	Sacred and secular polyphony
1592, 1593	SALES, Franz	Imperial	10 years each	Sacred polyphony
1594	CALVISIUS, Seth	Saxon	6 years	Hymnal
1594	RATZ, Abraham	Saxon	Perpetual	German-texted editions of Jacob Regnart's secular songs
1598	STEUERLEIN, Johann	Saxon	4 years	Sacred polyphony (no works issued under protection of privilege)
1600	KNÖFEL, Johann	Imperial	10 years	Vocal polyphony (posthumous privilege; no works issued under its protection)
1601	VULPIUS, Melchior	Saxon	10 years	Sacred polyphony
1604	WEISSENHAN (Weisshahn), Adolph	Imperial	5 years	Lute book (no printed works survive)
1611	CALVISIUS, Seth	Saxon	10 years	Hymnal
1611	GROPPENGIESSER, Johann	Saxon	[application only]	No printed works survive
1611	VULPIUS, Melchior	Saxon	10 years	Sacred polyphony
1613	STRAUSS, Christoph	Imperial	10 years	Sacred polyphony
1614	BOLLIUS, Daniel, and his father Marcus Bollius	Imperial	5 years	Sacred polyphony (no printed works survive
1614	PRAETORIUS, Michael	Saxon	10 years	Theoretical treatises (*Syntagma musicum*)
1617	SCHEIN, Johann Hermann *	Saxon	10 years	Sacred vocal concertos. Also issued secular songs and hymnal protected by privilege
1618	SCHÜTZ, Heinrich *	Saxon	8 years	Sacred vocal concertos (*Psalmen Davids*)
1619	DEMANTIUS, Christoph	Saxon	10 years	Treatise and sacred polyphony
*c.*1622	KRAF, Michael	Imperial	[application only]	Sacred polyphony
1622	SCHULTZ, Johannes *	Saxon	10 years	Sacred and secular polyphony
1627	SCHÜTZ, Heinrich	Saxon	10 years	Hymnal of metrical psalms (Becker Psalter)

Privileges as Princely Protection

Table 4.1 (*cont.*)

Date	Composer	Type	Duration	Genres protected by privilege
1628	ROBERTI, Johann Christoph	Imperial	10 years	Sacred polyphony (no printed works survive)
1628	SCHEIN, Johann Hermann *	Saxon	10 years	General privilege for all music publications
1636	LOHR, Michael *	Saxon	10 years	Sacred vocal concertos
1636	SCHÜTZ, Heinrich *	Saxon	10 years	Sacred vocal concertos
1637	SCHÜTZ, Heinrich *	Imperial	5 years	Sacred vocal concertos and instrumental music
1638	HAMMERSCHMIDT, Andreas	Saxon	10 years	Sacred vocal concertos
1638	KITTEL, Caspar *	Saxon	[application only]	Secular songs
1640	SCHOP, Johann	Imperial	10 years	Sacred concertos
1642	SCHÜTZ, Heinrich *	Imperial	10 years	Sacred vocal concertos and instrumental music
1648	ALBERT, Heinrich *	Imperial	12 years	Songbooks
1651	SCHOP, Johann	Imperial	[application only]	Instrumental music
1658	ERHARD, Lorenz	Saxon	10 years	Hymnal
1662	HAMMERSCHMIDT, Andreas *	Saxon	10 years	Sacred vocal concertos
1662	STENGER [Stengler], Wilhelm Hieronymus	Saxon	10 years	Keyboard music (no printed works survive)

holder of the privilege). Uniquely, imperial privileges permitted holders to take the law into their own hands and confiscate unauthorised copies themselves: for example, Schütz's 1637 privilege ordered imperial subjects that: 'you should allow the aforementioned supplicant, wherever he or his heirs might find the [unauthorised books], to confiscate them by his own force, without impediment, and trade and do with them as he wishes, whereby he shall have committed no crime'.[53] Such a sweeping provision reflected the Emperor's status as the supreme power over German territories, but also the difficulties in upholding imperial edicts without a coherent apparatus of state.

Applications for privileges were ritualistic acts, requiring the applicants to show their humility before the prince's authority. Such a process

---

[53] 'Alß lieb euch seÿ . . . den vielgenanter supplicant, wo er oder seine erben dergleichen bey euer ieden finden werden, alß gleich auß einem eigenen gewalt, ohne verhinderung menniglichs zu sich nehmen, vnd damit nach ihren gefallen handlen vnd thun mögen, daran sie auch nicht gefrävelt haben sollen. . .' A-Whh, Impressoria, Karton 61, Konvolut 1, no. 3, fols. 5v–6r.

130   *Rites of Musical Ownership*

Table 4.2   *Publishers who held imperial or Saxon printing privileges for music 1550–1700, as documented by archival evidence.*

For details of archival sources and publications protected by privileges, see Rose, 'Protected Publications'.

Date	Composer/editor	Publisher (place)	Type	Duration	Genres protected by privilege
1603	PRAETORIUS, Hieronymus	Philipp de Ohr (Hamburg)	Imperial	5 years	Sacred polyphony
1611	BODENSCHATZ, Erhard	Abraham Lamberg (Leipzig)	Saxon	Unspecified	Sacred polyphony
1616	PRAETORIUS, Hieronymus	Georg Ludwig Frobenius (Hamburg)	Imperial	Unspecified	Sacred polyphony
1624	VINCENTIUS, Caspar	Johann Volmar (Würzburg)	Imperial	10 years	Organ part for Lassus motets
1632	CALVISIUS, Seth	Bartholomäus Voigt (Leipzig)	Saxon	15 years	Hymnal (posthumous privilege)
1641	SCHEIN, Johann Hermann	Jakob Schuster (Leipzig)	Saxon	8 years	All Schein's works, including sacred and secular polyphony and a hymnal (posthumous privilege)
1649	SCHEIN, Johann Hermann	Jakob Schuster (Leipzig)	Saxon	8 years	All Schein's works, including sacred and secular polyphony and a hymnal (posthumous privilege)
1656	HAMMERSCHMIDT, Andreas	Christian and Melchior Bergen (Dresden)	Saxon	Unspecified	Sacred vocal concertos
1656	KRIEGER, Adam	Martin Maier (Leipzig)	Saxon	10 years	Songbook
1657	CRÜGER, Johannes	Balthasar Mevius (Wittenberg)	Saxon	10 years	Hymnal (*Praxis pietatis melica*)
1661	HINTZE, Jacob	Völcker, Rupert (Berlin)	Saxon	10 years	Hymnal
1665	CRÜGER, Johannes	Balthasar Mevius (Wittenberg)	Saxon	10 years	Hymnal (*Praxis pietatis melica*)
1667	KRIEGER, Adam	Anna Krieger (composer's mother)	Saxon	10 years	Songbook (posthumous privilege)
1667	ZIANI, Pietro Andrea	Georg Beuther (Freiberg)	Imperial	10 years	Sonatas
1673	HORN, Johann Caspar	Georg Heinrich Frommen (Dresden)	Saxon	10 years	Secular songs
1675	CRÜGER, Johannes	Balthasar Christoph Wust (Frankfurt am Main)	Saxon	10 years	Hymnal (*Praxis pietatis melica*)

Privileges as Princely Protection

Table 4.2 (cont.)

Date	Composer/editor	Publisher (place)	Type	Duration	Genres protected by privilege
1678	KRIEGER, Adam	Martin Gabriel Hübner (Dresden)	Saxon	10 years	Songbook (posthumous privilege)
1679	HORN, Johann Caspar	Johann Christoph Mieth (Dresden)	Saxon	10 years	Sacred vocal concertos
1679	QUIRSFELD, Johann	Christoph Klinger (Leipzig)	Saxon	10 years	Hymnal

might seem akin to the 'submission to an absolute power or authority' that Stephen Greenblatt identified as a prerequisite of self-fashioning in sixteenth-century England;[54] I interpret it, however, as a negotiation defining the power and status of both author and ruler. In the Holy Roman Empire, privilege applications were handled by the imperial chancery (*Reichskanzlei*), which was the main administrative organ of imperial government. Decisions on privileges may have been taken by the vice-chancellor or the chancery secretary, whose signatures often appear on the privilege documents.[55] In Saxony, applications were managed by the upper consistory (*Oberkonsistorium*), which was responsible for church discipline and for regulating the book trade via its subsidiary, the Leipzig book commission. The upper consistory was staffed by clergy (including the senior court chaplain and the superintendent of Dresden's churches) and jurists who acted as electoral court councillors. The Elector was probably not directly involved in decisions on applications, although a scribbled note filed with Michael Praetorius's draft privilege indicates it was 'most graciously granted' by the Elector himself.[56] The Elector's signature, found on privileges such as that pictured in Figure 4.1, has not yet been verified as autograph.[57]

As the first step in obtaining a privilege, an individual submitted a petition, addressed to the Emperor or Elector as appropriate. In Saxony some applicants evidently presented their submissions in person to the upper consistory: their petitions were typically dated the day before the

---

[54] Stephen Greenblatt, *Renaissance Self-Fashioning: From More to Shakespeare* (Chicago: University of Chicago Press, 1980), 9.

[55] Schütz's 1637 imperial privilege, for instance, is signed by the chancery secretary Johann Söldner. A-Whh, Impressoria, Karton 61, Konvolut 1, no. 3, fol. 6r. See also Maclean, *Scholarship, Commerce, Religion*, 144, 148.

[56] D-Dla, Loc. 10757/1, fol. 538r.

[57] D-LEsm, Sammlung Autographen, A/4298/2009; transcription in Wilibald Gurlitt, 'Ein Autorenprivileg für Johann Hermann Schein', in Heinrich Hüschen (ed.), *Festschrift Karl Gustav Fellerer zum sechzigsten Geburtstag am 7. Juli 1962* (Regensburg: Gustav Bosse, 1962), 200–204.

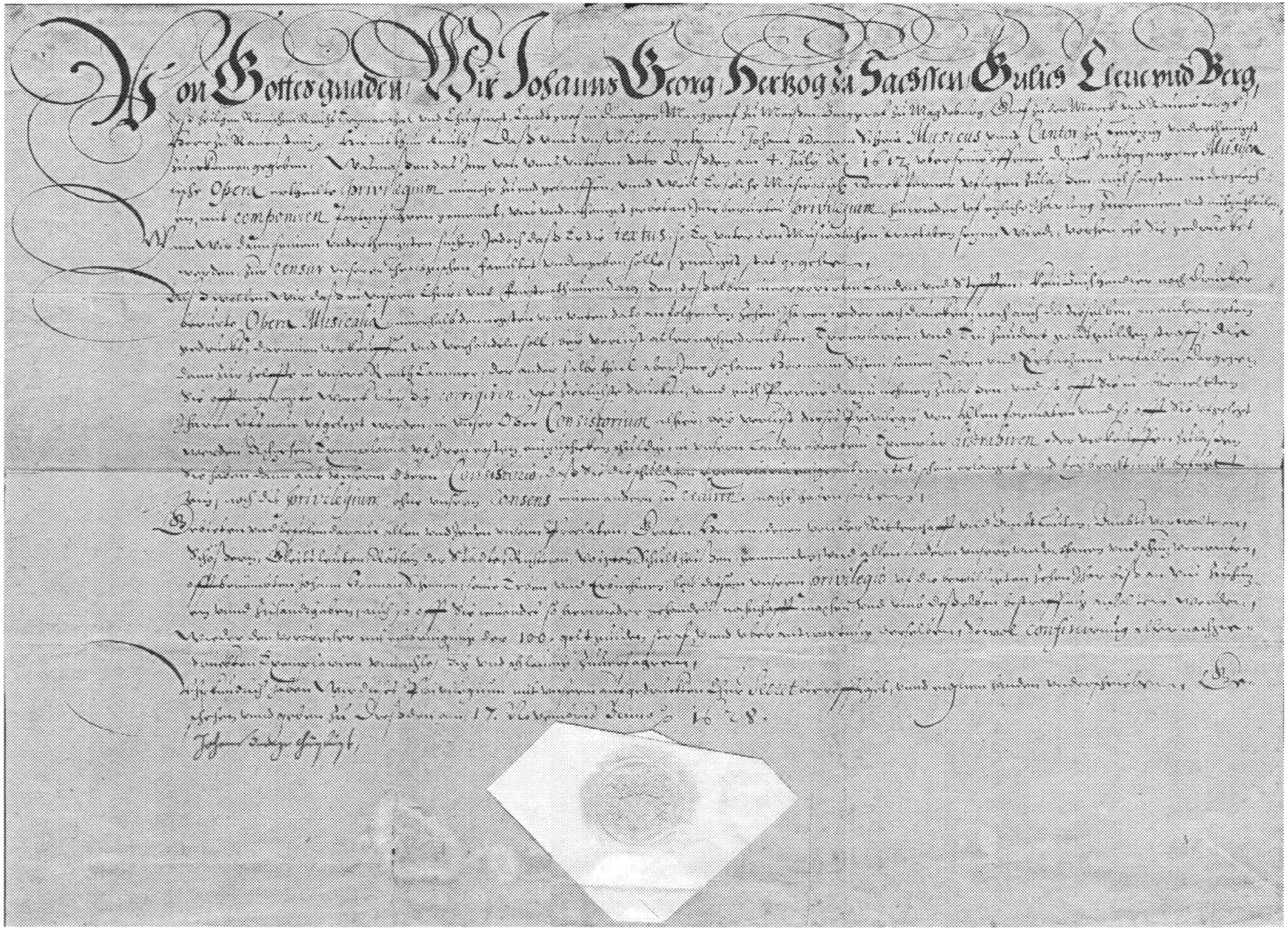

Figure 4.1 Fair copy of Saxon printing privilege issued to Johann Hermann Schein, 17 November 1628.
Leipzig, Stadtgeschichtliches Museum, A/4298/2009.

Privileges as Princely Protection 133

privilege was drafted, which would have been insufficient time for a letter to travel in the post and be processed by the court. Indeed, Schein's 1617 application was signed by the composer in Dresden rather than his current place of residence, Leipzig.[58] Some applicants also lobbied members of the chancery or upper consistory for favourable treatment of their petition. In 1614 Michael Praetorius wrote to the Dresden chief court chaplain Matthias Hoë von Hoënegg, the assessor on the upper consistory, mentioning his wish for a privilege for his series of treatises *Syntagma musicum*, and saying that the consistory would shortly receive his other letter (presumably a petition addressed to the Elector, which does not survive).[59] An applicant might enclose supporting material, such as an endorsement from a patron or sample pages from the proposed book. Lassus accompanied his 1581 application for an imperial privilege with a letter of support from Wilhelm V of Bavaria.[60] Schütz's 1627 application for a renewal of his Saxon privilege included a handwritten mock-up of the title page of his Becker Psalter.[61] The draft of Hammerschmidt's 1638 Saxon privilege survives with an unbound printed partbook of his *Musicalischer Andacht Erster Theil*, presumably submitted for the upper consistory to scrutinise as they considered his application.[62]

If the chancery or upper consistory reached a favourable decision, a draft privilege was prepared by a secretary; this is the document that usually survives in the imperial or Saxon archives, often with evidence of redrafting (sometimes in more than one hand). A calligraphic fair copy of the privilege was then made and sent to the applicant. Figure 4.1 shows the fair copy of Schein's 1628 printing privilege, with the signature and seal of Johann Georg I of Saxony. The grandeur of these Saxon documents asserted the Elector's authority, perhaps with the aim of convincing lesser officials to uphold the privilege.

Several aspects of the application process show how princes sought to assert their authority over the holder of a privilege. Firstly, a substantial fee was often charged for a privilege. In the 1520s the correspondence between Erasmus and Willibald Pirckheimer shows that a payment of 'twenty gold pieces' was usually necessary to secure a general imperial privilege, but the fee could be avoided by petitioning sympathetic officials.[63] With regard to Saxon privileges, Jürgen Gramlich asserts there is no evidence of fees being

---

[58] D-Dla, Loc. 10757/2, fol. 61r; transcribed in Rose, 'Protected Publications', 305.

[59] D-Dla, Loc. 10757/1, fol. 539r; transcribed in Rose, 'Protected Publications', 303.

[60] Lassus's and Wilhelm V's letters are transcribed in Henri Vanhulst, 'Lasso et ses éditeurs: remarques à propos de deux lettres peu connues', *Revue belge de musicologie* 39–40 (1985–86), 80–100 (pp. 94–96).

[61] D-Dla, Loc. 10757/2, fol. 592r.

[62] D-Dla, Loc. 10757/3, unpaginated insertion between fols. 467v and 468r.

[63] Letter of Willibald Pirckheimer to Erasmus, 28 January 1523; *CWE* 9, 407–8 (letter no. 1344).

charged;[64] yet my archival research suggests otherwise. Michael Praetorius's 1614 letter to the Saxon chief court chaplain refers to the payment of a 'chancery fee', a task he had delegated to the Dresden court instrumentalist Michael Mölich.[65] At the time, Praetorius was working as guest capellmeister at the Saxon court (although the privilege uses his official title of capellmeister at the Brunswick court), so it is somewhat surprising that he expected to pay a fee. His letter raises the possibility that even musicians with official Saxon posts such as Schütz and Caspar Kittel paid a fee to obtain their privileges.

Princes also sought to enhance their authority by censoring the books covered in a privilege. Most territories had a system of censorship by church or university authorities, whereby books were approved prior to publication.[66] Applicants for imperial privileges sometimes submitted certificates to show their books had been approved by the censor in their local jurisdiction, and from the late 1570s imperial privileges often included a proviso that the books contain nothing damaging to the Catholic faith.[67] Imperial privileges drafted in Latin occasionally show attempts by the chancery to censor the texts of vocal music. The 1588 imperial privilege to Jacobus Handl for his 'church songs' (*canti ecclesiastici*) specified that the texts and preface should contain nothing scandalous or contrary to the imperial constitution.[68] The privileges granted in 1603 and 1616 to the Hamburg publishers Philipp de Ohr and Georg Ludwig Frobenius for the music of Hieronymus Praetorius went further: presumably because Praetorius was Protestant, these instructed 'that the songs should contain nothing in the preface or in the texts that is scandalous or opposed to Roman Catholic orthodoxy, or to the imperial constitution'.[69] Praetorius's published collections contained Latin liturgical texts that would not offend the censor, and indeed several of them were subsequently reprinted in the strongly Catholic territory of Antwerp.[70] Nonetheless the Emperor wished to endorse only those books that did not undermine his political and religious position.

---

[64] Jürgen Gramlich, 'Rechtsordnungen des Buchgewerbes im Alten Reich: genossenschaftliche Strukturen, Arbeits- und Wettbewerbsrecht im deutschen Druckhandwerk', *Archiv für Geschichte des Buchwesens* 41 (1994), 1–145 (p. 90).

[65] D-Dla, Loc. 10757/1, fol. 539r; transcribed in Rose, 'Protected Publications', 303.

[66] Hans-Peter Hasse, *Zensur theologischer Bücher in Kursachsen im konfessionellen Zeitalter. Studien zur kursächsischen Literatur- und Religionspolitik in den Jahren 1569 bis 1575* (Leipzig: Evangelische Verlagsanstalt, 2000).

[67] Koppitz, 'Die Privilegia impressoria', 195–96; Maclean, *Scholarship, Commerce, Religion*, 144.

[68] A-Whh, Impressoria, Karton 27, no. 46, fols. 481r–2v; transcribed in Pohlmann, *Die Frühgeschichte*, 272–73.

[69] 'Hac tamen specialiquoque lege adiecta: ut cantiones haec tam in praefationibus, quam in contextu nihil quicquam scandalosum, aut adversum orthodoxae religioni Catholicae, vel etiam Imperii constitutionibus in se contineant.' A-Whh, Impressoria, Karton 21, no. 32, fol. 231v.

[70] Phalèse reprinted Hieronymus Praetorius's *Cantiones sacrae* in 1622 (RISM A/I P5356) and his *Missae* in 1625 (RISM A/I P5329).

Privileges as Princely Protection 135

In Saxony the upper consistory used privileges to uphold the system of censorship specified in a 1594 electoral ordinance. This edict commanded that books should be approved prior to publication by the theological faculties in Wittenberg and Leipzig, or by the court preachers in Dresden.[71] Accordingly, several privileges for musicians – including those for Schein (1617 and 1628), Schultz (1622) and Hammerschmidt (1662) – instructed these composers to submit the texts of their works to the Leipzig theological faculty for approval before printing.[72] In his 1617 application, Schein volunteered to send a manuscript of each future work to the Elector for approval; nonetheless, a consistory member annotated the letter, saying that the privilege was granted on condition that the theological faculty censored the texts.[73] Schütz's 1618 and 1627 privileges make no mention of censorship, but his 1636 privilege states that his works are subject 'to the usual advance censor'.[74] Further research is necessary to show how rigorously music publications were censored. The Saxon system of censorship was shaped by the efforts of clergy and state in the 1570s to suppress Calvinism and to promote Lutheran orthodoxy.[75] Perhaps the censors treated polyphony with a light touch, because something so musically elaborate would have had connotations of Lutheran orthodoxy.

A final way in which rulers asserted control over privilege holders was by requiring them to deposit, at their own expense, copies of the book thereby protected. Imperial privileges usually required the holder to submit between three and seven copies to the chancery: Schütz's 1637 privilege stated he should submit four copies of each book issued under its protection.[76] Saxon privileges were more onerous, typically demanding eighteen copies from 1612 onwards despite the protests of bookdealers.[77] Schein's 1617 privilege stipulated he supply eighteen copies of the first work issued under the privilege, and then nine copies of any subsequent titles; Schütz's 1618 privilege required him to submit twelve copies of the initial publication and six copies of any subsequent books. In 1636 Schütz tried to reduce this obligation, asking to submit just six copies of the *Kleine geistliche Concerte* if he published it himself, but twelve copies if a bookseller were the publisher.[78] The upper consistory ignored his request,

[71] Ludwig Gieseke, 'Die kursächsische Ordnung für Buchhändler und Buchdrucker von 1594', *Archiv für Geschichte des Buchwesens* 60 (2006), 176–83 (p. 178).

[72] D-Dla, Loc. 10757/2, fol. 59v, 335r; Loc. 10757/3, fol. 76r; Loc. 10758/3, fols. 34v.

[73] 'Diss privilegium ist bewilligen, dass er die texten durch die theologische faculten in Leÿpzigk censirt lassen'. D-Dla, Loc. 10757/2, fol. 61v.

[74] 'auf vorhergehende gewöhnliche censur'. D-Dla, Loc. 10757/3, unfoliated privilege before fol. 406r.

[75] Hasse, *Zensur theologischer Bücher*, 69–182.

[76] Koppitz, 'Die Privilegia impressoria', 197; A-Whh, Impressoria, Karton 61, Konvolut 1, no. 3, fol. 6r.

[77] Johannes Franke, *Die Abgabe der Pflichtexemplare von Druckerzeugnissen mit besonderer Berücksichtigung Preussens und des deutschen Reiches* (Berlin: Asher, 1889), 81–85.

[78] D-Dla, Loc. 10757/3, undated autograph note inserted before fol. 406r.

instead specifying that he should submit eighteen copies of each book.[79] If composers obeyed the stipulation to submit so many copies, the Elector would have accrued countless books whose current location is unknown. One copy may have been placed in the electoral library, and another in Leipzig's university library,[80] but there would still have been a substantial number for the Elector to use as gifts or even re-sell. Perhaps the requirement for so many deposit copies was primarily symbolic, an ostentatious show of the Elector's power over the applicant. Through such demands, rulers demonstrated the power that enabled them to bestow the favour of a privilege on authors.

Despite their formulaic nature, privileges and applications reveal underlying ideas about musical authorship, including the balance between individual recognition and social obligation. The earliest printing privileges, issued in the decades around 1500, argue that these temporary favours to an individual publisher or author would nonetheless serve the common good.[81] The first known privilege granted to a musician, the 1511 imperial privilege to Arnolt Schlick, explained that his treatise on organ-building 'will reduce the high cost of organ-building caused from time to time by uncertain standards, by making this knowledge generally available to all in one book'.[82] Schlick's ten-year privilege for his book was accordingly 'for the furthering of the common good'.[83] Another early imperial privilege, granted in 1545 to the publisher Hans Ott for Heinrich Isaac's *Choralis Constantinus*, opens with a typical preamble. It praises 'those who strive to aid public studies at their own expense, labour and industry, and take it upon themselves that every book by good authors ... should be printed and published in the most accurate editions possible for distribution to the public'. Ott's publication of the *Choralis Constantinus* is described as an 'act of public beneficence', which deserved protection from pirate publishers 'who unjustly abuse the labour and industry of others for their own gain'.[84] Thus the privilege system aimed to incentivise authors and publishers to overcome the artisanal reluctance to share specialist knowledge.

In the decades around 1600, applicants for privileges still invoked the notion of the common good. Calvisius's 1594 application for a Saxon

---

[79] D-Dla, Loc. 10757/3, unfoliated privilege before fol. 406r.

[80] Franke, *Abgabe der Pflichtexemplare*, 85.   [81] Gieseke, *Vom Privileg zum Urheberrecht*, 60–2.

[82] 'dardurch der mercklich vncosten. so bißher auf die werch der Orgeln jrer vnbestanndigkeit halben yezüzeitten gangen ist. verhütte werdt. in ainen druckh. solhs menigelich zü offen waren/ zü bringen willens sey.' Privilege printed in Arnolt Schlick, *Spiegel der Orgelmacher und Organisten* (Speyer, 1511), sig. A2v.

[83] 'sonnderlich zür fürdrung des gemainen nütz'. Ibid.

[84] Translation from Royston Gustavson, 'Commercialising the *Choralis Constantinus*: The Printing and Publishing of the First Edition', in David J. Burn and Stefan Gasch (eds.), *Heinrich Isaac and Polyphony for the Proper of the Mass in the Late Middle Ages and Renaissance* (Turnhout: Brepols, 2011), 215–68 (pp. 264–65).

Privileges as Princely Protection   137

privilege for his *Hymni sacri latini et germani* mentioned the hindrance caused by erroneous scribal copies, thereby implying the public benefit of having these hymns available in print.[85] In his 1611 application to renew his Saxon privilege, Calvisius explained: 'With this [privilege] your Electoral Grace will promote the prosperous state of the Christian church and the profit of the studious youth ... and ... will increase my diligence to do other things that I hope will serve the common good'.[86] As late as 1662, Hammerschmidt explained that his *Kirchen- und Tafel Music* was intended to 'seek not mine, but God's honour and the profit of the Holy Church'.[87] Through such statements about the common good, composers justified protection of their individual enterprise while avoiding accusations of self-interest.

Applicants for printing privileges often requested protection from the reputational or financial damage caused by unauthorised editions. Echoing Luther's attacks on profiteering merchants and publishers, applicants often castigated the makers of illicit editions as seeking to cause disadvantage (*Schaden, Nachteil*). Several composers claimed in applications that their reputation would be damaged by misprints in pirated editions. In his 1617 petition for a Saxon privilege, Schein explained that 'many times, carefully disseminated things are liable to be reprinted by others with mistakes, not without special prejudice and disadvantage to the author'.[88] Lassus's application for an imperial privilege stated the difficulties involved in proofreading music (see Chapter 3, p. 85). He then declared: 'For the first edition [the printers] are following my will closely, but afterwards where my works are reissued, either they follow their own taste or they abandon the care they previously showed, so I can scarcely recognise my own work'.[89] James Haar regards Lassus's comment as an example of 'the rhetorical vividness for which his music was celebrated',[90] yet his fears were arguably justified. As is shown below, unauthorised editions often contained misprints. Errors in partbook editions might not be spotted until the music was performed, and then it might be unclear whether the resulting harmonic clashes were caused by misprints or by the composer's

---

[85] D-Dla, Loc. 7300/2, Bd. 1, fols. 511r–v.

[86] 'Befordern hiermit Eꝰurerꝰ Churfꝰürstlichenꝰ Gnꝰadenꝰ der Christlichen kirchen wolstand vnd der studierenden iugend nutz ... vnd sonsten meines fleißes so ich auf andere sachen, welche gemeinem besten meines verhoffens dienstlich, zulegen gesinnet'. D-Dla, Loc. 10757/1, fol. 354v; transcribed in Rose, 'Protected Publications', 301.

[87] 'ich nicht meine, sondern Gottes ehre und deselbigen heilꝰigenꝰ kirchen nutzen suche', D-Dla, Loc. 10758/3, fol. 35r; transcribed in Rose, 'Protected Publications', 312.

[88] 'Vndt aber vielmahl wolabgesande sachen von andern, nicht ohne sonderliches praejudiis vndt nachtheil der authorn vitiose nachgetrucket zuwerdꝰeꝰn pflegen ...' D-Dla, Loc. 10757/2, fols. 60v–61r; transcribed in Rose, 'Protected Publications', 304.

[89] 'Nam ut prima aliqua vice vel maxime agant ex voluntate mea, postmodum ubi recudenda sunt opera mea, vel sibi ipsis morem gerunt solum, vel a prima sua diligentia ita recedunt ut quod meum prius fuerat, vix agnoscam statim'. Musée royal de Mariemont, Inv. Aut. 1112/4; transcribed in Vanhulst, 'Lasso et ses éditeurs', 95.

[90] Haar, 'Orlando di Lasso', 141.

incompetence. A privilege, by contrast, assured purchases that an edition contained an accurate text.

Composers also argued that a privilege would protect them from the financial damage caused by unauthorised editions. Such views were mainly voiced by composers who acted as their own publishers and who wished to recoup the capital they had invested in a run of copies. The asterisks in Table 4.1 indicate which composers holding privileges were also publishers of their music. Applying in 1618 for a privilege for his *Psalmen Davids*, Schütz explained the financial risk borne by self-publishers. As a novice to the publishing business, he fretted that 'on completion of the opus, experienced booksellers and printers might immediately undertake to publish, reprint and sell it; consequently my copies might remain unsold and cause me significant and considerable harm'.[91] A privilege would help him 'recoup all the more quickly the effort and considerable expense'[92] of publishing this substantial partbook set.

Vivid detail on why self-publishers needed economic protection was offered by Hammerschmidt in his 1662 application for a Saxon privilege for his *Kirchen- und Tafel Music*: 'There might be selfish people who ... would reprint my work and sell it, through which not only my great labour would be turned to water, but also at the worst I would be ruined'.[93] He claimed his expenses exceeded 600 florins 'and I must therefore myself go back and forth into debt'.[94] Hammerschmidt's concern about unauthorised editions was a legitimate one: all of his other works were published by commercial booksellers and often appeared in several editions, indicating strong demand for his music.

That a considerable number of composers with privileges were also self-publishers suggests that they primarily sought to protect their publications as business ventures rather than from a nascent sense of intellectual property. Pohlmann, by contrast, interpreted a limited selection of privilege applications as early examples of authors asserting their economic right to profit from creative work. Examining a 1598 application for a Saxon privilege by the Thuringian composer Johann Steuerlein, Pohlmann declared: 'Here the relevant consideration is that the author by rights must reap the economic fruits of his intellectual work, and should not thereby

---

[91] 'nach verfertigung des operis, geübte buchhändtler vndt drucker vntterstehen, daßelbe also baldt aufzulegen, aufs newe widrumb nachzudrucken, vndt ferner zuvorhandlen, dannenhero mir dann meine exemplaria, ersitzen bleiben, vndt mercklicher großer schade, zugefügt werden möchtte'. D-Dla, Loc. 10757/2, fol. 85r.

[92] 'auch meiner müh vndt ziemblichen großen vncosten, desto baß [besser] wieder beÿkommen möge'. Ibid.

[93] 'es möchten sich eigennütziger leuthe finden, welche dieses mein werk nachzudrucken und zue verhandlen, sich unterstehen und belieben laßen möchten, dardurch mier meine große arbeit nicht allein zue wasser gemacht sondern auch ich ins euserste verderben gesetzet würde.' D-Dla, Loc. 10758/3, fol. 35r; transcribed in Rose, 'Protected Publications', 312.

[94] 'ich mich also hin und wieder in schulden stecken muß'. Ibid.

Privileges as Princely Protection 139

be exposed to any injury or loss of rights'.[95] Yet Steuerlein was concerned to recoup the costs of printing and showed no sense that his compositions were the products of his intellect. Near the start of his petition he described how for his previous publications, 'I have had ... to pay a fee to the printer, generally one thaler for each sheet, as is usual'.[96] He continued in his petition to the Elector: 'With your princely reputation and authority ... and by means of a privilege transmitted from your princely grace to me ... I would humbly like to taste the profit from my musical work, and thereby remain unscathed by the printer's fees'.[97] 'Musical work' could refer to either his published opus or the labour he invested in preparing this publication; either way, Steuerlein sought protection to ensure a return on his publication costs, not as recompense for the creative act.

Pohlmann made a similarly anachronistic interpretation of Melchior Vulpius's 1601 privilege application as articulating 'the imminent legal awareness of the human creator'.[98] He focused on Vulpius's statement that 'my work is not for my private hoarding, and I am hoping through it to earn a modest crust of bread for me and my family'.[99] But here again, Vulpius was concerned specifically about the costs of printing: 'As everyone knows, my income cannot stretch in the slightest to the printing of a publication'.[100] Whether because of modesty or a deep-seated view that true creativity belonged to God, composers never mentioned their intellectual abilities as justifications for their privileges.

That privileges could reward a range of types of labour and investment is evident from the fact that they were also granted to publishers and editors. Table 4.2 lists the publishers who are documented archivally as holding privileges for music. Some musicians who edited collections claimed that their labour justified the protection of a privilege. In 1594 and 1611, Calvisius applied for Saxon privileges for hymnals he had edited, arguing that a privilege 'would secure gratification for my expended labour'.[101]

---

[95] Pohlmann, *Die Frühgeschichte*, 212.

[96] 'Ich habe aber ... vor jedem bogen, meistes theils, dem typographo, allweg ein thaler, zu truckgebuer entrichten müssen, wie dann gewöhnlich'. Thüringisches Staatsarchiv, Meiningen, Hennebergica Weimar, Akten Nr. 679, fol. 1r.

[97] 'mit ihrer fürstlichen reputation vnd auctoritet, meine musicalische arbeit ... damit vermittelst Euer Fürstliche Gnade mir gnedigst mittheilendten privilegij ... ich desselben vnderthenigst nützbarlich genießen, vnd also hinfüro, der trückgebühr dardurch verschont bleiben möge'. Thüringisches Staatsarchiv, Hennebergica Weimar, Akten Nr. 679, fol. 1v.

[98] Pohlmann, *Die Frühgeschichte*, 212.

[99] 'zu meinem schatz oder vorrath nichts denn meine arbeit, vnd hoffend bin ich wolts dadurch mihr vnd den meinen ein geringes stucklein brots zu wegen bringen ... ' D-Dla, Loc. 08844/4, fol. 177v.

[100] 'Wann aber iederman bewust, das mein vermögen den verlag zu trucken sich im geringsten nicht erstrecket.' Ibid, fols. 177r–177v.

[101] 'mir zu ergetzung gehabter arbeit gereichen würde'. D-Dla, Loc. 7300/2, Bd. 1, fol. 511v. For a similar phrasing, see Calvisius's 1611 application, D-Dla, Loc. 10757/1, fol. 354v; transcribed in Rose, 'Protected Publications', 301.

(The term 'gratification' (*Ergötzung*) usually indicated the author receiving an honorarium or a set of free copies.[102]) The nature of Calvisius's labour is indicated on the title page of his 1597 hymnal, which described his role as setting the tunes 'in four voices in contrapuntal style correctly' and bringing them together 'in good order'.[103] That arrangements could be protected by a privilege is confirmed by the 1624 privilege obtained by the Würzburg publisher Johann Volmar, for the figured bass part made by the organist Caspar Vincentius for Lassus's *Magnum opus musicum* (1604).[104] Vincentius was not the author of the 516 motets contained in the *Magnum opus musicum*. But he must have invested considerable labour in making the figured bass part, a task for which he would have had to intabulate or score up all these motets in order to discern their harmonies.

My archival research shows that, contrary to Pohlmann's teleological interpretations, privileges did not recognise authorship in terms of creative or intellectual work. Instead these legal instruments could be held by publishers, arrangers, editors and composers alike. Privileges were granted for publications that served the common good and to protect the time and money that applicants invested in their books. The favour thus shown to individuals was therefore justified on the basis of its benefit to wider society. At the same time, privileges had a strong symbolic element, seen in how applicants had to participate in a ritualistic performance of princely power, abasing themselves before the ruler in order to gain a modicum of individual recognition.

PRIVILEGES VERSUS PIRACY

The question remains whether privileges offered effective protection against unauthorised editions. Because polyphony was an elite product for a small market, there are only a few documented examples of collections with sufficient commercial appeal to attract unauthorised editions. The following section considers how Schütz, Schein and Heinrich Albert sought to use their privileges against pirate publishers.

Because of its complexity and technical demands on performers, Schütz's music had limited commercial appeal. None of his authorised publications was sufficiently popular to appear in a second edition during his lifetime, apart from the simple four-voice metrical psalms in his Becker Psalter (1628) that subsequently appeared in editions of 1640 and 1661

---

[102] Rose, 'Protected Publications', 283.

[103] 'Mit Vier Stimmen *contrapuncts* weise/ richtig gesetzt/ vnd in gute Ordnung zusammen gebracht/ Durch Sethum Calvisium'. Seth Calvisius, *Harmonia cantionum ecclesiasticarum* (Leipzig, 1597), title page. RISM A/I C258.

[104] *In magni illius magni boiariae ducis symphoniarchae Orlandi de Lasso Magnum opus musicum Bassus ad organum nova methodo dispositus studio et opera Gasparis Vincentii* (Würzburg, 1625), RISM A/I L1033, VV1648 II,1; A-Whh, Impressoria, Karton 74, no. 63, fols. 288r–289v.

Privileges versus Piracy

sponsored by central German courts.[105] However, several of Schütz's pieces were reprinted in the two volumes of *Geistliche wolklingende Concerte* made for Nordhausen music-lovers and issued in Goslar in 1637–38. Chapter 2 detailed how these anthologies contain unauthorised reductions of Schütz's polychoral psalms, including *Lobe den Herren* (SWV39) arranged for two voices and continuo, and *Alleluja! Lobet den Herren* (SWV38) arranged for three voices with continuo and now attributed to Andreas Oehme. The anthologies also reprinted a set of duos from the *Historia der Aufferstehung* (SWV50) and the concerto *Schaffe in mir, Gott* (SWV291) for two voices and continuo.[106]

Schütz would have regarded the reprinting of *Schaffe in mir, Gott* as a prohibited act, given that it was taken from the first book of his *Kleine geistliche Concerte*, which had been published two years earlier under a ten-year Saxon privilege. As discussed in Chapter 2, he doubtless also considered the few-voiced arrangements of his polychoral psalms as detrimental to his reputation. However, his Saxon privilege could not have been upheld against the Nordhausen anthologies, which claim on their title pages to be likewise covered by a Saxon privilege (possibly a false claim, as no corroboratory evidence survives in the archives). Instead Schütz sought an imperial privilege, presumably in direct response to the Nordhausen volumes.[107] His imperial privilege invoked a higher authority than the purported Saxon privilege protecting the Nordhausen anthologies. But his imperial privilege may have had little more than symbolic power, for it was likely to be upheld only by the imperial book commission at the Frankfurt book fair. It is best interpreted as part of a package of measures Schütz took to protect his editions, along with his use of paper with a personalised watermark (see Chapter 3, p. 94).

Privileges again had limited effectiveness for Schein against unauthorised editions. As mentioned in Chapter 3, Schein's self-published music had a strong commercial appeal, with many volumes being reprinted within a few years of their first publication. Particularly popular were his secular villanellas in the three volumes of *Musica boscareccia*, which were reprinted in 1628 by Paul Ledertz in Strasbourg. Ledertz's editions reproduce closely the composer's authorised versions, except they omit the

---

[105] RISM A/I S2282, 2283, 2284.

[106] *Fasciculus primus geistlicher wolklingender Concerten* (Goslar, 1638), RISM B/I 1638[5], nos. 50, 52; *Fasciculus secundus geistlicher wolklingender Concerten* (Goslar, 1637), RISM B/I 1637[3], nos. 12, 55. For comments on both anthologies, see Werner Braun, 'Bemerkungen zu den "Nordhäusischen Concerten" von 1637/38', *Schütz-Jahrbuch* 25 (2003), 85–104.

[107] The chronology of the relevant documents is not straightforward: the earliest Nordhausen volume has a dedication dated 25 March 1637, whereas Schütz's imperial privilege is dated 3 April 1637 (A-Whh, Impressoria, Karton 61, Konvolut 1, no. 3). Unless these dates reflect the use of different calendars, Schütz would have required advance warning of the Nordhausen volumes to have gained an imperial privilege so soon after their publication.

engraved title pages and have no reference to a privilege.[108] Ledertz probably believed he was acting legitimately, given that Schein's first Saxon privilege had expired the previous year. Moreover, it was accepted practice in the book trade for publishers to reprint a work if they served a different geographical market from the original publisher. But Schein complained bitterly about Ledertz's editions in his 1628 application to renew his Saxon privilege, describing them as causing him 'insurmountable harm'.[109] Undoubtedly Schein was irked by the appearance of Ledertz's reprints in the autumn 1628 book fair at Leipzig, where they were in direct competition with his own stock.[110] But because he had let his previous Saxon privilege expire, Schein could not petition the Leipzig council to confiscate Ledertz's copies at the fair. Nor did his renewed Saxon privilege prevent Ledertz's heirs printing further editions in 1632 of *Musica boscareccia* after Schein's death, and these unauthorised copies were again advertised for sale at the Leipzig fair.[111] An imperial privilege might have offered better protection, given that Strasbourg was under imperial control; but Schein's struggle against Ledertz shows the difficulty of enforcing a privilege across the fragmented jurisdictions of German-speaking lands.

The best documented example of a mid-seventeenth-century musician clashing with pirate publishers is provided by the Königsberg organist Heinrich Albert. Albert's *Arien* (which he published himself between 1638 and 1650) comprise eight volumes of strophic songs, setting verse by poets such as Simon Dach and Robert Roberthin (who met in Albert's garden in an informal society dubbed the *Kürbs-Hütte*).[112] The *Arien* were highly popular for several reasons. They were the first German songbooks in score format, printed on elegant folio pages with eye-catching engravings on the title pages. The songs included an attractive mix of sacred and secular topics, plus some homage compositions written for dignitaries visiting Königsberg. The musical settings could be realised in a variety of ways, ranging from a singer self-accompanying on the keyboard, to a group of singers alternating with instrumental ritornelli. With such versatility, the *Arien* appealed to many burghers in the cities along the Baltic coast.

---

[108] RISM A/I S1381, 1391 and 1401.

[109] D-Dla, Loc. 10757/3, fol. 77v; transcribed in Rose, 'Protected Publications', 307.

[110] *Catalogus Universalis ... Verzeichnüß aller Bücher/ so zu Franckfurt in der Herbstmeß/ Leipzigischen Michaelsmarckt dieses jetzigen 1628. Jahres ... zu befinden* (Leipzig, 1628), sig. C4v.

[111] RISM A/I S1382, 1392, 1402; see *Catalogus Universalis ... Verzeichnüs aller Bücher/ so zu Franckfurt in der Herbstmeß/ vnd Leipzigischen MichaelsMarckt dieses jetzigen 1632. Jahrs ... zu befinden* (Leipzig, 1632), sig. C1v (publisher stated as Caspar Dietzel); *Catalogus Universalis ... Verzeichnüs aller Bücher/ so zu Franckfurt in der FastenMeß/ vnd Leipzigischen Ostermarckt dieses jetzigen 1633. Jahrs ... zu befinden* (Leipzig, 1633), sig. B4r (publisher stated as Ledertz's heirs).

[112] For studies of Albert's *Arien* from literary and musical perspectives, see Anthony J. Harper, *German Secular Songbooks of the Mid-Seventeenth Century* (Aldershot: Ashgate, 2003), 83–110; Werner Braun, *Thöne und Melodeyen, Arien und Canzonetten. Zur Musik des deutschen Barockliedes* (Tübingen: Niemeyer, 2004), 172–79.

Most of the eight volumes received second or third editions within a few years of their first publication, and the folio format was imitated by other songbooks such as Johann Weichmann's three-volume *Sorgen-Lägerin* (1648).

In June 1642 Albert obtained his first printing privilege, from the Elector of Brandenburg and Duke of Prussia: 'We Friedrich Wilhelm ... command graciously and earnestly the printers and booksellers in all our electoral and inherited lands, that they should not print the *Arien* in any format, neither in whole nor in part, neither melodies nor texts within ten years, nor possess or sell [unauthorised] copies printed by others'.[113] Subsequently the privilege was ratified by Władysław IV Vasa of Poland, who held sovereignty over Prussia.[114] The wording of the privilege overlooked the collaborative nature of the *Arien*, specifically the contribution of the poets such as Dach. By giving Albert the exclusive right to control the publication of the texts and tunes, the privilege recognised primarily his role in assembling and publishing the *Arien*, rather than his role as a composer.

In 1645 the first unauthorised edition appeared: the *Poetisches Lust-Gärtlein*, a duodecimo book containing the texts of 57 secular songs from books 1 to 5 of the *Arien*.[115] Like most illict editions, the *Lust-Gärtlein* bears no place of publication and no publisher's name; according to a catalogue from the Leipzig book-fair, however, the publisher was Andreas Hünefeld in Danzig.[116] The book epitomised the spirit of appropriation and popularisation common in the transmission of secular song: it made the lyrics available in a pocket-sized format, suitable for those who could not read music or could not afford Albert's folio books. The *Lust-Gärtlein* gives correct attributions for the authors of almost all of the poems, and omits the melodies that were Albert's authorial contribution to the *Arien*. Yet Albert considered it to be 'an unjust work'[117] and a breach of his 1642 privilege that protected the texts of the *Arien*.[118]

More serious for Albert were three pirated editions of 1648 that mimicked the folio format of his authorised editions, in a deliberate attempt to deceive buyers. These counterfeits comprised the *Poetisch-Musicalisches*

---

[113] 'Wir Friederich Wilhelm ... befehlen derowegen gnädigst und ernstlich den Buchdruckern und Buchhändlern in allen unsern Chur- und Erb-Landen/ daß sie dieselbige in keinerley Format/ weder gantz noch zum theil/ weder Melodeyen noch Texte innerhalb 10 Jahren nicht nachdrucken noch von andern gedruckt feil haben oder verkauffen sollen'. Reprinted in Heinrich Albert, *Erster Theil der Arien*, 4th edn (Königsberg, 1652), sig. A1v. RISM A/I A620.

[114] For extracts from the Polish privilege, see ibid.

[115] *Poetisches Lust-Gärtlein, darinnen schöne anmuthige Gedichten, lustige Lieder, zur Anleitung guter Tugend u. höfflichen Sitten* ([Danzig], 1645). US-NH, Zg17 D11 645.

[116] *Catalogus universalis ... Verzeichnüß aller Bücher/ so zu Franckfurt in der HerbstMeß/ auch Leipzigis. MichaelisMarckte/ dieses ietzigen 1645. Jahrs* (Leipzig, 1645), sig. D4r.

[117] 'eine ungerechte Arbeit'. Albert, *Siebender Theil der Arien* (Königsberg, 1648), sig. G1v. RISM A/I A636.

[118] Because Danzig was under Polish jurisdiction, the *Poetisches Lust-Gärtlein* infringed the version of the privilege confirmed by the Polish king.

Lustwäldlein, containing the words and music of 144 songs from Albert's books 1 to 6; an unauthorised edition of the *Siebender Theil der Arien*; and an unauthorised edition of the *Musicalische Kürbs-Hütte* (a 1645 set of three-part compositions commemorating the poetic circle that met in Albert's garden).[119] To a casual buyer and even to some modern bibliographers, these editions might look genuine.[120] They claim on their title pages to be printed in Königsberg and they contain forewords bearing Albert's name; an extant copy of the *Poetisch-Musicalisches Lustwäldlein* even has an engraved frontispiece depicting Mount Parnassus, reminiscent of the engraved title pages on Albert's authorised editions.[121] Yet these editions give no information about the publisher, and in the spring 1648 book-fair catalogue the *Lustwäldlein* was ascribed to the fictitious bookseller 'Christian Castuben' of Christiana (Oslo).[122] Furthermore they are inaccurately printed, with no vertical alignment of the barlines in the score. Evidently the pirate typesetter had followed the notational symbols in Albert's authorised editions by rote, unaware that a score needs to be read vertically as well as horizontally.

Albert complained bitterly about the pirated editions, even issuing a pamphlet condemning the *Lustwäldlein*.[123] Confirming the fears of Lassus and Schein about misprints in unauthorised editions, he argued that the inaccuracies of these pirated editions would damage his reputation. Regarding the 1645 *Lust-Gärtlein*, he claimed that 'not a single song-text, whether reprinted in Danzig or here in small format, can be read without finding a mistake, not to mention that the same people have modified entire words and hence suppressed the correct meaning of each song'.[124] Given the vagaries of early modern orthography, this was perhaps an exaggerated grievance; but more pertinent were his complaints about the errors in the 1648 editions. Besides listing misprints in specific songs, he bemoaned the lack of vertical alignment in the score format: 'As is apparent already from the first song, this [compositor] must be an ignoramus, for he does not set a single bar correctly, as it should stand in a score. The evil man continues in this inept way until the end of all

---

[119] Copies of all three counterfeits are bound together as GB-Lbl, G.62.b, and D-Mbs, 2 Mus.pr. 231.

[120] Gerhard Dünnhaupt's bibliography of Albert's output does not recognise the pirated *Siebender Theil der Arien* and *Kürbs-Hütte* as unauthorised editions; see his *Personalbibliographien zu den Drucken des Barock*, 2nd edn, 6 vols. (Stuttgart: Hiersemann, 1990–93), i, 170–90.

[121] D-Mbs, shelfmark 2. Mus.pr.231.

[122] *Catalogus Universalis ... Verzeichnüß aller Bücher/ so zu Franckfurt in der Fasten-Meß/ auch Leipzigischen Oster-Marckte/ dieses ietzigen 1648. Jahrs ... zu befinden* (Leipzig, 1648), sig. C1v. The pirated *Siebender Theil der Arien* is an exception to this statement, in that the imprint on the title page audaciously reads 'Königsberg/ bey dem Autor'.

[123] *Heinrich Alberts/ abgenötigte/ Nachricht vnd Verwarnung/ Wegen eines ... Nachdrucks seiner Arien* (Königsberg, 1648), bound into the copy of *Achter Theil der Arien* (Königsberg, 1650), GB-Lbl, G.61.

[124] 'Wie dann nicht ein einiges Lied/ so wol die zu Dantzig/ als auch/ welche dieses Orts in klein Format nachgedruckt/ zu lesen ist/ da nicht Fehler drinnen zu finden seyn solten/ zugeschweigen/ daß selbige Leute unterweilen gantze Wörter geendert vnd damit des Liedes rechten Verstand verdrucket haben.' Albert, *Siebender Theil der Arien*, sig. G1v.

Privileges versus Piracy   145

the songs'.[125] Afraid that these botched editions would expose him to the 'scolding and mockery of learned musicians',[126] Albert declared: 'I protest solemnly, that I did not set the music in such confusion'.[127]

Equally irksome for Albert was the economic damage caused by the pirate publishers. Echoing Luther's 1545 attack on avarice in the book trade (see p. 119 above), Albert claimed that booksellers and printers are particularly prone to greed, 'which in disregard of their conscience, against the prohibition of high princes, yes even against our God, they have no scruple in doing disadvantage to their neighbour'.[128] Elaborating these comments in his 1648 pamphlet, he lambasted 'these greedy printers and booksellers who take away the reward for my musical work'.[129] Here 'work' (*Arbeit*) could denote the published product or the process of composing and compiling it.

Albert then articulated his notion of musical property, explaining that 'this my work, so to speak (with Nathan) is my own little sheep, which can give me milk and wool, [but] some greedy people who have many sheep and cattle want to take it away from me'.[130] Here he invoked the parable told by Nathan (2 Samuel 12. 1–13), in which the rich man stole the poor man's only sheep. In the Old Testament, Nathan used this parable to rebuke King David for murdering Uriah the Hittite and committing adultery with his wife Bathsheba. As adapted by Albert, the rich men are the unscrupulous booksellers who steal the composer's few publications. The pastoral analogy does not refer to Albert's authorial role, overlooking the mental or physical labour that might mark his metaphorical 'sheep' as his own. By comparing himself to a smallholder with livestock, Albert clarified his desire to subsist from his publications, while distancing himself from any connotations of commerce.

Albert's privileges provided some legal protection against the pirated editions. In 1648 he reported that his Polish privilege was upheld by the city council of Danzig, which confiscated unauthorised copies of the *Lust-Gärtlein* and interrogated a possible suspect, a bookdealer's servant

---

[125] 'Wie dann bald erscheinet aus dem Ersten Lied, welch ein Vnwissender es muß gewesen seyn/ der fast nicht ein *Tempus* richtig/ als es *in partitura* stehen sol/ gesetzet vnd geordnet hat; In welcher Vngeschicklicheit der böse Mensch bey nah in allen Liedern biß an das Ende geblieben ist'. *Heinrich Alberts/ abgenötigte/ Nachricht vnd Verwarnung*, sig.):(1r.

[126] 'Schimpff vnd Spott bey gelährten *Musicis*'. Ibid.

[127] 'Ich *protestire solennissimè/* daß ich die Noten in solche *Confusion* nicht gesetzet'. Ibid, sig.):(1v.

[128] 'Der Geitz/ wie er unter allerhand Leüte sich einschlieret/ also befällt er auch unterweilen erst die Buchführer vnd Buchdrucker/ welche mit hindansetzung ihres Gewissens/ wider das Verbot hoher Potentaten/ ia selbst unsers Gottes/ kein bedencken tragen/ ihrem Nechsten schaden zu thun.' Albert, *Siebender Theil der Arien*, sig. G1v.

[129] 'etliche geitzige Buchdrücker vnd Buchführer ... den Lohn meiner Musicalischen Arbeit mir zu entziehen vnd weg zunehmen'. *Heinrich Alberts/ abgenötigte/ Nachricht vnd Verwarnung*, sig.):(1r.

[130] 'diese meine Arbeit/ so zusagen (mit Natan) mein einiges Schäfflein/ das mir Milch und Wolle geben könte/ wollen etliche Geitzige/ deren doch ieder sehr viel Schafe und Rinder hat/ mir wegnehmen'. Albert, *Achter Theil der Arien*, sig. H1v.

from Rostock.[131] The servant declared in a sworn testimony that he was unaware of the author's privilege, and that he did not have more than eight unauthorised copies. He claimed these copies were acquired from a journeyman printer (a group often suspected of involvement in book piracy).[132] If Albert's report is true, it can be added to the list of known occasions when privileges were upheld against unauthorised publishers.[133]

In 1648 Albert obtained a twelve-year imperial privilege for his *Arien*,[134] but it is unclear whether or not this was upheld. Its jurisdiction did not include the Prussian and Polish lands that were the main markets for his music and the probable location of the printer of the 1648 pirated editions. Nor did it prevent the Breslau musician Ambrosius Profe issuing in 1657 a two-volume octavo edition of the songs from books 1 to 6 of the *Arien*, reduced to a two-voice texture of cantus and bass.[135] Although Albert had died in 1651, the imperial privilege remained in force until 1660 and forbade anyone from reprinting the *Arien* 'in larger or smaller formats'.[136]

In his preface, Profe justified his edition by arguing it served the common good. All previous editions had sold out, he noted, yet many people still wished to buy them, and there was nobody except Profe willing to print further copies. He also argued that his pocket-sized octavo edition was 'better and more useful' (*besser und nützlicher*) than the folio format of Albert's songbooks, in which only the first verse of each song was provided as underlay, with the remaining strophes printed at the bottom of the page. Some musicians even copied out the songs with all the strophes underlaid, 'but with much complaint and annoyance. To save you such effort and work, I have put the words of each strophe under the melody'.[137] Through such arguments, Profe presented his edition as a legitimate enterprise that neither infringed the composer's printing privileges nor disadvantaged Albert's heirs.

Although the legal power of Albert's privileges was limited, they had symbolic power, investing his editions with authority. Such a statement of authority is shown in Figure 4.2, the 1650 engraved frontispiece of the

---

[131] *Heinrich Alberts/ abgenötigte/ Nachricht vnd Verwarnung*, sig.):(2r.

[132] On *Gesellen-Exemplarien* (journeymen's copies) as a cause of piracy, see Adrian Beier, *Kurtzer Bericht von der nützlichen und fürtrefflichen Buchhandlung* (Jena, 1690), 53.

[133] These disputes include those between Caspar Peucer and Sigmund Feyerabend over the *Chronicon Carionis* (1568) and between Peter Kopf and Ernst Vögelin over a legal treatise (1595). Gramlich, 'Rechtsordnungen des Buchgewerbes', 99–102.

[134] A-Whh, Impressoria, Karton 1, no. 7, fols. 25r–26v; an excerpt is printed on the reverse of the title page of Albert, *Achter Theil der Arien*.

[135] *Heinrich Albert Arien Erster Theil/ Darinnen die jenige Geistliche Lieder/ so in seinen 6. unterschiedenen Theilen vorhin in Folio gedruckt*, ed. Ambrosius Profe (Leipzig, 1657); *Heinrich Albert Arien Ander Theil/ Darinnen die jenige Weltliche Lieder/ so in seinen 6. unterschiedenen Theilen vorhin in Folio gedruckt*, ed. Ambrosius Profe (Brieg, 1657). RISM A/I A641–2.

[136] 'weder in größer- oder kleinerer Form/ nit nachgedruckt'. Quoted in Albert, *Achter Theil der Arien*, sig. H1v. On the disputed question of whether privileges remained valid after the death of their holder, see Lehne, 'Zur Rechtsgeschichte der kaiserlichen Privilegien', 385.

[137] '[a]ber mit vielem Beschwer und Verdruß. Solcher Mühe und Arbeit nun euch zu überheben/ hab ich die Texte/ oder ieden Vers/ unter die gesetzte Melodey und Noten.' *Heinrich Albert Arien Erster Theil*, ed. Profe, sig. A3v.

Privileges versus Piracy 147

Figure 4.2 Engraved title page of Heinrich Albert, *Achter Theil der Arien* (Königsberg, 1650). British Library, G.61. By permission of the British Library Board

eighth book of *Arien,* where the three eagles symbolise the rulers who granted Albert his privileges. In the centre, the double-headed eagle represents the Holy Roman Emperor; on the left, the eagle symbolising the Polish crown is identifiable from the heraldic sheaf of the Vasa dynasty; and on the right, the eagle representing the Elector of Brandenburg is identifiable by the 'FV' initials of Friedrich Wilhelm (ruled 1640–88). Above the eagles, light radiates from the Hebrew initial YHWH, the divine authority from which these secular princes drew their power. Under the protection of the eagles' wings are stylised scenes of Königsberg life that represent the poetic world of the *Arien*: on the left, a funerary procession entering the city gates, and on the right, a convivial garden scene with musicians around a table and a lutenist and female singer. The theme of protection is reinforced by the nesting hen in the foreground, whose chicks are surrounded by the text 'Sub his alis' (under these wings), an allusion to Psalm 90.4 and its promise of God's shelter.[138] Just as the hen protects her chickens, so too do the princely eagles guard Albert's sense of ownership over his *Arien.* Such eyecatching iconography demonstrated how Albert's authorial status depended on the authority of the princes who granted his privileges.

The experiences of Schütz, Schein and Albert show that privileges had limited legal power to protect musicians from unauthorised editions. Partly because of the patchwork of jurisdictions in German-speaking lands and partly because of the nature of privileges as exemptions from common law, it was hard to uphold these legal instruments. Yet in the early seventeenth century, composers and publishers repeatedly underwent the ritualistic process of obtaining privileges, presumably because of the symbolic value these added to editions. Nowhere is this clearer than in Albert's engraved frontispiece shown in Figure 4.2, where the eagles indicate the authority carried by the edition. A privilege acted as an authentication device, differentiating authorised editions from counterfeit ones, and reasussuring potential purchasers that an edition was worth buying. Thus the symbolic power of a privilege could enhance the commercial value of a published book.

MUSICAL OWNERSHIP IN THE AGE OF MANUSCRIPT

From 1650 onwards, composers rarely applied for printing privileges. Table 4.1 shows that the handful of musicians to hold privileges after this date included Andreas Hammerschmidt and the Halle organist Wilhelm Hieronymus Stenger. Instead most of the printing privileges for music after 1650 were held by publishers of lucrative items such as hymnals or secular songbooks (see Table 4.2). The dwindling use of privileges

---

[138] Psalm 90:4: 'In scapulis suis obumbrabit tibi et sub alis eius sperabis' (He shall cover thee with his feathers, and under his wings shalt thou trust).

Musical Ownership in the Age of Manuscript 149

primarily reflected the decline of music printing, as outlined in the introduction. After 1650 fewer editions were printed and there was less commercial incentive for unauthorised publications as occurred with Schein and Albert. This section explores changing notions of musical ownership in the second half of the seventeenth century, showing how the altered material forms of music circulation affected attitudes to attribution and unauthorised copying.

As shown in the first section of this chapter, Luther's ideal of individuals serving the common good persisted among musicians of the early eighteenth century such as Kuhnau and Bach. Yet newer attitudes to self-identity and individual property were also emerging. Theorists of natural law such as Samuel von Pufendorf and Christian Thomasius argued that the natural order bestowed individual rights and duties on humans. The historian Winfried Schulze claims that attitudes towards *Eigennutz* (self-interest) changed such that it was no longer seen negatively, but rather as benefitting the wider community. Schulze traces this development through seventeenth-century discussions of taxation (which argued that individual prosperity can boost the state's revenues) and a 1658 treatise by Christian Herold (which claimed that humans by nature seek to make their lives better, more comfortable and more secure).[139] For Schulze, such sources anticipate later doctrines such as Adam Smith's theory of free market economics, according to which the greatest public benefit results from individuals following their own interests.[140] While Schulze's account verges on the teleological, newer attitudes undoubtedly existed alongside older Lutheran ideals of serving the common good.

By the late seventeenth century, legal writings acknowledged that authors and publishers had inherent rights of property in books. In a 1689 ruling, the law faculty at Leipzig University advised:

We consider that a book, which either the author himself publishes or the bookdealer purchases from the author, is true and correct property that nobody should take against his will. Therefore it is an unjust thing, for another to take without payment this book for reprinting. ... In respect of the books that are made public for the benefit of the commonweal, the author and publisher have not thereby abdicated their possessive right, but rather they thereby seek in respect of their effort, work and expense a permissible profit for their upkeep.[141]

---

[139] Schulze, 'Vom Gemeinnutz zum Eigennutz', 606–12, 617, 620–21.   [140] Ibid., 614.

[141] 'Nachdem aber, unsers Ermessens, hierbey billig zu *considerir*en, daß ein Buch, so entweder der *Autor* selbsten verleget, oder ein Buchführer von demselben erkauffet, derselben wahres und rechtes Eigenthum sey, auch wie insgemein niemand das Seinige wider seinen Willen zu entziehen, also es ebenmäßig eine ungerechte Sache, einem andern sein Buch durch den Nachdruck zur Ungebühr zu nehmen ... in Betrachtung zwar hierdurch zu Nutz des gemeinen Wesens der Gebrauch der Bücher gemein gemachet wird, iedoch besagter *Auctor* und Verleger deswegen ihr daran habendes Recht nicht *abdicir*en, sondern vielmehr vor ihre Mühe und Arbeit, auch Kosten, einen zuläßigen Gewinn zu ihrem Unterhalt darmit zu suchen'. Legal ruling reprinted in Johann Heinrich von Berger, *Electa discreptationum forensium secundum seriem*, vol. 1 (Leipzig, 1738), 1009–10.

Thus Luther's doctrine of sharing with neighbours was partly replaced by a notion of proprietorial rights; these rights were conferred by ownership of the copy-text, not by creative effort on the part of the author.[142]

Such nascent awareness of proprietorial rights led to dissatisfaction with the system of privileges. In 1690 the Jena jurist Adrian Beier lamented:

Up to the present time, one could say that bookdealers must protect themselves through privileges. Consequently where there is no privilege, the unauthorised reprints will go unheeded and unpunished. Not so, my friend! In such cases the process is at fault and the system of privileges should be lamented . . . . It does not follow that where there is no privilege, there is no law, no help, no sin, no punishment. Natural law and reason command you to leave alone what is not your own.[143]

Beier criticised the privilege system for its presumption that books could be protected only as exceptional cases. Proponents of natural law instead assumed that every individual had propertorial rights and the duty to respect others' property. Beier's views did not enter the statute books, and Martha Woodmansee has shown how debates about literary property continued throughout the eighteenth century.[144] Yet the growing dissatisfaction with privileges may help explain why few musicians after 1650 applied for them.

More specific reasons for the dwindling use of privileges by composers can be found in the changing state of the German music trade. After the 1650s music printing declined, and engraved editions became an increasingly significant part of the trade. But privileges were almost never used for engraved editions of music in German-speaking lands.[145] None of the engraved editions of keyboard music issued in Leipzig by Kuhnau (the two parts of his *Clavier Übung*, his *Frische Clavier-Früchte* and *Biblische Historien*) or by Bach (the four volumes of his *Clavier-Übung*) mentions a privilege on its title page, even though all were published by the composer.

Arguably the technology of engraving gave composers greater control over the publication process. Although it has been disproved that Kuhnau or Bach did their own engraving,[146] they presumably retained ownership

---

[142] Gieseke, *Vom Privileg zum Urheberrecht*, 102–5.

[143] 'Hats Zeit biß dorthin/ möcht einer sagen und müssen die Buchhändler sich durch *Privilegia* vorher bewahren/ So folgt/ wo deren keines/ wird der Nachdruck ungewehrt und ungestrafft seyn. Nicht also/ mein Freund! der *Process* ist in solchen Fall/ da uff *privilegia* geklagt wird . . . . Folgt aber drumb nicht/ wo kein *Privilegium*, da sey kein Recht/ keine Hülff/ keine Sünde/ keine Strafe. Das natürliche Recht/ die Vernunfft weiset einen jeden an/ liegen zu lassen was nicht ist'. Beier, *Kurtzer Bericht*, 52–53.

[144] Martha Woodmansee, 'The Genius and the Copyright: Economic and Legal Conditions of the Emergence of the "Author"', *Eighteenth-Century Studies* 17 (1984), 425–48.

[145] A 10-year privilege is stated on Johann Heinrich Schmelzer's engraved *Sonatae unarum fidium, seu a violino solo* (Nuremberg, 1664), RISM A/I S1659; and Wilhelm Hieronymus Stenger's Saxon privilege of 1662 was for a proposed engraved book (probably of keyboard music) (see Table 4.1).

[146] Christoph Wolff, *Bach. Essays on His Life and Music* (Cambridge, MA: Harvard University Press, 1991), 194; on Kuhnau's engravers and his ownership of the plates, see Johann Kuhnau, *The Collected Works for Keyboard*, ed. C. David Harris, 2 vols. (New York: The Broude Trust, 2003), i, p. xxi.

Musical Ownership in the Age of Manuscript

of the copper plates on which their music was engraved. In the technology of movable type used previously, the type was redistributed as soon as all copies had been printed. If there was demand for a second edition, the book would have to be newly typeset, and in this respect the maker of an authorised second edition had no advantage over a pirate. For engraved editions, by contrast, the owner of the plates could have extra copies printed whenever required, whereas any other prospective publisher would have to commission a new set of plates. Kuhnau regularly made further impressions of his keyboard works from his plates: for his *Neue Clavier Übung*, the copies dated 1689 exist in several different states with small variants of musical ornamentation and page decoration, while there are also extant impressions dated 1695, 1710 and 1718.[147] Bach similarly re-used the plates of his Partitas, printed individually from 1726 onwards, for the collected edition (*Clavier Übung ... opus I*) in 1731.[148] Perhaps Kuhnau and Bach regarded privileges as an unnecessary expense when they had such control over the publication of their engraved music.

In more competitive sectors of the music market such as England and the Low Countries, the use of engraving did not deter unauthorised editions. Between 1708 and 1711, many of the engraved editions of the Amsterdam publisher Estienne Roger were copied by his rival Pieter Mortier, who made new sets of plates for his own editions of music by such figures as Albinoni and Corelli.[149] Dutch publishers even offered unauthorised editions of keyboard collections of some German composers: the *Composizione musicali per il cembalo* of Conrad Friedrich Hurlebusch, published by the composer in Hamburg in 1735, had already been illicitly published a few years earlier by Gerhard Fredrik Witvogel in Amsterdam.[150] Within central Germany, however, the sluggish nature of the music trade made unauthorised reprinting less of a hazard for composers such as Bach who published their own engraved editions.

By the early eighteenth century, the main threat to printed editions in central German lands came instead from scribal copying. In 1736 the Weimar organist Johann Gottfried Walther wrote to the Wolfenbüttel cantor Heinrich Bokemeyer, describing his difficulty finding a bookseller to publish his set of keyboard variations on the chorale *Allein Gott*: 'The publishers fear that such an undertaking would expose them to harm, because for every music-lover who buys it, ten or more copy it out'.[151] Similarly, the Erfurt organist Jakob Adlung noted that 'if a publisher sinks

---

[147] Kuhnau, *Collected Works*, ed. Harris, ii, 131–33.

[148] RISM A/I B480. Wolff, *Bach. Essays*, 196–200.

[149] Rudolf Rasch, 'De muzierkoorlog tussen Estienne Roger en Pieter Mortier (1708–11)', *De Zeventiende Eeuw* 6 (1990), 89–97.

[150] Conrad Friedrich Hurlebusch, *Opera scelte per il clavicembalo* (Amsterdam, *c*.1733). RISM A/I H8022.

[151] 'die Verleger befürchten, es möchte ihnen solch Unternehmen zu Schaden gereichen, weil, wenn 1 Liebhaber Geld anwendet, ihrer 10 und mehr es abschrieben'. Letter to Bokemeyer, 4 August 1736. Walther, *Briefe*, 195.

his fortune into engraving a piece, sometimes he sells only one copy in a big town, from which thirty amateurs make their own scribal copies, and the publisher is left with his own [unsold] copies'.[152] Evidence of such scribal copying is provided by manuscripts that duplicate all (or almost all) the contents of such engraved editions as Bach's *Clavier-Übung III* (1739)[153] or Kuhnau's *Biblische Historien* (1700).[154] Such copying could not be prevented by princely privileges, and it presented new challenges to composers seeking to control the circulation of their music.

Scribal transmission arguably maintained the ideals of sharing music for the common good, although access to copies might be restricted to those with the necessary contacts among elite musicians. Yet there were concerns that the liberties taken in scribal transmission could mar the reputation of composers. Adlung complained about the 'free-spiritedness' (*Freygeisterei*) of scribes, recommending that when copying music 'you should change nothing intentionally, unless a copyist's mistake is observed, which you should correct provided it is not contrary to the laws of composition. Otherwise what Gaius alters, Crispus will also change in his copy, so that finally the master will no longer recognise his work'.[155] This comment on textual corruption alluded to 1 Corinthians 1, where St Paul lamented the different doctrinal views spread by early Christian converts in Corinth.

Even worse, in Adlung's opinion, were misguided attempts at improvement:

Still less should one change another's ideas deliberately; he who believes himself to be qualified to improve another's work (as Balhorn imagines) should preferably compose something himself, and leave another's work in peace. Many do not change the ideas, but the key or the clefs; again I believe this not to be good, should such things be disseminated further.[156]

Here Adlung evoked a proverb about the Lübeck printer Johann Balhorn, whose name was a byword for emendations that did not improve the original.[157] Such comments echoed the concerns for textual accuracy

---

[152] 'Wenn ein Verleger sein Vermögen dran gewendet, so wird bisweilen in einer großen Stadt 1 Exemplar verkauft; 30 und mehr Liebhaber nehmen davon die Abschrift, und der Verleger muß seine Exemplarien behalten'. Jakob Adlung, *Anleitung zu der musikalischen Gelahrtheit* (Erfurt, 1758), 727.

[153] GB-Lbl, R.M.21.a.9; I-Bc, Ms. DD.77; and the lost manuscript PL-GD, Mus. ms. 4203/4204.

[154] D-LEm, Ms.III.8.4 (Andreas-Bach-Buch), fols. 6–23.

[155] 'Man ändere nichts mit Vorsatz, und wenn im Abschreiben ein Fehler begangen worden, so corrigire man solchen, wenn auch gleich solcher der Setzkunst nicht entgegen wär. Denn wenn Caius etwas ändert, mit dessen Abschrift macht es Crispus wieder also, so wird endlich der Meister seine Arbeit nicht mehr kennen'. Adlung, *Anleitung*, 728–29.

[156] 'Noch weniger muß man eines andern Einfälle mit Vorsatz ändern; wer sich vor geschickt hält, eines andern Arbeit zu verbessern, (wie Ballhorn sich einbildet) der setze lieber selbst etwas, und lasse anderer Arbeit mit Frieden. Manche ändern die Einfälle nicht, wohl aber die Tonart oder die Schlüssel; auch dieses halte ich nicht vor gut, zumal, wenn solche Sachen sollen weiter communicirt werden'. Ibid., 729.

[157] Hans-Bernd Spies, '"Verbessert durch Johann Balhorn". Neues zu einer alten Redensart', *Zeitschrift des Vereins für Lübeckische Geschichte und Altertumskunde* 62 (1982), 285–92.

Musical Ownership in the Age of Manuscript 153

voiced in applications for printing privileges, and resonate with the debates about textual fidelity discussed in Chapter 6.

Adlung also criticised scribes who failed to attribute music correctly, thus depriving composers of the opportunity to receive recognition for their works: 'Yet another copyist omits from naivety the name of the composer. That is like those who tear the title page from books, as spiteful enviers do'.[158] Here he alluded to jealous scholars who removed crucial information from the spine or initial pages of books, in order to hide their sources from visitors to their libraries.[159] Even worse was the practice of deliberately misattributing compositions in order to deceive listeners or those selecting music for performance. In the opinion of Andreas Werckmeister:

[H]e, the unskilled author, writes on his composition the names of other honest composers and capellmeisters, and will convince others that it is the work of these distinguished people, in order that he initially can bring his pieces to be performed; then they are accepted and admired by those who do not understand composition, and he reveals they are his compositions.[160]

Werckmeister noted that these tricks slandered the better-known composers whose names became thereby attached to lesser pieces; it also undermined the practice of judging composers' skill from their notated works (see Chapter 3).

Yet several musicians admitted to misattributing pieces, often for playful reasons. In his autobiography, Johann Friedrich Fasch claimed as a student to have passed off one of his orchestral suites as the work of Telemann at a collegium musicum meeting in Leipzig, 'and they thought, to my joy, that it was by him'.[161] Kuhnau recommended novice composers circulate their works anonymously: 'For if [the novice] let the people know that he is the composer of the works put before them, he would always have to be suspicious of these judges who approve of and praise his works'.[162] Such advice was followed by Walther when sending one of his compositions to Bokemeyer in 1730. Walther explained that: 'I have diligently omitted my

---

[158] 'Noch andere schreiben aus Einfalt den Namen des Setzers nicht hin. Das ist eben so viel als von den Büchern das Titleblat wegreissen, wie einige Neidhämmel thun'. Adlung, *Anleitung*, 729.

[159] On such secretive scholars, see Sari Kivistö, *The Vices of Learning: Morality and Knowledge at Early Modern Universities* (Leiden: Brill, 2014), 117.

[160] 'Er der untüchtige *Autor* schreibet vor seine *Composition* den Nahmen anderer rechtschaffenen *Componi*sten und Capellmeister/ und wil andere bereden/ als ob es solcher vornehmen Leute Arbeit wäre/ umb daß er erstlich seine Stücke zu *musici*ren anbringet/ wenn sie dann von denen/ so die *Composition* nicht wohl verstehen/ angenommen und *admiri*ret worden/ so ziehet er dann loß/ daß es seine *Composition* sey'. Andreas Werckmeister, *Cribrum musicum* (Quedlinburg and Leipzig, 1700), 24–25.

[161] 'und sie glaubten, zu meiner Freude, daß solche von Ihm wäre'. Friedrich Wilhelm Marpurg, *Historisch-kritische Beyträge zur Aufnahme der Musik* 3 (1757–58), 124.

[162] 'Denn wenn er die Leute wissen lässet/ daß er der Meister von denen ihnen vorgelegten Stücken sey/ so sollen ihm diese Richter allezeit verdächtig vorkommen/ die seine Wercke *approbi*ren und loben werden'. Kuhnau, *Der musicalische Quack-Salber*, 512.

name from it, because from experience I know that one values the piece according to [the name of] the person, rather than the person according to the piece (as it should properly be)'.[163] He recounted how he had passed off some of his compositions as those of Telemann, and some of Telemann's works as another's compositions; he had found that any works ascribed to Telemann were praised, regardless of their true authorship.[164] Thus some musicians used deliberate misattributions to test the judgement of their listeners and provoke thought about why certain composers had been canonised.[165]

Other composers, however, objected strongly to the misattribution or corruption of their works in scribal transmission, notably the Munich court organist Johann Caspar Kerll. His objections concerned his keyboard works, a genre where copyists and performers often took liberties in adapting compositions to their individual needs. In his 1686 book of organ versets on the Magnificat, *Modulatio organica*, Kerll claimed he had entered print to avoid the pieces circulating under other names:

In truth I have seen, and not just in one place, my works ascribed to other names. In this way any little crow, decked with assumed plumage, triumphs. Consequently, let the author receive the credit, that the honey-making bee may enjoy the fruit of its own labours.[166]

As discussed in Chapter 2, the metaphor of Aesop's crow was shorthand for plagiarists; by contrast, the metaphor of the honeybee evoked the honest labour required to fill one's mental storehouse with noteworthy ideas. Kerll added: 'I would like to warn keyboardists not to subject the themes to their own discretion, or to improve on them as they wish: food once cooked is bad when reheated'.[167] This was an unprecedented attempt to restrict the freedom usually enjoyed by keyboardists in improvising on pre-existing material and tailoring notated compositions to suit their own performance style (see Chapters 1 and 6).

Kerll's concerns about misattribution and corruption were not simply justifications for entering print, but reflected the transmission of his keyboard works. In one of the most authoritative sources of his music,

---

[163] 'Ich habe mit Fleiß meinen Nahmen nicht drauf setzen wollen, weil aus der Erfahrung inne worden bin, daß man öfters die Sache nach der Person, und nicht dieser nach jener (wie es doch billig seyn solte) zu schätzen pfleget'. Walther, *Briefe*, 104.

[164] Ibid.

[165] For further examples of misattributions in relation to canonisation, see Stephen Rose, 'Plagiarism at the Academy of Ancient Music: A Case-Study in Authorship, Style and Judgement', in Alan Howard and Rebecca Herissone (eds.), *Concepts of Creativity in Seventeenth-Century England* (Woodbridge: Boydell & Brewer, 2013), 181–98.

[166] 'Et vero inspexi non uno in loco, alieno Nomini laboris mei partus adscriptos. Ita triumphat, mutuatis pennis, ornata Cornicula. Ut ergo de Authore constaret, & suus api mellificanti honos redderetur'. Johann Caspar Kerll, *Modulatio organica* (Munich, 1686), sig. A3v. RISM A/I K457.

[167] 'Organaedos hic monitos velim, ne subjecta themata, ad suum quisque arbitrium, placitumque deflectant: & coctum bene cibum, male recoquant', Ibid., sig. A4r.

Musical Ownership in the Age of Manuscript

the Göttweig manuscript copied by Georg Muffat, there are no attributions given for Kerll's compositions.[168] In another early manuscript source, the keyboard book of Emanuel Benisch (compiled in the 1680s), Kerll's Toccatas Prima and Ottava have no attribution, and his Toccatas Quinta and Sesta are ascribed to Poglietti.[169] Further misattributions of his toccatas to Poglietti and Frescobaldi occur in early eighteenth-century manuscripts,[170] and a 1693 printed edition attributes a short-ened version of Kerll's Toccata Settima to Froberger.[171] Even by the relatively fluid standards of transmission for keyboard music, these are high levels of misattribution, suggesting the difficulty of identifying personal style in keyboard compositions largely assembled from formulae (see Chapter 1, p. 40).

Kerll sought to stem the false attributions by appending to the *Modulatio organica* a thematic catalogue of his other keyboard works. Spanning 10 pages, it included engraved incipits of eight toccatas, six canzonas, fourteen movements from dance suites, and four other pieces. This is the first known printed thematic catalogue of a single composer's output.[172] Musicians sometimes recommended making a thematic catalogue to show what manuscript music they had available for sharing.[173] Kerll, by contrast, used it to claim authorship over his compositions circulating scribally. As Figure 4.3 shows, he thereby fixed in notation the opening of toccatas, imposing a sense of workhood on pieces that were usually characterised by improvisation. The thematic catalogue might seem to suggest Kerll was concerned with his moral rights as an author, although he was probably primarily motivated by a humanist ideal of transmitting his name and reputation for posterity.

Yet Kerll's assertion of his authorial claims rested on princely authority. The dedication of *Modulatio organica* indicates that it and the thematic catalogue were printed as a wedding gift to Maria Antonia of Austria, who married Elector Max Emanuel of Bavaria in 1685. They were engraved and published by Michael Wening, the Munich court engraver whose other work included lavish illustrations of the court and its entertainments; many of his projects were undertaken at the Elector's commission or with his financial backing.[174] Details of the financial support for *Modulatio*

---

[168] A-GÖ, Ms. Kerl. 2.   [169] US-NH, LM 5056.

[170] A-Wm, Ms. 721; I-Bc, Ms. DD.53; details in Johann Caspar Kerll, *The Collected Works for Keyboard*, ed. C. David Harris, 2 vols. (New York: The Broude Trust, 1995), vol. ii.

[171] Johann Jacob Froberger, *Diverse ingegnosissime, rarissime & non maj più viste curiose partite, di toccate, canzone, ricercate, alemande, correnti, sarabande e gique* (Mainz, 1693). RISM A/I F2026.

[172] Barry S. Brook, 'The Earliest Printed Thematic Catalogues', in Nils Schiørring, Henrik Glahn and Carsten E. Hatting (eds.), *Festskrift Jens Peter Larsen. 1902–14 VI–1972* (Copenhagen: Wilhelm Hansen, 1972), 103–12 (pp. 107–8).

[173] Adlung, *Anleitung*, 727.

[174] Gertrud Stetter, *Michael Wening: der Kupferstecher der Max Emanuel-Zeit. Ausstellung im Münchner Stadtmuseum, 28. September 1977 bis 28. Januar 1978* (Munich: Lipp, 1977).

Figure 4.3 Johann Caspar Kerll, *Modulatio organica* (Munich, 1686), start of thematic catalogue. Munich, Bayerische Staatsbibliothek, 4 Mus.pr. 37847, urn:nbn:de:bvb:12-bsb00090323-9

organica remain unknown but given the dedication to Maria Antonia, it seems likely that the book and thematic catalogue were underwritten by the Elector. Thus only with princely support could Kerll claim authorship of his keyboard pieces circulating in manuscript, in much the same way that only princes could grant the privileges that recognised the labour of musical authors in earlier decades. And just as privileges were largely symbolic objects, so too could it be argued that Kerll's thematic catalogue had limited power to enforce accurate attribution, given its restricted circulation and probable high price, and the impossibility of regulating the habits of copyists.

Throughout the long seventeenth century, musicians from German-speaking lands asserted that they should receive recognition for their labour in composing and publishing. This recognition could take the form of a financial return on their investment, an enhancement of their musical reputation, or the assurance that their compositions circulated with correct attributions. There was no legal basis for individual authorial rights in the period, particularly given the emphasis on the common good in Lutheran doctrine and legal cases until the late seventeenth century. Even privileges had limited effectiveness as protection against unauthorised reprints. The efforts by composers to assert ownership over their works were largely symbolic rituals that drew on princely authority; but through these rituals they confronted age-old questions about the balance between individuals' rights and their responsibilities to the surrounding community.

CHAPTER 5

The Regulation of Novelty

On 14 January 1651, the 65-year-old Heinrich Schütz wrote to the Elector of Saxony, requesting retirement from his regular duties as capellmeister at the Dresden court. In his letter he painted a vivid picture of the changing demands on church musicians in towns, recounting a cautionary tale about

an old, not badly qualified cantor living in a renowned town and well known to me, who wrote to me some time ago, complaining bitterly that the young councillors were extremely dissatisfied with his old style of music and thus would happily dismiss him. They said straight to his face in the town hall that a tailor of thirty years' service and a cantor of thirty years' service are of no more use in the world. And it is to be agreed that the young world quickly grows tired of the old customs and styles and wants to change them.[1]

Schütz's anecdote must be read in its context of an eloquent plea for retirement, in which his rhetorical tactic was to emphasise his advanced age and the risk that his skills would be overtaken by the fast pace of musical fashion. In other letters of the 1650s, he projected a more dynamic self-image, for instance when writing to the Wolfenbüttel court to recommend prospective musicians and to send his own compositions.[2] Yet the tale probably contains an element of truth; it may even describe Schütz's correspondent Henricus Baryphonus, cantor in Quedlinburg until his death in 1655, who regularly commiserated with Schütz on the foolishness of the younger generation of composers.[3] Whatever its veracity, the anecdote pointed to a wider change in attitudes to authority and individuality in church music after the Thirty Years War, a change that is vital to understanding how notions of musical authorship altered between the generations of Schütz and Bach.

In 1580 a Saxon ordinance forbade cantors and organists from performing their own compositions in church, instead stipulating that they should

---

[1] D-Dla, Loc. 8687/1, fol. 293r; *SDok* 1, 325; translation adapted from *HSR*, 185.
[2] See, for instance, Schütz's letter dated 27 November 1655 to Sophie Elisabeth of Brunswick-Lüneburg; *SDok* 1, 388–91; *HSR*, 219–21.
[3] Excerpts of the correspondence between Baryphonus and Schütz were published by Andreas Werckmeister in his *Musicae mathematicae hodegus curiosus* (Frankfurt am Main, 1686), 3, 114 and *Cribrum musicum* (Quedlinburg and Leipzig, 1700), 30, 39–41.

158

The Regulation of Novelty

use works by 'old, outstanding composers who are experienced in this art, such as Josquin, Clemens non Papa and Orlande de Lassus'.[4] The edict envisaged a uniform musical repertory in Saxon churches, as opposed to the disruption potentially caused by cantors performing their own untested pieces. The authorised repertory was in the polyphonic 'old style' mentioned by Schütz and was typically available in printed editions.

By the end of the seventeenth century, however, attitudes to composition by church musicians had reversed completely. In 1688 Johann Kuhnau, then organist at the Thomaskirche in Leipzig, wrote: 'Truly nobody can be a cantor, which involves directing the whole music (evidently in those places, which do not have a capellmeister), unless he can compose'.[5] When he became cantor at Leipzig's Thomasschule in 1701, Kuhnau adhered to this statement, writing numerous cycles of church music. On his death in 1722, his obituary noted: 'It is very hard to count the number of church pieces that he composed, for in his frequent musical performances he never or only very rarely relied on others' compositions'.[6] Kuhnau's practices were emulated by his successor Johann Sebastian Bach, who in his first two years in Leipzig wrote a new cantata for almost every Sunday in the liturgical calendar. In regularly performing their own new compositions, Kuhnau and Bach represented the norm expected of church musicians in the early eighteenth century. The church repertory thus became increasingly individualised and ephemeral: cantatas were written for a specific occasion and were rarely memorialised in print. To adapt Schütz's anecdote: just as a tailor provided clothes in the latest fashion and cut for specific individuals, so too should church musicians write compositions tailored for the tastes and ensembles of specific places.

This chapter explores why attitudes to authority and individuality in church music changed so radically across the long seventeenth century. The developments described here applied to ecclesiastical music in towns, especially to cantors (the school teachers who were responsible for directing vocal music in church); sacred music at courts was not regulated

---

[4] 'derer alten und dieser Kunst wolerfahrnen und fürtreffentlichen *Componisten*, als *Josquini, Clementis non Papae, Orlandi* und dergleichen Gesänge gesungen werden'. *Des Durchlauchtigsten/ Hochgebornen Fürsten und Herrn Augusten/ Hertzogen zu Sachsen ... Ordnung/ Wie es in seiner Churf. G. Landen/ bey den Kirchen/ mit der Lehr und Ceremonien/ deßgleichen in derselben beyden Universiteten/ Consistorien/ Fürsten und Particular Schulen/ Visitationen/ Synodis, und was solchem allem mehr anhanget/ gehalten werden sol* (Leipzig, 1580), 149.

[5] 'Nullus enim Cantoris officio, quod in dirigenda tota Musica consistit (nimirum in iis locis, ubi specialis Capellae Magister non habetur) satis facere potest, nisi sciat componere'. Johann Kuhnau, *Jura circa musicos ecclesiasticos* (Leipzig, 1688), sig. B4r.

[6] 'Was er nächstdem an *Musicali*schen Kirchen-Stücken ... *componir*et habe, mag wohl schwerlich zu zehlen seyn, gestalt er bey seinen häuffigen *Musicali*schen Aufführungen sich fremder *Composition* niemahls oder doch gar selten bedienet ... ' Obituary of Kuhnau in Christoph Ernst Sicul, *Annalium Lipsiensium maxime academicorum sectio XVI oder des Leipziger Jahr-Buchs zu dessen Dritten Bande erste Fortsetzung*, vol. 1 (Leipzig, 1723), 60–67 (p. 66).

in the same way. The 1580 ordinance was a product of the emphasis on social discipline in the late sixteenth century. Church and state worked together to impose social, spiritual and moral control on the German people. Pastors and legislators followed the writings of Plato, viewing music as having such powers over society that innovative or highly individualised compositions could arouse disorder. Yet after the Thirty Years War, town councils increasingly required novelty in church music, largely from a belief that sacred music was a fashionable accessory to be produced, consumed and then discarded. Church music was no longer an authoritative canon with absolute power over human emotions, but an object of taste and a platform for individual cantors to show their musical aspirations.

SOCIAL DISCIPLINE AND MUSIC

In Saxony the preference around 1600 for an authoritative, unchanging repertory of sacred music stemmed from the efforts of church and state to impose social discipline. As historians such as Gerhard Oestreich and Heinz Schilling have shown, the rise of Lutheran churches and the embedding of Lutheran beliefs within schools occurred in parallel with attempts to create a society of obedient subjects.[7] The new institutions of the Lutheran church, bolstered by the authority of territorial princes, sought to shape the morals, beliefs and behaviour of individuals in several ways. Foremost among these techniques was education, through which reformers aimed to create pious subjects as well as the next generation of leaders. Philipp Melanchthon explained in a 1531 oration *De ordine discendi* (*On the order of learning*) that 'your studies do not concern only you, but also the state ... they are provided for giving of advice for the state, for teaching in the churches and for upholding the doctrine of religion'.[8] Ecclesiastical practices and school life were regulated by edicts (*Kirchenordnungen* and *Schulordnungen*), whose stipulations ranged from the liturgy to the books used in school and the responsibilities of church officials and school teachers. The implementation of these edicts was policed by visitations, in which committees of ecclesiastical officials

---

[7] Heinz Schilling, 'Die Konfessionalisierung von Kirche, Staat und Gesellschaft – Profil, Leistung, Defizite und Perspektiven eines geschichtswissenschaftlichen Paradigmas', in Wolfgang Reinhard and Heinz Schilling (eds.), *Die katholische Konfessionalisierung. Akten eines von Corpus Catholicorum und Verein für Reformationsgeschichte veranstalteten Symposions (Augsburg 1993)* (Gütersloh: Gütersloher Verlagshaus, 1995), 1–49 (p. 4); Winfried Schulze, 'Gerhard Oestreichs Begriff "Sozialdisziplinierung in der frühen Neuzeit"', *Zeitschrift für historische Forschung* 14 (1987), 265–302.

[8] Philip Melanchthon, *Orations on Philosophy and Education*, ed. Sachiko Kusukawa, trans. Christine F. Salazar (Cambridge: Cambridge University Press, 1999), 5–6.

Social Discipline and Music

inspected churches, schools and congregational behaviour. Susan Karant-Nunn has shown how in electoral Saxony the efforts of the visitations intensified between *c*.1575 and the mid-1590s into a full-blown attack on popular cultures which were regarded as disorderly.[9]

Lutheran thinkers justified their programme of social discipline via reference to classical philosophers, notably Plato's vision of a republic where individuals were harnessed in harmonious unity. Luther, in his 1534–35 commentary on Psalm 101, a *Regentenspiegel* ('mirror of sovereignty') aimed at Elector Johann Friedrich I of Saxony, recommended Plato, Aristotle and Cicero as indispensible reading for a secular ruler.[10] Melanchthon, despite his suspicion of pagan philosophers, commended Plato's *Laws* as providing 'useful precepts for the leading of cities'.[11] Particularly pertinent to Lutheran education was the Platonic view of the child as a wild creature in need of taming.[12] Plato argued that individuals should be chiselled into conformity to ensure the stability of the state. In his *Laws*, the Athenian Stranger was wary of creative innovation even in the dances and songs of children: 'There is no greater mischief a State can suffer than ... the man ... who is always innovating or introducing some novel device ... since he privily alters the characters of the young, and causes them to condemn what is old and esteem what is new'.[13]

Plato regarded music as one of the most powerful ways to control individuals within society. In *The Republic*, Socrates advised that the education of children should begin with music (in the form of declaimed stories), to mould youngsters when their characters are most pliable.[14] Later in *The Republic*, he commended music's rhythm and harmony as the best way to insinuate ideas into the soul.[15] These Platonic notions about music's power were adopted by sixteenth-century reformers. Melanchthon declared: 'Our ears are drawn to song, and delightful harmonies penetrate deeper into our minds and stick more tenaciously in our memory'.[16] The Rostock theologian David Chytraeus explained that God had invented music 'so that His Word and all godly doctrines ... may the more eagerly and joyfully be learned, the more easily kept in the memory, and the more

---

[9] Susan Karant-Nunn, 'Neoclericalism and Anticlericalism in Saxony, 1555–675', *Journal of Interdisciplinary History* 24 (1994), 615–37.

[10] *WA* 51, 242–43.   [11] Melanchthon, *Orations on Philosophy and Education*, 202.

[12] Plato, *Laws* 7.808d.

[13] Plato, *Laws* 7.797c; trans. R. G. Bury, Loeb Classical Library 192 (Cambridge, MA: Harvard University Press, 1926).

[14] Plato, *Republic* 2.376e–377b; trans. Paul Shorey, Loeb Classical Library 237 (Cambridge, MA: Harvard University Press, 1930).

[15] Ibid., 3.401d.

[16] 'Citius enim arripiunt aure carmina, et harmoniae gratae penetrant altius in animos, et haerent in memoria tenacius'. Melanchthon's preface to Lucas Lossius, *Psalmodia, hoc est cantica sacra veteris ecclesiae selecta* (Nuremberg, 1553), sig. A3v. RISM A/I L2874.

deeply received into Christian hearts ... and the dear youth are brought through dear music with pleasure and joy to a true recognition of God, faith and thanksgiving, and all God-pleasing virtues and services'.[17]

Also influential were Plato's fears that musical innovation could undermine state authority. In *The Republic*, Socrates asserted: 'A change to a new type of music is something to beware of as a hazard of all our fortunes. For the modes of music are never disturbed without unsettling of the most fundamental political and social conventions'.[18] In *The Laws*, the Athenian stranger attributed the decline of Athens to the 'unmusical illegality' of poets who were 'unduly possessed by a spirit of pleasure': a confusion of genres (mixing 'dirges with hymns and paeans with dithyrambs') caused 'a spirit of lawlessness in regard to music' and fostered disdain for general laws. 'Next after this form of liberty would come that which refuses to be subject to the rulers'.[19] This warning was summarised by Cicero in *De legibus*: 'There can be no change in the laws of music without a resulting change in the laws of the state'.[20] He conceded, however, that such change was 'neither so greatly to be feared, nor on the other hand, to be considered of no importance at all'.[21]

To prevent music from damaging the structure of the state, Plato's *Laws* recommended strict controls on musical individuality and novelty. According to the Athenian stranger, repertories should be chosen by 'men not under fifty years of age', whose seniority should make them avoid immoderate innovation.[22] He commended the practice in ancient Egypt of preserving an unchanging musical repertory in the temples, with expulsion of anyone who attempted something new.[23] Any new compositions and poems should be censored by state-appointed judges, to ensure that they are 'legal and right, fair and good'.[24] In summary, 'every unregulated musical pursuit becomes, when brought under regulation, a thousand times better'.[25]

These Classical prescriptions on regulating musical novelty were cited by several German writers of the late sixteenth century. In his article on music, Philipp Camerarius's 1591 encyclopedia included Cicero's

---

[17] 'Damit aber Gottes wort/ vnd alle göttliche lehr ... mit grösserem lust vnd frewden gefasst/ leichter im bedechtnus behalten/ vnd desto tieffer in der Zuhörer hertzen durchdringen ... vnd die liebe jugent vnd andere durch die liebliche Musica/ mit lust vnd freuden/ zu warer erkentnus Gottes/ Glauben/ Dancksagung/ vnd allen gottgefelligen tugenden vnd gottesdiensten'. David Chytraeus, *Der fürnemsten Heubtstuck Christlicher Lehr nützliche vnd kurtze Erklerung* (Rostock, 1578), 251r–251v. On Chytraeus's notion of music's rhetorical power, see Inga Mai Groote, 'Musikalische Poetik nach Melanchthon und Glarean: Zur Genese eines Interpretationsmodells', *Archiv für Musikwissenschaft* 70 (2013), 227–53.

[18] Plato, *Republic* 4.424, trans. Shorey.   [19] Plato, *Laws* 4.700D–701B, trans. Bury.

[20] Cicero, *De legibus* 2.15.39, trans. C. W. Keyes, Loeb Classical Library 213 (Cambridge, MA: Harvard University Press, 1928).

[21] Ibid.   [22] Plato, *Laws* 7.802, trans. Bury.   [23] Ibid. 2.656, 7.799b.

[24] Ibid. 7.801d, trans. Bury.   [25] Ibid. 7. 802, trans. Bury.

summary of Plato's warning.[26] Another Latin version of Plato's warning ('Mutata Musica, mutatur Respublica') is among the inscriptions on a set of partbooks copied in the Saxon town of Löbau in the 1590s and early 1600s.[27] A more detailed discussion of these matters appears in an unpublished 1598 treatise on music by Cyriacus Spangenberg, a pupil of Luther who subsequently served as a pastor and teacher in Eisleben, Mansfeld and Sangerhausen. In a chapter on the abuses of music, Spangenberg endorsed Plato's recommendation that the music of the young should be censored by those in authority. 'For the maintenance of good order he gives the following rule: it should always be ensured that the young should not undertake to introduce anything new in singing or dancing'.[28] Spangenberg also praised the Egyptian practice of maintaining unchanged music as sanctioned by the priests.

Within the prevailing mindset of social discipline, the revival of Platonic ideas produced an atmosphere hostile to musical displays of individuality. Consequently pastors, princes and town councils alike favoured a sober and decorous musical repertory for the churches under their control. Chytraeus, writing in his preface to Matthias Ludecus's *Vesperale et matutinale* (Wittenberg, 1589), advised that: 'Simple, dignified, mature melodies corresponding to the text must be used in church. No singer should be free to change the music as he wishes. Otherwise if each organist played according to his own style, and each instrumentalist followed only his own imagination, the music would be like Africa, daily producing a new beast'.[29] Here Chytraeus invoked the Roman historian Pliny the Elder, who asserted that African lands were always producing new marvels, including monstrous hybrids such as men with dogs' heads.[30] For Chytraeus, freedom for musicians to follow their imagination or add virtuosic ornamentation would produce similar monstrosities, undermining the conformity that late-sixteenth-century thinkers saw as socially desirable.

---

[26] Philipp Camerarius, *Operae horarum subcisivarum, sive meditationes historicae, auctiores quam antea editae ... Centuria prima*, 2nd edn (Frankfurt am Main, 1602), 100.

[27] D-Dl, Mus. Löb. 8 + 70, tenor partbook, no. 32.

[28] 'Wie dann Auch der Heidnische Meister Plato weißlich vnndt wol solche Ordnung gestellet, vnnd Zu Erhalttung guetter Regimentt ein solche guette Regell gegeben vnnd gesagt, Eß ist Inn Allwege Zu verhuettenn, Daß die Jugent In Singen vnnd Springen sich nicht vnterwinde ettwas Newes auffzubringen'. Cyriacus Spangenberg, *Von der Musica und der Meistersängern* [1598], ed. Adelbert von Keller (Stuttgart, 1861), 161–62.

[29] 'Melodias simplices, graves, concinnas, & verbis textus, notulis subiecti, quantum omnino fieri potuit, congruentes adiunxit. Quas in Ecclesiis conservari, nec cuivis cantori liberum esse, suo libitu Musicae modos variare, rectissimum est, ne dum quilibet sibi Organista propriam applicationem, & quilibet Symphonista suam propriam phantasiam, ut loquuntur, affingit, Musica perinde ut Africa quotidie novam feram producat'. David Chytraeus, preface to Matthias Ludecus, *Vesperale et matutinale, hoc est, cantica, hymni et collectae, sive precationes ecclesiasticae, quae in primis & secundis vesperis, itemque Matutinis precibus ... cantari usitate solent. Prior pars. De tempore* (Wittenberg, 1589), sig. A4v.

[30] Pliny, *Naturalis historia* 8.17.42; see also Italo Ronca, '*Semper aliquid novi Africam adferre*: Philological Afterthoughts on the Plinian Reception of a Pre-Aristotelian Saying', *Akroterion* 37 (1992), 146–58.

164 *The Regulation of Novelty*

Such suspicion of musical individuality explains why the Saxon 1580 ordinance outlawed composition by cantors, as will be explored in the next section.

THE 1580 EDICT AND ITS IMPLEMENTATION

The 1580 church ordinance marked the climax of efforts in Saxony to enforce Lutheran orthodoxy and create a disciplined, moral society. It was issued by Elector August (reigned 1553–86), who in the mid-1570s sought to purge his territory's churches and universities of Calvinist sympathisers. To create a new religious consensus in Saxon lands, August recruited the Tübingen theologian Jakob Andreae. With other theologians, Andreae drafted the Formula of Concord, the statement of Lutheran orthodoxy to which all Saxon pastors were required to subscribe. Using a 1559 Württemberg edict as a model, Andreae wrote the 1580 church ordinance, which sought to create a centralised state church with strong electoral control over universities and schools.[31] The wording of the 1580 ordinance was subsequently echoed in local edicts for specific schools and churches, and its provisions were upheld by visitations inspecting each parish.[32]

The relevant passage in the 1580 ordinance is a clause on the duties of the cantor, within a section on the employment of teachers in *Particular-Schulen* (the grammar schools that prepared students for university). It is not present in the Württemberg edict that was the model for the Saxon order, and hence may have been added by Andreae:

Likewise the cantors should always sing that which is specified by their pastor. They should diligently pay attention to the pastors, and earnestly ensure that they do not perform any of their own songs (should they be composers) or other new things. Instead they should use pieces by old, outstanding composers who are experienced in this art, such as Josquin, Clemens non Papa and Orlande de Lassus. In particular they should avoid songs that are based on dances or shameful tunes; instead they should use pieces that are dignified, stately and strong, and that will move the people to Christian devotion when sung in church.[33]

---

[31] Helmar Junghans, 'Die kursächsische Kirchen- und Schulordnung von 1580. Instrument der "lutherischen" Konfessionalisierung?' in Helmar Junghans (ed.), *Die sächsischen Kurfürsten während des Religionsfriedens von 1555 bis 1618. Symposium anläßlich des Abschlusses der Edition 'Politische Korrespondenz des Herzogs und Kurfürsten Moritz von Sachsen' vom 15. bis 18. September 2005 in Leipzig* (Leipzig: Verlag der Sächsischen Akademie der Wissenschaften, 2007), 209–38.

[32] The reports of the visitations are summarised in Karl Pallas (ed.), *Die Registraturen der Kirchenvisitationen im ehemals sächsischen Kurkreise*, 7 vols. (Halle, 1906–18).

[33] 'Deßgleichen sollen die *Cantores* jederzeit in der Kirche singen, was sie von ihren Pfarrherrn geheißen werden, derowegen denn die Pfarrherren mit Fleiß darauf Achtung geben, und ernstlich verschaffen sollen, daß in der Kirche nicht ihre, da sie *Componisten* seyn, oder anderer neuen angehenden, sondern derer alten und dieser Kunst wolerfahrnen und fürtreffentlichen *Componisten*, als *Josquini, Clementis non Papae, Orlandi* und dergleichen Gesänge gesungen werden, fürnemlich aber sich derer Gesänge enthalten, so auf Tantzmäß- oder Schand-Lieder-Weise nachcomponiret, sondern es also anstellen, was in der Kirche gesungen, daß es *grave*, herrlich, tapffer sey, und zur

The 1580 Edict and Its Implementation

In specifying decorous music that moves congregations to devotion, the ordinance resonates with other sixteenth-century attempts to regulate sacred repertories. The ban on music with dance rhythms or secular tunes echoes the 1562 prescription of the Council of Trent to 'banish all music that contains, whether in the singing or in the organ playing, things that are lascivious or impure'.[34] Secular styles were also banned in subsequent German ordinances, for instance in the provinces of Hoya (1581) and Lauenburg (1585).[35] The preference for 'dignified' compositions partly stemmed from a belief that the seriousness of Biblical words demanded musical settings with *gravitas*, as argued by Hans Ott in the preface to his 1539 anthology of masses.[36] The predilection for *gravitas* also had patriotic undertones, because this quality was associated with the masculine bravery that had been regarded as a stereotype of Teutonic culture since Tacitus's *Germania*.[37]

The notable features of the 1580 Saxon ordinance are its stipulation that cantors should not perform their own compositions, and its choice of three polyphonists as exemplars of church music. In seeking to restrict the compositional activities of cantors, the edict implemented the curbs on individual creativity recommended in Plato's *Laws*. By prescribing the music of 'old' and 'experienced' composers such as Josquin, it echoed Plato's preference for the 'fine old pieces' of the ancients.[38] Although the ordinance did not explicitly mention Plato, the magistrates and town councils who upheld its provisions often did so with references to Plato and Cicero, as will be shown below.

Josquin, Clemens non Papa and Lassus were celebrated figures in Lutheran lands during the late sixteenth century. Their compositions were widely available in print, and they were recommended as models to aspiring composers by theorists including the Magdeburg cantor Gallus Dressler in his 1563–64 treatise *Praecepta musicae poeticae*.[39] Rather than

---

Christlichen Andacht die Leute reitzen mag'. *Des Durchlauchtigsten/ Hochgebornen Fürsten und Herrn Augusten/ Hertzogen zu Sachsen ... Ordnung*, 149. Quoted after modern edition in Reinhold Vormbaum, *Die evangelischen Schulordnungen des 16. Jahrhunderts* (Gütersloh, 1860), 256.

[34] Quoted in Allan W. Atlas, *Renaissance Music: Music in Western Europe, 1400–600* (New York: Norton, 1998), 581.

[35] In Hoya, organists 'should refrain from secular songs and other pesky texts and tunes' ('sie sich der weltlichen lieder und anderer ergerlichen geticht und melodeyen enthalten sollen'); see Emil Sehling (ed.), *Die evangelische Kirchenordnungen des XVI. Jahrhunderts*, vol. 6.i.2 (Tübingen: Mohr, 1957), 1144. In Lauenburg, the organist should neither play secular songs nor improvise ('nicht Weltliche Lieder/ oder allein sein sortizieren und fantasieren'); see Emil Sehling (ed.), *Die evangelische Kirchenordnungen des XVI. Jahrhunderts*, vol. 5 (Leipzig: Reisland, 1913), 422.

[36] 'Cum enim in istis Ecclesiae vocibus maxima insit gravitas, etiam Musicis sonis decentem gravitatem induerunt artifices'. *Missae tredecim quatuor vocum* (Nuremberg, 1539), tenor partbook, sig. AA3r. RISM B/I 1539².

[37] Werner Braun, *Der Stilwandel in der Musik um 1600* (Darmstadt: Wissenschaftliche Buchgesellschaft, 1982), 26–27.

[38] Plato, *Laws* 7.802, trans. Bury.

[39] *Gallus Dressler's* Præcepta musicæ poëticæ, ed. Robert Forgács (Urbana: University of Illinois Press, 2007), 188–99. See also Inga Mai Groote, "'Quod pium, quod grave, quod dignum ...

being uniformly 'ancient', these composers belonged to three different generations, as Dressler implied when he classified them as representing separate stylistic groups (*genera*).[40] Josquin des Prez (*d*.1521) achieved enormous posthumous fame in German lands, with extensive printed dissemination of works attributed to him (sometimes wrongly). In the *Novum et insigne opus musicum* of 1537, containing fourteen pieces ascribed to Josquin, the editor Hans Ott wrote: 'Everyone easily acknowledges Josquin as the most famous hero of this art; he has something truly divine and inimitable, and his fame will not be resented by a thankful and just world'.[41] Jacobus Clemens non Papa (*c*.1510–*c*.56) belonged to a younger generation of composers, and his dense counterpoint could make his text-setting less clear than Josquin's. Yet his music, too, was extensively available in print: the revised edition of the *Novum et insigne opus musicum*, issued in Nuremberg in 1558–59, included 67 motets attributed to him (along with 26 pieces ascribed to Josquin).[42] Dressler commended Clemens's compositions for their use of syncopated dissonance, cadences and imitation, and quoted extracts from several of them in his treatise.[43] Lassus (*c*.1532–94) was in his late forties at the time of the Saxon edict and was recognised as the leading contemporary musician of his age. Dressler praised Lassus 'as surpassing all in sweetness . . . he applies the harmony to the words aptly and fittingly through seemliness'.[44]

Motets by Josquin, Clemens non Papa and Lassus appealed to Lutheran church authorities partly because of the skill with which they communicated Biblical texts. Such compositions therefore served the exegetical purposes of the church, rather than simply displaying the ego of their authors. In a sermon on the value of vocal music, Conrad Dieterich (the church superintendent in Ulm) commended these three polyphonists because 'their compositions are lovelier and more graceful, because they follow the affections and movements of the heart, or otherwise accommodate the given words'.[45] Dieterich praised Josquin's *De profundis*, in which 'he delicately climbs from the lowest note to the highest, to show how

---

compositum est": Impulse aus der Musiktheoriegeschichte für die Kirchenmusikforschung', *Kirchenmusikalisches Jahrbuch* 98 (2014), 23–37 (p. 34).

[40] *Gallus Dressler's* Præcepta musicæ poëticæ, 190–91.

[41] 'Josquinum celeberrimu‹m› huius artis Heroem facile agnoscent omnes, habet enim vere divinum et inimitabile quiddam. Neq‹ue› hanc laudem grata et candida posteritas ei invidebit'. *Novum et insigne opus musicum*, ed. Hans Ott (Nuremberg, 1537) (RISM B/I 1537[1]), tenor partbook, sig. A4v–A5r. The sequel *Secundus tomus novi operis musici* (Nuremberg, 1538) (RISM B/I 1538[3]) contained 10 compositions ascribed to Josquin.

[42] RISM B/I 1558[4], 1559[1], 1559[2].   [43] *Gallus Dressler's* Præcepta musicæ poëticæ, 164–65.

[44] 'Orlandus qui omnes suavitate antecellere videtur . . . verbis harmonium apte et convenienter per decorum applicat'. Ibid., 190–91.

[45] 'Sind auch deren *Compositiones* so viel desto lieblich- vnd anmutigher/ wann sie dieselbige nach den *Affection* vnd Bewegungen des Hertzens richten/ oder sonsten auff die vntergebene *Materi accommodiren*'. Conrad Dieterich, *Sonderbarer Predigten von unterschiedenen Materien. Teil 1: Jubel und Kirch-weyh Predigten* (Leipzig, 1632), 218.

Example 5.1 Josquin (attrib.), *De profundis*, initial bass entry (from *Tomus secundus psalmorum selectorum quatuor et quinque vocum* [Nuremberg, 1539], no. 31).

David sighs from the depth of his heart, and his sighs climb from below up to heaven'[46] – presumably a reference to the upward octave leap in the bass voice after the initial point of imitation (Example 5.1). This piece was widely known in German-speaking lands through the version printed in Nuremberg in 1539[47]; it was quoted in its entirety in Glarean's *Dodekachordon* (1547), although the attribution to Josquin has been recently challenged by Patrick Macey.[48] Dieterich also extolled a motet *Pater Abraham, miserere mei* that he ascribed to Clemens non Papa (probably he was referring to Hubert Waelrant's setting), noting how the fauxburden setting of 'quia crucior' 'sounds as if one heard the rich man in hell moaning and screaming' (Example 5.2).[49] Finally he singled out Lassus's *Pater peccavi*, where the words 'Hic famo pereo' 'sound as if one heard the prodigal son lamenting his extreme ruin'.[50] That Dieterich gave such musical detail within a sermon shows the significance he placed on composers' abilities to convey Biblical meanings. Dieterich's sermon, published in 1632 but probably originally delivered in the 1620s, suggests how the 1580 ordinance helped perpetuate the canonisation of Josquin, Clemens non Papa and Lassus into the early seventeenth century.

The question remains whether the 1580 edict was followed in musical practice in Saxony in the decades around 1600. Many churches held printed and manuscript copies of music by Josquin, Clemens non Papa and Lassus, alongside polyphony by other composers from the period. In Leipzig until at least 1679, the Thomasschule owned two sets of the anthology *Novum et insigne opus musicum* – probably separate copies of the 1537 edition and the 1558–59 expanded edition, which contained numerous pieces by Josquin and Clemens. The school also owned five volumes of the choirbook series *Patrocinium musices* (Munich, 1573–76)

---

[46] 'er fein von den untersten Noten biß auff die höchste steiget: anzuzeigen/ wie David von Grund seines Hertzens geseufftzet/ und seine Seufftzen von unten herauff bis oben hinan in Himmel gestiegen'. Ibid.

[47] *Tomus secundus psalmorum selectorum quatuor et quinque vocum* (Nuremberg, 1539). RISM B/I 1539⁹.

[48] Patrick Macey, 'Josquin and Champion: Conflicting Attributions for the Psalm Motet *De profundis clamavi*', in M. Jennifer Bloxam, Gioia Filocamo and Leofranc Holford-Strevens (eds.), *Uno gentile et subtile ingenio: Studies in Renaissance Music in Honour of Bonnie J. Blackburn* (Turnhout: Brepols, 2009), 453–68.

[49] 'sie klingen/ als wann einer den reichen Mann in der Höllen hörete jammern vnd schreyen'. Dieterich, *Sonderbarer Predigten*, 218.

[50] 'lauten/ als wann einer den verlornen Sohn in seinem eussersten Verderben schreyen hörete'. Ibid.

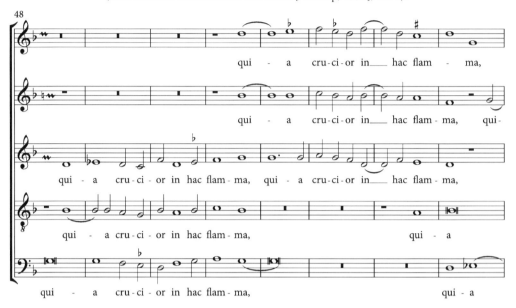

Example 5.2 Hubert Waelrant, *Pater Abraham, miserere mei*, bars 48–55 (from *Sacrarum cantionum . . . liber sextus* [Antwerp, 1558], no. 1).

that contained motets, canticles and masses by Lassus, plus manuscript copies of masses by Thomas Crecquillon and Philippe de Monte, and Magnificats by Matthaeus le Maistre.[51]

In the town of Delitzsch, approximately 14 miles north of Leipzig, a 1634 inventory of the church's music again included a copy of the *Novum et insigne opus musicum* (either the 1537 or the 1558–59 edition).[52] Other items included a Josquin mass in manuscript, books of motets by Lassus, seven of the parody masses by Clemens printed in Leuven between 1556 and 1563, plus printed polyphony by composers of the late sixteenth century such as Jacobus Handl (Gallus) and Gallus Dressler.[53] In Pirna, 11 miles southeast of Dresden, the church's large collection of manuscript music included masses and motets by Clemens (copied 1556) and a choirbook with music by Clemens, Lassus and central German composers such as Joachim a Burck (copied in the 1570s).[54] Thus

---

[51] D-LEsa, Stift. IX. A. 35, fols. 3r, 6r. Partial transcription in Arnold Schering, 'Die alte Chorbibliothek der Thomasschule in Leipzig', *Archiv für Musikwissenschaft* 1 (1918–19), 275–88 (p. 277).

[52] The book can be identified from the inventory's reference to its first motet as '*Veni sancte, Josquini*'. Arno Werner, 'Zur Musikgeschichte von Delitzsch', *Archiv für Musikwissenschaft* 1 (1918–19), 535–64 (p. 540).

[53] Ibid., 539–40.

[54] D-Dl, Mss. Mus. Pi. Cod. VII; Mus. Pi. Cod. III; for inventories and information on dating and scribal hands, see Wolfram Steude, *Die Musiksammelhandschriften des 16. und 17. Jahrhunderts in der Sächsischen Landesbibliothek zu Dresden* (Wilhelmshaven: Heinrichshofen, 1974), 201–2, 206.

The 1580 Edict and Its Implementation

the repertory prescribed by the 1580 edict had a strong presence in Saxon churches, although it was not the only music performed in these places.

Some church musicians were praised for following the 1580 ordinance, such as Christian Graefenthal, organist in Wittenberg from 1593 until his death in 1628. The funeral sermon (written by the local church superintendent, Paul Röber) commended Graefenthal as follows: 'It is known to everyone how faithfully and with what honour he served as organist. For he himself used the stately and moving style of performance, frequently and diligently playing the old and devout songs, as is prescribed in the electoral church edict'.[55] The sermon continued with a paraphrase of the relevant passage in the 1580 ordinance, singling out the 'old, highly experienced and superior composers Josquin, Clemens non Papa and the like'. Read literally, the sermon suggests that Graefenthal played keyboard intabulations of sixteenth-century motets, perhaps taken from Johannes Rühling's *Tabulaturbuch* (1583), an anthology of keyboard versions of motets by such composers as Clemens and Lassus, ordered according to the liturgical year.[56] Rühling's intabulations lack coloration, and if played unadorned would provide the dignified and depersonalised performance style preferred by the 1580 ordinance. Another interpretation of the sermon is that the pastor wished to extol Graefenthal for performing in an approved style, and accordingly praised the deceased organist with the language of the 1580 ordinance. Whichever was the case, Graefenthal also served as chief notary to the Saxon court,[57] and his juridical responsibilities probably encouraged him to stay on the right side of the law in his organ playing.

Yet many church musicians of the early seventeenth century were active as composers, and some of their performances must have contravened the terms of the edict. It must be recognised that many composers of the era worked at courts (such as Michael Praetorius at Wolfenbüttel or Heinrich Schütz at Dresden), whereas the edict applied only to town musicians in Saxony. For a town cantor such as Johann Hermann Schein (cantor at the Thomasschule in Leipzig between 1616 and 1630), some of his sacred compositions may have been performed outside the church (for instance in funeral processions) or in private devotion. Indeed, the dedication to his

[55] 'welchem Dienste/ wie treulich vnd mit was ehren er vorgestanden/ ist jederman bekand. Denn er sich herrlicher beweglicher art zu *musiciren* gebrauchet/ die alten andächtigen Lieder offt und fleissig geschlagen/ wie solches auch Churf. Kirchenordnung gemes ist ... daß sie mit fleis achtung drauff geben/ vnd ernstlich verschaffen sollen/ daß in der Kirchen nicht angehender newer/ sondern der alten vnd dieser Kunst wolerfahrnen vnd fürtreffentlichen *Componisten*, als *Josquini, Clementis non Papae*, vnd dergleichen Gesänge *musiciret* werden/ etc. daß es *grave*, tapffer vnd zur Christlichen Andacht die Leute reitzen möge'. Paul Röber, *Sichere Schiffart ... bey Christlicher Leichbestattung/ des ... Christiani Grefenthals* (Wittenberg, 1628), sig. G2v.

[56] RISM B/I 1583[24]; on the possible functions of Rühling's collection, see David Crook, 'The Exegetical Motet', *Journal of the American Musicological Society* 68 (2015), 255–316.

[57] Röber, *Sichere Schiffart*, title page, sig. G3v.

Opella nova Erster Theil (1618) indicates that these sacred concertos were sung 'publicly as well as privately'.[58] Yet Schein undoubtedly performed his compositions in worship, and his 1628 application for a printing privilege described his works as suitable for town churches.[59] The Leipzig city council presumably tolerated Schein's infringements of the 1580 ordinance, not least because it sought to boost the city's prestige through musical innovations similar to those found at courts.[60]

In other Saxon towns, however, cantors found themselves in trouble for performing their own compositions. In Freiberg in 1608, the cantor Christoph Demantius was reprimanded thus by a visitation: 'It is said that the cantor, as a good composer, performs only his own motets, usually new and unknown things. [But] the edict ordains that the old pieces, which are known to the burghers, should not be omitted.'[61] Subsequently Christoph Fröhlich, Demantius's successor from 1643, claimed that the council 'did not want a composer, having had one previously and having been able to hear nothing but his own compositions, with annoyance. They would prefer that I assiduously used various pieces from their own collection'.[62] Indeed Fröhlich purchased a music library that included older examples of polyphony (such as the motet anthology *Florilegium portense*, 1603 and 1621), as well as the up-to-date music of Andreas Hammerschmidt and Heinrich Schütz.[63]

The Platonic linkage between musical and social change remained in the minds of clerics and teachers into the 1640s, as the Thirty Years War caused unparalleled disruption to German society. As already mentioned, the town of Delitzsch possessed a relatively conservative musical repertory of sixteenth-century polyphony. On 23 June 1643, the cantor Christoph Schultze reported to the town council on how the war had undermined the state of school music. The council replied with an *Apologia* attacking Schultze and his choristers for cultivating musical novelties: 'In the ancient songs there was much dignity, just as there was dignity in men [of that era]. But now the riding songs (*ReuterLiedlein*) arise, and many wars are

---

[58] 'so wol *publicè*, als *privatim*'. Schein, *Opella nova Erster Theil* (Leipzig, 1618), tenor partbook, sig. A2r. RISM A/I S1377.

[59] D-Dla, Loc. 10757/3, fol. 77v; transcribed and translated in Stephen Rose, 'Protected Publications: The Imperial and Saxon Privileges for Printed Music, 1550–700', *Early Music History* 37 (2018), 247–313 (pp. 306–9).

[60] On the desire of Schein's patrons for church music in courtly style, see Michael Maul, *"Dero berühmbter Chor". Die Leipziger Thomasschule und ihre Kantoren (1212–804)* (Leipzig: Lehmstedt Verlag, 2012), 45–57.

[61] 'Es wirt gesagt, daß der *Cantor* als ein guter *Componist* nur seine modetten vnd sonst new vnbekannte Dinge singe, deshalb ist die Verordnung gemachet, daß die alten stücke, so der bürgerschaft bekant sind, nicht gar selten aussen gelassen werden'. Ernst Müller, 'Musikgeschichte von Freiberg', *Mitteilungen des Freiberger Altertumsvereins* 68 (1939), 1–144 (p. 27).

[62] 'sie begehreten keinen *Componisten*, Sie hetten bißher einen gehabt, hetten nichts als seine Sachen mit Verdruß anhören müssen. Es were Ihnen lieber, wenn ich mich *variorum musicorum* ihrer Sachen befließe und gebrauchte'. Ibid., 33.

[63] Ibid., 31–33.

The 1580 Edict and Its Implementation

the consequence. Our singers do not like dignified things, but rather they prefer Italian songs'.[64] *Reuterliedlein* ('riding songs') were rowdy or bawdy outdoor songs favoured by young men and soldiers; the council saw these songs as inciting the ongoing military hostilities. To reinforce its argument, the council cited the dictum of Plato and Cicero that: 'There can be no change in the laws of music, without a resulting change in the public laws'. It then reiterated the preference of 'our school elders for the sweetness of [Hieronymus] Praetorius and the dignity of Lassus'.[65] (Hieronymus Praetorius's polychoral motets have the full-voiced texture favoured by many Germans in the early seventeenth century, and omit the obbligato melody instruments that proved contentious in some locations.) In its preference for polyphonic church music with decorum and dignity, the council upheld the ethos of the 1580 ordinance.

On 27 July 1643, Schultze retaliated with a 24-page document that defended himself against the council's accusations and justified his viewpoint on musical innovation. Responding to the council's allegation about Italian songs and *Reuterliedlein*, he denied using these compositions in worship. He declared that he could neither read nor sing Italian; as for 'the songs that soldiers are accustomed to howl before the table, at the command of their unmusical laws, I always hate these more than a dog or a snake'.[66] But he admitted that secular songs might have been used by singers in convivial gatherings outside church. Regarding the relationship between musical style and social change, Schultze stated: 'Plato's argument is not displeasing to me, as the author of the [council's] *Apologia* presents as his sole opinion, that the musical modes can never change without the republic's laws also being changed'.[67] However, he inverted the cause and effect, arguing that the chaos of war was damaging musical life. The school choir was so depleted that 'the sacred music is sung incomplete in the church, thus depriving it of the gravitas of Orlando and the sweetness of Praetorius'.[68] Schultze also blamed the town council for not investing in

---

[64] 'In cantilenis veterum fuit magna gravitas: fuit etiam in viris magna tum gravitas. Do aber die Reüter Liedlein aufkommen seind, secuta sunt bella plurima. Nostri Cantores non delectantur gravitate ista; Sed magis amant Italicis Cantiones'. Partial transcription of documents of dispute in Werner Braun, 'Die Musik im Delitzscher Kulturkampf (1643)', *Archiv für Musikwissenschaft* 60 (2003), 1–30 (p. 5); see also Werner Braun, 'Cantiones veterum und neue Reuterliedlein (1643): aus einem Streitfall in Delitzsch', in Paul Mai (ed.), *Im Dienst der Quellen zur Musik: Festschrift Gertraut Haberkamp zum 65. Geburtstag* (Tutzing: Schneider, 2002), 279–85.

[65] 'Annis superioribus scholastici nostri suavibus Praetorii, aut gravibʋusʋ Orlandi delectabantur cantibus'. Cited in Braun, 'Die Musik im Delitzscher Kulturkampf', 5.

[66] 'Illas autem cantilenas quas caculae ante mensas ad nutum suorum extra leges Musicas vociferari assvefacti sunt, semper cane peius et angve odi . . . ' Ibid., 15.

[67] 'Nec mihi displicet Platonis disputatio *quam Autor Apologeticus ut suam solam opinionem apponit, nempe*: Musicos modos nusquam mutari absque maximarum legum civilium mutatione'. Ibid., 15.

[68] 'quod hymni sacri in templo imperfecti canuntur, inde fit, quod Gravitate Orlandinae, et Svavitate Praetorianae ~~privantur~~ adimuntur'. Ibid., 13.

any copies of Lassus's or Praetorius's music, apart from some scribal copies made by the schoolmaster in the nearby town of Bitterfeld.[69]

Despite declaring his sympathy for Plato's arguments, Schultze attacked the notion that only the music of the ancients was worthwhile: 'I praise the composers who have crowned the present age and the churches of the Holy Roman Empire with numerous affecting motets and all kinds of sweetly sounding concertos'.[70] He singled out Schütz, Schein, Scheidt and Daniel Selich for acclaim, commending the clear text-setting in their compositions. He then quoted an elegy by the sixth-century poet Maximianus that had been set to music in 1596 by Jacobus Handl:

> Different things please different people
> Not everything suits every age;
> What was once the right thing may now do harm.
> The boy delights in his swiftness, the aged man in his dignity,
>   and the grace of youth has its place between the two.[71]

Schultze thereby implied that the dignity of the 'ancients' might suit only the senior members of the congregation. But he did not pursue this argument at length. The Platonic link between musical novelty and social disorder was still fundamentally unchallenged in the 1640s.

Echoes of the 1580 edict could still be heard in Halle in 1661, in the revised ordinance for the grammar school. It instructed the cantor to uphold the sixteenth-century repertory in his teaching (prescribing texts such as Dressler's *Praecepta musicae poeticae*) and in his choice of music for church performance. Especially on feast days, the cantor should choose compositions by Josquin, Senfl, Johann Walter, Lassus and other polyphonic composers.[72] The edict contrasted the sweetness yet gravity of the music of these sixteenth-century composers with the 'frivolity and garrulousness' (*volubilitas et garrulitas plurimarum vocum*) and dance rhythms of newer repertories. It then instructed:

The cantors should not perform a new composition unless it has been approved by the pastor and church overseers, and previously tried out in the school. For as

---

[69] Ibid., 16, 23.

[70] 'Interea ego eos eveho melopoeos, qui praesens speculum, et Romani Imperij templa, innumeris patheticis mutetis, et omnis generis dulcisonis concertatio[nibus] Musicis ... quasi coronârunt'. Ibid., 15.

[71]

> 'Diversos diversa iuvant, non omnibus annis
> omnia conveniunt, res prius apta nocet.
> Exultat levitate puer, gravitate senectus,
> inter utrumque manens stat iuvenile decus'.

Maximianus *Elegiae* 1.103–6, cited in Braun, 'Die Musik im Delitzscher Kulturkampf', 16. Set to music in Jacobus Handl, *Moralia* (Nuremberg, 1596), no. 1. RISM A/I H1989.

[72] 'solennes illae probatissimaeque de praecipuis festis compositiones, a Josquino, Senfelio, Gualtero, Orlando et aliis'. *Leges scholae Hallensis* (Halle, 1661), transcribed in Reinhold Vormbaum, *Die evangelischen Schulordnungen des 17. Jahrhunderts* (Gütersloh, 1863), 540.

The Cantor as Composer

Plato said: A change in the music leads to changes in the state. And in recent history we have experienced the saddest example of this, to our sorrow.[73]

The 'saddest example' is a reference to the Thirty Years War, in which Halle suffered atrociously. Between 1635 and 1642, the city was repeatedly invaded and occupied by the rival armies of Saxony, Sweden and the Emperor. There were several outbreaks of the plague, including one in 1636 that led to the death of all the pupils in the school. In 1645 much of the city was destroyed by fire.[74] Such calamitous events were attributed in the school ordinance to the arrival of newer styles of music; perhaps the writer of the edict had in mind the concerted music with voices and instruments that Samuel Scheidt had introduced into Halle in the 1620s. The Halle school ordinance was no legalistic irrelevance, but shaped the curriculum at least until George Frideric Handel studied there in the 1690s; it may have been read aloud regularly to pupils, as happened at Leipzig's Nicolaischule.[75] Through such local edicts, the Platonic association between individuality, novelty and social chaos persisted until the end of the seventeenth century.

The 1580 Saxon ordinance was a product of an era that valued adherence to religious and princely authority. Underpinning its prescriptions of an authoritative sixteenth-century musical repertory was a Platonic belief that music had a unique grasp over human souls, and therefore had to be regulated as a tool of social discipline. The 1580 ordinance remained on the statute book in Saxony until the mid-eighteenth century, being reprinted in editions of the law code during Bach's lifetime.[76] By this date, however, its vision of unified princely and religious authority was receding. As part of this reshaping of authority and individuality, a new paradigm of church music emerged, requiring cantors to ignore the ordinance and instead perform their own compositions.

THE CANTOR AS COMPOSER

The science of musical composition is a characteristic virtue in musicians, and for music and musicians it is as indivisible a requisite as an arrow is to a bow. For an organist or a cantor it is as necessary as

---

[73] 'Nullum igitur novum et inusitatum carmen exhibento Cantores, praesertim in festis celebrioribus: nisi Pastorum et ecclesiae praefectorum suffragiis fuerit comprobatum, et in schola prius exploratum: quod enim Plato dixit: mutata musica, mutatur resp. cuius rei nuper tristissima, pro dolor, vidimus exempla'. Ibid.

[74] Wolfgang Stolze, 'Samuel Scheidt und der 30-jährige Krieg', in Konstanze Musketa and Wolfgang Ruf (eds.), *Samuel Scheidt (1587–654). Werk und Wirkung. Bericht über die Internationale wissenschaftliche Konferenz am 5. und 6. November 2004 ... in der Stadt Halle und über das Symposium in Creuzburg zum 350. Todesjahr, 25.–27. März 2004* (Halle: Händel-Haus, 2006), 393–410.

[75] Richard Sachse (ed.), *Acta Nicolaitana et Thomana: Aufzeichnungen von Jakob Thomasius während seines Rektorates an der Nikolai- und Thomasschule zu Leipzig (1670–84)* (Leipzig: Wörner, 1912), 35.

[76] See, for instance, *Corpus Juris Ecclesiastici Saxonici* (Dresden and Leipzig, 1735), 245–46.

a stick to the blind. A musician without compositional skill is like a house built without a roof, on which it rains in all places.[77]

Thus wrote Martin Heinrich Fuhrmann, cantor at Berlin's Friedrich-Werder Gymnasium from 1704 until his death in 1745. The vivid analogies, typical of his prose, highlight the importance of compositional skill in a church musician: a cantor lacking such ability will stumble like a blind man without a guide, or will be as ineffective as a leaky roof. Other writers of the early eighteenth century, including Johann Mattheson and Johann Gottfried Walther, agreed that compositional ability was essential in a cantor.[78] Fuhrmann explained that such skill allowed cantors to make a discerning choice of music for the church, to correct errors in scribal copies, and to supply missing parts for polyphonic works. Above all it allowed cantors to adorn worship with their own compositions, particularly by setting new poetic texts to music.[79] This section discusses how cantors in Leipzig and elsewhere used their compositional skills to produce cycles of cantatas, and asks why town councils permitted such a contravention of the 1580 edict. I argue that church music was increasingly regarded as a fashionable commodity, to be produced and consumed according to capitalist notions of over-production and rapid obsolescence.

The increasing tendency for church musicians to perform their own compositions can be seen in the activities of the cantors at Leipzig's Thomasschule during the seventeenth century. As already mentioned, Schein (cantor 1616–30) wrote extensive quantities of sacred music, much of which was intended for weddings or funerals. From the 1650s, as Leipzig recovered from the depredations of the Thirty Years War, its cantors increasingly used their own works for the *Haupt-Music* before or after the sermon at the main Sunday Communion service. Sebastian Knüpfer, cantor between 1657 and 1676, appears to have been the first cantor in Leipzig to compose a cycle containing a new piece for each Sunday in the church year. Around 1665 he made a series of settings of David Elias Heidenreich's *Geistliche Oden*, a year-long cycle of libretti for church music, from which 10 pieces survive.[80]

---

[77] 'Daß *Musica Poëtica* eine *Virtus Characteristica in Musico*, und ein unzertrennlich *Requisitum Musicae & Musici* als Pfeil und Bogen, und dieselbe insonderheit einem Organisten und *Cantor*, so nöthig als einem Blinden der Stab, und ein Musicus ohne *Composition* wie ein aufgerichtet Haus ohne Dach/ darinn es an allen Orten einregnet'. Martin Heinrich Fuhrmann, *Musicalische Striegel* ([Leipzig], *c*.1719–21), 13.

[78] Johann Gottfried Walther, *Musicalisches Lexicon* (Leipzig, 1732), 137; Johann Mattheson *Grundlage einer Ehren-Pforte* (Hamburg, 1740), xxxiii.

[79] Fuhrmann, *Musicalische Strigel*, 18–24.

[80] Gottfried Gille, 'Der Kantaten-Texdruck von David Elias Heidenreich, Halle 1665, in der Vertonungen David Pohles, Sebastian Knüpfers, Johann Schelles und anderer', *Die Musikforschung* 38 (1985), 81–94. For Knüpfer's surviving and lost settings of Heidenreich's libretti, see the works-list in Michael Maul, 'Knüpfer, Sebastian', *Die Musik in Geschichte und Gegenwart: Personenteil* 2nd edn, vol. 10 (Kassel: Bärenreiter, 2003), 355–58.

The Cantor as Composer

The practice of composing annual cycles of church music intensified during the tenure of Knüpfer's successor Johann Schelle, who was cantor from 1677 to 1701. He wrote at least six annual cycles, from each of which rarely more than a few pieces survive: a 1683–84 cycle using texts by Paul Thymich; a 1689–90 cycle of chorale concertos; a 1690–91 cycle on texts by Gottfried Erdmann; a cycle using texts by Johann Neunhertz (performed 1700–01); and two undated cycles of Heidenreich's *Geistliche Oden*.[81] Contemporary accounts of the reception of Schelle's music indicate a shift away from the earlier notion of church music as a form of social control. Erdmann Neumeister, commenting on Schelle's settings of Gottfried Erdmann's *Evangelisches Honig* cycle of poems, wrote: 'When one considers the lovely melodies which the well-known Schelle, the director of the Leipzig choirs, cultivated every Sunday, one can say that listeners swarmed here like bees to the hive'.[82] Referring to the sweetness of Schelle's melodies, Neumeister's image indicates the increasing importance of attracting and pleasing listeners, and compares the act of listening to that of consumption: the cantor's compositions are like honey, to be eagerly eaten and regularly replenished.

The extant evidence suggests that Schelle was the first Leipzig cantor to sell printed booklets containing the texts of his church music. Booklets survive for a vocal concerto he performed at Whitsun 1693 and a series of pieces for Whitsun 1699.[83] For his Neunhertz cycle of 1700–01, a volume containing the entire sequence of texts was printed in 1701, with the information on the title page that the cycle was being performed by Schelle that year.[84] Text booklets also survive from the tenure of Schelle's successor Kuhnau (including for sections of the liturgical years 1709–10, 1710–11, 1715–16 and 1720–21), documenting his own cycles of church music.[85] Such booklets were purchased by affluent members of the congregation, in order to help them follow the words of the newly written texts for the church music. The printed libretti linked the cantata to proto-capitalist forms of production and consumption: the composer acted as an entrepreneur, building demand for these ephemeral pamphlets and profiting by supplying them. For members of the congregation, the ability

---

[81] For surviving pieces from each cycle, see the works-list in Peter Wollny, 'Schelle, Johann', *Die Musik in Geschichte und Gegenwart: Personenteil*, 2nd edn, vol. 14 (Kassel: Bärenreiter, 2005), 1267–70.

[82] 'Accedentibus vero etiam modulis suavissimis, quas diebus Dominicis adhibere solet CL. *Schellius, chori Musici Lips. moderator*, auditores, perinde ac apes ad tintinnabula, dixeris convolare'. Erdmann Neumeister and Friedrich Grohmann, *De poëtis Germanicis huius seculi praecipuis dissertatio compendiaria* (n. p., 1695), 30.

[83] RUS-SPsc, shelfmarks 15.7.4.39 and 6.34.5.132; described in Tatjana Schabalina, '"Texte zur Music" in Sankt Petersburg: neue Quellen zur Leipziger Musikgeschichte sowie zur Kompositions- und Aufführungstätigkeit Johann Sebastian Bachs', *Bach-Jahrbuch* 94 (2008), 33–98 (pp. 43–46).

[84] Johann Neunhertz, *Evangelische Hertz-Ermunterung* (Leipzig, 1701), RUS-SPsc, shelfmark 15.17.3.92; see Schabalina, '"Texte zur Music" in Sankt Petersburg', 47–51.

[85] Wolf Hobohm, 'Neue "Texte zur Leipziger Kirchen-Music"', *Bach-Jahrbuch* 59 (1973), 5–32.

to afford a printed libretto was a mark of social distinction, similar to how their choice of clothing might indicate their social status.

When Bach was appointed as cantor in 1723, he too embarked on an ambitious programme to write his own compositions for the Leipzig liturgy: two cycles of cantatas for every Sunday and feast day requiring concerted music in the liturgical years 1723–24 and 1724–25, and subsequently at least one further annual cycle of cantatas. Previous scholars viewed Bach as exceptional in his effort to provide his own cycles of cantatas. Christoph Wolff's 2000 biography of Bach described the composer as undertaking 'an enormously challenging task (especially during the first several years) demanding extraordinary concentration and discipline'.[86] Yet our increasing awareness of Schelle's and Kuhnau's achievements shows that Bach was following the example of his predecessors by writing annual cycles. The productivity of Schelle and Kuhnau made it all the more important for Bach's professional pride that he performed his own works. Whereas Schelle and Kuhnau had acquired the music libraries of their predecessors for the use of the Thomasschule, Bach showed no interest in purchasing Kuhnau's musical estate.[87]

The task of regular composition enabled Bach to tailor his cantatas to the tastes of Leipzigers. As Martin Geck has suggested, with reference to the 1723–24 and 1724–25 cycles: 'Bach composed both cantata cycles not as an entity but in short phases of work. Between each phase was the opportunity to evaluate experiences, assimilate the congregation's reactions, and to rethink the situation afresh. In view of these external conditions he found himself in a working situation which always had new possibilities for interaction'.[88] Geck suggests that Bach's choice of chorales reflected the tastes of specific Leipzigers, such as funerary hymns established by local traditions including 'Welt ade, ich bin dein müde' in Cantata 27, and 'Liebster Gott, wenn wird ich sterben' in Cantata 8. Bach's cantatas for consecutive weeks sometimes share unusual features of scoring, suggesting that he was writing for a specific performer or exploring a musical preoccupation: for instance, several cantatas from autumn 1726 have an organ obbligato (including Cantatas 27, 47 and 169, performed on 6 October, 13 October and 20 October, respectively). Thus Bach conceived his cantatas as ephemeral works for specific occasions, without the timeless connotations they gained in twentieth-century revivals.

---

[86] Christoph Wolff, *Johann Sebastian Bach: The Learned Musician* (New York: Norton, 2000), 253–54.

[87] Ibid., 269, 332.

[88] Martin Geck, 'Bachs Leipziger Kirchenmusik. Diskurs zwischen Komponist und Kirchgängern', in Ulrich Leisinger (ed.), *Bach in Leipzig. Bach und Leipzig. Konferenzbericht Leipzig 2000*, Leipziger Beiträge zur Bach-Forschung 5 (Hildesheim: Olms, 2002), 403–11 (p. 404).

The Cantor as Composer

Bach's cantatas are merely the best-known part of a huge wave of compositional activity by central German cantors in the early eighteenth century. Even in locations where the 1580 ordinance had been upheld in earlier decades, now cantors were performing their own compositions. In Freiberg, the cantor from 1699 to 1744 was Johann Samuel Beyer, whose many extant cantatas suggest that he regularly performed his music in worship.[89] In Delitzsch, the cantor Christoph Gottfried Fröber performed a weekly cantata in a cycle between Easter 1735 and Easter 1736, with texts printed in advance; according to the preface of the text booklet, the cantatas were sometimes the work of Telemann or Johann Friedrich Fasch, and sometimes his own creations.[90] In Halle, the organist at the Ulrichskirche, Johann Gotthilf Ziegler, reported in 1721 that he had 'taken the great trouble to compose and perform three whole years' worth of new church pieces'.[91] Church music was no longer a uniform repertory but one whereby even small towns and provincial musicians could express their musical aspirations.

Why did town councils encourage this move to novelty and the ephemeral in church music? Bettina Varwig has traced changing attitudes to musical novelty in relation to Schütz in the 1640s and 1650s, linking it with expanding geographical and intellectual horizons caused by such diverse phenomena as the European discovery of the New World and the Copernican model of the cosmos.[92] The following paragraphs offer an explanation arising from the increased emphasis on the consumption of fashionable goods in eighteenth-century German society.[93] Town councils now regarded church music as a fashionable adornment to be consumed and then discarded. A central piece of evidence is Kuhnau's 1688 dissertation on the laws affecting church musicians.[94] Kuhnau had matriculated as a law student in Leipzig in 1682, two years before he became organist at the Thomaskirche, and his dissertation addressed the question of why the 1580 edict could now be flouted.[95]

---

[89] Manuscript cantatas in D-Dl; Beyer's *Geistlich-musicalische Seelen-Freude* (Freiberg, 1724) contains 72 arias 'auf alle Sonn- und Fest-Tage zu gebrauchen'. RISM A/I B2496.

[90] Werner, 'Zur Musikgeschichte von Delitzsch', 543–44.

[91] 'die große Arbeit auf sich genommen, drei gantze Jahr allezeit ein neu Kirchen-Stück zu componiren und aufzuführen'. Quoted in Walter Serauky, *Musikgeschichte der Stadt Halle. II/i: Von Samuel Scheidt bis in die Zeit Georg Friedrich Händels und Johann Sebastian Bachs* (Halle: Buchhandlung des Waisenhauses, 1939), 524.

[92] Bettina Varwig, *Histories of Heinrich Schütz* (Cambridge: Cambridge University Press, 2011), 173–80.

[93] Michael North, *'Material Delight and the Joy of Living': Cultural Consumption in the Age of Enlightenment in Germany*, trans. Pamela Selwyn (Aldershot: Ashgate, 2008).

[94] Johann Kuhnau, *Jura circa musicos ecclesiasticos* (Leipzig, 1688). The authorship of seventeenth-century university disputations is often unclear: the title page usually gives the names of the supervisor (*praeses*) and student (*respondent*), with no indication of who takes intellectual responsibility. Kuhnau's dissertation is an exception, as its title page describes him as the *autor*, working under the guidance (*sub moderamine*) of his supervisor Andreas Mylius.

[95] Kuhnau, *Jura circa musicos ecclesiasticos*, sig. B4r.

A major reason for the emphasis on compositional novelty in church music was that towns wished to emulate the cultural practices of courts. In the second half of the seventeenth century, courts were characterised by displays of conspicuous consumption. As Norbert Elias noted, an aristocratic family felt an 'obligation to spend on a scale befitting one's rank', signalling that they were not constrained by bourgeois ideals of economic productivity and balanced finances.[96] Aristocratic spending on clothing and ceremony ensured that courts were regarded as the fount of new fashions, with a lifestyle characterised by a constant stream of new entertainments.[97] The demand for incessant novelty took its toll on court musicians. Johann Beer, concertmaster at the Weissenfels court, commented: 'Today one must go with the court there, tomorrow somewhere else. There is no difference between day and night. Come storm, rain or sunshine it is all the same. Today one must be at church, tomorrow at table, the next day at the theatre'.[98] Musicians responsible for court chapels were obliged to write new cantatas regularly, as Christoph Graupner (capellmeister at Darmstadt) complained in his autobiography: 'I am so overburdened by my employment, that I can hardly do anything else but must always ensure that my compositions are finished in time for one Sunday or feast day after another, though other matters keep intervening'.[99]

In their provision of sacred music, town councils sought to follow the precedent of courtly chapels. Discussing the duties of cantors, Kuhnau asked whether they should be expected to use newly composed songs every Sunday in church worship. In answer, he reported: 'Nothing definite has been established, although this practice is usual in princely chapels, since princes are usually accustomed to it from their capellmeisters'.[100] Indeed several of the cantata cycles by Leipzig cantors were modelled on courtly precedents. The texts for Knüpfer's cycle were originally written by Heidenreich for musical settings for the Halle court by David Pohle (probably in the church year 1663–64). The 'Neumeister' form of cantata preferred by Bach, involving the alternation of arias and recitatives, was pioneered

---

[96] Norbert Elias, *The Court Society*, trans. Edmund Jephcott (Oxford: Blackwell, 1983), 67.

[97] Julius Bernhard von Rohr, *Einleitung zur Ceremoniel-Wissenschafft der Privat-Personen* (Berlin, 1728), 35.

[98] 'Heute muß man mit dem Hof da/ morgen dorthin. Tag und Nacht leiden da keinen Unterscheid. Sturmwind/ Regen und Sonnenschein/ gilt da eines wie das andere. Heute muß man in die Kirche/ morgen zu der Tafel/ übermorgen aufs *Theatrum*'. Johann Beer, *Musicalische Discurse* (Nuremberg, 1719), 18–19.

[99] 'Ich bin also mit Geschäfften dermassen überhäuffet, daß ich fast gar nichts anders verrichten kann, und nur immer sorgen muß, mit meiner Composition fertig zu werden, indem ein Sonn- und Fest-Tag dem andern die Hand bietet, auch noch öffters andre Vorfälle dazwischen kommen'. Graupner's autobiography, printed in Johann Mattheson, *Grundlage einer Ehren-Pforte* (Hamburg, 1740), 412–13.

[100] 'An vero Directorum Musices partium sit singulis diebus dominicis noviter compositas cantiones cultui sacro adhibere, in hoc nihil certi constitutum, interim tamen in aulicis Capellis fere obtinet, qvod Principes a Capellæ Magistris id exigere non raro soleant'. Kuhnau, *Jura circa musicos ecclesiasticos*, sig. C3r.

The Cantor as Composer   179

at the Weissenfels court in cycles with texts by Neumeister and music by Johann Philipp Krieger. By encouraging such cantatas, town councils sought to emulate courtly prestige rather than uphold Platonic ideals of civic stability.

Cantors were also expected to compose regularly so they could tailor music to the requirements of a place or congregation, as Kuhnau explained via three examples. Firstly, a cantor may need to perform 'a unique text that has not been previously set by skilled musicians'.[101] Here Kuhnau recognised that church musicians increasingly set newly written poetry customised for local taste or specific occasions, rather than the Biblical texts that were the norm around 1600. Secondly, pieces may need to be written to suit the abilities of local performers. Thirdly, cantors could showcase their skill through their compositions, particularly full-scored pieces. Rather than church music being an authoritative repertory imposed across Saxony, Kuhnau advocated an empiricist awareness of the tastes and abilities of individuals.

Already in the 1680s, Schelle had showed the importance of responding to the tastes of the Leipzig congregation. As the Thomasschule headmaster Jacob Thomasius noted, Schelle intended his 1683–84 cycle to appeal to 'erudite' as well as 'plebeian' churchgoers, by including arias for elite listeners and also chorales that everyone would recognise.[102] Schelle wrote his 1689–90 cycle of chorale concertos to accompany sermons elucidating the texts of the respective chorales by the pastor of the Thomaskirche, Johann Benedict Carpzov: the cantata was performed before the sermon, after which the chorale was sung by the congregation.[103] Through these initiatives, Schelle created church compositions designed for the social make-up and religious preoccupations of the Leipzig congregation.

Kuhnau too was sensitive to the preferences of his listeners. In his dissertation he advised cantors to be guided by the tastes of congregations, either feeding their appetite for new music or maintaining a mixed diet of old and new styles. (To support a mixed approach, he cited the 1634 ordinance for the Leipzig Thomasschule, which instructed the cantor 'neither to use the new so frequently, nor completely forget the old motets, but instead to follow the [preferences of] citizens and inhabitants rather

---

[101] 'Saepissime textus singularis & ab aliis peritis Musicis nondum compositus ad aliqvam incidentem venit elaborandus'. Ibid, sig. B4r.

[102] Sachse (ed.), *Acta Nicolaitana*, 653. For a modern edition and analysis of *Durch Adams Fall*, one of two surviving pieces from the 1683–84 cycle, see *Leipzig Church Music from the Sherard Collection: Eight Works by Sebastian Knüpfer, Johann Schelle, and Johann Kuhnau*, ed. Stephen Rose (Madison, WI: A-R Editions, 2014).

[103] Schelle's surviving chorale cantatas are edited in Johann Schelle, *Six Chorale Cantatas*, ed. Mary S. Morris, Recent Researches in the Music of the Baroque Era, vols. 60–61 (Madison, WI: A-R Editions, 1988); for a recent study, see Markus Rathey, 'Schelle, Carpzov und die Tradition der Choralkantate in Leipzig', *Jahrbuch des Staatlichen Instituts für Musikforschung Preußischer Kulturbesitz* (2011), 185–210.

than those who only like modern things'.[104]) He had a relativistic view of music's command over the emotions. In the preface to his *Biblische Historien* (1700) he noted: 'But that [the musician] should have universal power over his listeners, and be able to move every one of them now to joy, now to sadness ... now to some other emotion – this only a few will believe'.[105] Music's affective power is limited because 'the temperaments of men are entirely dissimilar. ... A cheerful spirit can be led to joy or compassion without difficulty, while on the other hand the composer will have great trouble if he wants to gain the same effect on a melancholy or choleric temperament'.[106] Such an empiricist awareness of human diversity meant that a uniform sacred repertory (as envisaged in the 1580 edict) could no longer claim to move all churchgoers to devotion; instead church music had to be adapted to local requirements and tastes.

A final reason why town councils now encouraged regular new music in church stemmed from their increasing acceptance of the role of fashion. At the start of the seventeenth century, the Leipzig town council feared that displays of fashionable clothing would destabilise the social order, and sought to regulate the clothing of different social groups via sumptuary ordinances (*Kleiderordnungen*). By the early eighteenth century, however, such ordinances were no longer issued; instead fashion was viewed as a sign of progress. As the Merseburg administrator Julius Bernhard von Rohr (who had studied at Leipzig in his youth) said: 'It is rational and praiseworthy when you choose not the hard, inconvenient and unhelpful, but instead the easier, more convenient and more useful'.[107] Kuhnau showed a similar approval of musical fashion when he commented on how the repertory sanctioned by the 1580 edict was now outmoded: 'The motets of Lassus and Clemens are incompatible with instrumental music [i.e., the use of obbligato instruments], which is not unpleasing to other musicians, and in our churches is regularly used and received'.[108] Showing confidence in historical progress, he commented: 'The virtues of the musicians of

---

[104] 'weder die newen so gar offt einführen vnd gebrauchen/ noch auch der alten *Moteten* gar vergessen/ Sondern sich hierinn mehr nach den Bürgern vnd Einwohnern/ als nach den jenigen/ so allein die *moderna* belieben/ richten'. *Des Raths zu Leipzig Vornewerte Schul-Ordnung* (Leipzig, 1634), sig. C3r.

[105] 'Aber daß er über die Zuhörer einerley Gewalt habe/ und einen ieden bald zur Freude/ bald zur Traurigkeit ... bald wieder zu was anders bewegen könne/ das wollen noch die wenigsten glauben'. Johann Kuhnau, *Musicalische Vorstellung einiger Biblischer Historien* (Leipzig, 1700), sig. B1v. RISM A/I K2997.

[106] 'die *Complexiones* der Menschen gantz unterschieden sind. ... Ein lustiger Geist kan ohne Schwierigkeit zur Freude oder zum Mitleiden gebracht werden/ da hingegen ein Künstler grosse Mühe haben wird/ wenn er dergleichen bey einem *Melancholico* oder *Cholerico* ausrichten soll'. Ibid., sig. B1v–B2r.

[107] 'Daß man statt des schweren, unbequemern und unnützern etwas leichters, bequemers und nützlichers erwehlt, ist vernünfftig und löblich'. Rohr, *Einleitung*, 40.

[108] 'Orlandi & Clementis Motetae Instrumentali Musica non concomitantur, qvod alias Musices non exigua gratia est & in Ecclesiis nostris ubiqve usitata & recepta'. Kuhnau, *Jura circa musicos ecclesiasticos*, sig. B4r.

ɔur time have climbed to a peak of perfection, so far as to surpass the wondrous feats of the so-called celebrated composers, namely Lassus and Clemens'.[109] By rejecting the canonised repertory of the 1580 ordinance, Kuhnau indicated that cantors should follow present-day musical taste. Bach similarly prioritised the new in his 1730 *Entwurff* appealing for more performers for Leipzig's church music, claiming that: 'The state of music is quite different from what it was, since our artistry has increased very much, and the taste has changed astonishingly, and accordingly the former style of music no longer seems to please our ears'.[110] A cantor who could supply the latest style of music was essential for the prestige of Leipzig. As Kuhnau said in a petition to the city council, it was imperative that 'especially on feast days and during trade fairs, foreign visitors and distinguished men judge there is something good to hear in the main churches'.[111]

The shift to a notion of church music as a fashionable commodity did not completely displace older attitudes. Andreas Werckmeister, one of the most eloquent advocates of a theological understanding of musical creativity, ingeniously reconciled his viewpoint with the imperative for musical novelty. He regarded innovation as an expression of God's never-ending gifts: 'Our dear forefathers exerted themselves to sing and play new songs to dear God. So we must not avoid this, especially as we see that God has given each and every musician always good new inventions and ornaments. Who would be reluctant to use such good gifts to the glory of God?'[112] He claimed the public's desire for musical innovation resulted from the movements of the constellations, which influence the 'humours and mores of mankind from one time to another'.[113] Such movements explain 'why the styles in music are so changeable, for those which ten, twenty, thirty or more years ago were the most pleasing, are now derided and not valued'.[114] Yet the shifts of constellations did not alter the fundamental

---

[109] 'nostri temporis Musicorum virtutes ad ejusmodi perfectionis culmen adscendisse, ut supra dictos celebres Melopoetas, ut Orlandum & Clementum, qvoad mirificam movendi felicitatem superare'. Ibid, sig. C1r.

[110] *BDok* 1, 63 (no. 22); *NBR*, 149.

[111] 'sonderlich in Feyer Tagen und Meßzeiten, da frembde Leüte und vornehme Herren in den Haupt Kirchen etwas gutes zu hören gedencken'. Johann Kuhnau, Memorial of 17 March 1709, D-LEsa, Stift. VIII.B.2c, fols. 356r–361v.

[112] 'Haben nun unsere lieben Vorfahren sich bemühet/ dem lieben GOtt neue Lieder zu singen/ und zu spielen/ so müssen wir auch nicht ablassen/ sonderlich da wir sehen daß Gott einem und dem andern *Musico* noch immer neue gute *inventiones* und Manieren eingiebet/ wer wolte denn nun den guten Gaben/ so einem gegeben worden/ widerstreben/ und nicht zur Ehre GOTTes wieder anwenden?' Andreas Werckmeister, *Der edlen Music-Kunst Würde, Gebrauch und Mißbrauch* (Frankfurt am Main and Leipzig, 1691), 22.

[113] 'das von einer Zeit zu andern die *humores* und *mores* der Menschen verändert werden'. Agostino Steffani, *Send-Schreiben darinn enthalten wie grosse Gewißheit die Music*, trans. and expanded by Andreas Werckmeister (Quedlinburg, 1699), 51. The portions quoted are from Werckmeister's additions.

[114] 'warum die Manieren in der *Music* so veränderlich sind/denn dasjenige, was vor 10. 20. 30 und mehr Jahren am angenehmsten gelautet/ dasselbe wird anjetzo verlachet, und gar nicht *aestimiret*'. Ibid., 51–52. 'Manieren' usually translates as 'ornaments' but here has the sense of 'styles'.

harmonies designed by God at the heart of the cosmos: 'The consonances stay unchanged, but the constellations change the styles'.[115]

Despite Werckmeister's attempts to accommodate musical novelty within his mindset of immutable harmonic ratios, church music was increasingly regarded as a fashionable object to be consumed. Here it is useful to recall the analogy between the cantor and the tailor, as suggested by Schütz's anecdote at the start of this chapter. Like fashionable clothes, cantatas were valued for their novelty, and cantors were required to update the musical repertory regularly with new compositions to maintain this sense of innovation. The comparison between church music and fashionable clothing underpinned another of Fuhrmann's metaphors explaining why cantors should compose. A cantor who did not supply his own bespoke compositions, Fuhrmann wrote, 'is the same as a naked and poor thief, who took some expensive clothes from the Jew's store for a few groschen, so on Sundays he can look resplendent, yet often the bag does not have a whole shirt in it'.[116] To perform another's compositions was akin to buying secondhand clothes from Jews (who dominated this trade, being barred from the guilds which regulated the tailors who supplied new clothes).[117] Fuhrmann's anti-Semitic analogy highlighted the deceit of the non-composing cantor, who has purchased what he thinks are valuable goods at a cut price; but this musician has himself been hoodwinked into buying tatty garments from the Jew. By contrast with earlier views of the cantor as the executant of an authorised repertory of canonised polyphony, now the church musician was akin to a tailor supplying fashionable adornments to the congregation.

CHOOSING A NEW CANTOR

The increasing importance of compositional ability in cantors is shown by the changing ways in which church musicians were recruited. In Leipzig before the 1650s, there is little evidence that candidates were tested for their compositional ability, although in its 1616 search for a new cantor the city council invited Schein to be heard in a trial at the Thomaskirche.[118] After 1650 systems for auditioning compositional skill developed, indicating the social and economic status that musicians could gain by proving their ability to compose regularly.

---

[115] 'die *consonantien* bleiben zwar/ aber die *constellationes* verändern die Manieren'. Ibid., 52.
[116] 'und ist gleich einer nackigten und dabey stoltzen Dirne, so bey den Juden vor etliche Groschen sich ein kostbahr Kleid ausm Laden nimt, um des Sonntags in der Kirchen damit zu prangen/ da doch die arme Sacke oft nicht eine gantz Hembde darunter an hat'. Fuhrmann, *Musicalische Strigel*, 16.
[117] Marion A. Kaplan, *Jewish Daily Life in Germany, 1618–945* (New York: Oxford University Press, 2005), 58.
[118] Arthur Prüfer, *Johan Herman Schein* (Leipzig: Breitkopf & Härtel, 1895), 23.

Choosing a New Cantor

Among the candidates applying in 1657 for the Thomaskantorate, several highlighted their compositional skill in their letters of application. Adam Krieger presented himself as primarily a composer, to the extent that he asked to be excused from the cantor's usual duties of teaching Latin (see Chapter 1, p. 46). Elias Nathusius, then cantor at the Nicolaischule in Leipzig, promised to compose two new pieces a week should he be successful in his application. 'Should perhaps anyone be doubtful in me,' he wrote, 'I offer myself for a public test in composition and performance. [A draft setting of] Psalm 71 is now on my *cartella* and when it is finished, I wish to offer it to your noble … magnificences as a specimen of composition and practice'.[119] On this occasion, auditions were not held; the vacancy arose during the mourning period following the death of the Elector of Saxony, and church music was consequently silenced. Nathusius's letter nonetheless indicated the priority now given to compositional skills in the recruitment of church musicians.

In 1676–77 the Leipzig council held auditions when selecting Knüpfer's successor as Thomaskantor. An account of the auditions, given in the diary of Jacob Thomasius, shows the importance that the city council now attached to compositional ability in its cantor. Of the 13 applicants for the cantorate,[120] five were invited to audition by providing the music for church services during Advent and the Christmas season; this had the advantageous side-effect of supplying concerted music for major feast-days. Georg Bleyer, the candidate favoured by the burgomaster Lorenz von Adlershelm, was given the privilege of two auditions, at the Nicolaikirche on 26 November and the Thomaskirche on 3 December (1st Sunday of Advent). In an attempt to ingratiate himself with the town council, he had the text of his church music printed and presented copies to them.[121]

Between 25 December and 1 January, auditions were held for Joachim Ernst Spahn (cantor in Liegnitz), Johann Theile (titular capellmeister in Gottorf), Johann Schelle (cantor in Eilenburg) and Johann Pezel (Leipzig town musician). Spahn's and Theile's pieces were delivered to the school a week in advance, allowing a rehearsal on 21 December in the

---

[119] 'Solte vielleicht noch etwas weiters an mir dubitirt werden, erbiete ich mich zur öffentliche probe, in compositione und praxi: Wie denn der 71. Psalm gleich izzo auf der chartell ist, und, wenn es were fertig gewesen, hätte es Eurer Edlen‹ … Herrligkeiten, ich gleich izt zuglich, loco speciminis in melopoeiâ und praxi wollen offeriren'. D-LEsa, Tit. VII B 116, fol. 140v. See also Michael Maul, 'Elias Nathusius: ein Leipziger Komponist des 17. Jahrhundert', *Jahrbuch mitteldeutscher Barockmusik* (2001), 70–98. The *cartella*, an erasable tablet for drafting compositions, is mentioned in several German treatises of the early seventeenth century; see Jessie Ann Owens, *Composers at Work: The Craft of Musical Composition 1450–600* (New York: Oxford University Press, 1997), 74–107.

[120] Twelve applicants were recorded in the council minutes, but Thomasius mentioned a thirteenth applicant – the Leipzig resident Christian Boldaeus, formerly a village organist – who was never auditioned on account of his 'foolish head' ('närrischen Kopffs'). Sachse (ed.), *Acta Nicolaitana*, 538.

[121] Ibid., 184–85.

184   *The Regulation of Novelty*

presence of members of the council and the city's most senior musician, Werner Fabricius (organist at the Nicolaikirche and director of university music).[122] Presumably the council members sought to form an opinion on the quality of Spahn's and Theile's compositions, and their suitability for the city's performing forces. When the council met to elect the new cantor, they discussed the piety, teaching experience and compositional skill of the candidates. Spahn was ruled out of the competition because, according to one set of minutes, he 'had let nothing of his own composition be heard';[123] according to another set of minutes, 'he did not understand composition correctly, to the extent that the choirboys laughed at him in the audition'.[124] The successful candidate, Schelle, by contrast, satisfied the council in all respects. Compositional ability was now a deciding factor in the appointment of cantors.

Auditions were again held in 1722–23 to appoint Kuhnau's successor.[125] Each of the candidates called to audition presented at least one cantata. Telemann auditioned in August 1722; then between November 1722 and February 1723, audition cantatas were presented by Christoph Graupner, Andreas Christoph Duve, Georg Friedrich Kauffmann, Georg Balthasar Schott and Johann Sebastian Bach. Graupner presented three pieces, each appealing in different ways to the mixed tastes of the city's burghers. Congregants with modern tastes would appreciate the simple choruses in his cantata *Aus der Tiefe*, and the dramatic writing for solo oboe and unison strings in the alto aria of his cantata *Lobet den Herrn alle Heiden*. At the same time, Graupner acknowledged Leipzig traditions by ending *Lobet den Herrn* with the last verse of the chorale 'In allen meinen Taten' (a verse written by the Leipzig poet Paul Fleming); and his third piece, a Magnificat, showed his ability to write the Latin-texted liturgical works still favoured in Leipzig on feast-days.[126]

In his audition pieces, *Jesu nahm zu sich die Zwölfe* (BWV22) and *Du wahrer Gott und Davids Sohn* (BWV23), Bach too showed his ability to cater for the varied tastes of Leipzig's inhabitants. For lovers of modern secular styles, he included in Cantata 22 an aria with an attractive oboe obbligato ('Mein Jesu, ziehe mich nach dir'), and in Cantata 23 the chorus

---

[122] Ibid., 198–200.

[123] 'Spahn hätte nichts von seiner eigenen *composition* hören laßen', D-LEsa, Tit. VIII 39. Quoted in *Ausgewählte Kirchenkantaten: Sebastian Knüpfer, Johann Schelle, Johann Kuhnau*, ed. Arnold Schering, Denkmäler Deutscher Tonkunst, vols. 58–59 (Leipzig: Breitkopf & Härtel, 1918), xxiv.

[124] [Er] 'verstünde auch die *composition* nicht recht, inmaßen dann die Knaben ihn in seinen Proben verlachet'. D-LEsa, Tit. VIII. 51. Quoted in *Ausgewählte Kirchenkantaten*, ed. Schering, xxiv.

[125] For an account of the lengthy negotiations to select a new cantor in 1722–23, see Ulrich Siegele, 'Bach's Situation in the Cultural Politics of Contemporary Leipzig', in Carol K. Baron (ed.), *Bach's Changing World: Voices in the Community* (Rochester, NY: University of Rochester Press, 2006), 127–73.

[126] For extracts from Graupner's compositions, see Friedrich Noack, 'Johann Seb. Bachs und Christoph Graupners Kompositionen zur Bewerbung um das Thomaskantorat in Leipzig 1722–23', *Bach-Jahrbuch* 10 (1913), 145–62.

Choosing a New Cantor

'Aller Augen warten' evokes the rhythms of the minuet and the structure of the French rondeau. Yet both cantatas also invoked long-standing Lutheran musical traditions (particularly the Leipzig tradition of chorale settings cultivated by Schelle), with the inclusion of the 1524 chorale 'Herr Christ, der einig Gotts Sohn' in Cantata 22 and the 1528 chorale melody 'Christe, du Lamm Gottes' in Cantata 23. A newspaper account of Bach's audition asserted: 'The music performed by the said candidate was much praised by all those who value such things'.[127] In contrast with the 1580 edict's vision of an unchanging repertory of authorised polyphony, cantors were now judged on their ability to compose and perform music that satisfied public taste.

By holding such auditions, towns hoped to avoid appointing the kind of non-composing cantor as described by Bach's cousin Johann Gottfried Walther. Walther was organist at the Stadtkirche in Weimar, and in 1727 he applied to be cantor there, only to see the rival candidate Lorenz Reinhard appointed. Reinhard came from a non-musical background; previously he had been professor of eloquence and Greek literature at Hildburghausen Gymnasium. Walther complained in a letter to his fellow musician Heinrich Bokemeyer about Reinhard's incompetence: 'It so wondrously happened that Lorenz Reinhard ... took this post, because he understood composition; yet from his diposition he has done nothing but what I report: in two and a quarter years he has brought to the table the same cycle of cantatas and only three Kyries [i.e. *Missae breves*], when a new one is necessary each Sunday. (Here my lord can imagine what moved me to compose six Kyries of my own.)'[128] Walther went on to complain sarcastically that Reinhard 'composes without a score and directs without a score, and just continues the good pieces cultivated by the previous cantor'.[129] By the early eighteenth century, a cantor who did not regularly perform his own pieces was regarded as a disgrace to the music profession and a detriment to the prestige of the town.

The shifts described in this chapter show how efforts to regulate church music shaped notions of the musical author. The 1580 edict envisaged musical authorship as constituted by authority, sanctioning a church repertory of polyphonic motets by canonised composers such as Josquin and Lassus. This repertory was widely available in printed partbooks, and its virtues were extolled by clerics such as Conrad Dieterich and music

---

[127] *BDok* 2, 91 (no. 124); for a different translation, see *NBR*, 101.

[128] 'muste es sich wunderlich fügen, daß Hr. *Laurentius* Reinhardt ... diesen Dienst, weil Er die *Composition* verstehet, völlig überkam; von Beschaffenheit derselben will nichts, sondern nur so viel melden: daß in 2 ¼ Jahren nur einerley Jahr-Gang, und dabey nur 3 *Kyrie eleison*, da doch Sonntäglich eins nöthig ist, aufs Tapet gekommen sind. (Hierbey können Mein Herr abnehmen, was mich zu Setzung der 6 *Kyrie* bewogen!)'. Johann Gottfried Walther, *Briefe*, ed. Klaus Beckmann and Hans-Joachim Schulze (Leipzig: Deutscher Verlag für Musik, 1987), 73.

[129] 'Er ohne *Partitur componi*ret, und ohne *Partitur dirigi*ret, übrigens auch die mit dem vorigen *Cantore* gepflogene gute Harmonie *continui*ret hat'. Ibid.

theorists such as Gallus Dressler. Town councils regarded church musicians as executants of this repertory, discouraging them from exploring compositional or performerly innovations that might disrupt society. After the Thirty Years War, church musicians were increasingly regarded as the suppliers of ephemeral novelties, their compositions analogous to the fashionable goods made by tailors and other artisans. Town councils wanted their church repertory to be tailored for the moment of performance, rather than being fixed on paper as a permanent opus. Yet a legacy of the 1580 edict was the ongoing role of the Latin polyphonic motet in the Lutheran liturgy: sixteenth-century motets continued to be performed as introits in Leipzig until the late eighteenth century.[130] Different notions of musical authorship were therefore on display within a single church service during Bach's time in Leipzig.

[130] Wolff, *Johann Sebastian Bach*, 249, 255–56, 499 n. 84.

CHAPTER 6

Authorship and Performance

> In music everything depends on performance. The most wretched
> melodies often please the ear if they are well played. On the
> other hand, a piece in whose composition one can see the most
> beautiful harmony and melody certainly cannot please the ear if
> those who should perform it are neither able nor willing to fulfil
> their duty.[1]

Thus wrote the Leipzig scholar of rhetoric Johann Abraham Birnbaum in
his 1738 defence of Johann Sebastian Bach, whose music had been criticised as unduly complex by Johann Adolph Scheibe. Birnbaum highlighted
the role of performers in shaping the reputation of composers in the early
eighteenth century. Given the fashion for regular performances of new
music (as described in Chapter 5), compositions were rarely available for
perusal in print, and instead had to be appraised in the moment of
performance. The attention of listeners was primarily directed at aspects
of performing technique such as ornamentation and rhetorical delivery.
Birnbaum reacted against this emphasis on the event, arguing that performers had an obligation (*Schuldigkeit*) to present a composition to its best
effect. He blamed bad performers for creating the impression that Bach's
music was confused: 'When all this is performed as it should be, there is
nothing more beautiful than this harmony. If, however, the clumsiness or
negligence of the instrumentalists or singers causes confusion, it would be
very tasteless to attribute such mistakes to the composer'.[2]

Birnbaum's comments echoed an earlier reaction against the performance-
centred culture of the early eighteenth century, namely a letter by the
Zittau organist Johann Krieger. The letter was published by Johann
Mattheson in 1725, as one of many commenting on the controversy
caused by his treatise *Das neu-eröffnete Orchestre* with its manifesto for
music to be intelligible to the *galant homme*. Krieger politely disagreed
with Mattheson's assumption that music was best perceived as a sensory
experience through the ears. Like Birnbaum, Krieger noted that the
quality of performance affected listeners' opinions of a piece: 'The poorest
composition, when well performed, will always find more admirers, than

---

[1] *BDok* 2, 302 (no. 409); translation adapted from *NBR*, 344–45. [2] Ibid.

188   *Authorship and Performance*

the best composition if it has the misfortune of being poorly performed'.[3]
Krieger went further than Birnbaum, advising:

> It remains certain that one must make a precise distinction between the perform-
> ance and composition of a piece, and it is impossible to come to a correct
> judgement if both are not well observed. ... Therefore I deem a good evaluator
> to be someone who does not let himself be seduced by the performance, but who
> considers the actual fundament, namely the question of the inner and not the
> external virtue of a piece.[4]

By regarding composition as the 'fundament' and 'inner virtue' (he also
described it as a 'kernel' accessible only to those with an 'upright understanding'), Krieger disclosed a hierarchical conception of composition as
superior to performance. This was a view that Birnbaum would later take,
in a 1739 essay that recommended judging a composer's 'work as it has
been set down in notes'.[5]

Birnbaum and Krieger went against the tide of their times by prioritis-
ing the composer above the performer, and by arguing that judgements
of music should evaluate the compositional fabric rather than comprise
an impression gleaned from a performance. Birnbaum believed that the
performer should be beholden to the composer, a tool to realise the
meanings that the composer has embedded in the work. Such a viewpoint
appears to anticipate the twentieth-century vision of the performer as an
executant who represents the author's work: as Stravinsky wrote, 'the idea
of execution implies the strict putting into effect of an explicit will that
contains nothing beyond what it specifically commands'.[6] It also resonates
with the rhetoric used by some historically informed performers of the
1970s and 1980s such as Christopher Hogwood, for whom '[getting] as
close as possible to what the composer intended'[7] was shorthand for the
practices he sought to rehabilitate, as well as a marketing slogan for his
performances.

More recently, however, the idea that the performer is obliged to
represent the composer's intentions has been extensively critiqued. In
the late 1980s, Richard Taruskin attacked the emphasis on original meanings in the period-performance movement, arguing that performers

---

[3] 'Die schlimmste *Composition*, so wohl *executirt* wird, findet allemahl mehr Liebhaber, als die
allerbeste, so das Unglück hat, übel *executirt* zu werden'. Johann Krieger, letter printed in Johann
Mattheson, *Critica musica* 2 (1725), 223.

[4] 'Es bleibt aber gewiß, daß man zwischen *Execution* und *Composition* eines Stückes genauen
Unterscheid machen müste, und das *Judicium* unmöglich recht erfolgen könne, wenn nicht
beydes wohl *observir*et worden. ... Also halte ich denjenigen vor einen guten *Raisonneur*, der sich
die *Execution* nicht verführen läst, sondern das eigentliche *Fundament regardir*et, nehmlich in so weit
die Frage von der innerlichen, und nicht der äuserlichen Tugend eines Stückes ist'. Ibid.

[5] *BDok* 2, 355 (no. 441).

[6] Igor Stravinsky, *Poetics of Music in the Form of Six Lessons*, trans. Arthur Knodel and Ingolf Dahl,
preface by George Seferis (Cambridge, MA: Harvard University Press, 1970), 163.

[7] Christopher Hogwood, quoted in interview in *Los Angeles Times*, 7 December 1988.

should be faithful to their own age rather than an imagined past. Drawing on W. K. Wimsatt Jr and Monroe C. Beardsley's scepticism about the value of authorial intentions in literary criticism, Taruskin dismissed naïve appeals to the notion of composers' intentions: 'We cannot know intentions ... or rather, we cannot know we know them. Composers do not always express them. If they do express them, they may do so disingenuously. Or they may be honestly mistaken, owing to the passage of time or a not necessarily consciously experienced change of taste'.[8] In parallel to Taruskin's manifesto, the discipline of performance studies has developed methods to analyse and theorise the meanings created by performers. Building on the work of Richard Schechner, Nicholas Cook rejects a philological model for how music is transmitted in performance ('a kind of family tree in which successive interpretations move vertically away from the composer's original vision'), instead examining performances on a horizontal plane in relation to each other.[9] Recent studies of historical improvisation too have collapsed the hierarchy between performer and composer, showing how performers improvised counterpoint and composers used formulae from oral culture.[10] Such scholarly developments prompt a broader consideration of the porous boundaries between authors and performers, and between written and oral cultures.

This chapter seeks a better understanding of the prerogatives of the musical author, by uncovering seventeenth-century Lutheran debates about the relationship between composer and performer. After exploring the views of music theorists on this relationship, the chapter investigates different ways in which authority might be wielded by composer or performer. One viewpoint considered performers to be solely responsible for all musical parameters that were individualised or could not be effectively notated, such as ornamentation. Another view lionised the composer as the ideal performer, particularly in solo repertories that existed primarily in the embodied act of performance. The notion of composers' intentions was also used in the period, and can be understood in relation to the theological, humanist and artisanal models of creativity outlined in Chapter 1. Throughout the chapter, I recognise that the relationship between composer, notation and performance varied according to genre. In some genres, notation became more specific during the seventeenth and early eighteenth centuries, allowing composers to notate more aspects of

---

[8] Richard Taruskin, *Text and Act. Essays on Music and Performance* (New York: Oxford University Press, 1995), 97.

[9] Nicholas Cook, 'Music as Performance', in Martin Clayton, Trevor Herbert and Richard Middleton (eds.), *The Cultural Study of Music. A Critical Introduction*, 2nd edn (London: Routledge, 2012), 184–94 (pp. 186–87); see also Nicholas Cook, *Beyond the Score. Music as Performance* (New York: Oxford University Press, 2013), 135–37.

[10] Massimiliano Guido (ed.), *Studies in Historical Improvisation. From* Cantare super librum *to* Partimenti (Abingdon: Routledge, 2017).

190   *Authorship and Performance*

performance such as ornamentation; but John Butt has shown that several alternative notions of notation also existed in the period.[11] The relationship between authorship and performance was not a trans-historical universal, but rather can clarify which components of musical creativity were valued by seventeenth-century audiences.

MODELS FOR THE COMPOSER–PERFORMER RELATIONSHIP

German music theorists of the long seventeenth century recognised two basic models for the relationship between composer and performer. Most treatises in the *musica poetica* tradition viewed composition and performance as separate disciplines; rhetorical theory, by contrast, viewed performance as an integral part of the making of a speech or musical composition. Both of these models were connected with the humanist notion of creativity outlined in Chapter 1, and both were ambivalent towards performers, tending to view them as lowlier than composers.

The notion of composition and performance as separate spheres stemmed from the Aristotelian division of scientific knowledge into three branches: *theōretikē* (theoretical science), *praktikē* (practical action) and *poiētikē* (productive science).[12] This taxonomy underpinned the division of musical study into *theoretica*, *practica* and *poetica* as found in German *musica poetica* treatises from Nikolaus Listenius onwards. *Musica theoretica* comprised an exclusively intellectual understanding of music; *musica practica* put this understanding to practical use in the act of performance; *musica poetica* went one step further, by creating a durable product such as a composition (*opus*) (see p. 28).[13] This threefold division implied a clearer boundary between production and performance than existed in the predominantly oral culture of sixteenth- and seventeenth-century Europe,[14] leaving theorists uncertain where to categorise improvised counterpoint.[14] Yet the tripartite taxonomy was maintained by writers throughout the seventeenth century and even by Martin Heinrich Fuhrmann in 1706.[15]

Before Listenius, taxonomies of musical learning inspired by Aristotelian science had usually omitted composition and ranked performance as inferior to theoretical knowledge. Aristotle considered performing to be a menial occupation unsuitable for free men.[16] Transmitted via theorists

---

[11] John Butt, *Playing with History: The Historical Approach to Musical Performance* (Cambridge: Cambridge University Press, 2002), 96–124.

[12] Aristotle, *Metaphysics* 1025b, 1064a.

[13] Nikolaus Listenius, *Musica* (Wittenberg, 1537), sig. A4r–A4v. On the Aristotelian basis, see Heinz von Loesch, *Der Werkbegriff in der protestantischen Musiktheorie des 16. und 17. Jahrhunderts. Ein Mißverständnis* (Hildesheim: Olms, 2001), 87–94.

[14] Ibid., 63–68.

[15] Ibid., 130–37; Martin Heinrich Fuhrmann, *Musicalischer Trichter* (Frankfurt an der Spree, 1706), 34.

[16] Aristotle, *Politics* 1341a.

Models for the Composer–Performer Relationship   191

such as Boethius and Guido d'Arezzo, this dismissive attitude to performers was evident in the treatise *De musica* (1490) by Adam von Fulda, who in the same year was appointed to the chapel of the Elector of Saxony. Adam paraphrased Boethius to state that 'the science of music is much more excellent as the understanding of reason than as the work and act of performing, so much is the body surpassed by the mind'.[17] Theorists in the *musica poetica* tradition were less scathing of performance, insisting it required a modicum of theoretical knowledge. As Fuhrmann stated in 1706 (echoing a sentiment found as far back as Listenius): '*musica practica* is when someone not only understands the rules of music, but puts them into practice in singing and playing'.[18] Nonetheless the tripartite division implied composition was superior to performance, on account of its ability to produce a durable opus.

By the late seventeenth century, however, music theorists began to fuse the categories of *musica poetica* and *practica*, implying an erosion of the boundaries between composition and performance. Writers including Printz (1676), Walther (1708) and Mattheson (1739) divided the study of music into theoretical (*theoretica*) and practical (*practica*) branches, with *musica practica* subdivided into composition and performance.[19] Printz defined *musica practica* as 'an art through which a lovely harmony is awoken, to move the spirits of listeners', indicating that composers and performers shared the goal of arousing listeners' emotions.[20] Mattheson considered composition and performance to be united by their practical element: according to his definition, *musica practica* 'lies under the hand and makes the [mental] movements take external effect'.[21] With the collapse of music printing and the move to the frequent performance of new music (see Introduction and Chapter 5), composers were not necessarily associated any more with a durable opus.[22] This levelling of the respective status of composers and performers also reflected aspects of

[17] 'tanto enim praeclarior scientia musicae in cognitione rationis, quam in opere efficiendi atque actu, quantum corpus mente superatur'. Adam von Fulda, *De musica* (1490). Lost manuscript printed in Martin Gerbert, *Scriptores ecclesiastici de musica sacra potissimum*, 3 vols. (St Blasien, 1784), iii, 347.

[18] 'wenn jemand die Regeln der *Music* nicht nur verstehet/ sondern auch solche im Singen oder Klingen ausübet'. Martin Heinrich Fuhrmann, *Musicalischer Trichter* (Frankfurt an der Spree, 1706), 33.

[19] Wolfgang Caspar Printz, *Phrynis oder satyrischer Componist*, vol. 1 (Quedlinburg, 1676), sig. B2v; Johann Gottfried Walther, *Praecepta der musicalischen Composition*, ed. Peter Benary (Leipzig: Breitkopf & Härtel, 1955), 14–15; Johann Mattheson, *Der vollkommene Capellmeister* (Hamburg, 1739), 6–7.

[20] 'eine Kunst/ vermittelst welcher eine liebliche Zusammenstimmung erwecket wird/ um die Gemüther der Zuhörer zu bewegen'. Printz, *Phrynis*, vol. 1, sig. B2v.

[21] 'die … aber Hand anleget, und das erwogene äusserlich ins Werck setzet'. Mattheson, *Der vollkommene Capellmeister*, 6.

[22] Fuhrmann defined *musica poetica* as 'when a composer brings together the tones in an artful and lovely harmony' ('wenn ein *Componist* die *Tonos* in eine *Harmonie* künstlich und lieblich zusammen setzet'). Fuhrmann, *Musicalischer Trichter*, 34.

shared technique, with performers' ornaments increasingly being used as part of the compositional framework.[23]

A second model for the relationship between composer and performer was supplied by Ciceronian rhetoric and its fivefold division of poetic production into *inventio, dispositio, elocutio, memoria* and *pronuntiatio* (see Chapter 1, p. 34).[24] For orators, *memoria* involved the memorisation of a speech, and *pronuntiatio* (or *actio* or *executio*) concerned the vocal techniques, gestures and facial expressions involved in its delivery. Classical and early modern writers on poetics only rarely discussed the stages of *memoria* and *pronuntiatio*.[25] Yet the rhetorical model of creativity recognised performance as an integral part of the making of a poem or composition; its divisions allowed for performance to be by the same person as the composer, or by a separate individual. Hence rhetorical theory may seem to provide a historicised equivalent to the emphasis in performance studies on how the performer creates musical meaning.

Already in the early seventeenth century, some German musicians compared aspects of performance to rhetorical delivery: Joachim Burmeister described performance with the term *pronuntiatio*, and Michael Praetorius likened the role of a singer to an orator who decorates a speech with figures and moves the emotions.[26] However, until the end of the seventeenth century the rhetorical model of creativity was mainly used by musicians to theorise their notions of invention and disposition (see Chapter 1). Only in the eighteenth century was the rhetorical model systematically applied to the entirety of musical production from composition to performance. In 1713 Mattheson declared: 'Three things belong to a composition: *inventio* (discovering ideas), *elaboratio* (the working-out of those ideas), *executio* (the performance)'.[27] In 1739 he applied to music a full five-stage division of the creative process: *inventio* (invention), *dispositio* (disposition), *elaboratio* (elaboration), *decoratio* (embellishment) and *executio* (performance).[28] He replaced Cicero's *memoria* (memorisation) with *decoratio* (ornamentation), noting that embellishment could

---

[23] John Butt, *Music Education and the Art of Performance in the German Baroque* (Cambridge: Cambridge University Press, 1994), 148–64.

[24] Cicero, *Rhetorica ad Herennium* 1.2.3.

[25] Heinrich F. Plett, *Rhetoric and Renaissance Culture* (Berlin: De Gruyter, 2004), 91.

[26] See the section 'De vigore modulaminis comparato conservando, & de pronunciatione' (On acquiring and conserving strength in singing, and on delivery) in Joachim Burmeister, *Musica autoschediastike* (Rostock, 1601), sig. CC3v–DD3r; summarised in Benito V. Rivera, *German Music Theory of the Early Seventeenth Century: The Treatises of Johannes Lippius* (Ann Arbor: UMI, 1980), 54–55. Michael Praetorius, *Syntagmatis musici Michaelis Praetorii C. tomus tertius*, 2nd edn (Wolfenbüttel, 1619), 229.

[27] 'Es gehören sonst zu einer *Composition* dreyerley: *Inventio*, (Die Erfindung) *Elaboratio*, (Die Ausarbeitung) *Execution*, [*sic*] (die Ausführung oder Aufführung)'. Johann Mattheson, *Das neu-eröffnete Orchestre* (Hamburg, 1713), 104.

[28] Mattheson, *Der vollkommene Capellmeister*, 122.

Composition and Performance as Separate Spheres 193

be added by either composer or performer.[29] Through such statements, Mattheson conceived of performance as integral to composition.

Mattheson's use of the rhetorical model was in keeping with his empiricist beliefs. His emphasis on performance suited his conviction that music was primarily to be perceived aurally (see p. 12). Like Johann David Heinichen, he set little store on music that solely existed on paper as an opus.[30] Similar views were expressed in oratorical handbooks of the early eighteenth century: Johann Christoph Gottsched wrote that 'the most beautiful speech on paper has no effect on the listener, and does not promote at all the intention of the orator, if it is not properly performed'.[31] Indeed Birnbaum's views on the importance of performance, stated at the start of this chapter, may have stemmed from his background as a teacher of rhetoric. Yet the rhetorical model as advocated by Mattheson was ambivalent about the status of the performer. While recognising the performer's vital role in the communication of a composition, it could also establish a hierarchical relationship that obliged performers to project a composer's creation to the best of their ability. As Mattheson declared in his definition of composers and performers, 'the former are creators, the latter are readers or reciters of each and every melody'.[32] In this respect the rhetorical model may offer less to scholars seeking to recognise the creative role of the performer, than the Aristotelian model that separates composition from performance.

COMPOSITION AND PERFORMANCE AS SEPARATE SPHERES

In the first half of the seventeenth century, many musicians believed that composition and performance were separate spheres, according to the division between *musica poetica* and *musica practica* in treatises. The composer's domain was the notated opus, which might carry authority via the skill of its contrapuntal configurations or via the verification marks analysed in Chapter 3. The performer's domain, by contrast, comprised parameters such as scoring and ornamentation, which were typically described in terms that emphasised individuality, orality and the impossibility of fixing them in notation. Composers sometimes claimed to have no authority over these aspects of performance: thus Johann Hermann Schein in his madrigal collection *Diletti pastorali* (1624) wrote of his awareness

---

[29] Ibid., 242.

[30] See the dismissive comments about 'Pappierne Künste' in Johann David Heinichen, *Der General-Bass in der Composition* (Dresden, 1728), 10.

[31] 'Die schönste Rede auf dem Papiere thut bey dem Zuhörer keine Wirkung, und befördert die Absicht des Redners noch gar nicht, wenn sie nicht recht vorgetragen wird'. Johann Christoph Gottsched, *Ausführliche Redekunst* (Leipzig, 1739), 364.

[32] 'Die ersten sind Urheber; die andern Leser oder Vorleser von einerley und allerley Melodien'. Mattheson, *Der vollkommene Capellmeister*, 7.

'that a composer composes a song, but a cantor gracefully ornaments it'.[33] The present section examines this viewpoint in more detail, to develop a historically grounded awareness of the agency and prerogatives of the performer. It thereby offers a fresh perspective on the discipline of performance studies, which has tacitly used Barthes's notion of the 'death of the author' to justify a focus on how meaning is produced by performers rather than by authors.[34] The historical viewpoint, by contrast, suggests that the composer and performer are of equal status but engaged in different fields of activity: the notated source carries authority in its own right, but this authority is not necessarily to be imposed on performers.

A separation between the spheres of composition and performance was encouraged by the material characteristics of printed music of the early seventeenth century. Until 1650 most music circulated in partbook format, which typically presented compositions as a contrapuntal framework without performance details such as scoring or ornamentation. One reason for this neutral presentation was the difficulty of notating embellishment or idiomatic instrumental techniques, especially as short note-values and beamed passages were unwieldy in movable type (see p. 10). Another reason was to ensure that the music appealed to as many purchasers as possible. As Tobias Michael, cantor at Leipzig's Thomasschule from 1631 to 1657, explained: 'It would be a strangely absurd thing if an author wanted to publish his work for just two or three people'.[35] Performers, by contrast, worked within oral and memorised cultures, where the printed edition was a cue but not a prescription. In some cases they did not sing or play from the printed books, instead memorizing the composition or making a scribal copy.[36]

The prerogative of performers is illustrated by the freedom they enjoyed in terms of the scoring of polyphony. Even relatively simple pieces could be scored in numerous ways, as shown by Schein's villanellas, which he published in the trilogy *Musica boscareccia* (1621, 1626, 1628). These three-voice pieces are notated for two sopranos and bass, but Schein's preface indicated five further options for scoring: one or both of the sopranos could be replaced with tenors; instruments could be used to play the second soprano or bass line; and an additional bass could embellish the

---

[33] 'daß einem *Compositor*/ den Gesang zu *componiren*/ einem *Cantor* aber denselben zierlich zu *passeggioniren*'. Johann Hermann Schein, *Diletti pastorali* (Leipzig, 1624), Basso Continouo partbook, 'Auvertimento'. RISM A/I S1387.

[34] Cook, *Beyond the Score*, 24–25.

[35] 'So were ja ein seltzam vngereimt Ding/ wenn ein *Autor* seine Arbeit vor zwo oder drey Personen alleine *publici*ren . . .' Tobias Michael, *Musicalischer Seelen-Lust Ander Theil* (Leipzig, 1637), Quinta Vox, sig. B1v. RISM A/I M2637.

[36] In the preface to his 1624 keyboard collection *Tabulatura nova* (one of the first German music books printed in open score), Samuel Scheidt encouraged keyboardists to transcribe its pieces into tablature before performance. RISM A/I S1352.

Composition and Performance as Separate Spheres

second soprano line.[37] A similar variety of scoring was possible for full polyphonic works such as Orlande de Lassus's motets, with numerous possibilities involving instruments, voices and transpositions recommended by Michael Praetorius's treatise *Syntagma musicum*.[38] Music in the concerted style, with solo vocal lines and obbligato instrumental parts, was also amenable to adaptation. Praetorius encouraged many *ad libitum* practices with the vocal concertos in his *Polyhymnia caduceatrix et panegyrica* (1619), including the substitution of voices with instruments, and the replacement of instrumental sinfonias with movements from other sources such as dance collections.[39] Through such practices, performers could respond to circumstances and improve the compositions from their notated form. As Praetorius explained: 'As each music director and organist sees the occasion for himself in his church, and can think how to make the compositions better and improved'.[40]

From the mid-seventeenth century, the decline of music printing gave greater importance to manuscript sources that could incorporate more details of performance. Not restricted by the limitations of movable type, these manuscripts could have highly specific functions such as showing a novice how to perform in an ornamented style. Yet musicians increasingly voiced their awareness that aspects of performance could not be captured in notation. In 1668 Wolfgang Caspar Printz introduced the terms *quantitas intrinseca* and *quantitas extrinseca* to explain the difference between music as sounded and music as notated respectively. He presumably derived these concepts from Thomas of Aquinas's notion of intrinsic and extrinsic properties. (As Eleonore Stump explains, 'a change in x's extrinsic properties can occur without a change in x, while a change in x's intrinsic properties is as such a change in x'.[41]) Printz used these terms to explain why notes on strong beats are typically played longer than notated: 'The intrinsic property is the temporal quantity perceptible, which is longer or shorter than the note [as notated], and is permissible without similar extrinsic properties [in the notation]'.[42] Around 1690 Printz's terms were adopted by the Weissenfels court musician Johann Beer, who argued that ornaments were *quantitates intrinsecae* that could not be indicated in notation. As Beer explained: 'The intrinsic property

---

[37] Johann Herman Schein, *Musica boscareccia [Erster Theil]* (Leipzig, 1621), Basso partbook, sig. A3v. RISM A/I S1379.

[38] Praetorius, *Syntagmatis musici ... tomus tertius*, 152–68.   [39] Ibid., 174–75, 189–90.

[40] 'wie dann ein jeder *Musicus* vnd *Organist* selbsten in seiner Kirchen/ die gelegenheit sehen/ vnd der sachen besser vnd weitter nachdencken kan'. Ibid., 175.

[41] Eleonore Stump, *Aquinas* (London: Routledge, 2013), 97.

[42] 'Quantitas intrinseca est quantitas temporalis adparens, qua nota alia longa videtur, brevis alia, licet sine similis quantitates extrinsecae'. Wolfgang Caspar Printz, *Compendium musicae in quo breviter ac succincte explicantur et traduntur omnia ea, quae ad oden artificiose componendam requiruntur* (Guben, 1668), sig. B5v. For subsequent uses of these terms by Printz and other theorists, see George Houle, *Meter in Music, 1600–800: Performance, Perception and Notation* (Bloomington: Indiana University Press, 1987), 78–84.

cannot be shown through external signs ... it lies in the domain of listening, not of seeing'.[43] Such limitations of notation restricted how far a musical author could specify aspects of performance, leaving much to the prerogative of the performer.

Many musicians regarded the role of performers as involving the improvement and individuation of compositions in ways that could not be captured in notation. Such an attitude had roots in late sixteenth-century Italy, where Ludovico Zacconi described the obligation of performers to bring *gratia* (grace) and *vaghezza* (beauty) to a notated composition. These terms appeared in Italian art criticism of the period, where they indicated such elusive qualities as bodily proportions and feminine charm.[44] For Zacconi, *gratia* indicated something similar to Castiglione's *sprezzatura* (nonchalance): 'that quality possessed by men who, in performing an action, show that they do it effortlessly, supplementing agility with beauty and charm'.[45] In Zacconi's opinion, a singer should show the same combination of skill and grace as a knight on horseback, not the clumsiness of a peasant in the saddle.[46] Such usages of *gratia* were adopted by German exponents of Italianate styles. When describing different possible scorings for his *Historia der Aufferstehung*, Schütz noted that the use of concealed singers would add *gratia* and charm (*anmuth*) to the performance.[47] Michael Praetorius and Tobias Michael likewise used the term *gratia* to indicate the ineffable ways in which performers could improve a notated composition.[48]

The main way that performers could add grace was via ornamentation. As Zacconi explained: 'Music has always been beautiful and becomes more so each hour because of the diligence and study with which singers enhance it; it is not renewed or changed because of the figures [i.e., notes] which are always of one kind, but by graces and ornaments it is made to appear always more beautiful'.[49] Embellishment also permitted a performer

---

[43] 'Die *quantitas intrinseca* kan durch kein eusserlich Zeichen gewiesen werden ... Liegt also am hören/ nicht am sehen'. Johann Beer, *Musicalische Discurse* (Nuremberg, 1719), 136. The *Musicalische Discurse* was published posthumously; according to his manuscript autobiography, Beer wrote it in November 1690. See Johann Beer, *Sein Leben, von ihm selbst erzählt*, ed. Adolf Schmiedecke (Göttingen: Vandenhoeck & Ruprecht, 1965), 13.

[44] For instance, in Agnolo Firenzuola's treatise on female beauty, *Dialogo della bellezza delle donne* (1548) or the preface to Giorgio Vasari's *Le vite de' più eccellenti pittori, scultori, e architettori* (1550); see Philip Sohm, 'Gendered Style in Italian Art Criticism from Michelangelo to Malvasia', *Renaissance Quarterly* 48 (1995), 759–808.

[45] 'quella ch'hanno gli huomini quando in fare un attione dimostrano di farla senza fatica; et all'agilita, aggiungano le vaghezze e'l garbo'. Ludovico Zacconi, *Prattica di musica* (Venice, 1592), 55v.

[46] Ibid.

[47] Heinrich Schütz, *Historia ... der Aufferstehung* (Dresden, 1623), preface. RISM A/I S2277.

[48] Praetorius, *Syntagmatis musici ... tomus tertius*, 132, *recte* 112; Michael, *Musicalischer Seelen-Lust Ander Theil*, Quinta Vox, sig. B1v.

[49] 'la Musica e stata bella sempre, et ogni hora piu per la diligenza, et per lo studio che ci fanno i cantori si abellisce; la quale non si rinova, o si muta per via delle figure, che sempre le sono d'una sorte; ma con le gratie, et gl'accenti la si fa parer sempre piu bella'. Zacconi, *Prattica di musica*, 58r.

Composition and Performance as Separate Spheres 197

to customise a piece for his or her ability. As Hermann Finck wrote, 'the method for ornamentation depends on skill, natural ability and an individual's character. Every person has their own manner'.[50]

Throughout the seventeenth century, one school of thought emphasised that because of this individuality, ornamentation was the prerogative of performers and should not be notated by the composer. Detailed reasons for this viewpoint were given by Tobias Michael in 1637 and by Beer around 1690. Michael wrote that ornaments should flow from the innate talent and experience of the performer:

I have always held the opinion that authors, when they publish their works (both vocal and instrumental), act better if they do not mingle or add ornaments, for this reason: I myself have discovered that a skilful, trained and qualified musician, who not only has a good natural talent but also already has attained a good style, can better help the piece with his technique and give it a shape, than when one prescribes such things for him.[51]

Beer asserted that 'all throats are disposed differently ... the same ornament in two throats will rarely sound the same'.[52] For both writers, embellishment was a way for performers to tailor a piece to their talent and ability.

Like other writers on ornamentation, Michael and Beer emphasised that embellishment belonged to the oral sphere and could not be adequately indicated in notation. Michael explained that for many ornaments, a teacher's demonstration was preferable to a notated version:

I have omitted the smaller ornaments (such as the gruppo, trillo and the like), because such things can be taught not so much through notation as *viva voce*, and [by writing them down] a piece is made to appear more difficult and in many cases may lead to cat-calls and laughter rather than gracefulness; [hence] I have left them for the practised musician [to add] at his pleasure.[53]

Beer, as already mentioned, viewed embellishment as a *quantitas intrinseca* which could not be represented in notation. Unless the composer was

---

[50] 'Est vero ratio coloraturarum singularis cuiusdam dexteritatis, naturae et proprietatis. Suus cuicqᶜueᵓ mos est'. Hermann Finck, *Practica musica* (Wittenberg, 1556), sig. SS4r.

[51] 'ich allezeit der Meynung gewesen/ die *Autores* theten besser/ wenn sie ihre *opera* beydes *vocalia* vnd *Instrumentalia* also herausser gehen liessen/ daß sie keine *Coloratur*en einmengeten oder darzu setzeten/ vnd diß darumb: Weil ich selber erfahren/ daß/ wenn ein geschickter/ geübter/ vnd *qvalificir*ter *Musicus*, welcher nicht allein gute *naturalia*, sondern ihme auch allbereit eine feine Manier angewöhnet hat/ darüber kömmt/ daß er dem Stücke mit seiner Art besser helfffen vnd eine Gestalt geben kan/ als wann man ihme solches vorschreibet'. Michael, *Musicalischer Seelen-Lust Ander Theil*, Quinta Vox, sig. B1r.

[52] 'alle Gurgeln nicht gleich *disponi*rt seyn ... Einerley Manier in zweyen Gurgeln ... klinget selten einerley'. Beer, *Musicalische Discurse*, 135, 137.

[53] 'Daß die kleineren *Coloratur*en/ als den *gruppo trillo* vnnd dergleichen/ weil solche nicht so wol durch Vorschreiben als *viva voce* gelehrte werden können/ vnd das Stück im Anschawen nur desto schwerer machen/ auch bey manchem mehr ein Gekätter oder Gelächter als eine Zierde zu wege bringen/ gutwillig gantz aussen vnd dem geübten *Musico* zu seinem Vermögen gelassen habe'. Michael, *Musicalischer Seelen-Lust Ander Theil*, Quinta Vox, sig. B1v–B2r.

present to demonstrate the preferred embellishment, or unless the notation alluded to widely recognised conventions of decoration, most aspects of ornamentation were solely under the control of the performer.

In elaborating on why composers should not prescribe ornamentation, both Michael and Beer recognised that performance is pluralistic, giving rise to multiple interpretations of equal validity. Michael acknowledged that each singer develops a personal style depending on natural talent:

This is why I cannot be of the opinion of those who want to restrict everything to a single style [of performance], still less those who are pleased by nothing except that which they have created or baked. But I hold for my own unworthiness (though I gladly leave others to their opinions) that there are three, four, five or more entirely good styles to be found, each of which is acceptable and yet is easy to distinguish from the others.[54]

Beer added an awareness of changes in musical style and performers' dispositions. 'The ornaments themselves change from day to day: today this one but tomorrow another one flourishes'.[55] Furthermore, 'a singer, in consideration of his individuality, is disposed differently today from yesterday, and differently again tomorrow. Therefore the prescription [of ornaments] is like [wrangling over] goat's wool'.[56] Beer's culminating argument why composers should not intrude on this area of performance was an appeal to pluralistic liberty: 'Music is devoted to the shape of freedom, for it does not let itself be prescribed, still less compelled'.[57] In this manifesto for the performer individualising and adapting compositions, Beer indicated the limits on the powers of the musical author.

Although Michael acknowledged the problems involved in notating ornaments, he nonetheless supplied suggested embellishment as *ossia* lines in his 1637 publication of vocal concertos:

I have added for the pleasure of music-lovers ... something of the coloratura style in individual cases and in several pieces, yet in such a way that [the line] is doubled before the eyes. And anyone who carries a liking for my work can use which he wants, as far as is found to be unburdensome.[58]

---

[54] 'Daher ich derer Meynung nicht seyn kan/ welche alles nur an eine Manier binden wollen/ vielweniger derer/ welchen durchaus nichts gefället/ als was sie selber geschaffen vnnd was ihres Gebackes ist: Sondern halte vor meine Wenigkeit darfür (lasse aber einem andern gerne seine Meynung) daß wol 3/ 4/ 5 oder mehrerley/ sämptlich gute Arten anzutreffen/ da iede vor sich passiret/ vnd doch von der andern wol zu unterscheiden ist'. Ibid., sig. B1r–B1v.

[55] 'die *manier*en von Tag zu Tage ändern/ heute diese/ morgen eine andere florirt'. Beer, *Musicalische Discurse*, 135.

[56] 'ein Sänger/ in seinem *individuo consideri*rt/ heute nicht wie gestern/ und morgen nicht wie heute *disponir*t/ ist also die Vorschrifft *de lana caprina*'. Ibid.

[57] 'Die *music* ist der Freyheit dergestalten ergeben/ daß sie sich durchaus nichts vorschreiben/ noch vielweniger sich zwingen lässet'. Ibid.

[58] 'Als habe ich den Liebhabern zu Gefallen ... etwas von *Coloratur*en-Manier eintzeln vnd in etzlichen Stücken mit eingebracht/ doch also/ daß es duppelt vor Augen/ vnd der jenige/ so etwa Beliebung zu meiner Arbeit träget/ zu welchen er wil/ greiffen möge/ wobey ferner vnbeschweret zu mercken'. Tobias Michael, *Musicalischer Seelen-Lust Ander Theil*, sig. B1v.

By providing ornamented and plain versions of vocal lines, Michael followed the example of Italian musicians such as Bartolomeo Barbarino, whose *Il secondo libro delli motetti* (1614) explained how such dual lines should be used. The plain version was for singers who lacked the vocal ability (*dispositione*) to make ornaments, or for those with the necessary ability and contrapuntal knowledge to add their own divisions. The ornamented version (*passaggiata*) was for singers who had the requisite vocal ability (*dispositione*) but lacked the contrapuntal expertise to know where to add diminutions.[59] Michael's dual versions of vocal lines illustrate the tendency of certain seventeenth-century composers to incorporate more details of performance into their notation, yet in such a way that recognised different performers' interpretations as equally valid.

The view of performance as a separate domain from composition – characterised by such attributes as freedom, individuality and plurality – persisted in some genres until the first decades of the eighteenth century. In the 1700s the singers of Italian opera were among the leading proponents of this viewpoint: Pier Francesco Tosi's singing treatise idealised the extemporised ornamentation of singers as something that could not be captured in notation.[60] Early eighteenth-century opera, however, rarely showed the same polish on paper as polyphonic works of a century earlier. This repertory from the first half of the seventeenth century offers a corrective to the tendency of performance studies to prioritise the performer over the composer. Michael and Beer advocated a non-hierarchical relationship between composer and performer, whereby a notated composition could be complete in itself as an opus on paper, but it could also be beautified and individualised in the act of performance.

THE COMPOSER AS IDEAL PERFORMER

In contrast to the view of composition and performance as separate realms, another tradition idealised composers as authoritative performers of their works, responsible for all stages of production from *inventio* to *pronuntiatio*. This viewpoint was associated with solo repertories (including keyboard music and vocal monody) which primarily existed in the embodied act of performance. Although virtuoso soloists often aspired to courtly status, their emphasis on embodied knowledge connected them with artisanal notions of creativity. In the same way that the knowledge of craftworkers was shaped by their manual skill, so too was the compositional style of these solo musicians symbiotically connected with their techniques as performers. Whether their fingers were plucking gut strings or articulating notes on a keyboard, these musicians held embodied

---

[59] Bartolomeo Barbarino, *Il secondo libro delli motetti* (Venice, 1614), preface. RISM A/I B874.
[60] Pier Francesco Tosi, *Opinioni de' cantori antichi e moderni* (Bologna, 1723), 58–59.

knowledge of the sounding potential of their instrument's materiality. Just as artisans were reluctant to disclose their skills except to an apprentice, these composer-performers gained prestige from the exclusive nature of their performances. Some performed only in intimate venues, to select groups of connoisseurs or to the most privileged members of a court. They would normally disclose their performing styles only to apprentices or amateur pupils who paid dearly for this knowledge (as with Johann Heinrich Buttstett; see p. 122). Generally such composer-performers insisted that their styles could not be captured in notation, although a few manuscript or printed sources purported to do so, including Italian songbooks from the early seventeenth century that claimed to represent how pieces were sung by the author.[61]

In German lands of the seventeenth century, the notion of the composer's embodied performance as ideal was strongest in the keyboard music of Johann Jacob Froberger. This was a rarefied, performerly repertory that gave the highest cultural capital to its patrons and practitioners. Chapter 3 showed how the calligraphy of Froberger's autographs incorporated traces of his body, with stylised *manu propria scripsi* signs indicating the involvement of his hand in the making of the manuscript (see p. 99). Froberger's presence was also essential for a successful performance of his keyboard music. The Dutch connoisseur Constantijn Huygens commented that Froberger's 'compositions . . . can hardly be played properly without the original instruction of the author'.[62] Huygens praised a visiting virtuoso Franz Francken, who had worked with Froberger at the imperial court: 'This man has profited much from his talks with Froberger and is well versed in his method, as was apparent from the way he played some of his pieces, in a style more refined than I have ever heard before'.[63] Only by hearing Froberger play could a keyboardist understand how to perform his toccatas and suites.

Comments by Froberger's patron Sibylla of Württemberg emphasised how an effective performance of his music depended on skills within the composer's body. In a letter to Huygens, Sibylla referred to the Cologne

---

[61] Giulio Caccini's *Nuove musiche e nuova maniere di scriverle* (Florence, 1614) asserted that 'with this notation and with practice of it, all the exquisite things of this art may be learned, without the necessity of [hearing] the author sing them' ('che da tal Maniera di scrivere con la pratica di essa, si possano apprendere tutte le squistezze di quest'Arte, senza necessità del Canto dell'Autore'). RISM A/I C11. See Ellen Rosand, '"Senza Necessità del Canto dell'Autore": Printed Singing Lessons in Seventeenth-Century Italy', in Angelo Pompilio et al. (eds.), *Atti del XIV congresso della Società Internazionale di Musicologia, Bologna*, 3 vols. (Turin: Edizioni di Torino, 1990), ii, 214–24.

[62] 'compositions, qui . . . ne sçauroyent guères estre touchées proprement que de l'instruction originelle de l'auteur . . . ' Constantijn Huygens, letter of 4 August 1668 to Sibylla of Württemberg. Rudolf Rasch (ed.), *Driehonderd brieven over muziek van, aan en rond Constantijn Huygens*, 2 vols. (Hilversum: Verloren, 2007), ii, 1075.

[63] 'Cest homme tesmoignoit assez d'avoir proffité de la conversation du Sieur Froberger, donnant fort dans sa méthode et mesme en touchant quelqu'une de ses pièces, du plus haut stile que j'aye encor veu'. Constantijn Huygens, letter of 4 August 1668 to Sibylla of Württemberg. Ibid., 1076.

organist Caspar Grieffgens, who played the *Memento mori Froberger*, 'and has learned it from his [the composer's] hand, note by note. It is difficult to gather from the [written] notes'.[64] The emphasis on learning 'from his hand' recalls artisanal methods of education, where an apprentice imitated the master's techniques that could not be shared in writing. Sibylla told Huygens that since Froberger's death 'so many pieces have come to my sight and hands for which I should have needed his ingenious spirit and faithful tuition, and I was wanting his further indications'.[65] 'Ingenious spirit' invoked not only the humanist notion of *ingenium* but also those artisans such as Dürer who spoke of a power (*Gewalt*) present in everything they made[66]: such a power could not easily be transferred to others, except to pupils who laboriously imitated the master's technique. Sibylla continued: 'Compared to him I am only to be counted as a child, or as a copy against the living original'.[67] Even allowing for an element of false modesty here, her metaphor implied that Froberger's body is a point of origin and a patriarchal source of life for subsequent performances.

The unique quality of Froberger's performances, according to Sibylla, consisted of 'discretion'. As she said: 'Whoever has not learned the pieces from him, the late Froberger, could not possibly play them with the right discretion, as he played them'.[68] 'Discretion' appears to have involved a refined choice of tempo and careful use of rubato. The Froberger manuscript held by the Berlin Sing-Akademie (SA4450) contains the rubric 'lentement a la discretion' on several of his allemandes and toccatas. As noted in Chapter 3, this manuscript probably had a pedagogical purpose, instructing north German keyboardists how to perform in Froberger's style. The scribe marked the start and end of the sections requiring 'discretion', supporting the hypothesis that this term indicated the use of rubato.[69]

'Discretion' might also imply that the keyboardist should perform like an orator, projecting melodic figures or expressive harmonies.[70] Such a rhetorical style of performance could convey the biographical experiences

---

[64] 'und hat es von seiner Handt gelernt, Grif vor Grif. Ist schwer aus den Notten zu finden'. Sibylla of Württemberg, letter of 23 October 1667 to Constantijn Huygens. Ibid., 1069.

[65] 'mir seiter schon so viel Sachen under Gesicht und Handen komen, das ich seines herlichen sinreichen Geistes und getrewer Lernung wol von Nöten hete, und weitern Berichts bederfte'. Ibid., 1068.

[66] Joseph Koerner, *The Moment of Self-Portraiture in German Renaissance Art* (Chicago: University of Chicago Press, 1993), 213.

[67] '... gegen ihm nuhr wie ein unmündiges Künd oder Conterfait gegen dem lebendigen Original zu rechnen'. Sibylla of Württemberg, letter of 23 October 1667 to Constantijn Huygens. Rasch (ed.), *Driehonderd brieven*, ii, 1068.

[68] 'das wer die Sachen nit von ihme Hern Froberger seliger gelernet, unmüglich mit rechter Discretion zuschlagen, wie er sie geschlagen hat'. Ibid.

[69] D-Bsa, SA4450, 4.

[70] David Schulenberg, 'Crossing the Rhine with Froberger: Suites, Symbols, and Seventeenth-Century Musical Autobiography', in Claire Fontijn and Susan Parisi (eds.), *Fiori Musicali. Liber amicorum Alexander Silbiger* (Sterling Heights, MI: Harmonie Park Press, 2010), 271–302 (p. 301).

which Froberger claimed to represent in his allemandes (see Chapter 3, p. 97). In the *Allemande faite en passant le Rhin dans une barque*, rubato on some of the melodic flourishes and broken chords could highlight their role in representing the composer's experience of a perilous river journey; indeed, the copy in SA4450 annotates many of these gestures with numbers referring to a programmatic description.[71] Finally, 'discretion' might refer to the composer's distinctive ornamentation. Mattheson reported that Froberger 'sent Weckmann a suite written in his own hand, wherein he had notated all ornaments [*Manieren*], so that Weckmann could become familiar with Froberger's style of playing'.[72] The Berlin manuscript and the suite sent to Weckmann are rare examples of sources where a scribe specified aspects of performance such as rubato and ornamentation, in the belief that these are essential to the meaning of the compositions.

Keyboardists often expected to adapt repertory to their own performing styles, creating the illusion of their own improvisations even if they were playing another person's music. Such a process of appropriation is documented by the complex manuscript transmission of Froberger's music, with many variants of ornamentation, rhythm and texture found in manuscripts such as that copied by Michael Bulyowsky in Strasbourg in 1675.[73] Some musicians even arranged these highly idiomatic keyboard pieces for instrumental ensemble.[74] Yet Froberger objected to such appropriations, according to Sibylla: 'He often said to me that many gave out his compositions as though these were their own, and yet did not know what to do with them, but only spoilt them'.[75] Similar complaints were made by some French keyboardists who sought to represent their playing styles in authoritative printed or manuscript sources, yet faced a plethora of variants in manuscripts copied by other keyboardists.[76]

By the start of the eighteenth century, the notion of the composer as the ideal performer sometimes also occurred in ensemble music, particularly when parts were incompletely notated. In opera around 1700, the

---

[71] D-Bsa, SA4450, 33.

[72] 'Froberger sandte dem Weckmann eine Suite von seiner eignen Hand, wobey er alle Manieren setzte, so daß Weckmann auch dadurch der frobergerischen Spiel-Art ziemlich kundig ward'. Johann Mattheson, *Grundlage einer Ehren-Pforte* (Hamburg, 1740), 396.

[73] D-Dl, Ms. 1-T-595; modern edition published as *Vingt et une suites pour le clavecin de Johann Jacob Froberger et d'autres auteurs: Dresden, Sächsische Landesbibliothek, Ms. 1-T-595 (Strasbourg, 1675)*, ed. Rudolf Rasch (Stuttgart: Carus, 2000).

[74] See the instrumental ensemble arrangements of Froberger dance movements in the Ludwig Partiturbuch, D-W, Cod.Guelf. 34.7 Aug 2°, pp. 23–28. The Riga cantor Johann Valentin Meder recorded in a letter of 1709 how he arranged Froberger's *Memento mori* for viols, on the request of 'a known lover of music'; see Mattheson, *Grundlage einer Ehren-Pforte*, 222.

[75] 'Dan er mir offt gesagt das vil van seiner Composition vor ihre Composition ausgeben, und doch nit wisten mit umbzugehen, sondern selbige nuhr verderben'. Sibylla of Württemberg, letter of 23 October 1667 to Constantijn Huygens. Rasch (ed.), *Driehonderd brieven*, ii, 1068.

[76] Ronald Broude, 'Paris *chez l'autheur*: Self-Publication and Authoritative Texts in the France of Louis XIV', *Early Music* 45 (2017), 283–96.

Authorial Intentions and Performance 203

keyboard continuo was often played by the composer, who also directed from the harpsichord. Mattheson reported on the 1704 Hamburg performance of his opera *Cleopatra*, where he took the part of Antonius. 'Now I was previously accustomed, after this action [the death of Anthony], to go into the orchestra and accompany the rest of the opera myself; for such accompaniment can indisputably be done better by the author than anyone else'.[77] On this occasion Handel was playing continuo, and his refusal to cede his place to Mattheson provoked a duel between the two musicians.[78] Mattheson's insistence that the composer was the best continuo player partly reflected an egoistic desire to take as many roles in his opera as possible; but it also reflected the incomplete notation of a figured bass, where the full harmonic configurations might be preserved only in the mind of the composer.

The notion of the composer as the ideal performer was strongest in solo genres such as keyboard music and monodic song. When Sibylla of Württemberg described Froberger's performances as the 'living original' and her own renditions as a mere 'child', she upheld a vertical mode of transmission, where a performance is regarded as inferior the further away it is from the composer. Nicholas Cook has criticised this mode of transmission as constraining performers with a Romanticised notion of the composer and the musical work.[79] This section, however, has suggested an alternative origin for such attitudes, in the manual skill of early modern artisans and the secrecy of court virtuosos. By celebrating the unique nature of their embodied knowledge, composer-performers boosted their status and enhanced the value of their music.

AUTHORIAL INTENTIONS AND PERFORMANCE

In some cases the author was not the ideal performer, yet wished to control the interpretative decisions taken by singers and players. Such examples can be related to a rhetorical model of creativity where composition and performance are stages on a continuum, undertaken by separate people yet with an overall communicative purpose. Although Taruskin questioned the relevance and knowability of composers' intentions, subsequent scholars have offered more nuanced approaches. John Butt argues that intentionality can be present in different levels of compositional activity: active intentions (such as instrumentation or ornamentation) can be consciously notated, whereas passive intentions (such as compositional

[77] 'Nun war ich bisher gewohnt, nach dieser Action, ins Orchester zu gehen, und das übrige selbst zu accompagniren: welches doch unstreitig ein jeder Verfasser besser, als ein andrer, thun kann'. Mattheson, *Grundlage einer Ehren-Pforte*, 95.

[78] Ibid.; see also Stephen Rose, *The Musician in Literature in the Age of Bach* (Cambridge: Cambridge University Press, 2011), 197.

[79] Cook, *Beyond the Score*, 136.

style) tend to be assumed but are harder for the author to specify.[80] Quoting from a wide array of treatises from the sixteenth to eighteenth centuries, Andrew Parrott shows how composers referred to their intentions in order to specify their envisaged performance idiom, regulate ornamentation, and ensure that performances maintained their reputations.[81] This section builds on Parrott's survey, by analysing the contexts for comments about compositional intentions in Lutheran lands during this period. Such comments typically arose when composers were concerned that aspects of a notated work (such as its harmonic or contrapuntal structure) would be obscured in performance. I also relate the notion of compositional intentions to the theological, humanist and artisanal views of creativity outlined in Chapter 1, exploring its implications for an understanding of the agency of musicians.

In German-speaking lands during the seventeenth century, musicians frequently invoked the concept of compositional intentions when discussing notation that is purposefully incomplete, such as figured basses or melodic lines that omit ornamentation. Rather than celebrating the freedom of performers as a separate sphere of activity from notated music, composers feared that incomplete notation would prevent an understanding of the harmonic or contrapuntal structure. Thus the Nuremberg organist Johann Staden, in his 1626 instructions on continuo playing, explained that a lack of bass figuring or inconsistent use of figures 'sometimes leaves even experienced organists in doubt so that they cannot always know how the Bassus ad Organum is to be treated in accordance with the author's intention'.[82]

Around 1700 Andreas Werckmeister voiced a similar understanding of the composer's intentions as residing in the harmonic fabric. In his treatise on continuo playing, he advised 'those unable to play by touch, that when they precisely follow the figures, they can realise the harmony and the correct pulse according to the author's will'.[83] Warning continuo players not to double an expressive solo line, he explained that 'the figures and dissonances are not necessarily put in so that one should realise them, but rather so that someone who understands composition can thereby see what the composer's intention is, and how he should not contradict them with

---

[80] John Butt, *Playing with History*, 89–90.

[81] Andrew Parrott, 'Composers' Intentions, Performers' Responsibilities', *Early Music* 41 (2013), 37–43.

[82] 'auch wol bisweilen geübte Organisten zweifelhaftig macht/ dass sie nicht allezeit wissen können/ wie nach des Autoris Meinung der Bass ad Organum zu tractiren'. Johann Staden, *Kirchen-Music Ander Theil geistlicher Gesäng und Psamen* (Nuremberg, 1626), Bassus ad Organum partbook. RISM A/I S4239.

[83] 'die da nicht *tactuali*ter spielen können/ wann nur allemahl die *Signatur*en würden in acht genommen/ damit nebst der richtigen *Mensur* auch die *Harmonie* nach des *Autoris* Willen möchte heraus gebracht werden'. Andreas Werckmeister, *Die nothwendigsten Anmerckungen und Regeln wie der General-Baß wol könne tractiret werden*, 1st edn (Aschersleben, 1698), sig. B3v.

Authorial Intentions and Performance 205

anything that might ruin the harmony'.[84] That the composer's envisaged meaning resided in the harmonic structure is an example of Butt's 'active intentions'; this viewpoint reinforced the priority that Birnbaum and Johann Krieger gave to the compositional 'kernel' rather than the performed surface.

Debates about embellishment similarly addressed the importance of the composition's notated structure being audible in performance. From the mid-sixteenth to late seventeenth centuries, some composers voiced fears that florid improvised ornamentation would clash with their notated parts, or would obscure the planned interplay of dissonance and consonance. Such concerns are found during the second half of the sixteenth century in Italian treatises that would later be consulted and quoted by Lutherans such as Seth Calvisius and Michael Praetorius.[85] Gioseffo Zarlino advised: 'Therefore the singers should take care to sing those things as they are written according to the mind of the composer, intoning the voices well and putting the steps in the right places'.[86] Heavy ornamentation might prevent a performance displaying the harmonic or contrapuntal skill evident in the written opus. Zacconi remarked: 'On occasion composers have avoided the opportunity to have some of their pieces sung, not wishing to hand them over and have them sung by singers like this; for the sole reason that they liked to hear them with plain and simple ornaments, so they could hear the artifice that they had used in weaving and constructing them'.[87]

Lutheran musicians of the seventeenth century echoed these concerns about whether florid ornamentation obscured the intentions of the composer. As attitudes hardened against lavish embellishment, such concerns might seem to resemble a notion of moral rights, whereby authors are entitled to have their works circulate in undistorted forms (see p. 117). In 1704 Johann Georg Ahle complained that 'many [singers] favour fantasy and the great abuse of coloratura, with which the song itself is deformed and darkened, such that it can scarcely be recognised'.[88]

---

[84] 'darum sind die Signaturen/ und *Dissonantien* nicht allemal gesezet daß man sie so *crasse* mit mache/ sondern ein *Composition*-Verständiger kan dadurch sehen/ was des *Autoris* Meynung sey/ und wie er nichts dagegen bringe/ wodurch die Harmonia verlezet werde'. Andreas Werckmeister, *Die nothwendigsten Anmerckungen und Regeln wie der Bassus Continuus oder General-Baß wohl könne tractiret werden*, 2nd edn (Aschersleben, 1715), 42.

[85] See, for instance, Praetorius, *Syntagmatis musici ... tomus tertius*, sig.):(6v.

[86] 'Debbeno adunque li Cantori auertire, di cantar correttamente quelle cose, che sono scritte secondo la mente del Compositore; intonando bene le voci, & ponendole a i loro luoghi'. Gioseffo Zarlino, *Le istitutioni harmoniche* (Venice, 1558), 204.

[87] 'anzi che io ho trovato alle volte i Compositori haver fuggito l'occasione di far cantar alcune cose loro: per non farle cantare, et darle in mano a simili Cantori: non per altro solo perche haveano a piacere di sentirle con gli accenti schietti, et semplici: accioche s'udissero gli artificii con che le haveano tessute, et fatte'. Zacconi, *Prattica di musica*, 64v.

[88] 'viel davon vor Fantasei und großen misbrauch des *colorir*ens mag gehalten werden/ wormit der Gesang dermaßen *deformi*ret und verdunkelt wird/ daß er kaum mag erkennet werden'. Johann Rudolf Ahle, *Kurze, doch deutliche Anleitung zu der lieblich- und löblichen Singekunst ... mit ...*

In 1671 Andreas Hammerschmidt commented in his *Sechsstimmige Fest- und Zeit-Andachten*:

I would say that those immature instrumentalists from the choir are to be told that their hunting horns or cornetts should not adorn a single note, for otherwise their debased, ugly coloratura will most terribly stretch and twist the notes, so that against the author's intention all musical rules are contravened, and also the imitations, syncopations and the best impression of the whole composition are totally spoiled and torn.[89]

Hammerschmidt's music circulated widely among village churches, so this warning may have been aimed at rural instrumentalists rooted in vernacular and oral traditions. He wanted renditions to preserve the contrapuntal and harmonic configurations that made his work look polished on paper. Hammerschmidt's fear of performances that contravened 'musical rules' reflected the importance of such rules in proving the skill of musicians and their suitability for appointment as organists and cantors. Ensuring that a performance displayed the envisaged harmonic structure was therefore vital to a composer's professional and social status.

Some musicians claimed the notated version of a composition carried authority in its contrapuntal structure. Such rhetoric is occasionally found in sixteenth-century printed tablatures that contain arrangements of vocal polyphony. The vocal originals might already be canonised through their wide circulation, longevity in performance, or the endorsement given by the 1580 Saxon edict (see Chapter 5). The makers and users of intabulations had to choose whether to embellish the polyphonic originals: ornamentation suited solo performance on non-sustaining instruments such as the spinet or clavichord, but was less appropriate for intabulations used for accompaniment. To justify his addition of ornamentation in his *Tabulatur* of 1577, the Strasbourg organist Bernhard Schmid wrote:

I have adorned with modest coloraturas the motets and other pieces contained in this whole book, not with the intention of binding the experienced organists to my coloraturas (for they should be left free to make their own improvements) but solely for novice, young keyboardists; although I myself would prefer to leave the authority and art of the composers unaltered.[90]

---

nöthigen Anmerkungen ... zum drukke befördert durch des seeligen Verfassers Sohn Johan Georg Ahlen (Mühlhausen, 1704), 80.

[89] 'die jenigen unzeitigen *Instrumental*-Musicanten vom Chor gewiesen werden/ so mit ihren Jäger-Hörnern/ oder Zincken wolt ich sagen/ keiner eintzigen Noten schonen/ sondern selbe durch ihr gemeines unförmliches *colori*ren/ auffs ärgste dehnen und verdrehen/ dadurch so wohl des *Autoris Intention* wieder alle Musicalische Regeln verruckt/ als auch die *Fugen*/ *Syncopation* und der beste Nachdruck des gantzen Gesanges durchaus verderbet und zerstimmelt werden'. Andreas Hammerschmidt, *Sechsstimmige Fest- und Zeit-Andachten* (Dresden, 1670–71), Cantus 1 partbook, preface. RISM A/I H1954.

[90] 'Darnach hab ich die Motteten vnd stuck/ so im gantzen werck einverleibt/ mit geringen Coloraturen gezieret/ nit der meinung das ich die verständigen Organisten eben an mein Colloraturen wölle binde⟨n⟩/ sonder einem jetlichen sein verbesserung frei lassen/ vnd allein wie gemelt/ der angehenden jungen Instrumentisten halber angesehen worden/ wiewol ich selber auch

Authorial Intentions and Performance 207

Schmid's book mainly contained motets and secular songs by Lassus. Similar to the opinions of Tobias Michael discussed above, Schmid claimed to prefer that embellishment be left to the performer's discretion, unless it was added to assist the inexperienced. For him the 'authority and art' of the composers lay in the contrapuntal perfection of the original opus.

Beyond the notated contrapuntal configurations, musicians identified less tangible layers of authorial meaning in compositions. In his 1619 discussion of vocal ornamentation, Michael Praetorius advised that diligent articulation and pronunciation were necessary 'so that the natural power and grace of a song (which the master gives to it) are not dispelled by the deformation of diminutions, but instead are intelligible from each word and sentence'.[91] By 'natural power and grace', Praetorius probably meant the affections implied by the text, and he thereby echoed the concerns of Italians such as Giulio Caccini with the intelligibility of the sung words. Praetorius's description of these attributes as bestowed 'by the master' implies they may be a manifestation of the *ingenium* or personal style of the composer. As qualities that cannot be consciously notated, this 'natural power and grace' may be an example of Butt's 'passive intentions'; but Praetorius's account emphasised the agency of the composer in imbuing a notated composition with these characteristics.

From the early seventeenth century, as the notational conventions for certain genres expanded to specify more performance techniques, some composers argued that their intentions extended to the sounding realisations of their works. Schütz used the prefaces to his printed music to clarify his intentions in terms of performance effects. In the *Psalmen Davids* (1619), he requested that singers and instrumentalists avoid unduly fast recitation of the Biblical texts, 'otherwise a very unpleasant harmony will develop – nothing but a battle of flies, contrary to the intentions of the author'.[92] In the *Historia der Aufferstehung* (1623), he included detailed instructions for how a keyboardist or viol consort should accompany the Evangelist, to achieve the 'proper effect' and to ensure 'that the work is orderly and proceeds without confusion'.[93] However, he also conceded that performers could adapt the notated work for specific locations:

---

lieber gewolt/ das dem Componisten sein auctoritet vnd Kunst vnverändert blibe'. Bernhard Schmid, *Zwey Bücher einer neuen kunstlichen Tabulatur auff Orgel und Instrument* (Strasbourg, 1577), preface, p. [vi]. RISM B/I 1577[12].

[91] 'damit dem Gesange seine *naturalis vis* vnd *gratia*, die ihme der Meister gegeben/ durch solche *deformitet* des *diminuirens* nit benommen/ sondern von menniglichen jeder Wort vnd *Sententia* eigentlich verstanden werde'. Praetorius, *Syntagmatis musici ... tomus tertius*, 230.

[92] 'Im widrigen fall wird eine sehr vnangeneme Harmoney vnd anders nicht als eine *Battaglia di Mosche* oder Fliegenkrieg darauß enstehen/ der *intention* deß *Authoris* zu wider'. Heinrich Schütz, *Psalmen Davids* (Dresden, 1619), Basso Continouo partbook, sig.):(2v. RISM A/I S2275.

[93] 'jhren gebührlichen *effect* ... damit das Wercke fein ordentlich ohne *confusion* auffeinander folge'. Schütz, *Historia ... der Aufferstehung*, Bassus Generalis partbook, preface.

'informed musicians ... will take into account everything about the space and other circumstances of the place'.[94] Schütz's preoccupation with the sonic effect of his compositions stemmed from his concern that innovative techniques of performance should enhance his reputation. In the preface to *Symphoniarum sacrarum secunda pars* (1647), he worried that the quaver and semiquaver writing for the violins was unfamiliar to many German performers, and that 'pieces composed in this way are often so badly played, mishandled and downtrodden that they cause nothing but disgust and vexation to a discerning ear, even to the author himself'.[95] However, if performers rehearsed these works sufficiently, they could ensure that 'neither they nor the author himself, through no fault of his own, might receive unexpected derision instead of proper gratitude'.[96]

These historical discussions of authorial intention can shed light on the agency of composers in the sixteenth to eighteenth centuries, particularly in relation to the different concepts of creativity outlined in Chapter 1. The theological model of creativity did not permit the notion of authorial intention, for it regarded mankind as so sinful that willpower and agency were impossible without divine support. By contrast, the concept of the author's will had a strong affinity with humanist views of creativity as stemming from individual talent. The role of humanism in fostering discussion of compositional intentions is shown by the transmission of two anecdotes about Josquin's dealings with singers. Epitomising the view of the composer as having authority over the performer, these anecdotes were first printed by a Lutheran pedagogue in 1562.

The first anecdote involved Josquin chastising a singer for the profuse ornamentation that was frequently added in the sixteenth century:

When Josquin was living in Cambrai and a singer tried to add to his music *colores* or coloraturas which he had not composed, he went into the choir and scolded him severely with everyone listening: 'You ass. Why do you add embellishment? If I had wanted it I would have put it in myself. If you wish to improve completed compositions, make your own, but leave mine unimproved.'[97]

---

[94] 'verstendigen *Musicis* ... solches alles des Orts gelegenheit vnd andre Vmbstände jhnen selbsten an die hand geben werden'. Ibid.

[95] 'in deme ... dergleichen auffgesetzte Sachen offtmahls so übel angebracht/ zerlästert und gleichsam geradebrecht worden seynt/ das sie einen verständigen Gehöre nichts anders als Eckel und Verdruß/ ja auch dem Autori selbsten ... erwecken müssen'. Heinrich Schütz, *Symphoniarum sacrarum secunda pars* (Dresden, 1647), Bassus ad Organum partbook, preface. RISM A/I S2292.

[96] 'nicht etwa ihnen/ und dem Autori selbsten/ wieder seine Schuld/ vor gehörigen Danck/ ein unverhoffter Spott zuwachsen möge'. Ibid.

[97] 'Josquinus, vivens Cameraci, cum quidam vellet ei in suo cantu adhibere colores seu coloraturas, quas ipse non composuerat, ingressus est chorum, et acriter increpavit illum, omnibus audientibus, addens: Tu asine, quare addis coloraturam? Si mihi ea placuisset, inseruissem ipse. Si tu velis corrigere cantilenas recte compositas, facias tibi proprium cantum, sinas mihi meum incorrectum'. Johannes Manlius, *Locorum communium collectanea ... per multos annos tum ex lectionibus Philippi Melanchthonis tum ex aliorum doctissimorum virorum relationibus excerpta* (Basel, [1562]), 542.

Authorial Intentions and Performance

The second anecdote recounts how Josquin used performers to check how his compositions sounded, while he walked around: 'If he was dissatisfied, he stepped in: "Be silent," he said, "I will change it."'[98]

Both anecdotes present the singers as lowly figures, in accordance with the theoretical tradition stemming from Boethius. In the first anecdote, the unnamed performer who challenges Josquin's authority has as little sense and as little ability to create musical beauty as a donkey. Josquin, by contrast, is elevated by the *ingenium* that gives him the discrimination to make and amend compositions. Josquin does not deign to sing himself; instead the singers are, as Rob Wegman puts it, at his 'beck and call', tools for realising his compositional will.[99] The anecdotes give Josquin the status of a humanist author concerned with his legacy. It is no coincidence that both tales were first recorded in German-speaking lands in the mid-sixteenth century, a period when Josquin had been canonised via the acclaim of such diverse figures as Glarean and Luther (see pp. 18 and 25).

The humanist assumptions behind these anecdotes are clarified by the context of their first publication in Johannes Manlius's *Locorum communium collectanea* (1562), a collection allegedly assembled from the lectures of his teacher Philipp Melanchthon. (David Fallows has suggested that the anecdotes may derive from Melanchthon's Wittenberg associate Adrianus Petit Coclico, who claimed to be a pupil of Josquin's.[100]) Manlius printed the stories about Josquin in a chapter of commonplaces on the theme of studying, addressing such topics as 'Nothing in life is perfect' and 'Ignoring listeners is reprehensible'.[101] The Josquin anecdotes appear under the subheading: 'Whether it is right to emend another's inventions'.[102] Hence for Manlius they illustrated the importance of textual integrity, a central goal of humanist scholarship.

Humanists aimed to recover texts in uncorrupted forms and to read them to uncover the author's meanings. Erasmus had shown the importance of Biblical criticism that removed errors and unwanted emendations from the text, in order to expose the divine meaning. In his *Paraclesis*, the preface to his 1516 Greek-Latin edition of the New Testament, Erasmus claimed that his textual scholarship restored the voice of 'Christ Himself' and thereby clarified 'the truth itself, whose expression is the more

---

[98] 'Quoties novam cantilenam composuerat, dedit eam cantoribus canendam, et interea ipse circumambulabat, attente audiens, an harmonia congrueret. Si non placeret, ingressus: Tacete inquit, ego mutabo. Hoc nostrum aliquis non posset imitari: sed nobis iuxta aliorum praescriptum canendum, sive bene sive male harmonia consonet'. Ibid.

[99] Rob C. Wegman, '"And Josquin Laughed ... " Josquin and the Composer's Anecdote in the Sixteenth Century', *Journal of Musicology* 17 (1999), 319–57 (p. 330).

[100] David Fallows, 'Embellishment and Urtext in the Fifteenth-Century Song Repertories', *Basler Jahrbuch für historische Musikpraxis* 14 (1990), 59–85 (p. 59)

[101] 'Nullus in hac vita perfectus'; 'Auditorum negligentia reprehenditur'. Manlius, *Locorum communium collectanea*, 541, 544.

[102] 'Utrum recte faciat, inventa aliorum emendans'. Ibid., 542.

powerful, the simpler it is'.[103] He urged readers to return to the author's original: 'Why have we steadfastly preferred to learn the wisdom of Christ from the writings of men than from Christ Himself?'[104] A similar emphasis on authorial meaning can be found in Luther's 1539 advice on reading scripture, in the second stage of which 'you should meditate, that is read and re-read, with diligent attention and thought, on what the Holy Ghost means with this [passage]'.[105] Luther's prefaces to books of his German Bible translation likewise sought to identify the meaning intended by the writer.[106] Rhetorical tools to uncover the intention of the author were refined by Melanchthon in his analyses of texts such as Paul's letters to the Romans.[107] Such techniques of Biblical hermeneutics and textual criticism thus supplied the context for Manlius's anecdotes about Josquin and performers.

Manlius's book was extensively reprinted and used in Lutheran schools;[108] consequently his two anecdotes about Josquin were familiar to musicians until the early eighteenth century. Wolfgang Caspar Printz and Johann Georg Ahle used the first anecdote to support their recommendations that musicians apply ornamentation modestly.[109] Mattheson used the first and second anecdotes to support respectively his preference for music with natural simplicity, and his empiricist viewpoint that composers should trust the judgement of their ears.[110] The ongoing appeal of the Josquin anecdote suggests the continuing relevance of the humanist conception of musical authorship.

Indeed those musicians who recommended that performers follow authorial intentions sometimes advocated a type of hermeneutics similar to Biblical interpretation. In 1739 Mattheson declared that

The greatest difficulty in producing another's work probably consists in the fact that an acute power of discernment is required to capture correctly the sense and meaning of others' thoughts. Someone who has never experienced how the composer might prefer to have it himself, will scarcely be able to perform it well,

---

[103] Cited in John C. Olin (ed.), *Christian Humanism and the Reformation. Selected Writings of Erasmus*, 3rd edn (New York: Fordham University Press, 1987), 98–99.

[104] Ibid., 105.

[105] 'Zum andern soltu meditirn, das ist ... lessen und widerlesen, mit vleissigem auffmercken und nachdencken, was der heilige Geist damit meinet'. *WA* 50, 659.

[106] For instance, Luther's 1533 preface to the Acts of Apostles stated that the doctrine of justification by faith alone in Jesus Christ was Luke's 'chief meaning and cause for writing this book' ('Solchs stück ist seine furnemeste meinung vnd vrsache dieses buchs zu schreiben', *WA Deutsche Bibel* 6, 414).

[107] Kees Meerhoff, 'The Significance of Philipp Melanchthon's Rhetoric in the Renaissance', in Peter Mack (ed.), *Renaissance Rhetoric* (Basingstoke: Macmillan, 1994), 46–62 (p. 55).

[108] On the making and reception of Manlius's anthology, see Ian Maclean, *Learning and the Market Place: Essays in the History of the Early Modern Book* (Leiden: Brill, 2009), 121–22.

[109] Wolfgang Caspar Printz, *Historische Beschreibung der edelen Sing- und Kling-Kunst* (Dresden, 1690), 117; Ahle, *Kurze, doch deutliche Anleitung*, 80.

[110] Mattheson, *Der vollkommene Capellmeister*, 242–43, 483.

Authorial Intentions and Performance 211

but will often deprive the piece of its true force and charm, so that the author, if he should hear it himself, would scarcely know his own work.[111]

This viewpoint accorded with Mattheson's rhetorical model of production in which performers were 'readers' implementing the composer's work (see p. 193). The humanist notion of authorship therefore not only celebrated the talent and individuality of composers; it also strengthened the view that a composer's will should be recreated in subsequent performances.

Alternatively the notion of compositional intentions could relate to the artisanal model of musical creativity. Although the link between embodied knowledge and performance style was most closely associated with solo repertories such as Froberger's keyboard toccatas, it also shaped Bach's attitude to his ensemble works. In 1737 Scheibe criticised Bach's intricate lines for incorporating ornamentation into the compositional fabric, thereby denying performers any opportunity to assert their individuality: 'Every ornament, every little grace, and everything that one thinks of as belonging to the method of playing, he expresses completely in notes'.[112] Furthermore, he attacked Bach for imposing too many technical difficulties on performers: 'Since he judges according to his own fingers, his pieces are extremely difficult to play, for he demands that singers and instrumentalists should be able to do with their throats and instruments whatever he can play on the clavier'.[113] By emphasising Bach's reliance on the tactile knowledge within his fingers, Scheibe reinforced his insinuation that Bach was a mere practitioner (or to use his term, *Musikant*) out of step with the new taste for a 'natural' style.

Quick to defend Bach against such connotations, Birnbaum rehearsed the familiar argument that ornamentation at the performer's discretion risked obscuring the harmonic or contrapuntal meanings of a composition. Performers might,

by an inappropriate application of their method [of ornamentation][,] spoil the principal melody and indeed often introduce such passages as might easily be attributed, by those who do not know the true state of affairs, to an error of the composer. Therefore every composer . . . is entitled to set the wanderers back on the right path by prescribing a correct method according to his intentions, and thus to watch over the preservation of his own honour.[114]

Birnbaum thus asserted his view of performers as subordinate to composers, whose reputations relied on their pieces being presented without errors.

---

[111] 'Die grösseste Schwierigkeit eines andern Arbeit aufzuführen, bestehet wol darin, daß eine scharffe Urtheils-Krafft dazu erfordert werde, fremder Gedancken Sinn und Meinung recht zu treffen. Denn, wer nie erfahren hat, wie es der Verfasser selber gerne haben mögte, wird es schwerlich gut heräus bringen, sondern dem Dinge die wahre Krafft und Anmuth offt dergestalt benehmen, daß der *Autor*, wenn ers selber mit anhören sollte, sein eigenes Werck kaum kennen dürffte'. Ibid., 484.
[112] *BDok* 2, 286 (no. 400); *NBR*, 338.   [113] Ibid.
[114] *BDok* 2, 304–5 (no. 409); translation adapted from *NBR*, 347.

Yet Scheibe's insinuations that Bach relied on tactile knowledge could be regarded more positively, in line with the artisanal ethic outlined in Chapter 1. The status of artisans depended on the quality of their products and their bodily skills in shaping materials. Bach judged 'according to his own fingers' because his embodied knowledge was so compelling that he wanted performers on other instruments to mirror his keyboard technique. His desire to share his manual skill led him to intervene in other performances, as suggested by the reminiscences of his pupil Johann Christian Kittel of how Bach could not keep his hands away from the keyboard when a novice was playing continuo: 'One always had to be prepared to have Bach's hands and fingers intervene among the hands and fingers of the player and, without getting in the way of the latter, furnish the accompaniment with masses of harmonies'.[115] Bach's notion of compositional intentions stemmed less from humanist concerns about textual integrity, and more from a craftworker's desire to control every aspect of a finished product.

Debates about the relationship between composer and performer often have a strong moral or ideological tone. Historically informed performers such as Christopher Hogwood regarded themselves as ethically bound to investigate and respect the intentions of composers; Taruskin and theorists of performance studies, by contrast, attack such an approach for restricting the creative freedom of performers. This chapter has sought to defuse such passions by investigating historical debates about the prerogatives of composer and performer. In polyphonic motets around 1600, the composer's domain comprised the contrapuntal configurations of the notated opus, whereas the performer added the ineffable quality of grace via appropriate scoring and artful ornamentation. Keyboard toccatas of the late seventeenth century, by contrast, existed primarily in the embodied act of performance, which scribes struggled to capture in the imperfections of notation. Composers such as Beer and Tobias Michael welcomed the creative interventions of performers, while others such as Hammerschmidt and Schütz feared that botched performances would mar their reputation. Notions of musical authorship were shaped by the creative collaborations between composers and performers; and the sheer variety of these relationships reflect the dual status of music, existing both as notated artefacts and as sounding acts.

---

[115] *NBR*, 323.

Conclusion

When musicians such as Schütz and Bach described themselves as authors, they referred not only to the act of composition; their notions of authorship were also shaped by the negotiations involved in the reception and performance of their music. Primarily the term 'author' was used by composers making printed or manuscript books of their works. The production of such books was a collaborative endeavour, involving the participation of scribes, editors, printers, publishers and dedicatees. When deciding on the contents of a printed edition, composers and publishers balanced the symbolic value of the volume against the commercial requirement that it sold in sufficient quantities. In their dedications and prefaces, composers often reflected on the act of sending works out to public judgement, and on the relationships that the finished book would nurture with patrons, purchasers and performers. To show how musical authorship was defined by such negotiations, Chapter 3 explored the authentication marks and portraits which reassured purchasers of the involvement of the composer in the production of the book. Chapter 4 uncovered the legal manoeuvres necessary to gain printing privileges, whereby composers and publishers sought protection against unauthorised copies.

Besides its association with the making of books, the term 'author' could also denote an originator (as in Petrus Dasypodius's 1536 definition, p. 3). Yet it was problematic for humans to claim to create something out of nothing. Lutheran theologians held that the only true author was God, and that musicians were merely instruments for divine will. Notions of *imitatio*, as discussed in Chapter 2, viewed musical creativity as arising from the reception of existing works. Novice composers developed their craft and style by studying and imitating the works of authoritative musicians. Schütz created intertextual networks of allusions in his music, citing his teacher Giovanni Gabrieli and other prestigious Italian forebears. Even established composers such as Capricornus and Kuhnau justified their innovations by invoking the enabling past of authoritative models.

Practices for regulating music likewise show how notions of the musical author were constituted via authority. The negotiations to obtain printing privileges, studied in Chapter 4, required composers to submit to princely power in a ritualistic performance that clarified the status of both ruler and author. The 1580 church ordinance in Saxony, discussed in Chapter 5, was so suspicious of the agency of individual musicians that it forbade cantors and organists from performing their own compositions. Fearful of the social disruption that might result from displays of individuality or innovation, the edict upheld an unchanging musical repertory by established polyphonists such as Josquin, Clemens non Papa and Lassus.

Yet there were traditions that recognised the individuality and agency of musicians. Humanists believed every person had a unique nature that shaped their external appearance and behaviour, and that some individuals were endowed with the talent (*ingenium*) to create art, poetry or music. Schütz praised the range of *ingenia* for music found among his countrymen;[1] Bach recommended that his pupils tackle composition only if they had the necessary talent to invent ideas. Artisanal traditions too recognised human agency via the power of craftworkers to shape materials with their hands. Such traditions are evident in those musicians who assembled compositions from harmonic or contrapuntal formulae, drawing on their knowledge of manual skill and their awareness of the material properties of instruments. As Chapters 3 and 6 explained, solo keyboardists such as Froberger, Reincken and Bach prized the bodily techniques that enabled them to create improvisations and compositions characterised by their personal style.

At the end of the seventeenth century, attitudes towards individuality changed with the new emphasis on empiricism. Personal talent and judgement were increasingly prioritised over the example of authoritative predecessors, as shown by Mattheson's attitudes to musical invention and borrowing, and his adoption of Christian Thomasius's eclectic philosophy (pp. 12, 75). In Saxon towns the growth in consumer culture among individual citizens fostered a new understanding of church compositions as fashionable commodities, to be regularly supplied and discarded by cantors.

Yet it would be wrong to see a linear shift in attitudes regarding authority and individuality. Instead older and newer viewpoints were in constant dialogue, with different threads of ideas emerging and receding through the warp and weft of culture. Thus Schütz described his compositional vocation as God's calling and also something to which he was destined by nature (pp. 19, 27). Reincken celebrated the divine origin of his talent through the 'Soli Deo Gloria' inscription on his trio sonata collection *Hortus musicus*, yet on the same title page he immortalised himself via the triumphal arch emblazoned with his monogram (Figure 3.2). Bach invoked divine help at the start of many of his

---

[1] Heinrich Schütz, *Geistliche Chor-Music* (Dresden, 1648), Bassus Continuus partbook, preface. RISM A/I S2294.

manuscripts by writing 'Jesu juva', but also claimed that musicians with the necessary diligence could accomplish whatever they wanted (pp. 21, 33). Lutheran culture remained strongly theocentric yet recognised the capacity of humans to shape their place in the world. This study of authorship has exposed the rich complexities of Lutheran musical life between Schütz and Bach, as well as illuminating the many ways in which musicians interacted with the communities around them.

Bibliography

PRIMARY SOURCES

Printed and manuscript sources of music are not listed here. To aid identification, the footnotes indicate the RISM identifier or the library shelfmark of the consulted copy. Published items listed below are grouped by author and then chronologically.

Manuscripts

A-Whh, Impressoria.
D-Dla, Kopiale 407 (1575).
D-Dla, Loc. 8687/1, Kantoreiordnung.
D-Dla, Loc. 10757, Privilegia 1610–39 (3 vols.); Loc. 10758, Privilegia 1640–75 (4 vols.); Loc. 10759, Privilegia 1676–98, 1706–15 (4 vols.).
D-Dla, Loc. 32435, Rep. 28, Cantorey Ordnung (1568, 1592).
D-LEm, I.4° 37. Johann Beer, 'Schola phonologia'. Modern edition in Johann Beer, *Sämtliche Werke*, vol. 12/ii, ed. Michael Heinemann (Bern: Peter Lang, 2005).
D-LEsa, Stift. IX. A. 35; Tit. VII. B. 116.
GB-Eu, Ms. Dc.6.100. 'Instrumentalischer Bettlermantl'.
GB-Lbl, Add. Ms. 4910, fols. 11r–38v. Christoph Demelius (attrib.), untitled composition treatise.

Printed Primary Sources

Adam von Fulda, *De musica* (1490). Lost manuscript printed in Martin Gerbert, *Scriptores ecclesiastici de musica sacra potissimum*, 3 vols. (St Blasien, 1784), iii, 329–81.
Adlung, Jakob, *Anleitung zu der musikalischen Gelahrtheit* (Erfurt, 1758).
Ahle, Johann Rudolf, *Kurze, doch deutliche Anleitung zu der lieblich- und löblichen Singekunst ... mit ... nöthigen Anmerkungen ... zum drukke befördert durch des seeligen Verfassers Sohn Johan Georg Ahlen* (Mühlhausen, 1704).
Beer, Johann, *Der simplicianische Welt-Kucker*, book 1 (n.p., 1677).
  Teutsche Winter-Nächte ([Nuremberg], 1682).
  Musicalische Discurse (Nuremberg, 1719).

Bibliography

Sein Leben, von ihm selbst erzählt, ed. Adolf Schmiedecke (Göttingen: Vandenhoeck & Ruprecht, 1965).

Beier, Adrian, *Kurtzer Bericht von der nützlichen und fürtrefflichen Buchhandlung* (Jena, 1690).

Berger, Johann Heinrich von, *Electa discreptationum forensium secundum seriem*, vol. 1 (Leipzig, 1738).

Böhme, Jakob, *Sämtliche Schriften*, vol. 6: *De signatoria rerum (1622)* (Stuttgart: Frommann, 1957).

Brossard, Sébastien de, *Dictionaire de musique, contenant une explication des termes Grecs, Latins, Italiens, & François les plus usitez dans la musique* (Paris, 1703).

Burmeister, Joachim, *Musica autoschediastike* (Rostock, 1601).

Musica poetica (Rostock, 1606). Modern edn as *Musical Poetics*, trans. Benito V. Rivera (New Haven: Yale University Press, 1993).

Buttstett, Johann Heinrich, *Ut, mi, sol, re, fa, la, tota musica et harmonia aeterna* (Erfurt, n.d.).

Camerarius, Philipp, *Operae horarum subcisivarum, sive meditationes historicae, auctiores quam antea editae … Centuria prima*, 2nd edn (Frankfurt am Main, 1602).

Cardano, Girolamo, *De subtilitate* (Nuremberg, 1550).

Chytraeus, David, *Der fürnemsten Heubtstuck Christlicher Lehr nützliche vnd kurtze Erklerung* (Rostock, 1578).

Corpus Juris Ecclesiastici Saxonici (Dresden and Leipzig, 1735).

Crüger, Johannes, *Synopsis musica* (Berlin, 1630); 2nd edn (Berlin, 1654).

Dasypodius, Petrus, *Dictionarium Latinogermanicum* (Strasbourg, 1536).

Des Durchlauchtigsten/ Hochgebornen Fürsten und Herrn Augusten/ Hertzogen zu Sachsen … Ordnung/ Wie es in seiner Churf. G. Landen/ bey den Kirchen/ mit der Lehr und Ceremonien/ deßgleichen in derselben beyden Universiteten/ Consistorien/ Fürsten und Particular Schulen/ Visitationen/ Synodis, und was solchem allem mehr anhanget/ gehalten werden sol (Leipzig, 1580).

Des Raths zu Leipzig Vornewerte Schul-Ordnung (Leipzig, 1634).

Dieterich, Conrad, *Sonderbarer Predigten von unterschiedenen Materien. Teil 1: Jubel und Kirch-weyh Predigten* (Leipzig, 1632).

Felden, Johann von, *Elementa juris universi* (Frankfurt am Main and Leipzig, 1664).

Finck, Hermann, *Practica musica* (Wittenberg, 1556).

Fischart, Johann, *Das glückhafft Schiff von Zürich* [Strasbourg, 1576].

Fuhrmann, Martin Heinrich, *Musicalischer Trichter* (Frankfurt an der Spree, 1706).

Musicalische Strigel ([Leipzig], *c.*1719–21).

Gallus Dressler's Præcepta musicæ poëticæ, ed. Robert Forgács (Urbana: University of Illinois Press, 2007).

Gaurico, Pomponio, *De sculptura* (Nuremberg, 1542).

Glarean, Heinrich, *Dodekachordon* (Basel, 1547).

Gottsched, Johann Christoph, *Ausführliche Redekunst* (Leipzig, 1739).

Bibliography

Guazzo, Stefano, *De civili conversatione, das ißt von dem Bürgerlichen Wandel vnd zierlichen Sitten*, German edn (Frankfurt am Main, 1599).

Harsdörffer, Georg Philipp, *Frauenzimmer Gesprechspiele, so bey Ehr- und Tugendliebenden Gesellschaften ... beliebet und geübet werden mögen*, vol. 6 (Nuremberg, 1646).

Deß poetischen Trichters Dritter Theil (Nuremberg, 1653).

Nathan und Jotham: das ist geistliche und weltliche Lehrgedichte (Nuremberg, 1659).

Heinichen, Johann David, *Neu erfundene und gründliche Anweisung ... zu vollkommener Erlernung des General-Basses* (Hamburg, 1711).

Der General-Bass in der Composition (Dresden, 1728).

Herbst, Johann Andreas, *Musica poetica* (Nuremberg, 1643).

Arte prattica et pöetica (Nuremberg, 1653).

Heumann, Christoph August, 'Historia de gladio academico', in Johann Volkmar Bechmann, *Tractatus historico-juridicus de privilegiis ac juribus studiosorum* (Jena, 1741), 3–12.

Kircher, Athanasius, *Musurgia universalis sive ars magna consoni et dissoni*, 2 vols. (Rome, 1650).

Kuhnau, Johann, *Jura circa musicos ecclesiasticos* (Leipzig, 1688).

Der musicalische Quack-Salber (Dresden, 1700).

Kurtzer jedoch gründlicher Wegweiser/ vermittelst welches man aus dem Grund die Kunst die Orgel recht zu schlagen (Augsburg, 1689).

Leibniz, Gottfried Wilhelm, *Dissertatio de arte combinatoria* (Leipzig, 1666).

Listenius, Nikolaus, *Musica* (Wittenberg, 1537).

Locke, John, *Two Treatises on Government* (London, 1690).

Lossius, Lucas, *Erotemata dialecticae et rhetoricae Philippi Melanthonis* (Frankfurt an der Oder, 1554).

Manlius, Johannes, *Locorum communium collectanea ... per multos annos tum ex lectionibus Philippi Melanchthonis tum ex aliorum doctissimorum virorum relationibus excerpta* (Basel, [1562]).

Marpurg, Friedrich Wilhelm, *Historisch-kritische Beyträge zur Aufnahme der Musik* (Berlin, 1754–78).

Mathesius, Johann, *Historien von des ehrwirdigen ... Martini Luthers Anfang, Lehr, Leben und Sterben* (Nuremberg, 1566).

Mattheson, Johann, *Das neu-eröffnete Orchestre* (Hamburg, 1713).

Das beschützte Orchestre (Hamburg, 1717).

Das forschende Orchestre (Hamburg, 1721).

Critica musica, 2 vols. (Hamburg, 1722–25).

Der musicalische Patriot (Hamburg, 1728).

Grosse General-Bass-Schule (Hamburg, 1731).

Kleine General-Bass-Schule (Hamburg, 1735).

Der vollkommene Capellmeister (Hamburg, 1739).

Grundlage einer Ehren-Pforte (Hamburg, 1740).

Melanchthon, Philipp, *Elementorum rhetorices libri duo* (Wittenberg, 1532).

Orations on Philosophy and Education, ed. Sachiko Kusukawa, trans. Christine F. Salazar (Cambridge: Cambridge University Press, 1999).

Bibliography

Mizler, Lorenz Christoph, *Anfängs-Gründe des General Basses* (Leipzig, 1739).

Murschhauser, Franz Xaver, *Academia musico-poetica bipartita* (Nuremberg, 1721).

Neukirch, Johann Georg, *Anfangs-Gründe zur reinen teutschen Poesie itziger Zeit* (Halle, 1724).

Neumeister, Erdmann, and Friedrich Grohmann, *De poëtis Germanicis huius seculi praecipuis dissertatio compendiaria* (n. p., 1695).

Niedt, Friedrich Erhardt, *Handleitung zur Variation* (Hamburg, 1706).

   Friederich Erhard Niedtens Musicalischer Handleitung Anderer Theil/ Von der Variation, ed. Johann Mattheson (Hamburg, 1721).

Olin, John C. (ed.), *Christian Humanism and the Reformation. Selected Writings of Erasmus*, 3rd edn (New York: Fordham University Press, 1987).

Opitz, Martin, *Buch von der deutschen Poeterey* (Breslau, 1624).

Pantaleon, Heinrich, *Prosopographiae heroum atque illustrium virorum totius Germaniae*, 3 vols. (Basel, 1565–66).

Penna, Lorenzo, *Li primi albori musicali per li principianti della musica figurata*, 3 vols. (Bologna, 1672).

Petrarch, Francesco, *Le familiari*, 4 vols., ed. Vittorio Rossi (Florence: G. C. Sansoni, n.d.).

Praetorius, Michael, *Syntagmatis musici Michaelis Praetorii C. tomus tertius*, 2nd edn (Wolfenbüttel, 1619).

Printz, Wolfgang Caspar, *Compendium musicae in quo breviter ac succincte explicantur et traduntur omnia ea, quae ad oden artificiose componendam requiruntur* (Guben, 1668).

   Phrynis oder satyrischer Componist, 2 vols. (Quedlinburg, 1676–77).

   Historische Beschreibung der edelen Sing- und Kling-Kunst (Dresden, 1690).

   Musicus magnanimus oder Pancalus (n.p., 1691).

Quitschreiber, Georg, *De παρῳδία* (Jena, 1611).

Röber, Paul, *Sichere Schiffart . . . bey Christlicher Leichbestattung/ des . . . Christiani Grefenthals* (Wittenberg, 1628).

Rohr, Julius Bernhard von, *Einleitung zur Ceremoniel-Wissenschafft der Privat-Personen* (Berlin, 1728).

Scheibe, Johann Adolph, *Der critische Musicus* (Hamburg, 1737–40).

Schneegass, Cyriacus, *Nova et exquisita monochordi dimensio* (Erfurt, 1590).

Sehling, Emil (ed.), *Die evangelische Kirchenordnungen des XVI. Jahrhunderts*, vol. 5 (Leipzig: Reisland, 1913).

Sehling, Emil (ed.), *Die evangelische Kirchenordnungen des XVI. Jahrhunderts*, vol. 6.i.2 (Tübingen: Mohr, 1957).

Sicul, Christoph Ernst, *Annalium Lipsiensium maxime academicorum sectio XVI oder des Leipziger Jahr-Buchs zu dessen Dritten Bande erste Fortsetzung*, vol. 1 (Leipzig, 1723).

Spangenberg, Cyriacus, *Von der Musica und der Meistersängern* [1598], ed. Adelbert von Keller (Stuttgart, 1861).

Speer, Daniel, *Grund-richtiger . . . Unterricht der musicalischen Kunst oder vierfaches musicalisches Kleeblatt* (Ulm, 1697).

Steffani, Agostino, *Send-Schreiben darinn enthalten wie grosse Gewißheit die Music*, trans. and expanded by Andreas Werckmeister (Quedlinburg, 1699).

Telemann, Georg Philipp, *Briefwechsel. Sämtliche erreichbare Briefe von und an Telemann*, ed. Hans Grosse and Hans Rudolf Jung (Leipzig: Deutscher Verlag für Musik, 1972).

Thomasius, Christian, *Einleitung zur Hof-Philosophie* (Frankfurt am Main and Leipzig, 1710).

Höchstnöthige Cautelen . . . zu Erlernung der Rechts-Gelahrtheit (Halle, 1713).

Thomasius, Jacob, *Dissertatio philosophica de plagio literario* (Leipzig, 1673).

Walter, Johann, *Lob vnd Preis/ der himlischen Kunst Musica* (Wittenberg, 1564).

Walther, Johann Gottfried, *Musicalisches Lexicon* (Leipzig, 1732).

Praecepta der musicalischen Composition, ed. Peter Benary (Leipzig: Breitkopf & Härtel, 1955).

Briefe, ed. Klaus Beckmann and Hans-Joachim Schulze (Leipzig: Deutscher Verlag für Musik, 1987).

Werckmeister, Andreas, *Musicae mathematicae hodegus curiosus* (Frankfurt am Main, 1686).

Der edlen Music-Kunst Würde/ Gebrauch und Mißbrauch (Frankfurt am Main and Leipzig, 1691).

Die nothwendigsten Anmerckungen und Regeln wie der Bassus Continuus oder General-Baß wohl könne tractiret werden, 1st edn (Aschersleben, 1698), 2nd edn (Aschersleben, 1715).

Cribrum musicum (Quedlinburg and Leipzig, 1700).

Harmonologia musica (Frankfurt am Main and Leipzig, 1702).

Musicalische Paradoxal-Discourse (Quedlinburg, 1707).

Young, Edward, *Conjectures on Original Composition* (London, 1759).

Zacconi, Ludovico, *Prattica di musica* (Venice, 1592).

Zarlino, Gioseffo, *Le istitutioni harmoniche* (Venice, 1558).

SECONDARY SOURCES

Anttila, Miikka E., *Luther's Theology of Music: Spiritual Beauty and Pleasure* (Berlin: De Gruyter, 2013).

Arlt, Wulf, 'Zur Handhabung der "inventio" in der deutschen Musiklehre des frühen achtzehnten Jahrhunderts', in George J. Buelow and Hans Joachim Marx (eds.), *New Mattheson Studies* (Cambridge: Cambridge University Press, 1983), 371–92.

Ashcroft, Jeffrey, 'Zum Wort und Begriff "Kunst" in Dürers Schriften', in Alan Robertshaw and Gerhard Wolf (eds.), *Natur und Kultur in der deutschen Literatur des Mittelalters: Colloquium Exeter 1997* (Tübingen: Niemeyer, 1999), 19–28.

Atlas, Allan W., *Renaissance Music: Music in Western Europe, 1400–1600* (New York: Norton, 1998).

Baroncini, Rodolfo, '"Et per tale confirmato dall'auttorità del signor Giovanni Gabrieli". The Reception of Gabrieli as a Model by Venetian and Non-Venetian Composers of the New Generation (1600–1620)', in Rodolfo Baroncini, David Bryant and Luigi Collarile (eds.), *Giovanni Gabrieli: Transmission and Reception of a Venetian Musical Tradition* (Turnhout: Brepols, 2016), 5–31.

Bibliography

Barthes, Roland, *Image – Music – Text*, trans. and ed. Stephen Heath (London: Fontana, 1977).

Bedos-Rezak, Brigitte A., 'Loci of Medieval Identity', in Franz-Josef Arlinghaus (ed.), *Forms of Individuality and Literacy in the Medieval and Early Modern Periods* (Turnhout: Brepols, 2015), 81–106.

Benjamin, Walter, 'The Work of Art in the Age of Mechanical Reproduction', in *Illuminations*, ed. Hannah Arendt, trans. Harry Zohn (New York: Harcourt, 1968), 217–51.

Berglund, Lars, *Studier i Christian Geists vokalmusik* (Uppsala: Uppsala Universitet, 2002).

Bernardi, Marco, and Carlo Pulsoni, 'Primi appunti sulle rassettature del Salviati', *Filologia italiana* 8 (2011), 167–201.

Bianconi, Lorenzo, *Music in the Seventeenth Century* (Cambridge: Cambridge University Press, 1987).

Blankenburg, Walter, 'Bach', *Theologische Realenzyklopädie*, vol. 5 (Berlin: De Gruyter, 1979–80), 90–94.

Blume, Friedrich, 'Bach, Johann Sebastian', *Die Musik in Geschichte und Gegenwart*, vol. 1 (Kassel: Bärenreiter, 1949–51), 962–1047.

Bossuyt, Ignace, 'The Copyist Jan Pollet and the Theft in 1563 of Orlandus Lassus's "Secret" Penitential Psalms', in Albert Clement and Eric Jas (eds.), *From Ciconia to Sweelinck: Donum natalicium Willem Elders* (Amsterdam: Rodopi, 1994), 261–67.

Botstiber, Hugo, 'Ein Beitrag zu J. K. Kerll's Biographie', *Sammelbände der Internationalen Musikgesellschaft* 7 (1906), 634–36.

Braudel, Fernand, *Civilization and Capitalism, 15th–18th Century*, vol. 2: *The Wheels of Commerce*, trans. Siân Reynolds (London: Fontana, 1982).

Braun, Werner, 'Samuel Scheidts Bearbeitungen alter Motetten', *Archiv für Musikwissenschaft* 19–20 (1962–63), 56–74.

'Arten des Komponistenporträts', in Ludwig Finscher and Christoph-Hellmut Mahling (eds.), *Festschrift für Walter Wiora zum 30. Dezember 1966* (Kassel: Bärenreiter, 1967), 86–94.

Der Stilwandel in der Musik um 1600 (Darmstadt: Wissenschaftliche Buchgesellschaft, 1982).

'Die Mitte des 17. Jahrhunderts als musikgeschichtliche Zäsur', *Schütz-Jahrbuch* 21 (1999), 39–48.

Die Kompositionslehre des Christian Demelius (Nordhausen um 1702) (Nordhausen: Friedrich-Christian-Lesser-Stiftung, 2000).

'Cantiones veterum und neue Reuterliedlein (1643): aus einem Streitfall in Delitzsch', in Paul Mai (ed.), *Im Dienst der Quellen zur Musik: Festschrift Gertraut Haberkamp zum 65. Geburtstag* (Tutzing: Schneider, 2002), 279–85.

'Bemerkungen zu den "Nordhäusischen Concerten" von 1637/38', *Schütz-Jahrbuch* 25 (2003), 85–104.

'Die Musik im Delitzscher Kulturkampf (1643)', *Archiv für Musikwissenschaft* 60 (2003), 1–30.

Thöne und Melodeyen, Arien und Canzonetten. Zur Musik des deutschen Barockliedes (Tübingen: Niemeyer, 2004).

Brook, Barry S., 'The Earliest Printed Thematic Catalogues', in Nils Schiørring, Henrik Glahn and Carsten E. Hatting (eds.), *Festskrift Jens Peter Larsen. 1902–14 VI–1972* (Copenhagen: Wilhelm Hansen, 1972), 103–12.

Broude, Ronald, 'Paris *chez l'autheur*: Self-Publication and Authoritative Texts in the France of Louis XIV', *Early Music* 45 (2017), 283–96.

Bryant, David, 'Gabrieli, Giovanni', *Oxford Music Online*, oxfordmusiconline.com.

Burrows, Donald, 'What's in a Name? Handel's Autograph Annotations', in Nicole Ristow, Wolfgang Sandberger and Dorothea Schröder (eds.), *'Critica musica'. Studien zum 17. und 18. Jahrhundert. Festschrift Hans Joachim Marx zum 65. Geburtstag* (Stuttgart: Metzler, 2001), 25–47.

Butt, John, *Music Education and the Art of Performance in the German Baroque* (Cambridge: Cambridge University Press, 1994).

  Playing with History: The Historical Approach to Musical Performance (Cambridge: Cambridge University Press, 2002).

  Bach's Dialogue with Modernity: Perspectives on the Passions (Cambridge: Cambridge University Press, 2010).

Calella, Michele, *Musikalische Autorschaft. Der Komponist zwischen Mittelalter und Neuzeit* (Kassel: Bärenreiter, 2014).

Carruthers, Mary, *The Book of Memory. A Study of Memory in Medieval Culture* (Cambridge: Cambridge University Press, 1990).

Cavallar, Osvaldo, Susanne Degenring and Julius Kirshner (eds.), *A Grammar of Signs: Bartolo da Sassoferrato's* Tract on Insignia and Coats of Arms *(1358)* (Berkeley: Robbins Collection, University of California at Berkeley, 1994).

Chafe, Eric, *Analyzing Bach Cantatas* (New York: Oxford University Press, 2000).

Chapin, Keith, '"A Harmony or Concord of Several and Diverse Voices": Autonomy in Seventeenth-Century German Music Theory and Practice', *International Review of the Aesthetics and Sociology of Music* 42 (2011), 219–55.

Conermann, Klaus (ed.), *Die Deutsche Akademie des 17. Jahrhunderts: Fruchtbringende Gesellschaft*, Reihe I, Abteilung A: Köthen, Band 5: *Briefe der Fruchtbringenden Gesellschaft und Beilagen: Die Zeit Fürst Ludwigs von Anhalt-Köthen 1617–1650* (Berlin: De Gruyter, 2010).

Cook, Nicholas, 'Music as Performance', in Martin Clayton, Trevor Herbert and Richard Middleton (eds.), *The Cultural Study of Music. A Critical Introduction,* 2nd edn (London: Routledge, 2012), 184–94.

  Beyond the Score. Music as Performance (New York: Oxford University Press, 2013).

Copeland, Rita, *Rhetoric, Hermeneutics and Translation in the Middle Ages: Academic Traditions and Vernacular Texts* (Cambridge: Cambridge University Press, 1991).

Crook, David, 'The Exegetical Motet', *Journal of the American Musicological Society*, 68 (2015), 255–316.

Cucchiarelli, Andrea, 'Return to Sender: Horace's *Sermo* from the Epistles to the Satires', in Gregson Davis (ed.), *A Companion to Horace* (Oxford: Wiley-Blackwell, 2010), 291–318.

Bibliography

Curtius, Ernst R., *European Literature and the Latin Middle Ages*, trans. Willard R. Trask (London: Routledge, 1979).

Czerwenka-Papadopoulos, Karoline, *Typologie des Musikerporträts in Malerei und Graphik: das Bildnis des Musikers ab der Renaissance bis zum Klassizismus*, 2 vols. (Vienna: Verlag der Österreichischen Akademie der Wissenschaften, 2007).

David, Hans T., 'A Lesser Secret of J. S. Bach Uncovered', *Journal of the American Musicological Society* 14 (1961), 199–223.

Daybell, James, *The Material Letter in Early Modern England: Manuscript Letters and the Culture and Practices of Letter-Writing, 1512–1635* (Basingstoke: Macmillan, 2012).

Deeters, Walter, 'Alte und neue Aktenfunde über Michael Praetorius', *Braunschweigisches Jahrbuch* 52 (1971), 102–20.

Defant, Christine, 'Johann Adam Reinckens *Hortus musicus*: Versuch einer Deutung als Metapher für die hochbarocke Musikauffassung in Deutschland', *Die Musikforschung* 42 (1989), 128–48.

Deutsches Wörterbuch von Jacob Grimm und Wilhelm Grimm, auf CD-ROM und im Internet, http://dwb.uni-trier.de/de.

Douglas, Richard M., 'Talent and Vocation in Humanist and Protestant Thought', in Theodore K. Rabb and Jerrold E. Seigel (eds.), *Action and Conviction in Early Modern Europe: Essays in Honor of E. H. Harbison* (Princeton: Princeton University Press, 1969), 261–98.

Dreyfus, Laurence, *Bach and the Patterns of Invention* (Cambridge, MA: Harvard University Press, 1996).

Dünnhaupt, Gerhard, *Personalbibliographien zu den Drucken des Barock*, 2nd edn, 6 vols. (Stuttgart: Hiersemann, 1990–93).

DuPlessis, Robert S., *Transitions to Capitalism in Early Modern Europe* (Cambridge: Cambridge University Press, 1997).

'Capital Formations', in Henry S. Turner (ed.), *The Culture of Capital. Property, Cities, and Knowledge in Early Modern England* (New York: Routledge, 2002), 27–49.

Ehmer, Josef, 'Discourses on Work and Labour in Fifteenth- and Sixteenth-Century Germany', in Jürgen Kocka (ed.), *Work in a Modern Society: The German Historical Experience* (Oxford: Berghahn, 2010), 17–36.

Elias, Norbert, *The Court Society*, trans. Edmund Jephcott (Oxford: Blackwell, 1983).

Erler, Georg, *Die jüngere Matrikel der Universität Leipzig, 1559–1809*, 3 vols. (Leipzig, 1909).

Evans, G. R., *Getting It Wrong: The Medieval Epistemology of Error* (Leiden: Brill, 1998).

Fallows, David, 'Embellishment and Urtext in the Fifteenth-Century Song Repertories', *Basler Jahrbuch für historische Musikpraxis* 14 (1990), 59–85.

Foucault, Michel, *Language, Counter-Memory, Practice*, ed. Donald F. Bouchard (Ithaca, NY: Cornell University Press, 1977).

Frandsen, Mary, *Crossing Confessional Boundaries: The Patronage of Italian Sacred Music in Seventeenth-Century Dresden* (New York: Oxford University Press, 2006).

Franke, Johannes, *Die Abgabe der Pflichtexemplare von Druckerzeugnissen mit besonderer Berücksichtigung Preussens und des deutschen Reiches* (Berlin: Asher, 1889).

Friedrich, Felix, *Krebs-Werkeverzeichnis (Krebs-WV). Thematisch-systematisches Verzeichnis der musikalischen Werke von Johann Ludwig Krebs* (Altenburg: Kamprad, 2009).

Geck, Martin, 'Bachs Leipziger Kirchenmusik. Diskurs zwischen Komponist und Kirchgängern', in Ulrich Leisinger (ed.), *Bach in Leipzig. Bach und Leipzig. Konferenzbericht Leipzig 2000*, Leipziger Beiträge zur Bach-Forschung 5 (Hildesheim: Olms, 2002), 403–11.

Gieseke, Ludwig, *Vom Privileg zum Urheberrecht: die Entwicklung des Urheberrechts in Deutschland bis 1845* (Göttingen: Schwartz 1995).
  'Die kursächsische Ordnung für Buchhändler und Buchdrucker von 1594', *Archiv für Geschichte des Buchwesens* 60 (2006), 176–83.

Gille, Gottfried, 'Der Kantaten-Textdruck von David Elias Heidenreich, Halle 1665, in den Vertonungen David Pohles, Sebastian Knüpfers, Johann Schelles und anderer', *Die Musikforschung* 38 (1985), 81–94.

Giudici, Giacomo, 'The Writing of Renaissance Politics: Sharing, Appropriating, and Asserting Authorship in the Letters of Francesco II Sforza, Duke of Milan (1522–1535)', *Renaissance Studies* 32 (2018), 253–81.

Gmeinwieser, Siegfried, 'Die *Guida armonica* von G. O. Pitoni. Eine historisch-kritische Kompositionslehre in Beispielen', in Marcel Dobberstein (ed.), *Artes liberales: Karl-Heinz Schlager zum 60. Geburtstag* (Tutzing: Schneider, 1998), 245–81.

Goehr, Lydia, *The Imaginary Museum of Musical Works: An Essay in the Philosophy of Music* (Oxford: Clarendon Press, 1992).

Gramlich, Jürgen, 'Rechtsordnungen des Buchgewerbes im Alten Reich: genossenschaftliche Strukturen, Arbeits- und Wettbewerbsrecht im deutschen Druckhandwerk', *Archiv für Geschichte des Buchwesens* 41 (1994), 1–145.

Grapenthin, Ulf, 'Beziehungen zwischen Frontispiz und Werkaufbau in Johann Adam Reinckens *Hortus musicus* von 1688', in Sverker Jullander (ed.), *Proceedings of the Weckmann Symposium. Göteborg, 30 August–3 September 1991* (Göteborg: Department of Musicology, 1993), 199–210.

Greenblatt, Stephen, *Renaissance Self-Fashioning: From More to Shakespeare* (Chicago: University of Chicago Press, 1980).

Greene, Thomas, *The Light in Troy: Imitation and Discovery in Renaissance Poetry* (New Haven: Yale University Press, 1982).

Grimm, Heinrich, *Deutsche Buchdruckersignete des XVI. Jahrhunderts. Geschichte, Sinngehalt und Gestaltung kleiner Kulturdokumente* (Wiesbaden: Guido Pressler, 1965).

Groebner, Valentin, *Who Are You? Identification, Deception, and Surveillance in Early Modern Europe*, trans. Mark Kyburz and John Peck (Brooklyn, NY: Zone Books, 2007).

Groote, Inga Mai, 'Musikalische Poetik nach Melanchthon und Glarean: Zur Genese eines Interpretationsmodells', *Archiv für Musikwissenschaft* 70 (2013), 227–53.

'"Quod pium, quod grave, quod dignum ... compositum est": Impulse aus der Musiktheoriegeschichte für die Kirchenmusikforschung', *Kirchenmusikalisches Jahrbuch* 98 (2014), 23–37.

Guido, Massimiliano (ed.), *Studies in Historical Improvisation. From* Cantare super librum *to* Partimenti (Abingdon: Routledge, 2017).

Gurlitt, Wilibald, 'Ein Autorenprivileg für Johann Hermann Schein', in Heinrich Hüschen (ed.), *Festschrift Karl Gustav Fellerer zum sechzigsten Geburtstag am 7. Juli 1962* (Regensburg: Gustav Bosse, 1962), 200–204.

Gustavson, Royston, 'Commercialising the *Choralis Constantinus*: The Printing and Publishing of the First Edition', in David J. Burn and Stefan Gasch (eds.), *Heinrich Isaac and Polyphony for the Proper of the Mass in the Late Middle Ages and Renaissance* (Turnhout: Brepols, 2011), 215–68.

Haar, James, 'Orlando di Lasso, Composer and Print Entrepreneur', in Kate van Orden (ed.), *Music and the Cultures of Print* (New York: Garland, 2000), 125–62.

Halliwell, Stephen, 'Traditional Greek Conceptions of Character', in Christopher B. R. Pelling (ed.), *Characterization and Individuality in Greek Literature* (Oxford: Clarendon Press, 1990), 32–59.

Harper, Anthony J., *German Secular Songbooks of the Mid-Seventeenth Century* (Aldershot: Ashgate, 2003).

Hasse, Hans-Peter, *Zensur theologischer Bücher in Kursachsen im konfessionellen Zeitalter. Studien zur kursächsischen Literatur- und Religionspolitik in den Jahren 1569 bis 1575* (Leipzig: Evangelische Verlagsanstalt, 2000).

Herissone, Rebecca, *Musical Creativity in Restoration England* (Cambridge: Cambridge University Press, 2013).

Herissone, Rebecca, and Alan Howard (eds.), *Concepts of Creativity in Seventeenth-Century England* (Woodbridge: Boydell, 2013).

Herrmann, Hans Peter, *Naturnachahmung und Einbildungskraft. zur Entwicklung der deutschen Poetik von 1670 bis 1740* (Bad Homburg: Gehlen, 1970).

Higgins, Paula, 'Musical "Parents" and Their "Progeny": The Discourse of Creative Patriarchy in Early Modern Europe', in Anthony M. Cummings and Jessie Ann Owens (eds.), *Music in Renaissance Cities and Courts: Studies in Honor of Lewis Lockwood* (Warren, MI: Harmonie Park Press, 1997), 169–86.

'The Apotheosis of Josquin des Prez and Other Mythologies of Musical Genius', *Journal of the American Musicological Society* 57 (2004), 443–510.

Hill, Robert S., 'Stilanalyse und Überlieferungsproblematik: das Variationssuiten-Repertoire J. A. Reinckens', in Arnfried Edler and Friedhelm Krummacher (eds.), *Dietrich Buxtehude und die europäische Musik seiner Zeit. Bericht über das Lübecker Symposion 1987* (Kassel: Bärenreiter, 1990), 204–14.

Hirschmann, Wolfgang, '"Musicus ecclecticus". Überlegungen zu Nachahmung, Norm und Individualisierung um 1700', in Rainer Bayreuther (ed.), *Musicalische Norm um 1700* (Berlin: De Gruyter, 2010), 97–107.

Hobohm, Wolf, 'Neue "Texte zur Leipziger Kirchen-Music"', *Bach-Jahrbuch* 59 (1973), 5–32.

Houle, George, *Meter in Music, 1600–1800: Performance, Perception and Notation* (Bloomington: Indiana University Press, 1987).

Howell, Martha, *Commerce before Capitalism in Europe, 1300–1600* (Cambridge: Cambridge University Press, 2010).

Jaumann, Herbert, 'Öffentlichkeit und Verlegenheit. Frühe Spuren eines Konzepts öffentlicher Kritik in der Theorie des "plagium extrajudiciale" von Jakob Thomasius (1673)', *Scientia Poetica. Jahrbuch für Geschichte der Literatur und der Wissenschaften* 4 (2000), 62–82.

Jeanneret, Christine, 'La construction d'un monstre: la figure de Frescobaldi, virtuose génial et gribouilleur', in Caroline Giron-Panel and Anne-Madeleine Goulet (eds.), *La musique à Rome au XVIIe siècle: études et perspectives de recherche* (Rome: École Française, 2012), 321–39.

'Places of Memory and Invention: The Compositional Process in Frescobaldi's Manuscripts', in Andrew Woolley and John Kitchen (eds.), *Interpreting Historical Keyboard Music: Sources, Contexts and Performance* (Farnham: Ashgate, 2013), 65–81.

Junghans, Helmar, 'Die kursächsische Kirchen- und Schulordnung von 1580. Instrument der "lutherischen" Konfessionalisierung?' in Helmar Junghans (ed.), *Die sächsischen Kurfürsten während des Religionsfriedens von 1555 bis 1618. Symposium anläßlich des Abschlusses der Edition 'Politische Korrespondenz des Herzogs und Kurfürsten Moritz von Sachsen' vom 15. bis 18. September 2005 in Leipzig* (Leipzig: Verlag der Sächsischen Akademie der Wissenschaften, 2007), 209–38.

Kade, Reinhard, 'Der Dresdener Kapellmeister Rogier Michael', *Vierteljahresschrift für Musikwissenschaft* 5 (1889), 272–89.

Kamuf, Peggy, *Signature Pieces: On the Institution of Authorship* (Ithaca, NY: Cornell University Press, 1988).

Kaplan, Marion A., *Jewish Daily Life in Germany, 1618–1945* (New York: Oxford University Press, 2005).

Karant-Nunn, Susan, 'Neoclericalism and Anticlericalism in Saxony, 1555–1675', *Journal of Interdisciplinary History* 24 (1994), 615–37.

Kew, Graham David, 'Shakespeare's Europe Revisited. The Unpublished *Itinerary* of Fynes Moryson (1566–1630)', 4 vols. (PhD dissertation, University of Birmingham, 1995).

Kivistö, Sari, *The Vices of Learning: Morality and Knowledge at Early Modern Universities* (Leiden: Brill, 2014).

Koerner, Joseph, *The Moment of Self-Portraiture in German Renaissance Art* (Chicago: University of Chicago Press, 1993).

Kohls, Ernst-Wilhelm, *Die Schule bei Martin Bucer in ihrem Verhältnis zu Kirche und Obrigkeit* (Heidelberg: Quelle & Meyer, 1963).

Koppitz, Hans-Joachim, 'Die Privilegia impressoria des Haus-, Hof- und Staatsarchivs in Wien', *Gutenberg-Jahrbuch* 69 (1994), 187–207.

Krummacher, Friedhelm, *Die Überlieferung der Choralbearbeitungen in der frühen evangelischen Kantate. Untersuchungen zum Handschriftenrepertoire*

Bibliography

evangelischer Figuralmusik im späten 17. und beginnenden 18. Jahrhundert (Berlin: Merseburger, 1965).

Küster, Konrad, *Opus primum in Venedig. Traditionen des Vokalsatzes 1590–1650* (Laaber: Laaber Verlag, 1995).

Ladis, Andrew, and Carolyn Wood (eds.), *The Craft of Art: Originality and Industry in the Italian Renaissance and Baroque Workshop* (Athens, GA: University of Georgia Press, 1995).

Lamott, Bruce Alan, 'Keyboard Improvisation according to *Nova instructio pro pulsandis organis* (1670–ca.1675) by Spiridion a Monte Carmelo' (PhD thesis, Stanford University, 1980).

Landau, David, and Peter Parshall, *The Renaissance Print 1470–1550* (New Haven: Yale University Press, 1994).

Laube, Matthew, 'Materializing Music in the Lutheran Home', *Past & Present* 234, suppl. 12 (2017), 114–38.

Leaver, Robin A., *J. S. Bach and Scripture: Glosses from the Calov Bible Commentary* (St. Louis: Concordia Publishing House, 1985).

Ledbetter, David, *Bach's* Well-Tempered Clavier: *The 48 Preludes and Fugues* (New Haven: Yale University Press, 2002).

Lehne, Friedrich, 'Zur Rechtsgeschichte der kaiserlichen Privilegien', *Mitteilungen des österreichischen Instituts für Geschichtsforschung* 53 (1939), 323–409.

Lewis Hammond, Susan, *Editing Music in Early Modern Germany* (Aldershot: Ashgate, 2007).

Liebmann, Michael J., 'Die Künstlersignatur im 15.–16. Jahrhundert als Gegenstand soziologischer Untersuchungen', in Peter H. Feist, Ernst Ullmann and Gerhard Brendler (eds.), *Lucas Cranach: Künstler und Gesellschaft. Referate des Colloquiums mit Internationaler Beteiligung zum 500. Geburtstag Lucas Cranachs d. Ä. Staatliche Lutherhalle Wittenberg 1.–3. Oktober 1972* (Halle: Staatliche Lutherhalle, 1973), 129–34.

Loesch, Heinz von, *Der Werkbegriff in der protestantischen Musiktheorie des 16. und 17. Jahrhunderts: Ein Mißverständnis* (Hildesheim: Olms, 2001).

Loewenstein, Joseph, *Ben Jonson and Possessive Authorship* (Cambridge: Cambridge University Press 2002).

Lorenzetti, Stefano, '"Scritte nella mente"? Giovanni Gabrieli's Keyboard Music and the Art of Improvised Composition', in Rodolfo Baroncini, David Bryant and Luigi Collarile (eds.), *Giovanni Gabrieli: Transmission and Reception of a Venetian Musical Tradition* (Turnhout: Brepols, 2016), 135–48.

'Musical *Inventio*, Rhetorical *Loci*, and the Art of Memory', in Massimiliano Guido (ed.), *Studies in Historical Improvisation: From* Cantare super librum *to* Partimenti (Abingdon: Routledge, 2017), 25–40.

Lowinsky, Edward, 'Musical Genius: Evolution and Origins of a Concept', in *Music in the Culture of the Renaissance and Other Essays*, ed. Bonnie J. Blackburn, 2 vols. (Chicago: University of Chicago Press, 1989), vol. 1, 40–66. Originally published in *The Musical Quarterly* 50 (1964), 321–40 and 476–95.

Macey, Patrick, 'Josquin and Champion: Conflicting Attributions for the Psalm Motet *De profundis clamavi*', in M. Jennifer Bloxam, Gioia Filocamo and

Leofranc Holford-Strevens (eds.), *Uno gentile et subtile ingenio: Studies in Renaissance Music in Honour of Bonnie J. Blackburn* (Turnhout: Brepols, 2009), 453–68.

Maclean, Ian, *Learning and the Market Place: Essays in the History of the Early Modern Book* (Leiden: Brill, 2009).

Scholarship, Commerce, Religion: The Learned Book in the Age of Confessions, 1560–1630 (Cambridge, MA: Harvard University Press, 2012).

Macpherson, C. B., *The Political Theory of Possessive Individualism* (Oxford: Clarendon Press, 1962).

Mann, Alfred, 'Mattheson as Biographer of Handel', in George J. Buelow and Hans Joachim Marx (eds.), *New Mattheson Studies* (Cambridge: Cambridge University Press, 1983), 345–52.

Marissen, Michael, 'Bach against Modernity', unpublished typescript.

Martin, John, 'Inventing Sincerity, Refashioning Prudence: The Discovery of the Individual in Renaissance Europe', *The American Historical Review* 102 (1997), 1309–42.

Masten, Jeffrey, *Textual Intercourse: Collaboration, Authorship and Sexualities in Renaissance Drama* (Cambridge: Cambridge University Press, 1997).

Maul, Michael, 'Elias Nathusius: ein Leipziger Komponist des 17. Jahrhundert', *Jahrbuch mitteldeutscher Barockmusik* (2001), 70–98.

'Knüpfer, Sebastian', *Die Musik in Geschichte und Gegenwart: Personenteil*, 2nd edn, vol. 10 (Kassel: Bärenreiter, 2003), 355–58.

'Johann David Heinichen und der "Musicalische Horribilicribrifax". Überlegungen zur Vorrede von Heinichens *Gründlicher Anweisung*', in Rainer Bayreuther (ed.), *Musikalische Norm um 1700* (Berlin: De Gruyter, 2010), 145–65.

"Dero berühmbter Chor". Die Leipziger Thomasschule und ihre Kantoren (1212–1804) (Leipzig: Lehmstedt Verlag, 2012).

McKenzie, D. F., 'Typography and Meaning: The Case of William Congreve', in Giles Barber and Bernhard Fabian (eds.), *Buch und Buchhandel im Europa in achtzehnten Jahrhundert: The Book and the Book Trade in Eighteenth-Century Europe* (Hamburg: Hauswedell, 1981), 81–126.

Meconi, Honey, 'Does *Imitatio* Exist?', *Journal of Musicology* 12 (1994), 152–78.

Meerhoff, Kees, 'The Significance of Philipp Melanchthon's Rhetoric in the Renaissance', in Peter Mack (ed.), *Renaissance Rhetoric* (Basingstoke: Macmillan, 1994), 46–62.

Mentz, Georg, *Die Matrikel der Universität Jena. Band 1: 1548 bis 1652* (Jena: Gustav Fischer, 1944).

Milsom, John, 'The T-Mass: *quis scrutatur?*', *Early Music* 45 (2018), 319–31.

Mortimer, Ruth, 'The Author's Image: Italian Sixteenth-Century Printed Portraits', *Harvard Library Bulletin*, new series 7.2 (summer 1996), 7–87.

Moss, Ann, *Printed Commonplace-Books and the Structuring of Renaissance Thought* (Oxford: Clarendon Press, 1996).

Müller, Ernst, 'Musikgeschichte von Freiberg', *Mitteilungen des Freiberger Altertumsvereins* 68 (1939), 1–144.

Müller-Blattau, Joseph, *Die Kompositionslehre Heinrich Schützens in der Fassung seines Schülers Christoph Bernhard* (Leipzig: Breitkopf & Härtel, 1926).

Murphy, Stephen, *The Gift of Immortality: Myths of Power and Humanist Poetics* (Madison: Associated University Presses, 1997).

Newman, Jane O., 'The Word Made Print: Luther's 1522 New Testament in an Age of Mechanical Reproduction', *Representations* 11 (1985), 95–133.

Newman, W. S., 'Kirnberger's Method for *Tossing off Sonatas*', *Musical Quarterly* 47 (1961), 517–25.

Niemöller, Klaus Wolfgang, 'Parodia–Imitatio: Zu Georg Quitschreibers Schrift von 1611', in Annegrit Laubenthal (ed.), *Studien zur Musikgeschichte: Eine Festschrift für Ludwig Finscher* (Kassel: Bärenreiter, 1995), 174–80.

Noack, Friedrich, 'Johann Seb. Bachs und Christoph Graupners Kompositionen zur Bewerbung um das Thomaskantorat in Leipzig 1722–23', *Bach-Jahrbuch* 10 (1913), 145–62.

North, Michael, *'Material Delight and the Joy of Living': Cultural Consumption in the Age of Enlightenment in Germany*, trans. Pamela Selwyn (Aldershot: Ashgate, 2008).

O'Brien, John, *Anacreon Redivivus: A Study of Anacreontic Translation in Mid-Sixteenth-Century France* (Ann Arbor: University of Michigan Press, 1995).

Owens, Jessie Ann, *Composers at Work: The Craft of Musical Composition 1450–1600* (New York: Oxford University Press, 1997).

Owens, Samantha. '"Zum Fürstl: Hoff Staat gehörige Musicalien": The Ownership and Dissemination of German Court Music, 1665–c.1750', in Konstanze Musketa and Barbara Reul (eds.), *Musik an der Zerbster Residenz: Bericht über die internationale wissenschaftliche Konferenz vom 10. bis 12. April 2008 im Rahmen der 10. Internationalen Fasch-Festtage in Zerbst*, Fasch-Studien 10 (Beeskow: Ortus, 2008), 103–15.

'Music via Correspondence: A List of the Music Collection of Dresden Kreuzorganist Emanuel Benisch', *Understanding Bach* 11 (2016), 39–56.

Paas, John Roger, 'Inseparable Muses: German Baroque Poets as Graphic Artists', *Colloquia Germanica* 29 (1996), 13–38.

Palisca, Claude V., 'The Genesis of Mattheson's Style Classification', in George J. Buelow and Hans Joachim Marx (eds.), *New Mattheson Studies* (Cambridge: Cambridge University Press, 1983), 409–23.

Pallas, Karl (ed.), *Die Registraturen der Kirchenvisitationen im ehemals sächsischen Kurkreise*, 7 vols. (Halle, 1906–18).

Parrott, Andrew, 'Composers' Intentions, Performers' Responsibilities', *Early Music* 41 (2013), 37–43.

Perry, Ben Edwin, *Aesopica: A Series of Texts Relating to Aesop or Ascribed to Him or Closely Connected with the Literary Tradition That Bears His Name* (Urbana: University of Illinois Press, 1952).

Pigman, G. W., III, 'Versions of Imitation in the Renaissance', *Renaissance Quarterly* 33 (1980), 1–32.

Plett, Heinrich F., *Rhetoric and Renaissance Culture* (Berlin: De Gruyter, 2004).

Pohlmann, Hansjörg, *Die Frühgeschichte des musikalischen Urheberrechts (ca.1400–1800). Neue Materialien zur Entwicklung des Urheberrechtsbewußtseins der Komponisten* (Kassel: Bärenreiter, 1962).

Pons, Alain, 'Ingenium', in Barbara Cassin (ed.), *Dictionary of Untranslatables: A Philosophical Lexicon* (Princeton: Princeton University Press, 2014), 485–89.

Porter, Martin, *'Windows of the Soul': Physiognomy in European Culture 1470–1780* (Oxford: Oxford University Press, 2005).

Prüfer, Arthur, *Johan Herman Schein* (Leipzig: Breitkopf & Härtel, 1895).

Rahmatian, Andreas, 'The Elements of Music Relevant for Copyright Protection', in Andreas Rahmatian (ed.), *Concepts of Music and Copyright: How Music Perceives Itself and How Copyright Perceives Music* (Cheltenham: Edward Elgar Publishing, 2015), 78–122.

Rasch, Rudolf, 'De muzierkoorlog tussen Estienne Roger en Pieter Mortier (1708–1711)', *De Zeventiende Eeuw* 6 (1990), 89–97.

(ed.), *Driehonderd brieven over muziek van, aan en rond Constantijn Huygens*, 2 vols. (Hilversum: Verloren, 2007).

Rathey, Markus, 'Ein unbekanntes Mühlhäuser Musikalienverzeichnis aus dem Jahre 1617', *Die Musikforschung* 51 (1998), 63–69.

'Schelle, Carpzov und die Tradition der Choralkantate in Leipzig', *Jahrbuch des Staatlichen Instituts für Musikforschung Preußischer Kulturbesitz* (2011), 185–210.

Ravizza, Victor, 'Schütz und die Venezianische Tradition der Mehrchörigkeit', in Dietrich Berke and Dorothee Hanemann (eds.), *Alte Musik als ästhetische Gegenwart: Bach, Händel, Schütz: Bericht über den internationalen musikwissenschaftlichen Kongress, Stuttgart 1985*, 2 vols. (Kassel: Bärenreiter, 1987), vol. 1, 53–65.

Reichel, Jörn, 'Handwerk und Arbeit im literarischen Werk des Nürnbergers Hans Rosenplüt', in Rainer S. Elkar (ed.), *Deutsches Handwerk in Spätmittelalter und früher Neuzeit. Sozialgeschichte – Volkskunde – Literaturgeschichte* (Göttingen: Schwartz, 1983), 245–63.

Richter, Bernhard Friedrich, 'Eine Abhandlung Joh. Kuhnaus', *Monatshefte für Musikgeschichte* 34 (1902), 147–54. Trans. Ruben Weltsch as 'A Treatise on Liturgical Text Settings (1710)', in Carol K. Baron (ed.), *Bach's Changing World: Voices in the Community* (Rochester, NY: University of Rochester Press, 2006), 219–26.

Rifkin, Joshua, 'Schütz and Musical Logic', *The Musical Times* 113 (1972), 1067–70.

Rifkin, Joshua, et al., 'Schütz, Heinrich', *Oxford Music Online*, www.oxfordmusic online.com.

Ringler, William, 'Poeta nascitur non fit. Some Notes on the History of an Aphorism', *Journal of the History of Ideas* 2 (1941), 497–504.

Ritter, August Gottfried, *Zur Geschichte des Orgelspiels, vornehmlich des deutschen, im 14. bis zum Anfange des 18. Jahrhunderts*, 2 vols. (Leipzig, 1884).

Rivera, Benito V., *German Music Theory of the Early Seventeenth Century: The Treatises of Johannes Lippius* (Ann Arbor: UMI, 1980).

Roberts, John (ed.), *Handel Sources: Materials for the Study of Handel's Borrowing*, 9 vols. (New York: Garland, 1986).

Ronca, Italo, '*Semper aliquid novi Africam adferre*: Philological Afterthoughts on the Plinian Reception of a Pre-Aristotelian Saying', *Akroterìon* 37 (1992), 146–58.

Rosand, Ellen, '"Senza Necessità del Canto dell'Autore": Printed Singing Lessons in Seventeenth-Century Italy', in Angelo Pompilio et al. (eds.), *Atti del XIV congresso della Società Internazionale di Musicologia, Bologna*, 3 vols. (Turin: Edizioni di Torino, 1990), vol. 2, 214–24.

Rose, Mark, *Authors and Owners: The Invention of Copyright* (Cambridge, MA: Harvard University Press, 1993).

Rose, Stephen, 'The Composer as Self-Publisher in Seventeenth-Century Germany', in Erik Kjellberg (ed.), *The Dissemination of Music in Seventeenth-Century Europe. Celebrating the Düben Collection* (Bern: Peter Lang, 2010), 239–60.

  The Musician in Literature in the Age of Bach (Cambridge: Cambridge University Press, 2011).

  'Plagiarism at the Academy of Ancient Music: A Case-Study in Authorship, Style and Judgement', in Alan Howard and Rebecca Herissone (eds.), *Concepts of Creativity in Seventeenth-Century England* (Woodbridge: Boydell & Brewer, 2013), 181–98.

  'Protected Publications: The Imperial and Saxon Privileges for Printed Music, 1550–1700', *Early Music History* 37 (2018), 247–313.

Rose, Stephen, Sandra Tuppen and Loukia Drosopoulou, 'Writing a Big Data History of Music', *Early Music* 43 (2015), 649–60.

Rublack, Ulinka, 'Grapho-Relics: Lutheranism and the Materialization of the Word', *Past & Present* 206, suppl. 5 (2010), 144–66.

Ruhnke, Martin, *Joachim Burmeister. Ein Beitrag zur Musiklehre um 1600* (Kassel: Bärenreiter, 1955).

Saarinen, Risto, *Luther and the Gift* (Tübingen: Mohr Siebeck, 2017).

Sachse, Richard (ed.), *Acta Nicolaitana et Thomana. Aufzeichnungen von Jakob Thomasius während seines Rektorates an der Nikolai- und Thomasschule zu Leipzig (1670–1684)* (Leipzig: Wörner, 1912).

Salmen, Walter, *Musiker im Porträt*, vol. 2: *Das 17. Jahrhundert* (Munich: Beck, 1983).

Scanlon, Larry, *Narrative, Authority and Power: The Medieval Exemplum and the Chaucerian Tradition* (Cambridge: Cambridge University Press, 1994).

Schabalina, Tatjana, '"Texte zur Music" in Sankt Petersburg: neue Quellen zur Leipziger Musikgeschichte sowie zur Kompositions- und Aufführungstätigkeit Johann Sebastian Bachs', *Bach-Jahrbuch* 94 (2008), 33–98.

Schering, Arnold, 'Die alte Chorbibliothek der Thomasschule in Leipzig', *Archiv für Musikwissenschaft* 1 (1918–19), 275–88.

Schilling, Heinz, 'Die Konfessionalisierung von Kirche, Staat und Gesellschaft - Profil, Leistung, Defizite und Perspektiven eines geschichtswissenschaftlichen Paradigmas', in Wolfgang Reinhard and Heinz Schilling (eds.),

Die katholische Konfessionalisierung. Akten eines von Corpus Catholicorum und Verein für Reformationsgeschichte veranstalteten Symposions (Augsburg 1993) (Gütersloh: Gütersloher Verlagshaus, 1995), 1–49.

Schmid, Bernhold, 'Hassler-Bearbeitungen des frühen 17. Jahrhunderts', in Paul Mai (ed.), *Im Dienst der Quellen zur Musik. Festschrift Gertraut Haberkamp zum 65. Geburtstag* (Tutzing: Schneider, 2002), 249–58.

Schoch, Rainer, Matthias Mende and Anna Scherbaum, *Albrecht Dürer, das druckgraphische Werk*, 3 vols. (Munich: Prestel, 2001–4).

Schulenberg, David, 'Crossing the Rhine with Froberger: Suites, Symbols, and Seventeenth-Century Musical Autobiography', in Claire Fontijn and Susan Parisi (eds.), *Fiori musicali. Liber amicorum Alexander Silbiger* (Sterling Heights, MI: Harmonie Park Press, 2010), 271–302.

Schulze, Hans-Joachim, 'The Parody Process in Bach's Music: An Old Problem Reconsidered', *Bach: The Quarterly Journal of the Riemenschneider Bach Institute* 20 (1989), 7–21.

Schulze, Winfried, 'Vom Gemeinnutz zum Eigennutz. Über den Normenwandel in der ständischen Gesellschaft der frühen Neuzeit', *Historische Zeitschrift* 243 (1986), 591–626.

'Gerhard Oestreichs Begriff "Sozialdisziplinierung in der frühen Neuzeit"', *Zeitschrift für historische Forschung* 14 (1987), 265–302.

Serauky, Walter, *Musikgeschichte der Stadt Halle. II/i: Von Samuel Scheidt bis in die Zeit Georg Friedrich Händels und Johann Sebastian Bachs* (Halle: Buchhandlung des Waisenhauses, 1939).

Shephard, Tim, Sanna Raninen, Serenella Sessini and Laura Ştefănescu, *Music in the Art of Renaissance Italy c.1420–1540* (London: Harvey Miller, 2019).

Shrank, Cathy, '"These Fewe Scribbled Rules": Representing Scribal Intimacy in Early Modern Print', *Huntington Library Quarterly* 67 (2004), 295–314.

Siegele, Ulrich, '"I Had to be Industrious ... " Thoughts about the Relationship between Bach's Social and Musical Character', *Bach* 22 (1991), 5–12.

'Bach's Situation in the Cultural Politics of Contemporary Leipzig', in Carol K. Baron (ed.), *Bach's Changing World: Voices in the Community* (Rochester, NY: University of Rochester Press, 2006), 127–73.

Sittard, Josef. *Zur Geschichte der Musik und des Theaters am württembergischen Hof*, 2 vols. (Stuttgart: Kohlhammer, 1890).

'Samuel Capricornus contra Philipp Friedrich Böddecker', *Sammelbände der internationalen Musikgesellschaft* 3 (1901–2), 87–128.

Skowronek, Susanne, *Autorenbilder. Wort und Bild in den Porträtkupferstichen von Dichtern und Schriftstellern des Barock* (Würzburg: Königshausen & Neumann, 2000).

Smith, Pamela H., *The Business of Alchemy: Science and Culture in the Holy Roman Empire* (Princeton: Princeton University Press, 1994).

The Body of the Artisan: Art and Experience in the Scientific Revolution (Chicago: University of Chicago Press, 2004).

Snyder, Kerala J., *Dieterich Buxtehude: Organist in Lübeck*, 2nd edn (Rochester, NY: University of Rochester Press, 2007).

Bibliography

Sohm, Philip, 'Gendered Style in Italian Art Criticism from Michelangelo to Malvasia', *Renaissance Quarterly* 48 (1995), 759–808.

Spies, Hans-Bernd, '"Verbessert durch Johann Balhorn". Neues zu einer alten Redensart', *Zeitschrift des Vereins für Lübeckische Geschichte und Altertumskunde* 62 (1982), 285–92.

Sponheuer, Bernd, 'Reconstructing Ideal Types of the "German" in Music', in Celia Applegate and Pamela Potter (eds.), *Music and German National Identity* (Chicago: University of Chicago Press, 2002), 36–58.

Stetter, Gertrud, *Michael Wening: der Kupferstecher der Max Emanuel-Zeit. Ausstellung im Münchner Stadtmuseum, 28. September 1977 bis 28. Januar 1978* (Munich: Lipp, 1977).

Steude, Wolfram, *Die Musiksammelhandschriften des 16. und 17. Jahrhunderts in der Sächsischen Landesbibliothek zu Dresden* (Wilhelmshaven: Heinrichshofen, 1974).

'Das wiederaufgefundene *Opus ultimum* von Heinrich Schütz. Bemerkungen zur Quelle und zum Werk', *Schütz-Jahrbuch* 4–5 (1982–83), 9–18.

Stimmel, Eberhard, 'Die Familie Schütz. Ein Beitrag zur Familiengeschichte des Georgius Agricola', *Abhandlungen des staatlichen Museums für Mineralogie und Geologie zu Dresden* 11 (1962), 377–417.

Stolze, Wolfgang, 'Samuel Scheidt und der 30-jährige Krieg', in Konstanze Musketa and Wolfgang Ruf (eds.), *Samuel Scheidt (1587–1654). Werk und Wirkung. Bericht über die internationale wissenschaftliche Konferenz am 5. und 6. November 2004 ... in der Stadt Halle und über das Symposium in Creuzburg zum 350. Todesjahr, 25.–27. März 2004* (Halle: Händel-Haus, 2006), 393–410.

Stravinsky, Igor, *Poetics of Music in the Form of Six Lessons*, trans. Arthur Knodel and Ingolf Dahl, preface by George Seferis (Cambridge MA: Harvard University Press, 1970).

Strohm, Reinhard, 'Looking Back at Ourselves: The Problem with the Musical Work-Concept', in Michael Talbot (ed.), *The Musical Work: Reality or Invention?* (Liverpool: Liverpool University Press, 2000), 128–52.

'*Opus*: An Aspect of the Early History of the Musical Work-Concept', in Rainer Kleinertz, Christoph Flamm and Wolf Frobenius (eds.), *Musik des Mittelalters und der Renaissance. Festschrift Klaus-Jürgen Sachs zum 80. Geburtstag* (Hildesheim: Olms, 2010), 205–17.

Struever, Nancy, *The Language of History in the Renaissance: Rhetoric and Historical Consciousness in Florentine Humanism* (Princeton: Princeton University Press, 1970).

Stump, Eleonore, *Aquinas* (London: Routledge, 2013).

Taruskin, Richard, *Text and Act. Essays on Music and Performance* (New York: Oxford University Press, 1995).

Thompson, Robert, '"Francis Withie of Oxon" and His Commonplace Book, Christ Church, Oxford, MS 337', *Chelys* 20 (1991), 3–27.

Tully, James, 'The Possessive Individualism Thesis: A Reconsideration in the Light of Recent Scholarship', in Joseph H. Carens (ed.), *Democracy and*

Possessive Individualism: The Intellectual Legacy of C. B. Macpherson (Albany: State University of New York Press, 1993), 19–44.

van Asperen, Bob, 'A New Froberger Manuscript', *Journal of Seventeenth-Century Music* 13.1 (2007), https://sscm-jscm.org/v13/no1/vanasperen.html.

van Damme, Ilja, 'From a "Knowledgeable" Salesman Towards a "Recognizable" Product? Questioning Branding Strategies before Industrialization (Antwerp, Seventeenth to Nineteenth Centuries)', in Bert de Munck and Dries Lyna (eds.), *Concepts of Value in European Material Culture, 1500–1900* (Farnham: Ashgate, 2015), 75–101.

Vanhulst, Henri, 'Lasso et ses éditeurs: remarques à propos de deux lettres peu connues', *Revue belge de musicologie*, 39–40 (1985–86), 80–100.

van Orden, Kate, *Music, Authorship, and the Book in the First Century of Print* (Berkeley: University of California Press, 2014).

Varwig, Bettina, *Histories of Heinrich Schütz* (Cambridge: Cambridge University Press, 2011).

Vetter, Walther, *Der Kapellmeister Bach* (Potsdam: Athenaion, 1950).

Volz, Hans, 'Das Lutherwappen als "Schutzmarke"', *Libri* 4 (1954), 216–25.

Vormbaum, Reinhold, *Die evangelischen Schulordnungen des 16. Jahrhunderts* (Gütersloh, 1860).

  Die evangelischen Schulordnungen des 17. Jahrhunderts (Gütersloh, 1863).

Voss, Steffen, 'Händels Entlehnungen aus Johann Matthesons Oper *Porsenna* (1702)', *Göttinger Händel-Beiträge* 10 (2004), 81–94.

Waczkat, Andreas, *'Ein ehrenhaftes Spielen mit Musik': Deutsche Parodiemessen des 17. Jahrhunderts* (Kassel: Bärenreiter, 2000).

  'Samuel Scheidt und die neue Parodietechnik des 17. Jahrhunderts', in Konstanze Musketa and Wolfgang Ruf (eds.), *Samuel Scheidt (1587–1654). Werk und Wirkung. Bericht über die Internationale wissenschaftliche Konferenz am 5. und 6. November 2004 ... in der Stadt Halle und über das Symposium in Creuzburg zum 350. Todesjahr, 25.–27. März 2004* (Halle: Händel-Haus, 2006), 57–68.

Weber, Max, *Die protestantische Ethik und der 'Geist' des Kapitalismus* (1904–5). Modern edn as *The Protestant Ethic and the Spirit of Capitalism*, trans. and updated by Stephen Kalberg (New York: Oxford University Press, 2011).

Wegman, Rob C., 'From Maker to Composer: Improvisation and Musical Authorship in the Low Countries, 1450–1500', *Journal of the American Musicological Society* 49 (1996), 409–79.

  '"And Josquin Laughed ... " Josquin and the Composer's Anecdote in the Sixteenth Century', *Journal of Musicology* 17 (1999), 319–57.

Welch, Evelyn, 'The Senses in the Marketplace: Sensory Knowledge in a Material World', in Herman Roodenburg (ed.), *A Cultural History of the Senses in the Renaissance* (London: Bloomsbury Academic, 2004), 61–86.

Werner, Arno, 'Zur Musikgeschichte von Delitzsch', *Archiv für Musikwissenschaft* 1 (1918–19), 535–64.

Wiesner, Merry, *Gender, Church and State in Early Modern Germany* (London: Longman, 1998).

Bibliography

Wimsatt, W. K., Jr., and Monroe C. Beardsley, 'The Intentional Fallacy', in W. K. Wimsatt Jr. (ed.), *The Verbal Icon: Studies in the Meaning of Poetry* (Lexington: University of Kentucky Press, 1954), 3–18.

Wingren, Gustaf, *Luther on Vocation*, trans. Carl C. Rasmussen (Philadelphia: Muhlenberg, 1957).

Wolff, Christoph, *Bach. Essays on His Life and Music* (Cambridge, MA: Harvard University Press, 1991).

  Johann Sebastian Bach: The Learned Musician (New York: Norton, 2000).

Wollny, Peter, 'Bachs Sanctus BWV 241 und Kerlls *Missa superba*', *Bach-Jahrbuch* 77 (1991), 173–76.

  'Schelle, Johann', *Die Musik in Geschichte und Gegenwart: Personenteil*, 2nd edn, vol. 14 (Kassel: Bärenreiter, 2005), 1267–70.

  'Heinrich Schütz, Johann Rosenmüller und die *Kern-Sprüche* I und II', *Schütz-Jahrbuch* 28 (2006), 35–47.

  'From Lübeck to Sweden: Thoughts and Observations on the Buxtehude Sources in the Düben Collection', *Early Music* 35 (2007), 371–83.

  'On Johann Sebastian Bach's Creative Process: Observations from His Drafts and Sketches', in Sean Gallagher and Thomas Forrest Kelly (eds.), *The Century of Bach and Mozart: Perspectives on Historiography, Composition, Theory, and Performance* (Cambridge, MA: Harvard University Department of Music, 2008), 217–38.

  Studien zum Stilwandel in der protestantischen Figuralmusik des mittleren 17. Jahrhunderts (Beeskow: Ortus, 2016).

Woodmansee, Martha, 'The Genius and the Copyright: Economic and Legal Conditions of the Emergence of the "Author"', *Eighteenth-Century Studies* 17 (1984), 425–48.

Zirnbauer, Heinz, *Der Notenbestand der Reichsstädtisch Nürnbergischen Ratsmusik: Eine bibliographische Rekonstruktion* (Nuremburg: Stadtbibliothek, 1959).

Zohn, Steven, 'Telemann in the Marketplace: The Composer as Self-Publisher', *Journal of the American Musicological Society* 58 (2005), 275–356.

MODERN EDITIONS OF MUSIC

Ausgewählte Kirchenkantaten: Sebastian Knüpfer, Johann Schelle und Johann Kuhnau, ed. Arnold Schering, Denkmäler Deutscher Tonkunst, vols. 58–59 (Leipzig: Breitkopf & Härtel, 1918).

Froberger, Johann Jacob, *Seventeenth-Century Keyboard Music*, vol. 3: *Vienna, Österreichische Nationalbibliothek, Musiksammlung, Mus. Hs. 18706 (Froberger Autographs)*, introduction by Robert Hill (New York: Garland, 1988).

Kerll, Johann Caspar, *The Collected Works for Keyboard*, ed. C. David Harris, 2 vols. (New York: The Broude Trust, 1995).

Kuhnau, Johann, *The Collected Works for Keyboard*, ed. C. David Harris, 2 vols. (New York: The Broude Trust, 2003).

Lassus, Orlande de, *Sämtliche Werke*, Neue Reihe, vol. 26: *Sieben Busspsalmen*, ed. Horst Leuchtmann (Kassel: Bärenreiter, 1995).

Leipzig Church Music from the Sherard Collection: Eight Works by Sebastian Knüpfer, Johann Schelle, and Johann Kuhnau, ed. Stephen Rose (Madison, WI: A-R Editions, 2014).

Paris, Bibliothèque nationale de France, Rés. Vm^7 674–675: The Bauyn Manuscript, ed. Bruce Gustafson, 4 vols. (New York: The Broude Trust, 2014).

Schelle, Johann, *Six Chorale Cantatas*, ed. Mary S. Morris, Recent Researches in the Music of the Baroque Era, vols. 60–61 (Madison, WI: A-R Editions, 1988).

Schütz, Heinrich, *Sämmtliche Werke*, ed. Philipp Spitta, vol. 6: *Kleine geistliche Concerte* (Leipzig: Breitkopf & Härtel, 1887).

Neue Ausgabe sämtlicher Werke, vol. 39: *Der Schwanengesang*, ed. Wolfram Steude (Kassel: Bärenreiter, 1984).

Neue Ausgabe sämtlicher Werke, vol. 1: *Historia der Geburt Jesu Christi*, ed. Bettina Varwig (Kassel: Bärenreiter, 2017).

Vingt et une suites pour le clavecin de Johann Jacob Froberger et d'autres auteurs: Dresden, Sächsische Landesbibliothek, Ms. 1-T-595 (Strasbourg, 1675), ed. Rudolf Rasch (Stuttgart: Carus, 2000).

Index

Aaron, Pietro, 101
Adam von Fulda, 191
Adlung, Jakob, 151–53
aemulatio. See emulation
Aesop, 66, 154
agency, human, 13, 18, 24, 26, 29, 45–47, 62, 207–8, 214
Ahle, Johann Georg, 205–6, 210
Albert, Heinrich, 67, 142–48
Albinoni, Tomaso Giovanni, 151
Albrecht V, Duke of Bavaria, 125
Albrici, Vincenzo, 8, 125
Ammerbach, Elias Nikolaus, 121
Ammon, Hieronymus, 107
Andreae, Jakob, 164
Antico, Andrea, 101
Antiquis, Jacopo de, 64
apprenticeships, 31, 52, 121–22, 201
Aquinas, Thomas of, 195
Aristotle, 25, 118, 161, 190
Arlt, Wulf, 35
arrangements, musical, 64–65, 70–73, 80, 140, 202, 206–7
ars combinatoria, 43–45
artisans
    construction methods of, 32, 38–40, 46, 214
    makers' marks of, 82, 84
    manual skill of, 29–32, 38, 42–43, 113, 199–200, 203
    masterworks of, 32, 82, 113
    and notion of hard work, 30–33
    secrecy of, 121–23
    teaching methods of, 30–32, 52, 121–22, 201
arts
    liberal, 29, 31
    mechanical, 29, 31–32
August, Duke of Brunswick-Lüneburg, 1
August, Elector of Saxony, 124, 164
authentication signs and techniques, 14, 82–85, 100, 148, 213
    in manuscripts, 96–100
    watermarks, 94–96
author
    and fame, 28–29, 107–8, 155
    and notated works, 4–5, 155
    as maker of books, 3, 213

as originator, 3, 213
as proprietor, 4, 77, 116–17, 138–40, 145, 149–50
canonised, 11, 52–53, 58–61, 154, 167, 185
death of, 3, 194
definitions of, 3–4, 7, 10, 213
economic rights of. *See* author, as proprietor
God as true, 18–19, 213
intentions of. *See* intentions, intentionality
moral rights of, 117, 155, 205
musicians describing themselves as, 1–3, 213
portraits of, 14, 83, 100–9, 213
authority, 7, 10–11
    of Bible, 15
    of musical opus, 206–7
    of past, 10, 13, 53, 57–61
    of princes, 14, 129–31, 135–36, 140, 146–48
    of teacher, 54
authorship
    and authority, 10–11, 52, 56–61, 146–48, 155–56, 185
    as discursive construct, 3–4
    and individuality, 11–12, 111–12

Bach, Johann Christoph Friedrich, 79
Bach, Johann Ludwig, 23
Bach, Johann Sebastian, 3–4, 8, 14, 19, 52, 173, 178, 214
    artisanal mindset of, 33, 35, 212
    attacked by Scheibe, 33, 187, 211–12
    attitudes to creativity, 21, 23, 119, 214–15
    as author, 3, 213
    as cantor in Leipzig, 176, 181
    and church cantatas, 159, 176
    and invention, 34–35, 45, 214
    Marxist interpretations of, 21, 33
    and musical borrowing, 50, 78–80
    as teacher, 53, 212
Bach, Johann Sebastian, works
    Cantata *Du wahrer Gott und Davids Sohn* BWV23, 184–85
    Cantata *Gott soll allein mein Herze haben* BWV169, 176
    Cantata *Jesu nahm zu sich die Zwölfe* BWV22, 184–85

Index

Bach, Johann Sebastian, works (cont.)
  Cantata *Liebster Gott, wenn wird ich sterben* BWV8, 176
  Cantata *Wer sich selbst erhöhet* BWV47, 176
  Cantata *Wer weiß, wie nahe mir mein Ende* BWV27, 176
  Clavier-Übung I, 3, 150–51
  Clavier-Übung III, 152
  Orgel-Büchlein, 3, 119
  Sanctus, 78–80
  St Matthew Passion, 9, 15
  Wohltemperirte Clavier, 32
Banchieri, Adriano, 56
Barbarino, Bartolomeo, 199
Barthes, Roland, 3, 194
Baryphonus, Henricus, 53, 158
Baumann, Georg, 87
Beardsley, Monroe C., 3, 189
Becker, Dietrich, 21
Beer, Johann, 27, 31, 81, 111–12, 115, 178, 195–98, 212
Beier, Adrian, 143
Benisch, Emanuel, 78, 155
Benjamin, Walter, 84
Berg, Gimel, 124
Bernhard, Christoph, 29, 52–53, 56–58, 109, 111
Bertali, Antonio, 59
Beyer, Johann Samuel, 177
Birnbaum, Johann Abraham, 33, 187–88, 193, 205, 211
Blankenburg, Walter, 21, 24
Bleyer, Georg, 183
Blume, Friedrich, 21
Boccaccio, Giovanni, 87
Böddecker, Philipp Friedrich, 58
body
  of author, 85, 87, 97–98, 100, 107–8, 211–12
  of musician, 97, 199–201, 214
Boethius, 191, 209
Bohme, Jakob, 82
Bokemeyer, Heinrich, 75–76, 151, 153–54
borrowing, musical, 48–50, 64–65, 78–80
  See also emulation; *imitatio*
  honest, 67–68
  and invention, 75–78
  parody, 62
Braudel, Fernand, 83
Braun, Werner, 7
Briegel, Wolfgang Carl, 104
Brossard, Sébastien de, 110
Burmeister, Joachim, 26, 51, 53, 109–11, 192
Butt, John, 15, 19, 57, 190, 203–5, 207
Buttstett, Johann Heinrich, 44, 122, 200
Buxtehude, Dieterich, 22, 49, 65, 74

Caccini, Giulio, 200, 207
Calella, Michele, 5
Calvisius, Seth, 59, 64, 127–28, 130, 136–37, 139–40, 205

Camerarius, Philipp, 162
cantatas, church, 8, 13–14, 74, 175–77, 184–85
  printed libretti for, 175–77
cantors
  duties of, 164–65, 172–74, 185
  recruitment of, 182–85, 206
Capilupi, Gemignano, 65
capitalism, 12–13, 77–78, 149, 174–75
  and crisis of authentication, 13, 83–84, 87
  criticism of, 119–20
  modes of consumption, 14, 214
Capricornus, Samuel, 58–59, 213
Cardano, Girolamo, 63
Carissimi, Giacomo, 53, 59
Carpentras, 6
Carpzov, Johann Benedict, 179
Castaldi, Bellerofonte, 101
Castiglione, Baldassare, 196
censorship, 134–35, 162–63
Chafe, Eric, 21, 24
Chapin, Keith, 29
character. *See* identity, personal
Chiodino, Giovanni Battista, 36
church music
  and Biblical exegesis, 166–67
  regulation of, 165, 172–73, 214
Chytraeus, David, 36, 161–63
Cicero, 34, 51, 61, 69, 76, 109, 161–62, 171, 192
Clemens non Papa, Jacobus, 110, 159, 164, 166–69, 180–81
Coclico, Adrianus Petit, 209
common good, 14, 19, 117–20, 136–37, 140, 146, 149, 152, 157
commonplace books, 36–37, 40–41, 53, 68
commonplaces (*loci communes*), 36–37, 41–42, 53
composer
  figure of, 5, 16, 102–4
  as ideal performer, 189, 199–203
  prerequisites of, 27–28, 33–35
  as self-publisher, 88, 102, 138, 141, 150–51
composer–performer relationship, 187–99, 203–12
Cook, Nicholas, 189, 203
Copeland, Rita, 51
copyright law, 4, 116–17
Corelli, Arcangelo, 151
Council of Trent, 165
courts, 8, 56
  conspicuous consumption at, 178
  musicians' contracts at, 123–24
  secrecy at, 123–25, 203
Cranach, Lucas, 86, 89
creativity
  artisanal notions of, 13, 15–17, 29–34, 45–47, 82, 109, 199–200, 211–12
  as act of reception, 48, 61, 213
  as anachronistic term, 16
  collaborative, 4, 6–7, 143

Index

humanist notions of, 13, 15–17, 24–29, 45–47, 81–82, 109–12, 190, 208–9, 214
theological notions of, 12–14, 16–24, 45–48, 93, 117–19, 181–82, 208
Crecquillon, Thomas, 168
Crüger, Johannes, 52–53, 130

Danzig (Gdańsk), 143–45
Darmstadt, 178
Dasypodius, Petrus, 3, 213
David, Hans T., 79
Defant, Christine, 93
Delitzsch, 168, 170–72, 177
Demantius, Christoph, 128, 170
Demelius, Christian, 52–53
Descartes, René, 40
Dieterich, Conrad, 166–67, 185
discipline, social, 160–61, 163–64
dissonance, irregular, 56–61
Dresden, 8, 78, 123–25, 131–33
Dressler, Gallus, 26, 51, 53, 110, 165–66, 168, 172, 186
Dreyfus, Laurence, 17, 34, 42, 45
Dürer, Albrecht, 30, 85–86, 89, 100, 201
Duve, Andreas Christoph, 184

Ehmer, Josef, 31
Elias, Norbert, 178
empiricism, 11–12, 15, 29, 40, 179–80, 187, 193, 214
emulation, 13, 50, 61–63
in music, 64–65
Endter, Christoph, 10
Erasmus, Desiderius, 50, 61–62, 82–84, 96, 100, 110–12, 133, 209–10
Erdmann, Gottfried, 175
Erlebach, Philipp Heinrich, 22

Fabricius, Werner, 184
Fallows, David, 209
Fasch, Johann Friedrich, 153, 177
fashion, 174, 177, 180–82, 198
and the ephemeral, 8, 159–60
Felden, Johann von, 66
Finck, Hermann, 52, 197
Fischart, Johann, 30–31
Förster, Kaspar, 49
Foucault, Michel, 3–4, 11
Freiberg, 170, 177
Frescobaldi, Girolamo, 40, 101, 155
Friedrich Wilhelm, Elector of Brandenburg, 143
Fröber, Christoph Gottfried, 177
Froberger, Basilius, 123
Froberger, Johann Jacob, 15, 52, 97–100, 155, 200–2, 211, 214
Fröhlich, Christoph, 170
Fugger, Johann Jakob, 125
Fuhrmann, Martin Heinrich, 27, 31, 48, 173–74, 182, 190–91

Gabrieli, Andrea, 54, 69
Gabrieli, Giovanni, 36, 54–56, 69, 213
Gaffurius, Franchinus, 101
Gaurico, Pomponio, 104
Geck, Martin, 176
Geist, Christian, 49
Geistliche wolklingende Concerte (1637–38), 70–73, 96, 141
gifts, 1, 12, 17–18, 118–21, 155
Glarean, Heinrich, 25, 209
Gottsched, Johann Christoph, 193
Grabbe, Johann, 54
Graefenthal, Christian, 169
Graff, Johann Christoph, 37
Gramlich, Jürgen, 133
Grandi, Alessandro, 49, 53, 69
Grapenthin, Ulf, 93
Graupner, Christoph, 23, 178, 184
Graziani, Bonifazio, 65
Greenblatt, Stephen, 11, 129–31
Greene, Thomas, 50
Grieffgens, Caspar, 201
Guazzo, Stefano, 123

Haar, James, 137
Hahn, Johannes, 107
Halle, 172–73, 177–78
Hamburg, 76, 91–93
Hammerschmidt, Andreas, 3, 112, 119, 122–23, 170, 206, 212
as self-publisher, 137–38
printing privileges of, 129–30, 133, 135, 138, 148
Handel, George Frideric, 23, 50, 74, 76–78, 173, 202–3
Handl (Gallus), Jacobus, 128, 134, 168, 172
Harsdörffer, Georg Philipp, 26, 69–70, 89
Hassler, Hans Leo, 65, 70–71, 128
Haussmann, Valentin, 64
Heidenreich, David Elias, 174–75, 178
Heinichen, Johann David, 27, 44–45, 50, 74–75, 193
Herbst, Johann Andreas, 16, 28–29, 31–32, 36, 107
Herisson, Rebecca, 6, 16–17
Herold, Christian, 149
Higgins, Paula, 25, 52
historical progress, 62–64, 66, 180–81
Hoë von Hoënegg, Matthias, 133
Hogwood, Christopher, 188, 212
Horace, 24, 28–29, 61, 65–67, 76
Howell, Martha, 83
Hünefeld, Andreas, 143
Hurlebusch, Conrad Friedrich, 151
Huygens, Constantijn, 200–1

identity, personal, 11, 81–83, 87, 96, 100, 104–8, 110–12, 115, 214
imitatio, 50–51, 112, 213
in literature, 49–50, 54, 61–62, 68–70, 73
in music, 13, 50–61, 75–76

improvisation, 5, 189–90
  keyboard, 37–40, 112–13, 154–55
individuality, 11–12, 197–98, 214
ingenium, 24–26, 58, 110, 115, 201, 209, 214
inscriptions, pious, 20–24, 100, 214–15
inspiration, 6, 25, 27, 35, 46
intabulations, keyboard, 140, 169, 206–7
intentions, intentionality, 1, 3, 15, 49, 188–89,
  203–12
invention, 17, 34–36, 70
  and affections, 45
  definitions of, 34
  via formulaic material, 36–42
  and talent, 34–35, 42–45, 115
  via variation techniques, 42–45
Isaac, Heinrich, 5, 25, 136

Jeanneret, Christine, 40
Jesu juva. *See* inscriptions, pious
Johann Friedrich I, Elector of Saxony, 161
Johann Georg I, Elector of Saxony, 124–25, 133,
  183
Johann Georg II, Elector of Saxony, 95, 158
Josquin des Prez, 5, 18, 25, 64, 159, 164–67,
  172, 208–10

Kamuf, Peggy, 85
Karant-Nunn, Susan, 161
Kauffmann, Georg Friedrich, 184
Kerll, Johann Caspar, 14, 52, 78–80, 104, 118,
  154–56
Kircher, Athanasius, 59, 114
Kirnberger, Johann Philipp, 64
Kittel, Caspar, 134
Kittel, Johann Christian, 212
Klemm, Johann, 95
Knüpfer, Sebastian, 174, 178, 183
Koerner, Joseph, 86
Königsberg, 142, 144, 148
Kortkamp, Johann, 99
Kräuter, Philipp David, 53
Krebs, Johann Ludwig, 23
Krieger, Adam, 45–46, 81, 107–8, 115, 130,
  183
Krieger, Johann, 110, 187–88, 205
Krieger, Johann Philipp, 179
Kuhnau, Johann, 16, 75, 153, 184, 213
  on duties of cantors, 177–81
  on invention, 44–45, 67–68
  on Lutheran doctrine of service, 20, 23–24,
    119, 122–23, 149
Kuhnau, Johann, works
  Biblische Historien, 150, 152, 180
  church cantatas, 159, 175–76
  Clavier Ubung, 21, 104, 150–51
  Frische Clavier-Früchte, 59–61, 150

labour, human, 13, 19, 30–33, 138–40, 145,
  156
Lamberg, Abraham, 87

Lassus, Orlande de, 6, 53, 64, 125, 140,
  159, 164, 166–69, 171–72, 180–81,
  195, 207
  printing privileges of, 85, 127–28, 133, 137
Le Maistre, Matthaeus, 168
Leaver, Robin, 21
Lechner, Leonhard, 109, 123
Ledbetter, David, 32
Ledertz, Paul, 141–42
Leibniz, Gottfried Wilhelm, 43–44
Leipzig, 78, 136, 149, 153, 173, 180
  book fair, 127, 142–43
  cantors in, 127, 169–70, 174–76
  church music in, 167–68, 174–79, 184–86
  recruitment of cantors in, 45–46, 182–85
Liebmann, Michael, 86
Lippius, Johannes, 64
Listenius, Nikolaus, 25–26, 28, 190–91
Llull, Ramon, 43
Löbau, 163
loci communes. See commonplaces
Locke, John, 12–13, 15, 74, 116
Loewenstein, Joseph, 4
Lorenzetti, Stefano, 36, 114
Lossius, Lucas, 51
Lotti, Antonio, 76
Lowinsky, Edward, 25
Luther, Martin, 210
  denial of free will, 17–18
  doctrine of service, 14, 19–20, 118–21, 149
  doctrine of vocation, 19
  on gifts, 17–18, 118
  on humility, 20, 28
  on music, 18, 209
  personal seal of, 87
  on social discipline, 161
  unauthorised editions of, 84, 87, 119–20,
    137, 145

Macpherson, C. B., 12–13, 74
Macrobius, 63
Manlius, Johannes, 208–10
manuscripts, 9, 96–100, 151–55, 195
  autograph, 21–23, 97–99, 200
Marenzio, Luca, 64, 110
Maria Antonia of Austria, 155–56
Marissen, Michael, 23
Martial, 66
Masten, Jeffrey, 4
Mattheson, Johann, 11–12, 15, 93, 174, 187,
  202
  capitalist views of, 13, 50, 76–78, 80
  on composer–performer relationship, 191–93,
    202–3, 210–11
  on invention, 35, 41–45, 76–78, 214
  and musical borrowing, 75–78
  on prerequisites of composer, 27, 35
  on style, 110
Max Emanuel, Elector of Bavaria, 155–56
Maximianus, 172

Index

Meconi, Honey, 52–53
Melanchthon, Philipp, 36, 51, 160–61, 209–10
   on music's power, 116, 161
memory, arts of, 36–38, 42, 154
Merulo, Claudio, 101
Michael, Rogier, 123
Michael, Tobias, 14, 194, 196–99, 207, 212
Milsom, John, 49, 80
misattribution, 153–55
Mizler, Lorenz Christoph, 44
Mölich, Michael, 134
monograms, 85–87, 89–94, 96, 100
Monte, Philippe de, 168
Monteverdi, Claudio, 49, 53, 67, 69
Morales, Cristóbal de, 6, 101
Moritz of Hesse, 64
Mortier, Pieter, 151
Moryson, Fynes, 102
Muffat, Georg, 155
Munich, 125, 155–56
Murschhauser, Franz Xaver, 79–80
musica poetica, 25–26, 28–29, 31, 34, 190–91

Nathusius, Elias, 183
Nenning, Johann. *See* Spiridion
Neukirch, Johann Georg, 26
Neumeister, Erdmann, 175, 178–79
Neunhertz, Johann, 175
Neusidler, Melchior, 102
Newman, Jane, 84
Niedt, Friedrich Erhardt, 42–43, 45
Nielsen, Hans, 54
Niemöller, Klaus Wolfgang, 62
Nordhausen, 70–73, 141
notation, musical, 189–90
   limitations of, 193–201, 203–5
novelty, attitudes towards, 14, 59–61, 158–60, 162–64, 170–73, 177–82
Nuremberg, 86

Obrecht, Jacob, 5, 25
Ochsenkun, Sebastian, 102
Oehme, Andreas, 70–73, 80, 141
Oestreich, Gerhard, 160
operatic arias, 74–78, 199
Opitz, Martin, 26–31, 46, 69
opus, musical, 1, 4–5, 26, 28, 190–91, 193, 199, 207, 212
originality, 6, 76, 116–17
ornamentation, 10, 14, 163, 195–99, 202, 205–9
Ott, Hans, 136, 165–66
Ovid, 25–27, 68
Owens, Jessie Ann, 6

Palestrina, Giovanni Pierluigi da, 6, 53, 65, 80, 101, 112
Parrott, Andrew, 204
Pasquini, Bernardo, 79
Penna, Lorenzo, 40

Peranda, Marco Giuseppe, 8, 125
performance, 4–5, 14–15
   as judged by audience, 153–54, 187–88, 206, 208, 212
   as separate sphere from composition, 193–99
   See also composer–performer relationship
Petrarch, Francesco, 81, 111
Pezel, Johann, 183
physiognomy, 104–8, 112
Pietism, 11
Pigman, G. W., 50
Pinello, Giovanni Battista, 102
Pirckheimer, Willibald, 133
Pirna, 168
Pitoni, Giuseppe Ottavio, 37
plagiarism, 13, 48, 66–67, 70–73, 75, 141, 154
   as patchwork, 35, 40, 67–68, 80
Plato, 25, 27
   on musical novelty, 160, 162–63, 165, 171–73
   on social discipline, 161
Pliny the Elder, 163
poetics, 26, 28
Poglietti, Alessandro, 155
Pohle, David, 178
Pohlmann, Hansjörg, 117, 126, 138–40
Pollet, Jan, 125
possessive individualism, 12–13, 74, 77, 116
posterity, 5, 9, 107–8, 155
Praetorius, Hieronymus, 64, 130, 134, 171–72
Praetorius, Michael, 19, 65, 102, 124, 192, 195–96, 205, 207
   on gifts, 120–21
   on Lutheran doctrine of service, 121–22
   printing privileges of, 127–28, 131, 133
presence, 84, 86–88, 97, 115, 200–1
printing of music, 6–7
   costs of, 138–39
   decline of, 8–10, 14, 91, 118, 148–49, 195
   engraving, 10, 101, 150–51, 155–56
   in Italy, 101
   market for printed music, 10, 12, 84–85, 91, 151–52, 194
   movable type, 10, 194
   and patrons' consent, 124–25
printing privileges, 14, 85, 88, 117–18, 126
   application process for, 129–36, 140, 213
   dissatisfaction with, 143
   effectiveness of, 140–48, 156–57
   holders of, 127–31
   justifications for, 136–40
   symbolic authority of, 146–48, 156–57
   types and terms, 126–29, 143
Printz, Wolfgang Caspar, 27, 31, 33, 42, 91, 191, 195, 210
Profe, Ambrosius, 146
Pufendorf, Samuel, 149

Quickelberg, Samuel, 125
Quintilian, 24, 26, 61–62
Quitschreiber, Georg, 13, 50, 62–68, 74–75, 80

Raimondo, Marc'Antonio, 86
Reincken, Johann Adam, 214
    An Wasserflüssen Babylon, 32, 112–15
    Hortus musicus, 91–93, 214
    keyboard suites, 42
Reinhard, Lorenz, 185
Répertoire International des Sources Musicales (RISM), 9
rhetoric, 210
    and decorum, 109–10
    and performance, 192–93
    stages of composition, 14, 34, 190, 192–93, 203
Rifkin, Joshua, 57
Röber, Paul, 169
Roberts, John, 50
Rodio, Rocco, 64
Roger, Estienne, 151
Rohr, Julius Bernhard von, 180
Rose, Mark, 4, 116
Rosenmüller, Johann, 10, 49, 95, 119
Rosenplüt, Hans, 30
Rubens, Pieter Paul, 82
Rubert, Johann Martin, 108
Rühling, Johannes, 169

Sales, Franz, 127–28
Salviati, Lionardo, 87
Saxon 1580 church ordinance, 14, 51, 158–59, 164–66, 168–73, 180–81, 213–14
Scacchi, Marco, 109
Scandello, Antonio, 110, 123–24
Scanlon, Larry, 10
Schechner, Richard, 189
Scheibe, Johann Adolph, 33, 187
Scheidemann, Heinrich, 113
Scheidt, Samuel, 49, 71, 91, 102–4, 172–73
Schein, Johann Hermann, 3, 9, 14, 71, 169–70, 172, 174, 182
    as self-publisher, 88, 91, 137, 141–42
    as student, 105–7
    printing privileges of, 88, 127–30, 133, 135, 141–42, 170
Schein, Johann Hermann, works
    Diletti pastorali, 89–91, 193–94
    Israelis Brünlein, 88–89
    Musica boscareccia, 88–89, 141–42, 194–95
    Opella nova, 89, 110, 169–70
    Venus Kräntzlein, 105–7, 119
Schelle, Johann, 175–76, 179, 183–84
Schilling, Heinz, 160
Schlick, Arnolt, 136
Schmid, Bernhard, 206–7
Schneegass, Cyriacus, 63
Schott, Georg Balthasar, 184

Schultz, Johannes, 127–28, 135
Schultze, Christoph, 170–72
Schulze, Winfried, 149
Schuster, Jakob, 91
Schütz, Heinrich, 4–5, 7–9, 19, 27, 91, 123, 170, 172, 212, 214
    as author, 1–3, 213
    and musical borrowing, 49, 52–56, 67, 69, 213
    and musical novelty, 158, 177
    personal watermark of, 73, 94–96, 141
    printing privileges of, 73, 96, 127–29, 133–36, 138, 141
    scriptorium of, 95–97
    as self-publisher, 95–96, 138
Schütz, Heinrich, works
    Becker Psalter, 1, 95, 133, 140–41
    Cantiones sacrae, 18
    Geistliche Chor-Music, 7–8, 69, 95
    Historia der Aufferstehung, 141, 196, 207–8
    Historia der Geburt Jesu Christi, 95, 97
    Il primo libro de madrigali, 1, 54
    Kleine geistliche Concerte I, 1, 141
    Kleine geistliche Concerte II, 94
    Musicalische Exequien, 1
    Psalmen Davids, 32, 54–56, 69, 71–73, 124–25, 138, 141, 207
    Schwanengesang, 95, 97
    Symphoniae sacrae II, 67, 69, 95–96, 208
    Symphoniae sacrae III, 21, 69, 95
    Zwölff geistliche Gesänge, 95
scientific revolution, 11
self. *See* identity, personal
self-fashioning, 11, 105–7, 129–31
self-interest, 118–22, 137–38, 145, 149
self-publishing. *See* composer, as self-publisher
Selich, Daniel, 172
Seneca the Elder, 68
Seneca the Younger, 54, 69–70
Senfl, Ludwig, 172
Shrank, Cathy, 86
Sibylla of Württemberg, 200–1, 203
signatures, 85, 87, 96, 99
    doctrine of, 82
Smith, Adam, 149
Smith, Pamela, 29
Soli Deo Gloria. *See* inscriptions, pious
Soriano, Francesco, 64
Spahn, Joachim Ernst, 183–84
Spangenberg, Cyriacus, 163
Speer, Daniel, 34
Spiridion (Johann Nenning), 37–40, 45
Sponheuer, Bernd, 33
Staden, Johann, 110, 204
Stenger, Wilhelm Hieronymus, 148
Steuerlein, Johann, 65, 102, 128, 138–39
Strasbourg, 141–42
Stravinsky, Igor, 188
Striggio, Alessandro, 64

Index

243

Strohm, Reinhard, 4, 6
Struever, Nancy, 58
Strungk, Nicolaus Adam, 48, 76
Stump, Eleonore, 195
style (musical), 109–11
   concerted, 7, 10, 49, 173, 195
   fantasia, 114
   personal, 14, 61–62, 110–12, 155, 198, 214
   polyphonic, 7, 10, 159, 172, 195, 212
Sweelinck, Jan Pieterszoon, 64

talent, 24–28, 33–35, 44–46, 214
Taruskin, Richard, 188–89, 203, 212
Telemann, Georg Philipp, 9, 27–28, 153–54,
   177, 184
textual integrity, 137–38, 144–45, 152–53,
   209–10
Theile, Johann, 183–84
Thirty Years War, 7, 9, 11, 71, 158, 160,
   170–74, 185
Thomasius, Christian, 11, 15, 40–41, 149
   eclectic philosophy of, 11–12, 214
Thomasius, Jacob, 66, 179, 183–84
thoroughbass techniques, 42–43, 140, 202–5,
   212
Thymich, Paul, 175
Tinctoris, Johannes, 101
Tosi, Pier Francesco, 199
transmission (of texts, knowledge), 189,
   209–10
   misprints, 85, 137–38, 144–45
   patriarchal, 11, 51–52, 54, 56, 201, 203
   and variant texts, 152–55, 202

unauthorised editions, 73, 84, 86, 89–91, 96,
   137–38, 140–48, 151
Utendal, Alexander, 109

Valentini, Giovanni, 59
van Orden, Kate, 6
Varwig, Bettina, 177
Vetter, Walther, 33
Vincentius, Caspar, 130, 140

vocation
   humanist notions of, 24
   Lutheran doctrine of, 19
Volmar, Johann, 140
Vulpius, Melchior, 64, 128, 139

Waczkat, Andreas, 62
Waelrant, Hubert, 167
Walter, Johann, 172
Walther, Johann Gottfried, 27, 34, 40, 113, 151,
   153–54, 174, 185, 191
Weber, Max, 31
Weckmann, Matthias, 22, 202
Wegman, Rob, 209
Weichmann, Johann, 143
Weimar, 185
Weissenfels, 178–79
Wening, Michael, 155–56
Werckmeister, Andreas, 18–20, 27, 153,
   181–82, 204–5
Wert, Giaches de, 54
Wilhelm V, Duke of Bavaria, 133
Willaert, Adrian, 101
Wimsatt, W. K. Jr., 3, 189
Withy, Francis, 37
Wittenberg, 169
Witvogel, Gerhard Fredrik, 151
Władysław IV Vasa, 143, 148
Wolfenbüttel, 1, 5, 102, 124, 158
Wolff, Christoph, 176
Wollny, Peter, 7, 65, 74, 79
Woodmansee, Martha, 4, 150
work, musical, 4–5, 7, 155
   ambiguity of term, 139, 145
   concept of, 5
   durability of, 29, 32, 107–8

Young, Edward, 116–17

Zacconi, Ludovico, 196, 205
Zarlino, Gioseffo, 205
Ziani, Pietro Andrea, 127, 130
Ziegler, Johann Gotthilf, 177

Printed in the United States
by Baker & Taylor Publisher Services